Taking Stock of Air Liberalization

CENTRE FOR RESEARCH ON TRANSPORTATION
25TH ANNIVERSARY SERIES 1971 - 1996

EQUILIBRIUM AND ADVANCED TRANSPORTATION MODELLING
edited by
Patrice Marcotte and Sang Nguyen

TELECOMMUNICATIONS NETWORK PLANNING
edited by
Brunilde Sansó and Patrick Soriano

FLEET MANAGEMENT AND LOGISTICS
edited by
Teodor Gabriel Crainic and Gilbert Laporte

AUTOMOBILE INSURANCE: Road Safety, New Drivers, Risks, Insurance Fraud and Regulation
edited by
Georges Dionne and Claire Laberge-Nadeau

TAKING STOCK OF AIR LIBERALIZATION
edited by
Marc Gaudry and Robert Mayes

Taking Stock of Air Liberalization

Edited by
Marc Gaudry
Université de Montréal et Université Louis Pasteur
Robert Mayes
Transport Canada

Springer Science+Business Media, LLC

Electronic Services <http://www.wkap.nl>

Library of Congress Cataloging-in-Publication Data

A C.I.P. Catalogue record for this book is available
from the Library of Congress.

ISBN 978-1-4613-7309-4 ISBN 978-1-4615-5077-8 (eBook)
DOI 10.1007/978-1-4615-5077-8

Printed on acid-free paper.

Contents

PART II. SPECIFIC IMPACTS OF DEREGULATION

PART III. POLICY FORMULATION

PART IV. MODELLING DEMAND

Presenting Authors

PHILIPPE BARLA
Université Laval
philippe.barla@ecn.ulaval.ca

GEO BESSE
Internation Air Transport Association
BESSEG@iata.org

JAAP DE WIT
University of Amsterdam and Ministry of Transport of The Netherlands
j.g.wit@mail.uva.nl

MARC GAUDRY
Université de Montréal et Université Louis Pasteur
gaudry@crt.umontreal.ca

DAVID GILLEN
University of California at Berkeley and Wilfrid Laurier University
dgillen@euler.berkeley.edu

DEANNE JULIUS
Bank of England
deanne.julius@bankofengland.co.uk

RICHARD LAFERRIÈRE
Centre de recherche sur les transports
lafr@crt.umontreal.ca

BENEDIKT MANDEL
Centre de recherche sur les transports et MKmetric GmbH
mandel@mkm.de

WOLFGANG MICHALSKI
Organization for Economic Cooperation and Development
wolfgang.michalski@oecd.org

JOHN PANZAR
Northwestern University
jpanzar@nwu.edu

Louis RANGER
Transport Canada
rangerl@tc.gc.ca

Randal REED
Université de Montréal
rreed@crt.umontreal.ca

DANIEL P. RICH
Illinois State University
dprich@rs6000.cmp.ilstu.edu

IAN P. SAVAGE
Northwestern University
ipsavage@nwu.edu

ROBIN C. SICKLES
Rice University
rcs@rice.edu

LUDOLF VAN HASSELT
European Commission CHECK
Fax: 011-32-2-296-90-67

CLIFFORD WINSTON
The Brookings Institute
cwinston@brook.edu

JIM WOLFE
Department of transport of Australia
jwolfe@email.dot.gov.au

Preface

TEODOR GABRIEL CRAINIC, DIRECTOR

The Centre for Research on Transportation (C.R.T.) was founded in 1971 by the Université de Montréal. From 1988 on, it is jointly managed by the Université de Montréal and its affiliated schools, the École des Hautes Études Commerciales and École Polytechnique. Professors, students and researchers from many institutions in the Montreal area join forces at the C.R.T. to analyze transportation, logistics and telecommunication systems from a multidisciplinary perspective.

The C.R.T. pursues three major, complementary objectives: training of high-level specialists; the advancement of knowledge and technology; the transfer of technology towards industry and the public sector. Its main field of expertise is the development of quantitative and computer-based models and methods for the analysis of urban, regional and intercity transportation networks, as well as telecommunication systems. This applies to the study of passenger and commodity flows, as well as to the socioeconomic aspects of transportation: policy, regulation, economics.

The twenty-fifth anniversary of the C.R.T. offered the opportunity to evaluate past accomplishments and to identify future trends and challenges. Five colloquia were thus organized on major research and application themes that also reflected our main research areas. They gathered together internationally renowned researchers who linked recent scientific and technological advances to modeling and methodological challenges waiting to be tackled, particularly concerning new problems and applications, and the increasingly widespread use of new technologies.

The present book, together with its four companions, is the result of these meetings. I wish to thank my colleagues who organized these colloquia and also edited the books: PATRICE MARCOTTE and SANG NGUYEN for **Equilibrium and Advanced Transportation Modelling**, BRUNILDE SANSÓ and PATRICK SORIANO for **Telecommunications Network Planning**, TEODOR GABRIEL CRAINIC and GILBERT LAPORTE for **Fleet Management and Logistics**, GEORGES DIONNE and CLAIRE LABERGE-NADEAU for **Automobile Insurance: Road Safety, New Drivers, Risks, Insurance Fraud and Regulation** and MARC GAUDRY and ROBERT MAYES for **Taking Stock of Air Liberalization**.

I also wish to take this opportunity to thank all companies and institutions who financially supported the celebration of our twenty-fifth anniversary and the publication of the five books: BELL, BUREAU D'ASSURANCE DU CANADA, CANADIAN PACIFIC RAILWAY, ÉCOLE DES HAUTES ÉTUDES COMMERCIALES DE MONTRÉAL, INRO CONSULTANTS INC., LES ENTREPRISES GIRO INC., MINISTÈRE DES TRANSPORTS DU QUÉBEC, SOCIÉTÉ DE L'ASSURANCE AUTOMOBILE DU QUÉBEC, TRANSPORTS CANADA and the UNIVERSITÉ DE MONTRÉAL.

Préface

TEODOR GABRIEL CRAINIC, DIRECTEUR

Le Centre de recherche sur les transports (C.R.T.) fut fondé en 1971 par l'Université de Montréal. En 1988, deux institutions affiliées, l'École des Hautes Études Commerciales et l'École Polytechnique, se sont jointes à celle-ci pour former un centre multidisciplinaire conjoint. Des professeurs, étudiants et chercheurs provenant principalement des universités de la région montréalaise s'y regroupent pour mettre en commun leurs compétences diverses afin d'analyser les systèmes de transport, logistiques et de télécommunication.

La mission du C.R.T. s'articule autour de trois axes complémentaires : la formation de spécialistes de haut niveau; l'avancement des connaissances et des technologies; le transfert de ces technologies vers l'industrie et les organismes publics. L'expertise du C.R.T. est principalement associée au développement de modèles et méthodes quantitatifs et informatiques d'analyse des réseaux de transport urbains, régionaux, interurbains et internationaux ainsi que des réseaux de télécommunication. Celle-ci s'applique tout autant au transport de passagers et de marchandises qu'aux aspects socioéonomiques : réglementation, sécurité, économie du transport.

L'année du vingt-cinquième anniversaire nous a fourni l'occasion de faire le point et de nous tourner vers l'avenir. Cinq colloques portant sur des thèmes actuels et reflétant les axes majeurs de recherche du C.R.T. sont issus de cette réflexion. Ces colloques, qui ont rassemblé des chercheurs de réputation internationale, ont permis de discerner des liens entre les réalisations récentes et les défis de modélisation et méthodologiques qui nous attendent, particulièrement dans les nouveaux champs de recherche et d'application, et dans l'utilisation grandissante de nouvelles technologies.

Ce livre et ses quatre compagnons sont le résultat tangible de ces colloques. Je remercie mes collègues qui les ont organisés et animés et qui ont également produit ces livres : PATRICE MARCOTTE et SANG NGUYEN pour **Equilibrium and Advanced Transportation Modelling**, BRUNILDE SANSÓ et PATRICK SORIANO pour **Telecommunications Network Planning**, TEODOR GABRIEL CRAINIC et GILBERT LAPORTE pour **Fleet Management and Logistics**, GEORGES DIONNE et CLAIRE LABERGE-NADEAU pour **Automobile Insurance : Road Safety, New Drivers, Risks, Insurance Fraud and Regulation** et MARC GAUDRY et ROBERT MAYES pour **Taking Stock of Air Liberalization**.

Je tiens également à remercier les compagnies et institutions qui nous ont appuyé financièrement dans la réalisation des célébrations du vingt-cinquième anniversaire et la publication des cinq livres : BELL, le BUREAU D'ASSURANCE DU CANADA, CANADIAN PACIFIC RAILWAY, L'ÉCOLE DES HAUTES ÉTUDES COMMERCIALES DE MONTRÉAL, LES CONSEILLERS INRO INC., LES ENTREPRISES GIRO INC., le MINISTÈRE DES TRANSPORTS DU QUÉBEC, la SOCIÉTÉ DE L'ASSURANCE AUTOMOBILE DU QUÉBEC, TRANSPORTS CANADA et l'UNIVERSITÉ DE MONTRÉAL.

INTRODUCTION

Marc Gaudry and Robert Mayes

Technology, Economy, Policy (TEP). The practical collaboration required to bring together people belonging to the complementary streams of economic analysis and policy analysis present in this book started ten years ago as we discussed the relationship among transportation technology, transportation economics and transportation policy in the general *ambience* and under the general " cover " of the Canadian Royal Commission on National Passenger Transportation. Working over a 40-month period (1989-1992), this commission took stock of transportation and produced an up-to-date *État de la question* and policy framework (Hyndman *et al.*, 1992).

Our discussions started with the modern history of roads, where the TEP interaction is notorious. We discussed the first wave, defined by Trésaguet's (1716-1796) formulation of his technique in 1764, a year in which " the famous Scottish builders John Loudon McAdam (1756-1836) and Thomas Telford (1757-1834) were boys of seven and eight " (Kirby *et al.*, 1956). Although significant technological progress would have to await the use of cohesive materials instead of the finely graded and systematic broken stone technique defined by Trésaguet, the slowdown in technical progress did not prevent innovation in policy as Dupuit (1844), considering a problem of road pricing, invented demand analysis. His technique made it possible to understand the subjective nature of economic value and still constitutes the core of current evaluation methods (e.g. Ch. 15 below). Although Marx (1867) had drawn inspiration from Darwin's famous book (1859), which he had read, he unfortunately had not read Dupuit[1] or Cournot's (1838) supply-demand equations, long indecipherable to most. The policy framework was formulated, perhaps clearly for the first time in Duclos' famous 1759 *Essai*, where one can find, for instance :

> " [...]the State, badly served, sees its debts increase more and more and becomes incapable of reimbursing unless it mends its ways. In any case, disorder sets in as necessary expenditures are postponed while useless ones are made ahead of time because there is no barrier solid enough to resist connections and favouritism.
>
> This was the situation of Roads and bridges in 1726 when M. Dubois started his reformation of [...] ". (p. 24, our translation).

[1] There is no sign of it in his personal library.

Table 1. U.S. Scheduled Airline Enplanements, Passenger Miles, Revenues, and Employees, Selected Years, 1926-93

Year	*Enplanements (thousands)*	*Passenger miles (millions)*	*Passenger revenue (millions of 1993 dollars)*	*Employees*
1926	6	1	1	462[a]
1930	418	93	61	3,475
1940	2,966	1,152	641	22,051
1950	19,220	10,243	6,646	86,057
1960	57,872	38,863	11,657	167,603
1970	169,922	131,710	28,404	297,374
1985	205,062	162,810	33,180	289,926
1980	296,903	255,192	49,187	360,517
1985	382,022	336,403	52,691	355,113
1990	465,560	457,926	64,605	545,809
1993	487,249	489,137	63,951	537,111

Sources: Data before 1970 are from Civil Aeronautics Board, *Handbook of Airline Statistics, 1973 Edition* (March 1974). Data from 1970 on are from Air Transport Association, *Air Transport: The Annual Report of the U.S. Scheduled Airline Industry* (various years).

a. Figure is for 1927, the earliest available.

1.1 INDUSTRY STRUCTURE

Deregulation dramatically changed the structure of the airline industry. As some proponents had expected, competition exploded in the late 1970s and early 1980s as People Express, Air Florida, and other new carriers challenged the established airlines. But during the late 1980s the industry underwent severe consolidation. With the exception of Southwest, the new interstate entrants disappeared.

Of the carriers with annual revenues greater than $1 billion (the major carriers) that have remained in the industry, American is the leader in revenue, but United leads in passenger miles and Delta in enplanements (table 2). These three measures create an ambiguous ranking because airlines differ in the types of routes they fly, which is indicated by their average lengths of haul (that is, the average passenger trip distance, which is passenger miles divided by enplanements). United's long average length of haul (with its correspondingly low fare per mile) makes it a runner-up in revenue although it leads in passenger miles. Southwest's highly publicized regional service stands out clearly; its length of haul is the shortest of any major carrier. The size of the major carriers also varies considerably: American's revenue is more than eleven times greater than America West's.

To casual observers, deregulation seemed merely to have led to fewer airlines. But according to transportation officials, more operated at the end of 1993 (seventy-six) than at the end of 1978 (forty-three). A simple count, however, is a misleading indicator of the extent of competition because it assigns equal importance to a small carrier and a giant. One way to overcome this false comparison is to calculate the number of effective competitors, which is the inverse of the Herfindahl index.[3] Based on this index, figure 1 shows that the number of effective competitors at the national level increased from fewer than nine in the fourth quarter of 1978 to a peak of more than twelve in 1985. Then a wave of fourteen mergers between June 1985 and October 1987 reduced the number to slightly fewer than had existed before deregulation.

Table 2. Enplanements, Passenger Miles, Average Length of Haul, and Revenue, by Major Carrier, 1993

Carrier	*Enplanements (thousands)*	*Passenger miles (millions)*	*Average length of haul (miles)*	*Revenue (millions of 1993 dollars)*
American	82,536	97,062	1,176	14,737
United	69,672	100,991	1,450	14,354
Delta	84,813	82,863	977	12,376
Northwest	44,098	58,033	1,316	8,448
USAir	53,679	35,220	656	6,623
Continental	37,280	39,859	1,069	5,086
TWA	18,938	22,664	1,197	3,094
Southwest	37,517	16,716	446	2,067
America West	14,700	11,188	761	1,332

Sources: Air Transport Association, *Air Transport, 1994* (Washington, 1994), p. 5.

But if fewer effective competitors exist at the national level, deregulation has not necessarily decreased airline competition: for it is at the *route* level that airlines compete head to head. For example, four effective competitors at the national level can operate in two very different ways: with each having a monopoly share on one-quarter of the routes or with each having a one-quarter share on all routes. Although the number of airlines is the same either way, the second situation is obviously more competitive because more airlines serve each route. Thus fewer effective competitors at the national level does not necessarily mean that the industry is less competitive.

[3] Interpreting an inverted Herfindahl index as a "numbers-equivalent" was suggested by M.A. Adelman, "Comment on the 'H' Concentration Measure as a Numbers-Equivalent," *Review of Economics and Statistics*, vol. 51 (February 1969), pp. 99-101. The index approaches zero in the competitive case with a large number of small firms, and equals one in the monopoly case, so its inverse approaches infinity in the competitive case and equals one for monopoly. The inverse may be thought of as giving the number of equal-sized competitors that would provide a degree of competition equivalent to that actually observed in the market-share data. The index captures inequality in market shares by summing the square of each airline's market share. For example, if two airlines each have a 50 percent market share, the Herfindahl index is $0.50^2 + 0.50^2 = ½$. Inverting this gives 2 (effective competitors). Similarly, the index for three equal-sized airlines is $3 \times 0.33^2 = 1/3$, so inversion gives three effective competitors. But if there were three competitors with the largest serving 2/3 of the market and the other two each serving 1/6 of the market, the Herfindahl index would be ½, which also translates into two effective competitors. Thus *effective competitors* has a more intuitive interpretation than the Herfindahl index.

Figure 2-1. Airline Industry Effective Competitors, National Level, 1978-93

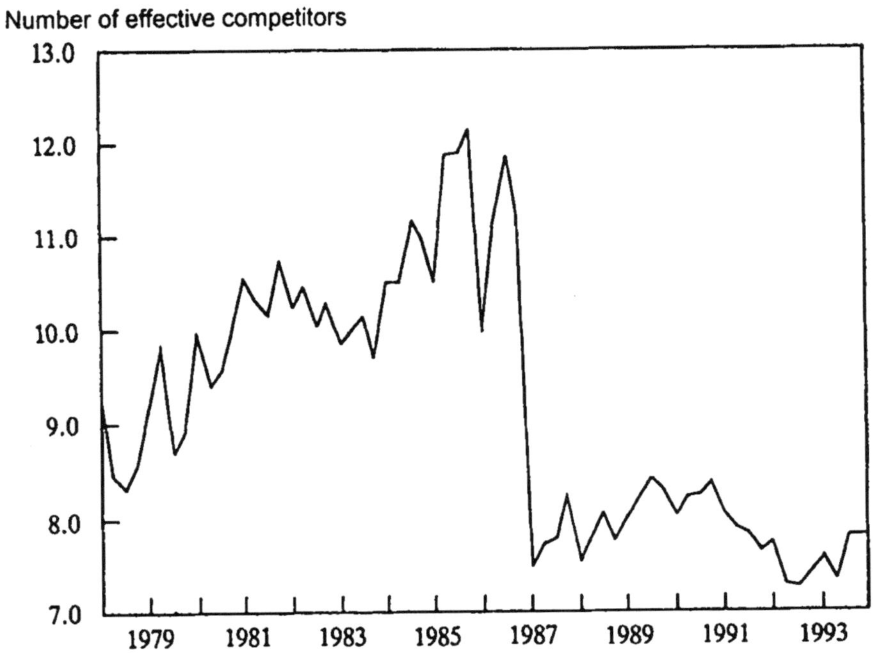

Sources: Authors' calculations using Department of Transportation Data Bank 1A, a 10 percent sample of airline tickets. The number of effective competitors at the national level is calculated based on each carrier's share of domestic passenger miles.

To measure competition at the route level, we calculated the number of effective competitors on each route; we then averaged over all routes, weighting both by passengers and by passenger miles (figures 2-2). The two measures diverge because more carriers have entered long-haul routes, and long-haul routes have a greater importance when passenger-mile weights are used than when passenger weights are used. But the trend is clear with either measure. Competition increased steadily until mid-1986, decreased because of mergers, then reversed course in mid-1989 and increased through the third quarter of 1990. The decline during the fourth quarter of 1990 and the first quarter of 1991 reflects the liquidation of Eastern Airlines and economic recession. Even so, at the route level airlines are clearly more competitive than they were under regulation.[4]

4 As an alternative measure to the number of effective competitors, we calculated from the Department of Transportation's Data Bank 1A ticket sample the percentage of passengers on carriers with different market shares. This calculation led to findings consistent with those obtained by using the number of effective competitors. In particular, the percentage of passengers flying on carriers with less than a 20 percent route market share more than doubled, from 7.2 percent to 15.2 percent, between 1978 and 1993. During that same period the percentage of passengers flying on carriers with route monopolies (100 percent route market share) fell from 102 percent to 5.6 percent.

Figure 2-2. Airline Industry Effective Competitors, Route Level, 1978-93

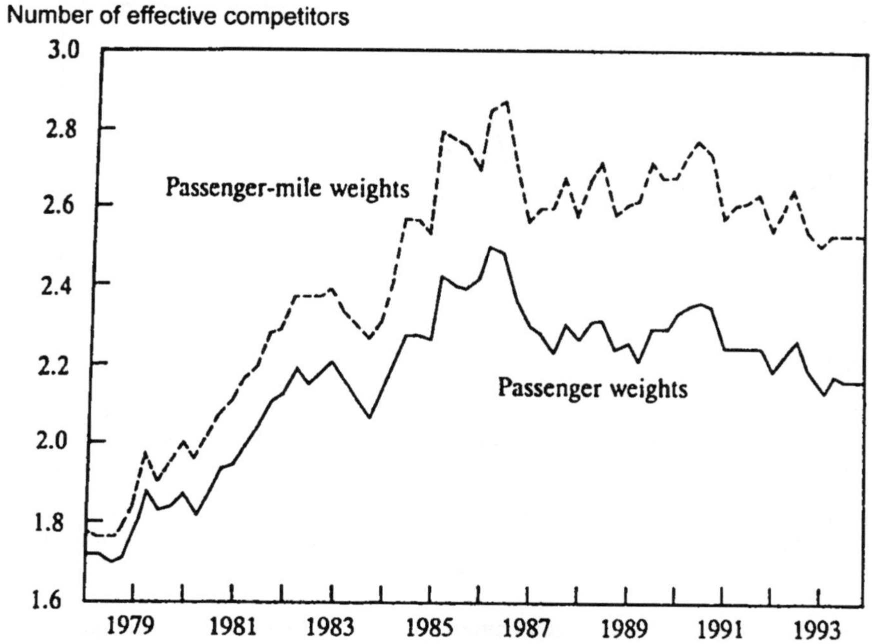

Sources: Authors' calculations using Department of Transportation Data Bank 1A. Each airline's share of passengers on each domestic route was calculated from a subsample of one-way tickets with two or fewer segments and round-trip tickets with two or fewer segments on the outbound and return legs. These route-level measures were aggregated across routes based on the percentage of sampled passengers and passenger miles on each route.

But as the difference between the passenger-weighted and passenger-mile-weighted figures suggest, competition has not been uniform on short and long routes. In particular, the number of effective competitors on routes shorter than 500 miles fell by 2 percent between 1978 and 1993, while the number on routes longer than 2,000 miles increased by 70 percent. Under deregulation, then, there are fewer effective competitors nationally, but carriers compete at the route level more often. What has been the effect on fares, services quality, profitability, and safety?

1.2 FARES

Fares are the focus of any discussion of the airline industry. As with competition, the measure used is important. The standard measure of fares, *yield*, is the average fare per mile for trips by paying customers. As figure 3 shows, yield adjusted for inflation had been falling even before deregulation. After more than a decade and a half of deregulation, real yield in 1993 was two-thirds of its value in 1976. Can this decrease be attributed to deregulation or, because of underlying factors such as technological change, would it have occurred with or without regulation?

Figure 2-3. Domestic Airline Average Fare per Passenger Mile (Yield), 1970-93

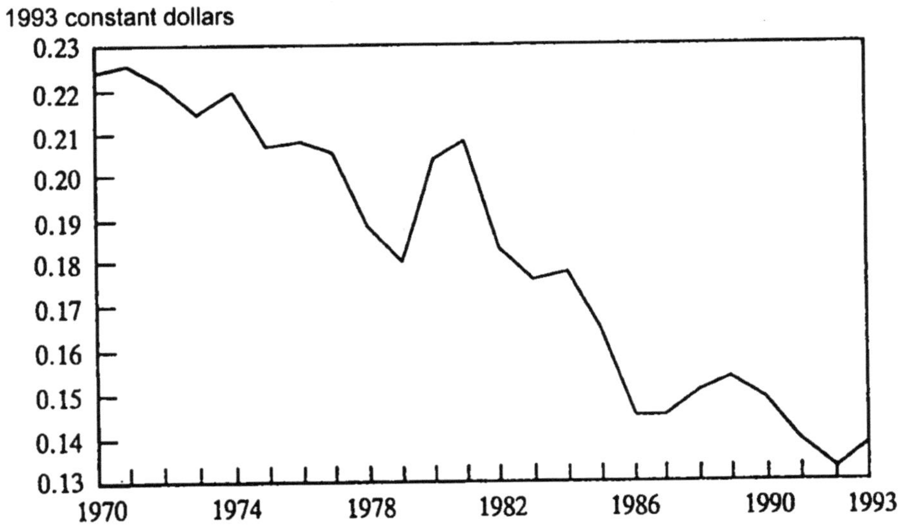

Sources: Domestic yield is from authors' calculations using Air Transport Association, *Air Transport: The Annual Report of the U.S. Scheduled Airline Industry*, various issues. Real yield was calculated by adjusting nominal yield using the consumer price index.

These questions can be analyzed empirically, but to do so we must compare the actual (nominal) deregulated yield with what fare formula (called the standard industry fare level, or SIFL) used by the CAB during the last few years of regulation. Although there is no way of knowing for certain what regulated fares would be today, there is no evidence to suggest that before deregulation the CAB was making or would have made fundamental changes in its fare structure. Indeed, the board believed that it was taking a rational cost-based approach to regulating fares.

The SIFL is calculated by the Department of Transportation, not for regulatory purposes but for use by the Internal Revenue Service in valuing free trips on corporate aircraft. Every six months the department calculates a SIFL cost adjustment factor based on observed changes in cost per available seat mile. But to use these factors to update the SIFL would have been misleading for our purposes. We need to know what the cost per available seat mile (and the SIFL) would have been if airlines were still regulated. If deregulation has kept costs lower than what they would have been, the unadjusted SIFL would be too low. Using data developed by Douglas W. Caves and his colleagues, we estimated that between 1976 and 1983 (when their study ended) deregulation increase passenger-mile productivity growth 1.3 to 1.6 percent a year.[5] We started with the midpoint of this range. But some of this productivity increase was due to greater load factors, which had to be excluded from the calculation because SIFL adjustments are based on

[5] Douglas W. Caves and others, "An Assessment of the Efficiency Effects of U.S. Airline Deregulation via an International Comparison," in Elizabeth E. Bailey, ed., *Public Regulation: New Perspectives on Institution and Policies* (MIT Press, 1987), pp. 285-320.

seat-mile costs, not passenger-mile costs. Adjusting for changes in load factor reduced the measured productivity change by 0.25 percentage point a year, resulting in a midpoint productivity change of 1.2 percent a year. We thus increased the observed SIFL by 1.2 percent a year from 1976 to 1983. By 1983 this resulted in an 8.7 percent increase. Arguably, productivity growth continued to increase after 1983 because of deregulation, although at a reduced rate, so the use of a midpoint figure only through 1983 should err on the side of conservatism; that is, in all likelihood the extent that deregulation has lowered fares is understated. We were also being conservative by assuming in this calculation that factor prices were unchanged by deregulation.[6]

The line for actual yield in figure 4 was calculated based on ticket prices in a subsample of Department of Transportation Data Bank 1A.[7] The line for regulated yield was calculated by pricing all the tickets in the actual yield calculation using an estimated fare implied by the adjusted SIFL. As the figure shows, actual yields have been consistently lower than regulated yields would have been, although the gap has varied. The largest percentage differences occurred during the 1981-82 and 1990-91 recessions, when rising fuel prices increased airline costs and thus would also have increased regulated fares. But during these recessions *deregulated* carriers lowered fares to attract what business was available. On average, deregulation has led to fares 22 percent lower than they would have been had regulation continued.[8] The annual saving to flyers has been about $12.4 billion in 1993 dollars.[9] During

---

6 According to previous research, deregulation, to the extent it had any impact, lowered the cost of labour. See, for example, David Card, "Deregulation and Labor Earnings in the Airline Industry," Princeton University, Princeton Industrial Relations Section working paper 247, January 1989.

7 The subsample was all domestic round-trip tickets with two or fewer segments on each of the outbound and return legs. Tickets with fares that were unreasonably high were excluded. Tickets with fares that seemed too low reflected coding errors and legitimate frequent flier awards. The percentage of tickets with low fares was stable (an average 1.7 percent of tickets and 2.5 percent of passenger miles) from the fourth quarter of 1978 to the fourth quarter of 1986, when it began to increase. We assumed that any subsequent increase in the percentage of low-fare tickets was due to frequent flier tickets. From the first quarter of 1987 to the fourth quarter of 1993 this averaged 4.0 percent of passengers and 5.5 percent of passenger miles. We then divided revenue earned on tickets with "good" fares by the sum of "good" passenger miles plus our estimate of frequent flier passenger miles to obtain actual yield.

8 It can be argued that this type of estimate becomes increasingly uncertain as time goes on, but this view is shaped by evidence based on the deregulated experience that reveals flaws in CAB regulation. That is, any belief that fare regulation would have caused less expense for travelers presumes that the regulatory authority would have learned from past errors and would have been able to avoid them when developing a new regulatory fare structure. There is not much evidence to support this view. Moreover, we were interested in calculating the difference between regulated and deregulated fares over time as opposed to calculating the difference between regulated and deregulated fares assuming that regulated fares are partly based on previous experience with deregulated fares.

9 This figure represents how much more money travelers would have paid if fares had remained regulated for trips they actually took under deregulated fares. The figure overstates travelers' gain because, on average, fares fell, generating more trips than would have occurred under higher regulated fares. The figure was obtained by multiplying, for each

1993, fares were 19 percent lower than they would have been under regulation. Real fares (figure 3) have declined about 33 percent since 1976 (that is, before any significant regulatory reforms by the CAB). Thus deregulation has accounted for 58 percent (19/33) of the observed decrease in real air fares.[10]

Although CAB fare regulation led to higher fares, is it possible that a more enlightened, less harmful type of regulation could be put into practice? The 1975-78 experience suggests that enlightened regulation is possible but that regulatory performance depends very much on the personalities involved, particularly that of the CAB chairman. Furthermore, for an alternative regulatory fare structure to improve very much on the CAB's effort, it would still have to adjust rapidly and accurately to carriers' costs and the demand on their capacity. It is unlikely that a regulatory body could design and implement a fare structure with that feature.

Figure 2-4. Airline Industry Average Fare per Passenger Mile (Yield), Actual under Deregulation and Projected under Regulation, 1978-93

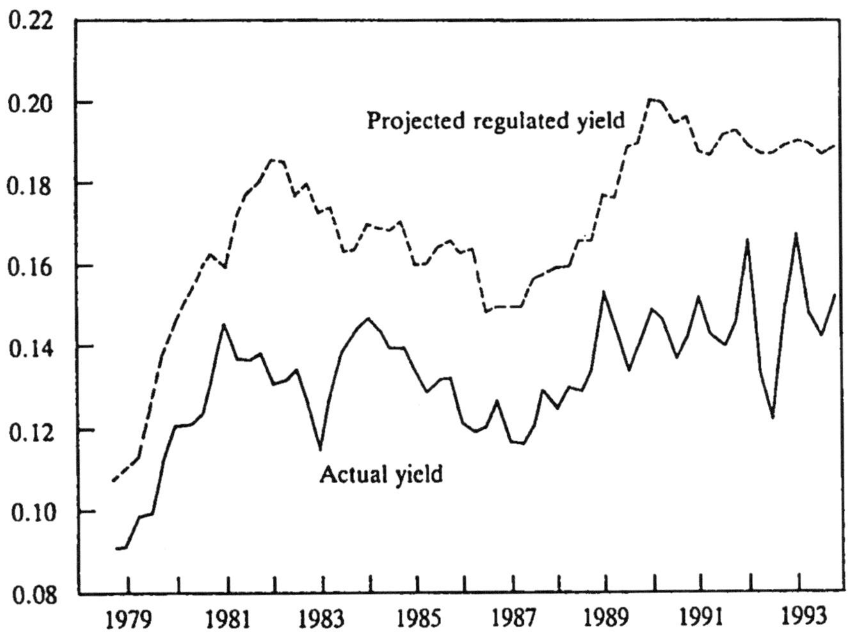

Source: Authors' calculations using data from Department of Transportation Data Bank 1A; see text.

quarter from the fourth quarter of 1978 to the fourth quarter of 1993, real domestic passenger revenue by the percentage that adjusted SIFL fares exceed actual (deregulated) fares and taking the annual average of the result.

10 Using data covering a much shorter time than is covered here, and without using methodologies that relied on adjusting the SIFL, we also found in 1986 that deregulation had lowered fares. See Steve Morrison and Clifford Winston, *The Economic Effects of Airline Deregulation* (Brookings, 1986). We obtained this result by comparing actual regulated fares in 1977 with predictions based on actual 1983 deregulated fares of what deregulated fares would have been during this period.

Table 3. U.S., North American, and World Airline Industry Average Fares per Passenger Mile (Yield), 1969, 1980, 1990, 1991[a]

Year	Distance (miles)	U.S. or North American yield (dollars)	World yield (dollars)	Percentage difference
1969	All	0.40 (U.S. only)	0.42	- 4.8
1980	All	0.76 (U.S. only)	0.88	- 13.6
1990	All	0.87 (U.S. only)	1.13	- 23.0
1991	150	0.35	0.37	- 5.4
	300	0.25	0.29	- 13.8
	600	0.18	0.23	- 21.7
	1,200	0.13	0.19	- 31.6
	2,400	0.09	0.15	- 40.0

Source: Authors' calculations based on unpublished data from the International Civil Aviation Organization.

a. Yields for 1991 are in dollars per revenue passenger mile; yields for other years are in dollars per ton-kilometers performed. World yield for 1991 includes the North American yield; world yield for other years does not include U.S. yield.

Figure 2-5. Distribution of Fares Travelers Paid Relative to Their Route's Average Fare, Fourth Quarter 1978, 1985, 1993

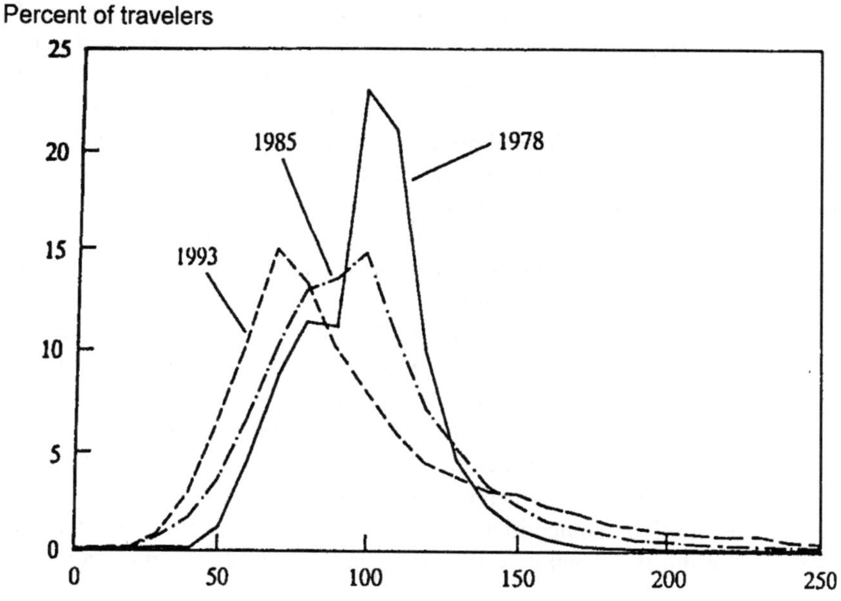

Source: Authors' calculations based on a subsample of Department of Transportation Data Bank 1A, a 10 percent sample of airline tickets. Subsample was all domestic round-trip tickets with two or fewer segments outbound and two or fewer segments return. To correct for possible coding errors in the data airlines submitted, tickets with fares that seemed unreasonably high or low were excluded. Thus frequent flier tickets were excluded.

Low U.S. airfares have not escaped the notice of other countries. Table 3 compares 1991 yields at various distances in North America with the world average for the same distances. The differential is what one would expect when comparing regulated and deregulated fares and provides additional evidence that U.S. fares would have been higher if left regulated. The table also shows that international fare differences have grown significantly since U.S. deregulation in 1978.[11] The widening gap has already prompted Japan, Canada, and Australia to deregulate their fares. Countries in the European Union plan to deregulate theirs in 1997.

Although deregulation has lowered average U.S. domestic fares, it has also led to the proliferation of fare categories, ranging from relatively expensive unrestricted coach seats to deeply discounted seats with a host of restrictions, on every carrier and for every route. To show this proliferation, figure 5 plots what percentage of travelers paid what percentage of the average fare on the route they traveled.[12] A glance confirms what travelers have believed for some time: the variability of fares has increased. Using the data to construct the figure, we found that in the fourth quarter of 1978, for instance, 37 percent of passengers paid fares that were less than or equal to the average fare, while only 2 percent paid more than 1.5 times the average. By the end of 1993, some 59 percent were paying fares less than or equal to the average, and 13 percent were paying more than 1.5 times the average.

Some of the variation reflects cost-based price differences, such as those between higher peak and lower off-peak fares. Cost differences also arise because business travelers place a much higher value than pleasure travelers on the convenience of booking a seat at the last minute. Airlines therefore carry a larger inventory of seats for business travelers relative to their expected demand than they do for pleasure travelers. The cost of these extra seats is reflected in the high unrestricted fares business travelers pay. Some additional price variation is due to the proliferation of so-called niche carriers such as Reno Air, which stimulates a greater range of fare offerings by all carriers. Finally, the wider variation reflects carriers' increased efforts to align their fares more closely with passengers' willingness to pay for air travel. The benefit for travelers and carriers is that carriers can use discount prices to fill seats that would otherwise be vacant.

The results in figure 5, in combination with the increase in competition at the route level shown in figure 2, suggests that the increase in airline competition has led to a wider dispersion of fares. Is this interpretation correct? Intuition suggests otherwise; perfect competition, for example, should cause prices to converge – the law of one price. To resolve this matter empirically, we constructed measures of a carrier's spread of fares on a route, then regressed this variable on characteristics of the route and the level of competition on it, including the number of effective competitors.[13] We did this separately for each quarter from the fourth quarter of

---

[11] Fare difference between countries could reflect differences in average trip distance. The significant finding here, however, is the trend in the percentage difference.

[12] To obtain a distribution for a given quarter, the variation on each route was weighted by the number of passengers traveling on that route.

[13] The basic unit of observation was the spread of a carrier's fares on a route. The data set was from the ten largest carriers nationwide in 1993 for the 1,000 most heavily traveled domestic routes. Separate regressions were run for each quarter from the fourth quarter of

Figure 2-6. Effect of an Additional Competitor on the Spread of Airline Fares on a Route, Fourth Quarter 1978 to Fourth Quarter 1993

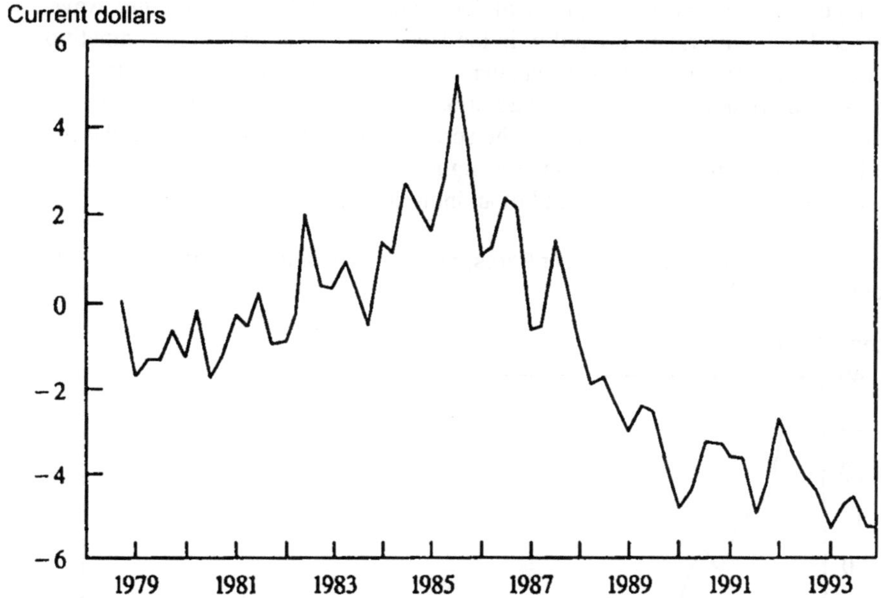

Source: Authors' calculations. Each entry is the effect of an additional effective competitor on the real standard deviation of each carrier's fares on each of its domestic routes (that is, the coefficient of the number of effective competitors from a regression for a given quarter). See text for additional details.

1978 to the fourth quarter of 1993, and for several definitions of spread. With spread defined as the real standard deviation, the effect of airline competition on the spread of fares (the estimated coefficient of the effective competition variable in the fare regressions) is shown in figure 6.[14] Increased competition widened the spread of fares only after deregulation had been under way for a few years, perhaps because of the introduction of discount fares by People Express and other new entrants. That

1978 to the fourth quarter of 1993. Four measures of the spread of fares were used: the real standard deviation of fares, the standard deviation divided by the mean (the coefficient of variation), the eightieth percentile of real fares minus the twentieth percentile of real fares, and that percentile difference divided by the fiftieth percentile fare. The results did not change regardless of which spread measure we used. We also considered alternative assumptions regarding the minimum number of passengers an airline had to carry to qualify as serving a route during a particular quarter. Our base case was 600 sampled passengers a quarter (Department of Transportation Data Bank 1A is a 10 percent sample of airline tickets), which is equivalent to one flight a day. The findings were not particularly sensitive to alternative assumptions. Finally, the dependent variables were route distance, carrier dummy variables to capture airline-specific effects, dummy variables for each airport on the route that is subject to capacity controls that effectively limit entry (there are four slot-controlled airports), the number of effective competitors on the route, and the minimum number of effective competitors at the origin and destination airports.

[14] The pattern of results was unchanged when a 95 percent confidence interval of the coefficients is plotted instead of the point estimates.

is, the established carriers lowered some of their fares to match those of the new entrants, but kept others unchanged.

Competition increased the spread of fares until the mid-1980s merger wave.[15] But since 1988, with relative stability in the level of national and route competition, the fares of carriers on routes with greater competition have less spread. Based on the data in the figure, during 1993 an additional competitor on a route decreased the spread 8 to 9 percent. Thus although the spread of fares for all carriers at the route level has grown since deregulation (see figure 5), after the late 1980s, increasing route competition reduced the spread of an individual carrier's fares.

Figure 2-7. Change in Domestic Air Fares, by Route Distance, Fourth Quarter 1978 to Fourth Quarer 1993

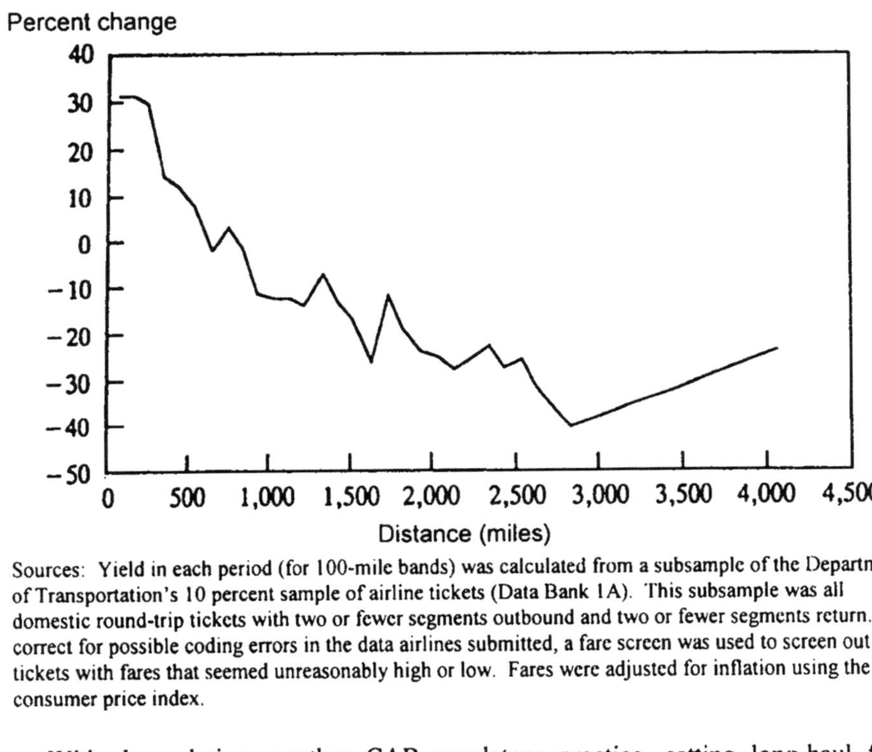

Sources: Yield in each period (for 100-mile bands) was calculated from a subsample of the Department of Transportation's 10 percent sample of airline tickets (Data Bank 1A). This subsample was all domestic round-trip tickets with two or fewer segments outbound and two or fewer segments return. To correct for possible coding errors in the data airlines submitted, a fare screen was used to screen out tickets with fares that seemed unreasonably high or low. Fares were adjusted for inflation using the consumer price index.

With deregulation, another CAB regulatory practice, setting long-haul fares higher than cost to subsidize short-haul fares that were set below cost, also ended. Now that competitive forces and not a regulatory formula determine prices, real

[15] Severin Borenstein and Nancy L. Rose, "Competition and Price Dispersion in the U.S. Airline Industry," *Journal of Political Economy*, vol. 102 (August 1994), pp. 653-83, also found a positive relationship between route-level competition and the spread of fares during the second quarter of 1986.

airfares have increased for distances of less than 800 miles and decreased for greater distances (figure 7).[16]

All these fare differences understandably obscure the finding that deregulation has substantially lowered average fares. Although 70 percent of passengers accounting for 78 percent of revenue passenger miles in the fourth quarter of 1993 paid fares less than or equal to what they would have had regulation continued (figure 8), not all travelers have benefited. Because of all the fare differences, 14 percent of passengers accounting for 10 percent of passenger miles are paying fares that are two or more times higher than they would have been had regulation continued. This new order is undoubtedly partly responsible for instances of public dissatisfaction with deregulation.

1.3 SERVICE QUALITY

Fare increases or decreases are not the only matter to affect passenger welfare, of course. There is also the question of how deregulation has affected service. Service is something of an amorphous concept: it can cover everything from the quality of food provided by carriers to the cheerfulness of flight attendants, from ease of check-in to the care taken in baggage handling, from the frequency of flights to how many direct flights are available to whether passengers need to switch airlines to reach their destination. Not all of these services are possible to quantify. But several key dimensions, including the frequency of service, how many passengers change flights, the length of travel time, and the level of restrictions on tickets, can be analyzed with some rigor.

By eliminating the old restrictions on which carriers could fly where, deregulation gave airlines increased freedom and flexibility to restructure their networks into hub-and-spoke systems that feed travelers from all directions into a major airport (hub) from which they take connecting flights to their destinations. The hub-and-spoke system has been adopted by nearly all carriers. American has established major hubs at Dallas-Fort Worth and Chicago, United at Denver and Chicago, Delta at Atlanta and Dallas-Fort Worth. Among smaller carriers, Southwest has hubs at Phoenix and Dallas Love Field and Reno Air at Reno. The system gives passengers from spokes and from the hub more frequent service than would be possible with single-plane service. The resulting benefits from the increased frequency over what was offered during regulation has been estimated at $10.3 billion a year in 1993 dollars.[17]

---

[16] Some low-density short routes are served by carriers receiving a subsidy under the essential air service provision of the Airline Deregulation Act. The subsidy was designed to ensure that no community that received air service by a CAB-regulated carrier would lose air service as a result of deregulation. Service to that community would be subsidized if no carrier was willing to offer unsubsidized service. Without the subsidy, short-haul fares would have risen somewhat more.

[17] This figure is from Morrison and Winston, *Economic Effects of Airline Deregulation*, p. 31 – a gain per traveler from increased frequency of $8.00 times 539.3 million intercity trips converted to 1993 dollars. It reflects the value of increased frequency through 1983. We are not aware of more recent estimates. This finding was somewhat surprising. The traditional view of regulation was that because carriers were prevented from competing through fares

Figure 2-8. Distribution of Domestic Air Fares Relative to Projected Regulated Fares, Fourth Quarter 1993

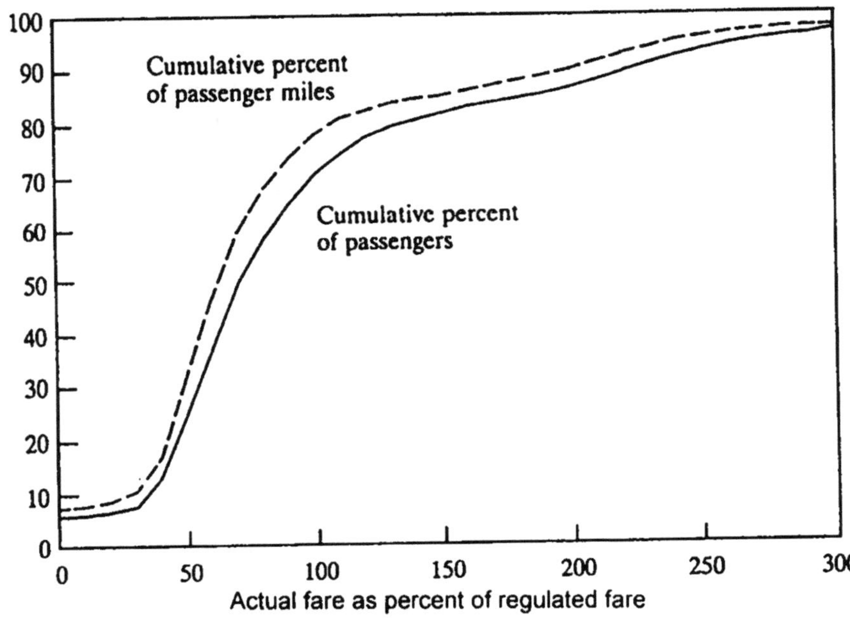

Data Source and Variable Construction: Fares actually paid in 1993:4 are from a subsample of the Department of Transportation's 10 percent sample of airline tickets (Data Bank 1A). This subsample was all domestic round-trip tickets with two or fewer segments outbound and two or fewer segments return. To correct for possible coding errors in the data the airlines submitted, a fare screen was used to eliminate tickets with fares that seemed unreasonably high. Tickets with low fares were not removed in order not to remove valid frequent flier tickets. However, the percentage of zero-fare tickets was reduced by 1.7 percent of total tickets (2.5 percent of total passenger miles) to correct for coding errors. (See footnote 6 in this chapter for the origin of these correction factors.) For each ticket in the subsample, the fare actually paid was compared with an estimate of the regulated fare that would have been charged if fares were based on our adjusted standard industry fare level (SIFL) fare formula.

A familiar complaint about the hub-and-spoke system is that passengers are not flown by the shortest route to their destinations, that instead they must take circuitous routings that require changing planes. But changing planes has not been much more frequent than it was before deregulation: 28 percent of passengers had to change in 1978 and about 32 percent in 1993 (figure 9). What has changed remarkably is the nature of the connections. In 1978 about half of passengers changing planes -- 14 percent of all passengers – also changed airlines. But with the freedom to enter new markets that was afforded by deregulation, airlines have been able to rationalize their route systems so that today only 1 percent of passengers much change airlines, an improvement in service because travelers prefer on-line to interline connections.[18] And despite the occasional apparent circuity of routing

they competed, in particular, through flight frequency. See, for example, George W. Douglas and James C. Miller III, *Economic Regulation of Domestic Air Transport: Theory and Policy* (Brookings, 1974).

[18] Dennis W. Carlton, William M. Landes, and Richard A. Posner, "Benefits and Costs of Airline Mergers: A Case Study," *Bell Journal of Economics*, vol. 11 (Spring 1980), p. 73,

required by the hub-and-spoke system, excess air mileage has increased only about 1 percentage point (figure 10).[19] Thus we found that the net effect on travelers' welfare of fewer interline connections combined with more connections overall would seem to be beneficial, if slight (see the appendix to this chapter).

Figure 2-9. Share of All Passengers on Domestic Flights Who Needed to Make Connecting Flights, 1978-93

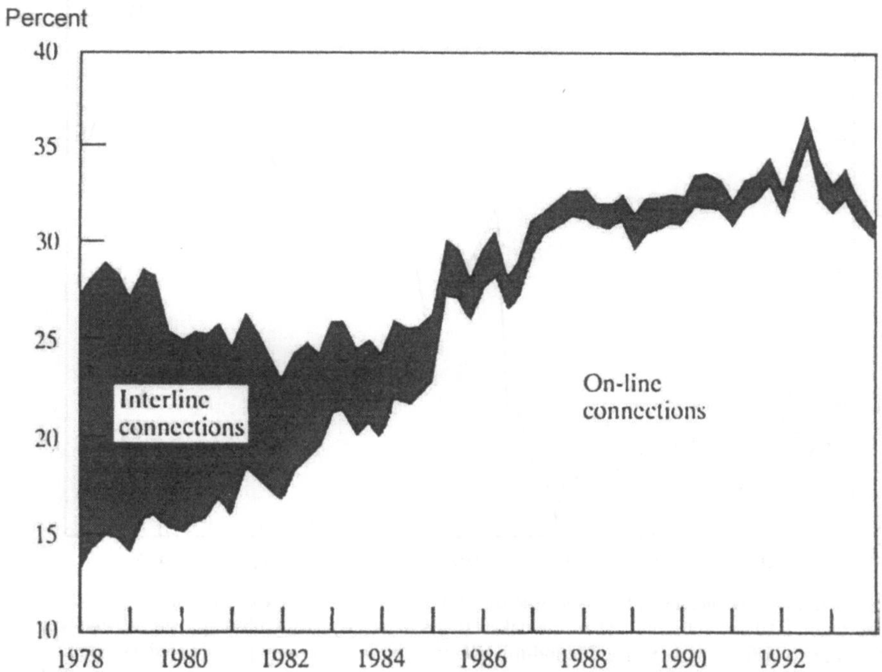

Sources: Percentage and composition of connecting passengers was calculated from a subsample of domestic trips in the Department of Transportation's 10 percent sample of airline tickets (Data Bank 1A). This subsample consisted of one-way tickets with two or fewer segments and round-trip tickets with two or fewer segments on the outbound and return legs.

---

estimate that travelers would be willing to pay between \$13.10 and \$17.75 (in 1977 dollars) more for a flight with an on-line connection than one with an interline connection. Using the midpoint of this range and converting it to 1993 dollars yields nearly \$37 a traveler. The benefits from on-line connections include a shorter walk in the terminal to catch the connecting flight, greater coordination with the originating flight (for example, if it is delayed), and less chance of lost luggage.

19 Excess air mileage was calculated by comparing the miles actually flown by all passengers in our subsample of Data Bank 1A with the great circle distance (the shortage distance) from their origin to their destination. The matter of circuity also affects the debate about fares. The conventional approach to calculating yield has been to divide revenue by passenger miles actually traveled, not the (shorter) great circle distance from origin to destination. To the extent that circuity has increased, yields will be artificially low, reflecting the increased miles required to make a given trip. However, because the change in circuity from 1978-93 was only one percent, the error in fare comparisons over the same period was small – only 1 percent.

Figure 2-10. Excess of Actual Distance Flown over Shortest Possible Distance to Destination, Domestic Trips, 1978-93

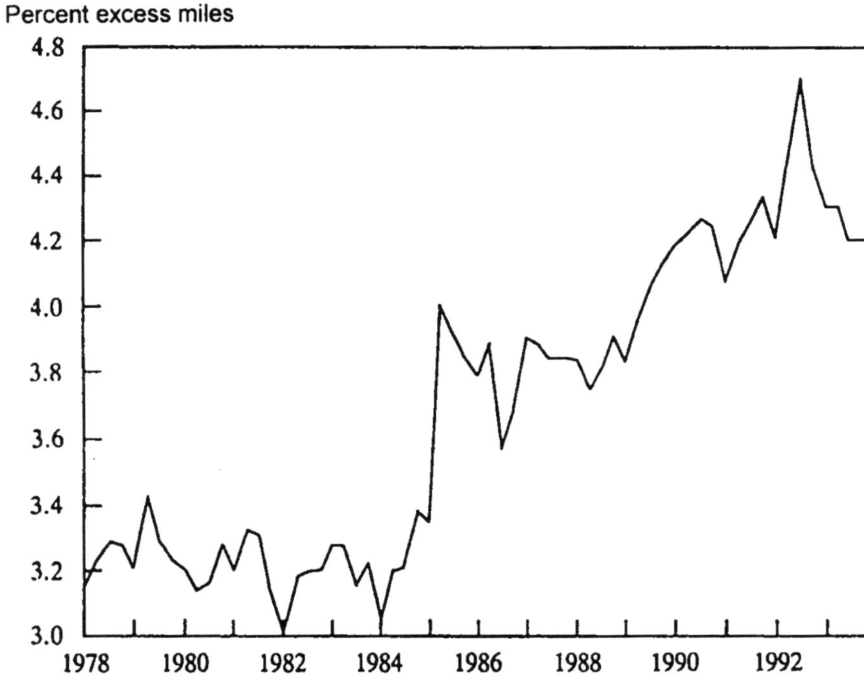

Sources: Circuity was calculated from a subsample of domestic trips in the Department of Transportation's 10 percent sample of airline tickets (Data Bank 1A). This subsample was all one-way tickets with two or fewer segments and round-trip tickets with two or fewer segments on the outbound and return legs. For all trips, the actual distance flown from origin to destination was compared with the shortest (that is, the great circle) distance from origin to destination. The circuity figures above involve the percentage of passengers connecting times the circuity of connections. Percentage of passengers connecting has increased from about 28 percent in 1978 to about 32 percent in 1993. During the same time the cuicuity of connections increased from about 11 percent to 13 percent.

The benefit from hub-and-spoke systems have been partly offset by increased travel time, both on the ground and in the air (figure 11). The ground time has increased by five minutes regardless of distance. (Because the data are for flight segments, time spent connecting between flights is not reflected.) This increase probably stems from greater airport and airway congestion in the wake of deregulation. The strike by air traffic controllers and the subsequent dismissal of trained personnel in 1981, events independent of deregulation may also have contributed to congestion.[20]

[20] As discussed more fully in the final chapter, the negative effects of increased airport and airway congestion could be reduced by congestion-based takeoff and landing fees at airports as well as by expedited introduction of new technologies and operating procedures.

The difference in travel time increases with distance, which is consistent with slower cruise speeds that are themselves perhaps the result of pilots' flying more slowly to conserve fuel and of the slower cruising speed of more recently developed aircraft. Because both influences are arguably independent of deregulation, this increase should not be entirely attributed to it. Nonetheless, if deregulation were responsible for the entire additional travel time, we estimate the cost to travelers at $2.8 billion in 1993 dollars.[21] The increase in flight time since deregulation, and its cost to travelers, does appear to have stabilized (figure 12). After expanding steadily since 1983, the additional flight time peaked in 1990 at about 8 minutes and has remained close to that level even though passenger enplanements have continued to expand.

Figure 2-11. Change in Components of Total Flight Time, Domestic Flights, by Flight Distance, 1978-93

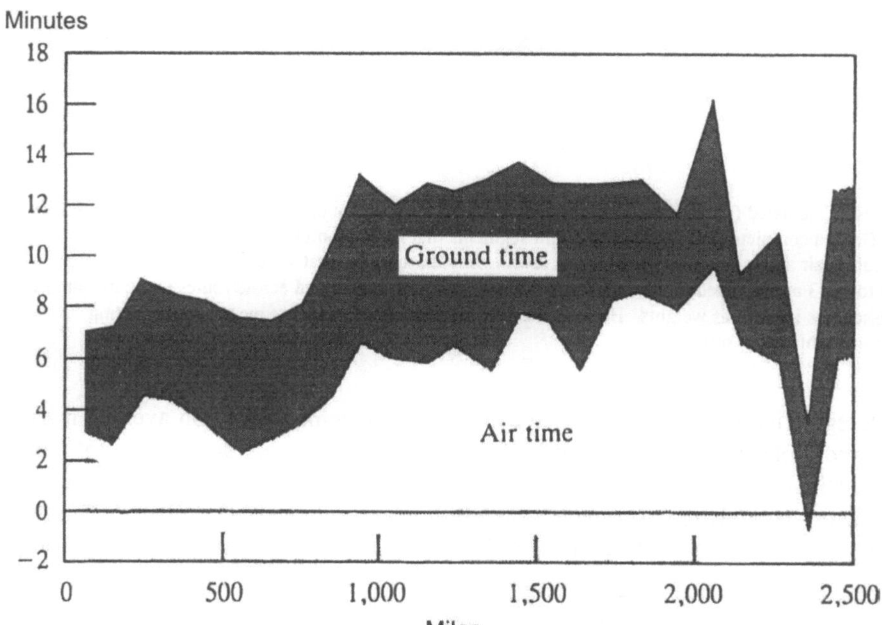

Sources: Calculated from the domestic flight data in the Department of Transportation Service Segment Data Base, a complete census of airline flight segments that gives monthly totals for actual (not scheduled) air and ground time at the route level. Because the data are for flight segments, time spent connecting between flights is not reflected. Variability for distances greater than 2,000 miles is because there are fewer routes over which to average.

---

21 From the data for figure 11, we derived a passenger-weighted average of 9.0 minutes' increase in total flight time for each flight segment. Multiplying the average number of passenger segments (enplanements) from 1978-93 by 9.0 minutes and using the value of travel time, updated to 1993 dollars, in Steven A. Morrison and Clifford Winston, "Enhancing the Performance of the Deregulated Air Transportation System," *Brookings Papers on Economic Activity: Microeconomics* (1989), p. 66 (the original estimate was $34.04 an hour in 1983 dollars), yields the figure in the text.

Figure 2-12. Change in Components of Total Flight Time, Domestic Flights, 1978-93

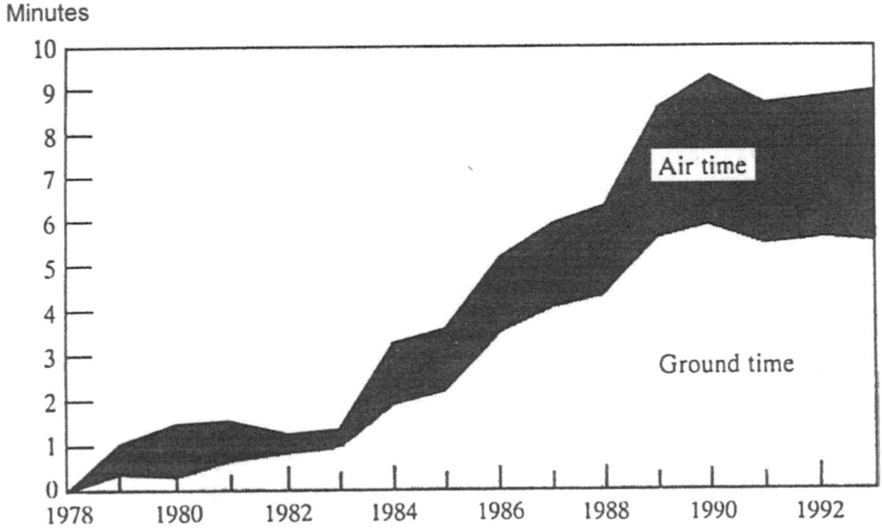

Sources: Calculated from the domestic flight data in the Department of Transportation Service Segment Data Base, a complete census of airline flight segments that gives monthly totals for actual (not scheduled) air and ground time at the route level. Only those routes that were served in all years from 1978 to 1993 are included in the calculation. Flight times are aggregated across routes using the number of passengers in 1978 as weights. Because the data are for flight segments time spent connecting between flights is not reflected.

Deregulation has reduced service convenience in some ways. On average it has filled more planes and made it harder for travelers to get a seat on the flight of their choice (figure 13). The increase in the percentage of seats filled, called the industry load factor, is likely to cost travelers $0.6 billion annually in 1993 dollars.[22] But the higher load factor has helped to hold average costs and fares down during

[22] This estimate used the schedule delay formula developed by Douglas and Miller, /*Economic Regulation of Domestic Air Transport*. We assume that without deregulation the load factor would have remained at its 1977 value of 55.9 percent (Morrison and Winston, *Economic Effects of Air Deregulation*, p. 35). This ignores any possible long-term growth in load factors that may have occurred during regulation, thus inflating our cost estimate. For each year from 1978 to 1993 we calculated the difference between schedule delay using the 1977 figure and the actual figure for that year (assuming routes had 1,000 passengers a day and an aircraft with 150 seats). Valuing schedule delay at the rate used by Morrison and Winston, *Economic Effects of Airline Deregulation*, and multiplying by the average number of enplanements from 1978 to 1993 yielded the figure in the text. To be sure, using an average load factor does not account for the variation in load factors across city pairs. However, because of the nonlinear relation between load factors and schedule delay, load factors probably need to be consistently in the 65-70 percent range, which is typically greater than current levels, to generate large welfare losses from the difficulty in obtaining a seat on a preferred flight.

deregulation. Between 1978 and 1993 load factors fell for flights shorter than 1,000 miles and rose for longer flights (figure 14) – an expected effect given the CAB's fare policies, which elevated long-haul fares in order to subsidize short-haul fares, and the postderegulation fare changes that increased fares on the shorter flights (see figure 7).[23] The inverse relationship between fare and load factor changes indicates that some of the benefits from lower long distance fares have been compromised by the greater difficulty of obtaining a seat on a desired flight. And some of the increases in short-distance fares have been counterbalanced by a better chance of getting a seat on a desired flight. But given an annual cost of only $0.6 billion, the effect on consumers of this deterioration in service quality has been slight.

Figure 2-13. Share of Airline Seats Filled by Paying Passengers (Load Factor), 1970-93

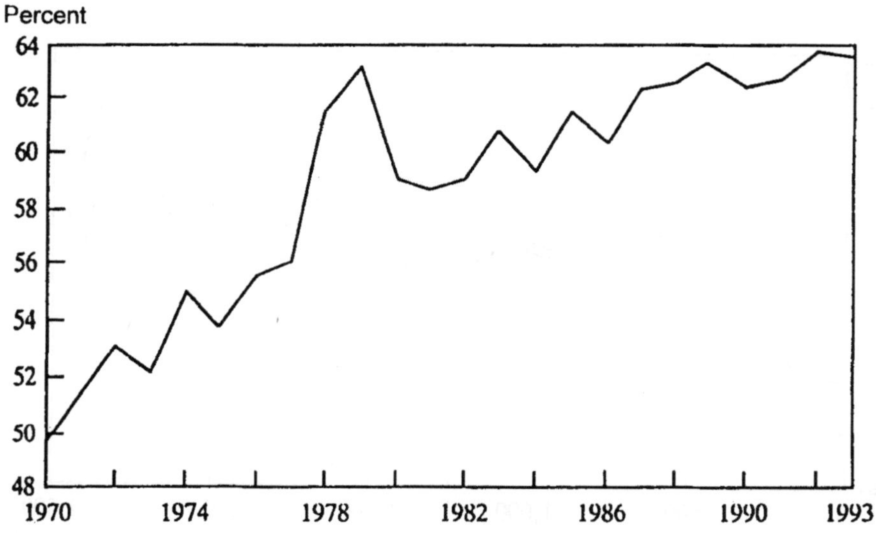

Source: Air Transport Association, *Air Transport: The Annual Report of the U.S. Scheduled Airline Industry* (various years). Load factor is the percentage of seats filled with paying passengers. It is calculated by dividing revenue-passenger miles by available seat miles (for both international and domestic service).

Service convenience has also been compromised by travel restrictions – advance purchase requirements, cancellation penalties, a mandatory Saturday night stay, and so on – attached to discount fares. Minimum stay and Saturday night stay requirements have perhaps caused more inconvenience than increase load factors because they may have forced customers to think about staying more days to get the

[23] The 1978 load factors reflect the effect of less stringent application of CAB fare policy leading up to deregulation. Douglas and Miller, *Economic Regulation of Domestic Air Transport*, found that load factors in 1969 actually decreased with distance because of CAB fare policies.

lower fare rather than consider traveling during off-peak hours or making other compromises.

Deregulation has, then, led to some significant improvements in service quality, especially more frequent flights and less necessity for changing airlines to make connections. These benefits must be balanced against reductions in service quality attributable to more crowded flights, slightly longer flight times because of more congestion, a few more connections, and fare restrictions, whose costs are quantified in chapter 4. We will assess these costs and benefits, along with the benefits from lower fares, after evaluating whether certain carrier practices could erode the benefits from deregulation.

Figure 2-14. Share of Airline Seats Filled by Paying Passengers, by Distance, Domestic Flights, 1978, 1993

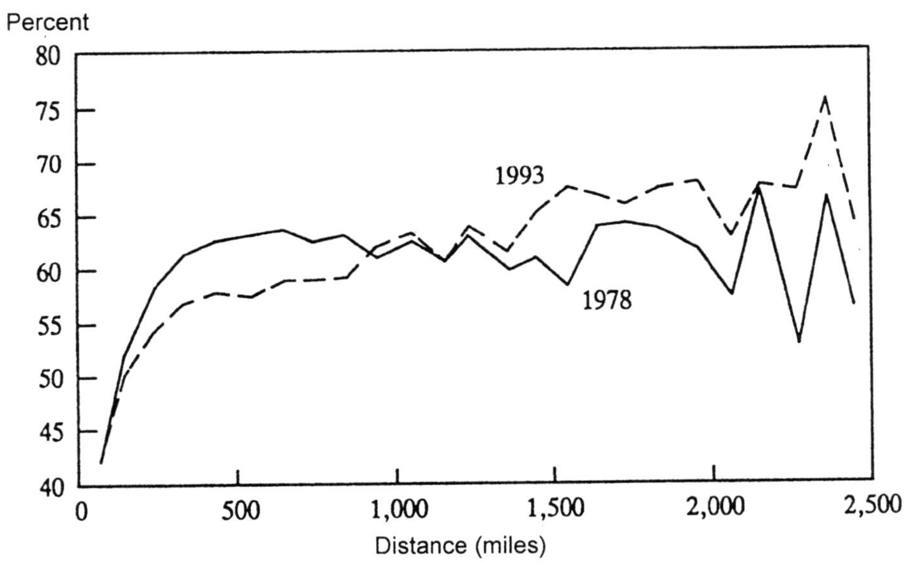

Source: Authors' calculations based on data in the Department of Transportation Service Segment Data Base, a complete census of airline flights.

TABLE 4. OPERATING PROFIT MARGINS, SELECTED AIRLINES, 1970-93
Percent

Year	American	Continental	Delta	Eastern	America West	Northwest	Pan American	TWA	United	USAir	Southwest
1970	- 1.33	6.98	12.20	4.42	...	13.49	- 3.61	- 7.32	- 1.40	6.12	n.a.
1971	2.30	9.16	8.97	3.40	...	4.30	- 3.04	1.19	2.27	3.66	n.a.
1972	3.05	9.36	11.45	4.58	...	3.88	- 1.12	5.29	4.40	6.59	n.a.
1973	- 2.45	3.93	11.01	- 1.55	...	8.84	- 0.21	4.80	7.73	6.06	n.a.
1974	2.38	10.23	12.03	4.62	...	10.20	- 6.21	- 1.05	7.96	5.00	n.a.
1975	-1.59	6.57	4.96	0.39	...	6.13	- 2.10	- 4.53	- 0.24	0.85	n.a.
1976	3.39	6.82	7.84	4.34	...	10.65	0.82	2.61	1.29	4.13	n.a.
1977	2.70	6.81	9.31	1.69	...	10.02	4.57	1.83	2.72	5.23	n.a.
1978	3.55	5.53	9.64	4.07	...	8.55	6.30	1.98	8.22	6.03	n.a.
1979	- 0.06	- 2.23	4.63	3.85	...	4.33	2.80	- 1.52	- 7.34	7.13	19.96
1980	- 3.07	- 6.27	4.97	0.05	...	- 1.46	- 3.56	- 1.09	- 1.55	9.40	22.92
1981	1.11	- 5.55	2.37	- 1.34	...	0.11	- 10.53	0.11	- 3.28	5.27	17.94
1982	- 0.46	- 5.06	- 2.37	- 0.50	...	- 0.42	- 10.74	- 3.22	- 1.49	6.23	11.84
1983	5.51	- 13.29	- 1.46	- 2.54	- 35.52	3.14	0.37	- 1.96	2.88	9.00	15.29
1984	6.66	8.99	6.39	4.35	- 7.01	3.93	- 4.00	2.06	9.02	11.83	12.81
1985	8.64	8.98	4.88	4.60	7.73	2.88	- 6.58	- 1.65	- 6.67	9.54	11.60
1986	6.69	6.98	5.00	1.44	1.20	4.16	- 13.63	- 2.38	- 0.15	9.19	13.13
1987	6.64	0.68	7.13	1.30	- 6.13	4.04	- 5.46	5.93	1.92	12.73	5.91
1988	9.37	1.72	7.10	- 5.39	2.32	3.50	- 2.93	5.95	7.14	5.13	10.00
1989	7.34	3.16	7.82	- 55.73	4.82	4.43	- 8.83	0.54	4.74	- 5.42	9.61
1990	0.62	- 4.65	- 2.69	- 24.45	- 2.39	- 1.95	- 12.48	- 3.52	- 0.50	- 8.93	6.88
1991	0.14	- 5.09	- 2.65	...	- 7.37	- 0.80	- 22.39	- 9.52	- 4.21	- 3.34	4.72
1992	- 0.57	- 3.73	- 7.09	...	- 5.74	- 3.88	...	- 10.35	- 3.90	- 6.02	10.79
1993	3.82	- 0.91	- 2.22	...	9.09	3.92	...	- 8.02	2.06	- 1.94	13.60

Source: Authors' calculations based on Department of Transportation form 41. Data include both international and domestic operations of the airlines. Operating profit margin is the difference between revenue and cost expressed as a percentage of revenue, where cost does not include interest on long-term debt and income taxes. (Eastern ceased operating in early 1991. Pan American ceased operating in late 1991. America West began operating in 1983. Although operating, Southwest did not have to file form 41 until 1979.)

n.a. Not available.

1.4 PROFITS

One thing is certain. The industry has not been earning excessive profits.[24] Although operating profits among individual carriers have always varied (table 4), from 1990 to 1993 nearly all carriers experienced heavy losses, for a total of several billion dollars. Some carriers went into bankruptcy, and Eastern, Pan American, and Midway Airlines were liquidated, prompting speculation that only a few carriers might survive the current shakeout.[25] But amidst all the bad news, Southwest Airlines, under the colorful and innovative leadership of Herbert Kelleher, developed into a highly profitable carrier, generating an average operating profit margin of nearly 9 percent between 1990 and 1993.[26] As we discuss later, although Southwest is the next-to-smallest major carrier, with revenues about one-seventh those of American Airlines, its low-cost operations offer an intriguing glimpse of the direction in which some parts of the industry appear to be headed.

Figure 15 shows the operating profit margin (for both domestic and international service) for U.S. scheduled airlines from 1970 to 1993. Given the amount of stockholders' equity outstanding and the carriers' long-term debt, earning a "normal" 12 percent pretax return on investment would require an operating margin of about 5 percent.[27] This rate has seldom been achieved either before or since

---

[24] There are many ways to measure profit. Economists' preferred approach is to estimate a return to capital. Other approaches are operating (gross) profit margin, net profit margin, return to equity, and so on. Return to capital, the best definition conceptually, suffers from the difficulty of obtaining the data, in particular, market values, needed to measure it. Although less appropriate for some purposes, the other measures are easier to calculate. For example, the operating profit margin is simply the difference between revenue and cost, where cost does not include income taxes or interest on long-term debt, expressed as a percentage of revenue. In this book we frequently focus on the operating profit margin because it could be constructed from readily available data and, because it excludes interest on long-term debt, was invariant to a firm's capital structure.

[25] A commonly cited estimate of the extent of losses during 1990-93 for both domestic and international service is $12.8 billion (after tax and interest payments), based on data in Air Transport Association, *Air Transport, 1994: The Annual Report of the U.S. Scheduled Airline Industry* (Washington, 1994), p. 3. This figure is potentially misleading because it includes losses due to changes in accounting practices (affecting all industries). Since 1992 the Financial Accounting Standards Board (through FASB 106) has required businesses to record retiree benefits and other liabilities that they always assumed but were not required to report. This change accounts for $2.2 billion of the losses reported earlier. In addition, the staggering losses of a few carriers (those that were in bankruptcy: Pan American, Eastern, TWA, and Continental), amounting to $5.6 billion, make the industry as a whole look sicker than it is. Finally, these losses exaggerate the true financial picture because the accounting charge for depreciation of airline assets (mostly airplanes) typically exceeds the true decline in the value of the assets. Notwithstanding these qualifications, by any measure the airlines did sustain considerable losses during the early 1990s.

[26] Richard S. Teitelbaum, "Southwest Airlines: Where Service Flies Right," *Fortune*, August 24, 1992, p. 115, estimated that Southwest generated a 26.5 percent annualized return to investors from 1987 to 1992.

[27] The 5 percent figure is the approximate operating profit margin that would be required from 1976 to 1993 to enable gross profits to be 12 percent of long-term debt and stockholders' equity.

deregulation. The industry's poor performance during regulation reflects another failing of regulatory policy, which was to have set fare levels that, at least in principle, would have enabled carriers to earn a normal rate of return. They did not, and deregulation has not remedied the situation. Indeed, the major concern today is whether the industry can be profitable at all for a protracted period.

Figure 2-15. Scheduled Airline Operating Profit Margin for Domestic and International Services, 1970-93

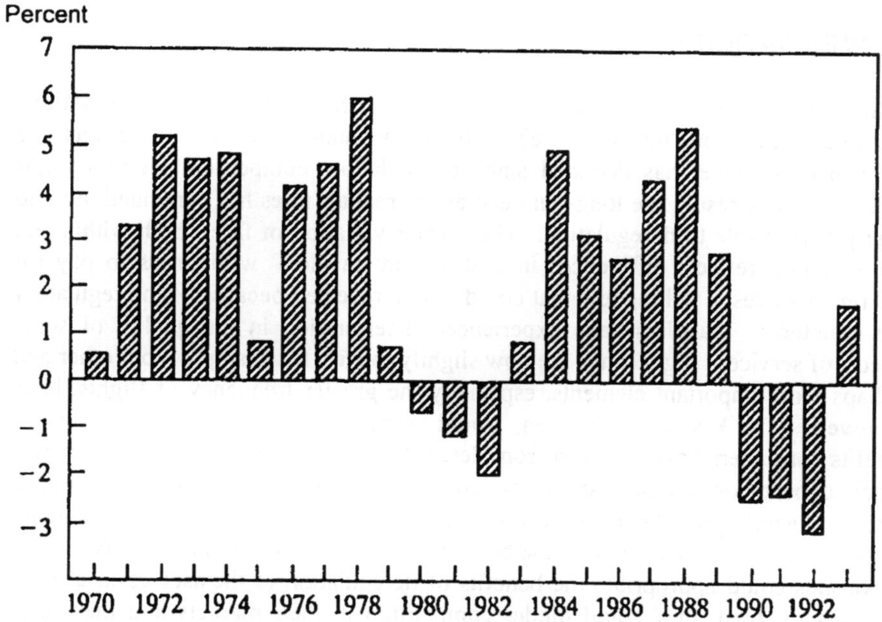

Source: Air Transport Association, *Air Transport: The Annual Report of the U.S. Scheduled Airline Industry* (various years). Operating profit margin is the percentage by which revenue exceeds cost, where cost does not include interest on long-term debt and income taxes and includes both domestic and international operations.

1.5 SAFETY

When deregulation took effect in 1978, industry analysts feared that the new competitive conditions could affect airline safety in two ways.[28] Some speculated that unregulated competition would lead to lower profits, prompting airlines to skimp on maintenance.[29] And there was also concern that as commuter airlines

---

[28] For complete discussion of airline deregulation and airline safety see Clinton V. Oster, Jr., John S. Strong, and C. Kurt Zorn, *Why Airplanes Crash: Aviation Safety in a Changing World* (Oxford University Press, 1992): and Nancy L. Rose, "Fear of Flying? Economic Analyses of Airline Safety," *Journal of Economic Perspectives*, vol. 6 (Spring 1992), pp. 75-94.

[29] Oster, Strong, and Zorn, *Why Airplanes Crash*, have noted that most researchers have found no relationship between lower profits and reduced safety. An exception is Nancy L. Rose. "Profitability and Product Quality: Economic Determinants of Airline Safety

replaced larger airlines at small cities, safety records might deteriorate because of the higher accident rate of commuter carriers. But in the past two decades, as figure 16 shows, air travel safety for commuter and larger airlines combined has improved. Because the raw data are so volatile from year to year, the figure uses a moving average to smooth out the fluctuations and emphasize the underlying trend. Safety therefore should be the least controversial concern about air transportation. Regardless of how it is measured, only one conclusion can be reached: the chance of dying in an airplane crash continues to diminish.

1.6 IMPLICATIONS

What does this empirical profile reveal about the current state of air transportation? And what does it bode for the future? Although the number of effective competitors at the national level has declined since deregulation, competition on routes has increased. As a result, the long-run decrease in real air fares has continued, a trend largely attributable to deregulation. The greater variation of fares, both within and across routes, reflects differences in cost and in travelers' willingness to pay for different services, a willingness that could not be revealed because of the regulatory fare structure. Travelers have experienced deterioration in the quality of some aspects of service – flight times are now slightly longer, for example – but other and perhaps more important elements, especially the greater frequency of flights, have improved. The key question, then, would seem to be can the fare and service benefits consumers have received from deregulation be sustained? And the answer largely depends on whether carriers can continue to maintain the benefits in the face of the industry's poor financial performance during the past few years or whether they will be able to appropriate these benefits to maintain their basic viability.

Airlines could appropriate the benefits of deregulation to themselves in at least three ways. First, they could hinder competition in their markets and then raise fares. One possible impediment to competition is that any carrier that might wish to compete on routes connected to another carrier's major hubs would have to enter the market on a large scale to match its competitor's large number of flights on those routes. Another impediment is the frequent flier programs that reward passengers for past patronage and encourage continued patronage by giving them free trips to domestic and international destinations served by the carrier. A final possible barrier to competition is computer reservation systems. The carrier that owns a

Performance," *Journal of Political Economy*, vol. 98 (October 1990), pp. 944-64, who found that lower profitability was associated with higher accident rates, particularly for smaller carriers. But, as Oster, Strong, and Zorn pointed out, the mechanism linking the two is unclear because, for example, there is little correlation between changes in profits and maintenance expenditures per available seat mile. D. Mark Kennet, "Did Deregulation Affect Aircraft Engine Maintenance? An Empirical Policy Analysis," *Rand Journal of Economics*, vol. 24 (Winter 1993), pp. 542-58, examined one aspect of maintenance and found that deregulated airlines have increased the time between major overhauls of jet engines. But he also found that this did not lead to any increase in the likelihood of an engine failure. Kennet suggests that airline maintenance was not optimized before 1978 but has been since.

system has a potential competitive edge because it is easier for travel agents who use the system to obtain information about that carrier's flights.

Figure 2-16. Chance of Death per Million Airline Departures, 1975-93

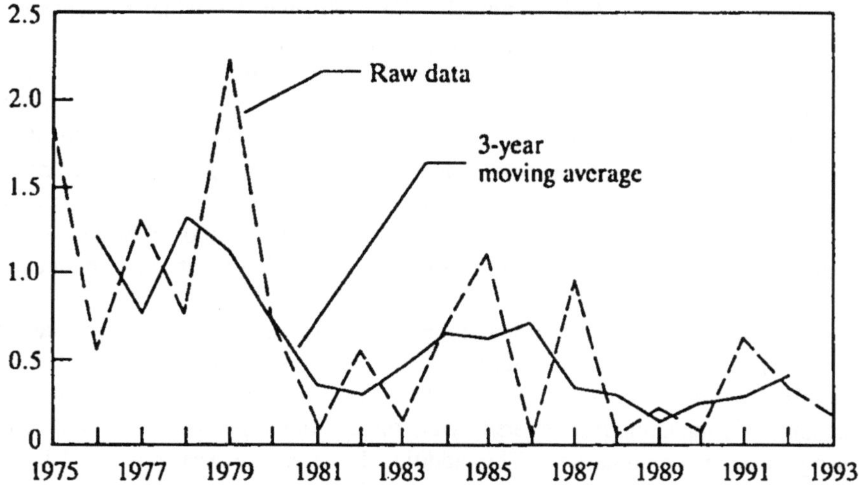

Source: Authors' calculations based on unpublished accident data from the National Transportation Safety Board for air carriers (part 121) and commuters (part 135). The probability of death is calculated by multiplying fatal accidents per departure by the percentage of passengers involved in fatal accidents who die.

With fewer effective competitors at the national level, carriers could find it easier to establish a cooperative arrangement that enables them to maintain fare increases and to avoid fare wars. Finally, travel restrictions already attached to discount fares could be tightened, forcing losses on travelers from higher (unrestricted) fares or greater service inconvenience.

Airline profits have continued to be cyclical, yet rarely during deregulation have they exceeded a normal return. In the past few years the industry has lost billions of dollars. This situation has prompted three classes of questions. What explains the large losses? What type of carriers – national, regional, commuter – will survive the slump? And is the only industry structure that is viable in the long run less competitive than the current structure?

Appendix

This appendix estimates the net effect on travelers' welfare of fewer interline connections but in the context of more connections overall. To obtain this estimate, we performed calculations based on the number of passengers taking one-way trips with two or fewer segments and round-trips with two or fewer segments on the outbound and return legs (the same data used in figure 9). Following this procedure reduced the likelihood that intermediate destinations were improperly viewed as points of connection because the data did not allow one to distinguish between a connection and an intermediate destination.

To estimate the benefits of fewer interline connections, we calculate the percentage of connections from the first three quarters of 1978 that were interline. This percentage was multiplied by the percentage of connecting passengers to yield an estimate of the percentage of passengers who would have had interline connections if regulation had continued. We subtracted the actual percentage of passengers making interline connections from this figure to yield the percentage of passengers who now have on-line connections but would have had 8 interline connections if regulation had continued. This resulting figure was multiplied by the number of passengers involved to obtain, for a given quarter, an estimate of the reduction in the number of interline connections due to deregulation. Multiplying this estimated reduction by $37 (the value of an on-line versus and interline connection reported in note 17) and averaging over the period 1979-93 gave an estimate of the average annual benefit to travelers from fewer interline connections of $0.85 billion in 1993 dollars.

To estimate the cost of additional connections, we calculated the percentage of travelers from the first three quarters of 1978 to estimate the percentage of connecting passengers under regulation. This figure was subtracted from the actual percentage of connecting passengers to yield the additional percentage of connecting passengers under deregulation. This additional percentage was multiplied by the number of passengers involved to give the number of extra connecting passengers. Based on findings in Steve A. Morrison and Clifford Winston, "Enhancing the Performance of the Deregulated Air Transportation System," *Brookings Papers on Economic Activity: Microeconomics* (1989), pp. 61-112, and assuming a 1,500 mile trip distance, an additional connection adds 66 minutes of transfer time and an additional 65 minutes to travel time. Based on the values of travel and transfer time obtained by Morrison and Winston, the average annual cost of additional connections is $0.69 billion in 1993 dollars. Because these calculations involved a subset of all passengers, both figures are understated, but their difference, approximately zero, should be reasonably accurate.

2 THE RECORD IN AUSTRALASIA

Jim Wolfe

2.1 INTRODUCTION

It is no small understatement to say that there has been a great deal of change in the way that air transport is regulated in Australia in the past ten years.

It has been a major transformation of thinking from regulation to deregulation.

Australia and New Zealand have moved from highly regulated, some would say strangled, policy approaches to aviation; to one where in Australia for example there is over 50 carriers serving the market.

I will try to avoid Australian bias in the following discussion but naturally I am better placed to concentrate on Australia's experience while in no way neglecting the achievements made in New Zealand.

In essence in Australia we have moved from an approach which saw:

- strict separation of the international and domestic aviation sectors;
- the two airlines policy in the domestic market;
- single designation in international markets; and
- government ownership of airlines in both the international and domestic sectors.

In its place we have taken away economic regulation of major interstate routes, enabled multiple designation of carriers on international routes, seen the privatisation of our major airline carrier and achieved excellent growth in domestic and international traffic. Our major carriers have also maintained their commitment to maintaining Australia's international safety record.

Since the mid 1980s policy changes by both the Australian and New Zealand governments have completely changed the nature of the domestic aviation markets within the two countries, the international market between the two countries and their international markets with other countries.

It is quite a big story so like any good novelist, I will try to break it down into small digestible chapters.

The first chapter covers domestic deregulation because this happened first.

2.2 DOMESTIC DEREGULATION

2.2.1 Australia

Up until the early 1990s Australia's domestic aviation market was extremely restricted.

It was ruled by what was known as the "Two Airlines" Policy. How did this come about and what led to the change?

Well, in the post second world war period of the late 1940s and early 1950s the Australian Government was keen to see the development of a commercial aviation industry in Australia. As many of you will know Australia has a proud tradition in aviation and many of its pioneers such as Sir Charles Kingsford Smith and Bert Hinkler has already graced the world stage.

However due to the small size of the Australian domestic market, government intervention was considered necessary to ensure the development and growth in an orderly manner of what was essentially an "infant" industry.

The policy setting established helped to ensure long term financial stability of the industry and to prevent the emergence of a monopoly. Whether the consequent regulation of an oligopoly of two was better in hindsight is an issue for the economic historians.

To this end the government created an environment that ensured the operation of both a government owned airline, Trans-Australia Airlines (or TAA), and a private airline, Australian National Airways (ANA), on Australia's major interstate routes.

Regulation of intrastate routes in Australia is the domain of individual State Governments, however, most of Australia's significant domestic markets are those featuring interstate routes between state capital cities.

The main features of the "Two Airlines" policy covered:

- control of aircraft imports into Australia;
- capacity restrictions to avoid excess capacity and major imbalances in market share;
- restriction of entry to trunk routes to the two major airlines (with some limited exceptions); and
- strict pricing controls for interstate operators (and some intrastate regular public transport operators) to ensure that fares were cost related, consistent for similar routes and avoided cross subsidisation between fare types.

In some quarters the two airlines policy was called the 50-50 policy, that is, the controls in place worked towards ensuring the two major carriers ended up at fifty percent of the market share each.

The main objective of the competition between the two carriers was to reach 50.3% at the expense of their rivals. Hardly inspiring competition but nevertheless it did have some benefits for consumers including a consistent quality of airline service and terminal investment, and the use of large aircraft serving markets where traffic levels and load factors would normally suggest smaller aircraft types.

All in all it was a very restrictive policy.

While the policy did achieve its objective of ensuring orderly growth of Australia's domestic aviation market, during the 1970s and early 1980s increasing levels of dissatisfaction over the policy emerged.

These concerns included complaints about parallel scheduling and a lack of innovation in fares and a fundamental questioning of what would be wrong with other Australian carriers injecting competition into the market place.

Against this background, the Federal Government announced a major review of domestic aviation (the May Review), which when completed in 1986, was critical of the two airlines policy and drew attention to public dissatisfaction with a number of aspects of airline services including the level and variety of air fares.

The outcomes of the May review clearly demonstrated that a policy that was originally framed to promote fair and workable competition between the two carriers was in fact stifling incentives in serving new and existing markets and was interfering with normal business responsibility for efficient utilisation of assets.

Consistent with increasing microeconomic reform of industry and the recommendations of the May Review, on 7 October 1987 the Australian Government gave the required three years notice that it would terminate the two airlines agreement hence paving the way for deregulation of Australia's domestic aviation market in 1990.

This meant the Government was be withdrawing from the detailed regulation undertaken previously and allowing the domestic aviation market to operate within the constraints of the established competition policy controls applicable to industry generally.

It has been six and half years since deregulation and by any measure the policy has been a success. This is true even though the Australian domestic market still has only two major airlines, Qantas and Ansett, with attempts by some other new entrant airlines being unsuccessful.

The success of domestic deregulation can be measured by increased responsiveness by airlines to consumer needs, a wider range of fares (especially discount fares) and types of service, increased competition between the two major carriers to win customers, increased airline efficiency through productivity grains and striving for greater cost efficiencies to improve profitability while continuing Australia's major airlines strong aviation safety record.

The statistics supporting the benefits of domestic deregulation provide compelling evidence.

Real average air fares in the June quarter of 1996 were still 23 percent lower than pre-deregulation levels (September 1990, the quarter just prior to deregulation).

Fare discounting is much more prevalent and one major by product of this was the large number of first time fliers taking to the skies after deregulation when air travel for the first time became affordable for many Australians. The airlines have continued to work hard to keep air travel within Australia an affordable option for those wishing to visit friends and relatives scattered across the continent.

Passenger growth on domestic services has seen a significant increase, averaging over 9 percent a year over the six years after deregulation compared with growth of just 2 percent for the six years prior to deregulation.

Overall domestic passenger traffic increased by almost 70 percent from September 1990 to September 1996.

In addition to price changes the quality of service offered by airlines has not diminished as some had feared. Research done by the Australian Bureau of Transport and Communications Economics has so far indicated increased consumer benefits including better frequency of flights, the introduction of frequent flier schemes and better airport lounges.

Deregulation has not been without some highs and lows.

The first major new entrant to complete with Qantas and Ansett, Compass, entered the domestic market shortly after deregulation in December 1990 and collapsed in December 1991.

Southern Cross Airlines, which had been planning to enter the domestic market, acquired the collapsed airline to take advantage of Compass' public support, market position, employee base and infrastructure. However this second "Compass" was shortlived, entering the marketing in August 1992 and ceasing operations in March 1993.

There was always many reasons why carriers fail. The Trade Practices Commission in Australia sighted many factors for the demise of the first Compass not the least of which was a poor capital base and failure to anticipate the price competition from the major two carriers, Australian Airlines (subsequently merged with Qantas) and Ansett.

Aviation is a tough business, its major start-up costs should never be underestimated and its returns are not always quick to show up in the first years of new entrant balance sheets.

It is of course even tougher when two strong incumbent carriers are already in the market with established experience and infrastructure, the latter being a part of the former policy approach where carriers invested in high quality terminals in return for long term leases on Federal airport sites.

Whether further carriers will seek to operate domestically in Australia remains to be seen, but it should be remembered that apart from some of the major capital city pairs, many of the other domestic markets are small and compared with the level of domestic traffic in the United States, wafer thin.

2.2.2 New Zealand

The deregulation of the New Zealand domestic aviation market essentially commenced in 1983 when licensing controls on entry to the market were liberalised and controls on tariffs were removed. Licensees were not subject to capacity controls and could offer services throughout New Zealand.

Licensing of domestic air services was subsequently abolished from 1 September 1990 leading to the total deregulation of the market.

The object of the policy changes were that carriers operating within the system should be made primarily responsible for their own performance while ensuring that their operations comply with safety standards overseen by regulatory authorities. Simply giving consumers a choice was an important outcome for New Zealand.

A major result of these changes was therefore the emergence of Ansett New Zealand to compete domestically with Air New Zealand and without question force the incumbent carrier to "lift its game" from what consumers may well have believed was monopolistic complacency.

The deregulation of the Australian and New Zealand domestic markets in 1990 created conditions that would allow for the creation of a unified Australia - New Zealand market.

2.3 THE AUSTRALIA - NEW ZEALAND SINGLE AVIATION MARKET (SAM)

The trans-Tasman market between Australia and New Zealand already had liberalization features before 1992 with market driven capacity approaches, deregulated freight, virtually no government control over tariffs and a liberal approach to charter flights.

The importance of this market is not lost on either Australia or New Zealand as over 2.4 million passengers travelled between the two countries in the year ended 30 June 1996 making it the largest market for both countries and Auckland-Sydney the highest city pair. It is also a market continuing to grow, with a growth rate of over 8 percent last year.

In February 1992, the Australian Government announced that it would be seeking to reach an agreement with New Zealand to integrate the aviation markets of the two countries to create a Single Aviation Market.

This was warmly received in New Zealand and in August that year led to the signing of an memorandum of understanding between the two countries establishing a clear path to multiple designation on all trans-Tasman routes and the ability for both countries to serve each other's domestic markets.

Like any true friendships, a few rough patches needed to be ironed out before in September 1996, the Australian and New Zealand Governments reached agreement on a Single Aviation Market, better known as SAM.

SAM allows airlines of each country to gain unrestricted rights to fly anywhere within the other country, and have unrestricted rights to fly trans-Tasman services.

For example, there will be no limit to the number of SAM airlines that can operate services linking cities within and directly between the two countries.

Each airline will be able to operate such capacity for passenger and/or freight services as it decides and air fares and freight rates will be set by the airlines without reference to Government.

The SAM arrangements have created a new market worth an estimated $5 billion and covering more than 31 million passengers a year by bringing together the domestic travel markets of each country, and the trans-Tasman market which links them.

This will provide a bigger economic base from which the host airlines can compete with each other and the rest of the aviation world.

Of course strengthening the international competitiveness of Australian airlines has occurred through firstly the Qantas alliance with British Airways and more recently with Ansett, through investment by, and a commercial alliance with, Air New Zealand.

These developments have occurred while the development of closer aviation ties between Australia and New Zealand have been negotiated.

The development of these alliances of course has occurred around the world and where they are beneficial for not only our carriers, but customers, tourism and trade then clearly can achieve net benefits for Australasia.

2.4 LIBERALIZATION IN AUSTRALIA'S INTERNATIONAL AVIATION POLICY

2.4.1 Scheduled Services (Bilateral Air Services Agreements)

Up until the late 1980s, Australia's international aviation policy covering scheduled services was based on:

- strict separation of the international and domestic aviation sectors;
- single designation; and
- government ownership of Qantas whose views were pre-dominant in determining bilateral air services negotiating positions.

Liberalization of international aviation policy commenced in June 1989 when the then Minister of Transport, announced a substantial change in the way Australia would negotiate its bilateral air services agreements.

The new approach would attempt to secure the best balance of overall benefits for Australia. This would include taking into account a wider range of interests in determining Australia's negotiating strategies, including tourism and trade interests as well as those of Qantas, the then only Australian international carriers.

This was a major policy shift for Australia which, until that time, had followed a fairly protectionist line. Adoption of this policy had a marked effect on Australia's approach to air services negotiations and the frequency with which new arrangements were entered into.

In particular, Australia began for the first time to initiate consultations and began to be seen internationally as a proponent of more liberal ideas and intentions.

The next major changes to Australia's aviation policy were announced in the "One Nation" Statement in 1992, changes which were far reaching and in many ways prepared Australian aviation for the 21st century.

It is not an exaggeration to say that this announcement took many in Australia by complete surprise and others with a degree of shock, heightened by their announcement on national television.

Five years later on there is little to suggest that it was not the right way to go.

One of the most important changes announced was the Government's decision to introduce a system of multiple designation on Australia's international air routes. This would allow other Australian carriers to enter international markets and complete with Qantas and of course more than one carrier to be designated by our bilateral partners.

Other changes included removing the policy of maintaining a strict separation between international and domestic aviation operations, providing Australian carriers with the opportunity to develop integrated domestic and international networks and the announcement that Australia would seek to implement a single aviation market with New Zealand, as outlined above.

Further reforms included the removal of investment barriers which had previously prevented equity investments between Australian carriers.

On the back of the 1990 announcement of the privatisation of Australian Airlines and the partial privatisation of Qantas, this cleared the way for the merging of Qantas and Australian Airlines, then both Government owned carriers.

This merger, which in hindsight seemed so sensible it was probably inadvertently overlooked, put a respected international carrier, with a respected domestic carrier under the banner of the flying kangaroo, Qantas. In any merger there is tension, heightened of course by the strong historical ties of both carriers, with their expertise in different markets and with different industrial and operating practices in place, but overall the merger was achieved relatively well, thanks to the cooperation of all parties concerned.

A subsequent decision was made to sell 125 percent of Qantas in a trade sale and the balance of shares by way of a public float. The sale of Qantas was completed in 1995.

This decision too was not an easy one for the Government, especially one which had previously fully supported Government ownership of public assets; and raised concerns amongst many Australians given Qantas role as the nation's flag carrier, and a Government institution.

However as the Minister at the time rather neatly put it when asked about this decision to sell the national icon, "Why on earth should the Government be running an airline business".

Another outcome of this process was the 25 percent investment in Qantas by British Airways and the effective working alliance between these two world renowned carriers. Clearly this development was a plus for both carriers given their respective strengths in different markets throughout the world.

Therefore, Australia's aviation markets are now characterised by:

- a deregulated domestic market;
- integrated international and domestic operations;
- multiple designation internationally; and
- private ownership of airlines.

The above changes to aviation policy have also been accompanied by a more liberalised Australian approach to bilateral air services negotiations.

Australia's approach to bilateral air services negotiations is aimed at liberalization, however, we are not advocating an "open skies" policy.

Our approach to negotiating air services agreements is represented by our pursuit of multiple designation and the negotiation of capacity ahead of demand.

The results of the pursuit of these two elements in our bilateral negotiations has led to a significant increase in competition and capacity, as well as leading to the opening of new markets previously only partially served by existing carriers.

2.4.2 Multiple Designation

The first element of our liberal approach to bilateral negotiations is to include in our aviation treaties with other governments the right for both sides to designate any number of national carriers to operate the capacity agreed.

This approach is designed to enhance competition and innovation in international aviation markets.

Australia now has more than 80 percent of our bilateral agreements with multiple designation, an increase of over 20 percent over the past five years.

At present more than 91 percent of origin-destination passenger traffic to and from Australia is covered by multiple designation agreements, up from less than 75 percent in 1992.

Only 4 percent of traffic is covered by single designation agreements and the remaining 5 percent of traffic flows to and from countries where demand is so low that agreements have not been concluded.

At the end of 1991 there were 40 international airlines operating around 430 scheduled passenger flights per week to and from Australia.

At present there are 54 international airlines operating almost 700 scheduled passenger flights per week. This amounts to a significant increase in the level of competition and capacity.

Importantly, most of Australia's top ten aviation markets are served by three or more national carriers and a number are also served additionally by third country carriers.

2.4.3 Capacity Ahead Of Demand

The second element of our liberal approach to bilateral air services agreements is to negotiate capacity ahead of demand.

This allows airlines, the travel and tourism industry, exporters and importers to better plan future operations, allows demand to determine supply rather than the other way around, gives the airlines flexibility to meet unanticipated increases in demand and allows greater competition on routes.

Capacity negotiated has increased by 70 percent since we moved to the multiple designation policy in 1992.

Australia's bilateral agreements allow operation by Australian and foreign carriers of 340,000 seats per week in each direction. At present only around 60 percent of this total, is actually operated by the airlines.

These increases in capacity have been particularly boosted by outcomes reached since the new Federal Government was elected just over a year ago on 2 March 1996.

In the first year of the new Government, Australia has held successful bilateral negotiations with 18 (over one-third) of its bilateral partners, which has also included the signing of four new air services agreements.

The outcome of these negotiations have been quite dramatic.

In some of our largest markets we have seen:

- a doubling of capacity in the UK market,
- a 25 percent increase in capacity to Indonesia and
- a 37 percent increase in capacity with Singapore.

There have also been important outcomes in some emerging markets such as a more than five fold increase in capacity to China and doubling of capacity to India and South Africa.

The above outcomes add up to an overall increase equivalent to 50,000 seats negotiated in bilateral air services agreements in the last year.

This equates to a 17 percent increase or the equivalent of an extra 130 Boeing 747 aircraft per week being able to fly to and from Australia.

In addition to the additional capacity just described, most of which could be used to operate freighter services, the Government has made significant progress in negotiating dedicated freight capacity, a policy it announced in the middle of 1996.

At the end of 1995 only five of Australia's bilateral air services agreements contained dedicated freight capacity. Unlimited capacity was allowed under the US and New Zealand agreements while 3 other agreements allowed for the equivalent of 3 B747 freighters. In the last year the ability to operate the equivalent of another 33 B747 freighters has been negotiated.

In addition to expanding capacity, many of the bilateral outcomes have provided significant increases in access for Australian carriers to third country markets and access for foreign carriers to the trans-Tasman market.

2.4.4 Non-Scheduled (Charter) Services

The pattern of change in Australia's charter policy has mirrored other changes in policy. The guidelines governing approval of international passenger and freight charter services has been progressively liberalized, commencing in 1987.

The most recent change occurred in June 1996, when the Australian Minister for Transport and Regional Development, John Sharp, announced changes to charter policy designed to develop charter markets as markets in their own right reflecting the unique characteristics of charter operations.

The passenger charter guidelines were liberalised to encourage tourism growth by providing for automatic approval of a wider range of passenger charter flights and removing previous quantitative limits on charter programs. The guidelines introduced the concept of test-and-develop charters. A test-and-develop charter is a program of charter flights which seeks to develop markets which are not yet served by scheduled services but which may, in time, develop sufficiently to sustain such services.

The freight charter guidelines were further liberalised to promote seasonal services to meet the needs of perishable exporters.

The effect of these progressive changes in charter policy is reflected in the large increases in the number of charter flights. For example, between 1990 and 1996 passenger charter flights more than quadrupled from just over 200 flights to almost 900 while freight charter flights almost doubled from just under 450 to around 830.

This has added significant flexibility to meet the seasonal needs of passengers and freight shippers and has enhanced international services to a wide range of Australian airports.

In making these changes however the Government has sought to ensure that consumers are adequately protected and has most recently passed legislation requiring charter operators to provide adequate evidence of consumer protection in the event of failure to meet their obligations to their passengers.

2.5 AIR SAFETY

Qantas and Ansett, the two major Australian carriers have continued to work toward maintaining their distinguished safety records, a tribute to the professionalism and commitment of these airline's staff and management.

The focus of attention on aviation safety in Australia however has been heightened by two tragic accidents in recent years involving smaller regional and charter carriers and as a result the Government has recently announced the establishment of higher standards for this sector of the industry.

Australia is also looking towards a more effective safety regulatory regime through the overhauling of its regulations, an initiative being undertaken with the full involvement of the aviation industry, in partnership with the safety regulatory authorities.

2.6 CONCLUSIONS AND THE FUTURE

Australia's approach to aviation liberalisation has already resulted in outcomes which have contributed to Australia's economic growth.

It has extended to many areas of aviation, including the Government's decision to lease its 23 Federal airports, the first three of which, Melbourne, Brisbane and Perth are expected to be leased to private sector operators by 30 June 1997.

Our international aviation policy has contributed to the country now being served by 54 international carriers including significant traffic carried by foreign carriers exercising fifth and sixth freedom rights.

As the same time Australian carriers market share has increased last year responding to this competition.

Being at the end of some of the longest international air routes in the world and, at the edge of its fastest growing region, presents Australia and New Zealand with opportunities that are both unique and challenging.

For Australia we have an unparalleled opportunity in the years leading up to the 2000 Olympics to set in place arrangements that will allow all regions of Australia, not only Sydney, to benefit from the influx of tourists and visitors that will occur during the time leading up to, during, and following the Games.

Australia does not see any surprises in the reaffirmation of support for the bilateral framework arising out of the International Civil Aviation Organization World wide Air Transport Conference in 1994 given that the framework has been flexible enough to enable Australia to achieve beneficial economic outcomes.

Within this bilateral system, Australia has been able to develop excellent relations with its major aviation trading partners and has been able to develop and implement a liberal, competitive and expansive approach to international air services.

Australia is watching with interest the approach being adopted by New Zealand in its bilateral negotiations and the implications for the SAM between two countries.

The two countries continue to have one or two areas for further discussion but that has not prevented us from putting the SAM into place.

Australia, because of its geographic location, immense size, relatively small population, and the significance of trade and tourism to its overall economic performance, must continue to pursue its own economic reform and innovation in its transport policies.

Informed dialogue on international aviation issues is important and we are committed to the continued role of the International Civil Aviation Organization (ICAO), encouraging ICAO to be able to improve its ability to achieve changes in areas of mutual interest such as better safety standards.

We also see an emerging role for forums such as APEC to contribute to the continued development of international aviation. The APEC Transportation Ministerial meeting in June is another opportunity to use the APEC forum to pursue areas of mutual benefit in aviation.

Australia and New Zealand will no doubt continue to work towards enhancing the development of strong and efficient Australian carriers in competing in our major international markets.

This in no way will diminish the important role overseas carriers such as Singapore Airlines and Cathay Pacific play in increasing competition in Australasian markets.

Our approach has come a long way from a "closed shop" protection of a single designated Government monopoly airline.

But aviation is an industry characterised by change.

Both Australia and New Zealand have demonstrated that their aviation policies have been flexible enough to successfully handle change. We will need to continue to maintain that flexibility in the future.

3 COMPETITION IN THE EUROPEAN AIRLINE INDUSTRY: 1976-1994

Anthony K. Postert
and Robin C. Sickles

3.1 INTRODUCTION

Until recently, the European airline industry has been sheltered from competition. Bilateral treaties were used to set fares and flight frequencies and flag carriers were heavily subsidized. With the ongoing liberalization of the industry, these carriers have been exposed to competitive pressures of the sorts that U.S. firms felt in the late 1970s and on.

It is widely agreed that fares charged on most routes in Europe have been significantly higher than those charged in the U.S. for routes of similar distance. This point is exemplified by the 1984 conference of the Federation of European Consumers where it was decided that it would be cheaper to fly all their delegates to Washington, D.C. than to meet anywhere in Europe (Sampson, 1988).

One possible explanation of the high prices is that European airlines are inefficient relative the U.S. airlines. When compared to the U.S. airline industry, Good, et al. (1993a,b, 1995) found that the European airline industry is highly inefficient. All the European airlines were technically less efficient than all the U.S. airlines for the period 1976-86. Pan Am and Eastern (both of whom have left the industry) had technical efficiency scores higher than those of the European carriers. A high cost structure for the European airline industry has also been noted by McGowan and Seabright (1989) who suggest that high costs in the European airline industry are due to poor utilization of labor and high indirect and overhead costs. They point out that all the non-U.K. airlines have very high labor costs when compared to U.S. airlines. Captain and Sickles (1997), using data largely based on the period 1976 through the mid-1980s, provide support for this in that labor is paid a wage above its marginal revenue product. They suggest strong labor unions as a reason.

In this paper, we also examine another possible reason for relatively high prices in the European airline industry: market power. With schedules set by treaty, the airlines in a market would constitute an oligopoly. We examine the European carriers in an oligopoly structure with product differentiation, using a newly developed panel of international carriers (Good, et al., 1997, Wingrove, et al., 1996, Kaplan, et al., 1997, and Johnson, et al., 1997) from which we extract data on eight air carriers from Europe with annual observations from 1976 through 1994.

The paper is organized as follows. We first discuss the institutional environment in the European industry as it has evolved through the mid-1990s. We next discuss the airline data we use and what it tells us about differences between carriers in Europe, which have operated in a highly regulated, albeit increasingly competitive economic environment, and carriers in the U.S., which have operated in a deregulated environment over the entire period. These comparisons point out the substantial differences in total productivity enjoyed by U.S. carriers vis-a-vis their European counterparts, and underscore the need to better understand the sources of these efficiency differentials. We pursue one possible source of productivity difference by considering the implications of a non-competitive model of cartel behavior to characterize the European carriers. We then implement this model empirically and test the extent to which European carriers' pricing decisions are at variance with marginal cost pricing. We conclude by suggesting that one way out of the European's conundrum of apparently competitive pricing at the margin and and moderate technical inefficiency may be to exploit the low cost structures of U.S. carriers via strategic alliances and code sharing arrangements.

3.2 A RECENT OF THE EUROPEAN AIRLINE INDUSTRY

Since their inception, European "flag carriers", subsidized and even owned by governments, have acted as duopolies: two carriers from two countries would carve up the market on every route and through bilateral agreements determine how many people each would carry and charge. Even as late as 1993, European international routes were oligopolistic. The airlines also engaged in "pooling" agreements whereby they would divide revenue, a practice that persisted until the late 1980s on three-fourths of European routes (*The Economist*, 1993). Before deregulation, the airlines had to get permission from national licensing offices and show financial strength to start operating. Established airlines even needed permission to start new routes. Competition was very limited and as a result of strong state protection and aid for five decades, these carriers were inefficient (Lowden, 1996).

All this began changing in 1987. Following the lead of Britain, the Aviation Directorate of the European Commission started a staggered set of deregulatory measures that lifted entry to barriers to new airlines and laid the foundations for a competitive environment in the industry (Lowden, 1996). Most significant of the three has been the "Third Package," which the Commission initiated in 1993 (Hotten, 1995) and whose entire provision came into full effect on April 1, 1997 (Lowden, 1996). The third EC liberalization package for air travel, also called the "open skies" program, allowed airlines to set fares starting in 1993 (Europe 2000, 1992) and to operate a route between any two EC countries. The open skies program also abolished pooling (*The Economist*, 1993) and allowed an airline to offer "cabotage" services, the right to offer flights within another country, for services starting in its own country (Europe 2000, 1992). As of April 1, 1997 airlines can provide full cabotage services regardless of a flight's origin (Lowden, 1996).

In keeping with the liberalization started with the Third Packages, the European Commission has also prepared guidelines for state aid to airlines. Although the Commission can not make a unilateral decision that it is the last time it approves aid to an airline, it is to consider further aid to an airline only if "external circumstances" require it (Feldman, 1997). These guidelines, based on the "one time, last time" principle, allow for a one time aid, except in unpredictable circumstances, so that airlines can adjust to new liberal market conditions (Lowden, 1996). In addition, the Commission created a subsidy test called the "market economy investor principle" (MEIP) whereby funds from public authorities will not be considered aid if such funds would have been invested by the private sector (Feldman, 1997).

The above provisions are in the spirit of the counsel of "The Committee of Wisemen" created by the Commission in 1993. The Committee advocated the continuation of deregulation to establish a Single Aviation Market to meet global challenges. Towards this end, it recommended harmonizing national regulations for effective cost cutting, eliminating infrastructural bottlenecks by creating an efficient Single Traffic Management System, enforcing internal market rules to address problems of slots and state aid, and curbing government intervention in the operation of air carriers (Agence Europe, 1994).

The consequences of the deregulatory undertaking have been manifold. The effort has created many challenges for the European established carriers, or "majors." Even without these threats, Europe's majors face a lot of problems including hub congestion, global competition from strong U.S. majors, lack of unlimited state aid and aircraft replacements. Yet, the most threatening issue has been upstarts that have sprang up following deregulation. These market opening efforts encouraged startups such as Gatwick's Air Europe, which failed in 1991, Ryanair of Ireland and easyJet of Greece. For instance, Ryanair's cheap aircraft, low overhead at its Dublin base and use of lower cost airports, such as Luton, allowed it to charge such low prices that British Airways (BA) was forced to pull its service in Dublin in 1991 (Lowden, 1996).

In fact one can say that the most visible impact of deregulation has been new entrants and lowered fares. Like Ryanair, Greek owned easyJet has offered fares that not only undercut BA's prices on British domestic routes but also those of train operators. These upstarts have largely been able to offer cheap fares by keeping sales and distribution costs low through the use of their own telephone reservations and ticket-less travel: these usually account for 15 to 20% of total operating expenses (Lowden, 1996).

Competition in the recent past has also come from low cost air travel made available by charter airlines. These "carriers," which initially catered to the leisure market by selling packed tours, have began selling tickets only for flights due to the relaxation of the rules. Estimates indicate that such "charter" flights account for about half cross border European travel. Like the recent startups, these also have costs well below those of the scheduled airlines since they employ only 8% of the airline workforce (*The Economist*, 1993).

To compete in the leisure market, which has become increasingly necessary due to the effects of deregulation, the majors realize the need to cut costs drastically: these costs have been high due to expensive service charges, such as those for airport handling and air traffic control fees, and low labor productivity (*The Economist*, 1993). One obvious target of cost cutting effort has been employment. Despite traffic growth and continued financial recovery, including a profit of $1.8 billion for IATA member European carriers in 1994 (Sparaco, 1995) and a record of 74.8% load factor on long haul routes in 1996 (Fiorino, 1997), job growth has been slow or falling. Prompted by growing competition from deregulation, scheduled airlines had cut about 40,000 jobs between 1990 and 1994, even in the face of social disputes and walkouts. Examples abound. Air France has frozen wages and cut 5,000 jobs to reduce cost by 30%. Alitalia and Iberia have made similar moves by cutting 2,000 and 3,500 jobs, respectively. By acquiring 49% stake in Sabena, Swissair has also cut ground staff to take advantage of synergy above the 1,600 jobs that it had already eliminated in 1994 (Sparaco, 1995).

The efforts towards greater market reliance have resulted in improvements. With deregulation and commercialization, mostly in northern Europe, airlines there have exhibited productivity and efficiency gains, especially BA, Lufthansa and KLM (Lowden, 1996). In addition, liberalization of aviation services, most advanced in the UK, has allowed BA to establish domestic services in Germany and France, and British Midland to become a third carrier by breaking traditional duopolies on many routes (Hotten, 1995).

Of course, competition from startups and pressures from liberalization might prompt the majors to retaliate by other than competition enhancing means. They may try to use political power to deter competition, for instance by monopolizing slots at congested airports. They may also launch advertisement campaigns at the time of entry of a new startup which will not be able to match these efforts. In reality, the majors have responded by undertaking "cloning strategies" whereby they have formed companies that match competitors' costs and operations: two cases in point of such strategic subsidiaries include Lufthansa's Cityline and BA's Deutsche BA and TAT France. The majors have also tried to increase market share by combining their network power. This latter concept has been behind many of the alliances of the majors in Europe and the US. Examples include alliances between KLM and Northwest, Lufthansa and United, Lufthansa and SAS, Delta and Sabena, and BA and American (Lowden, 1996). The benefits of deregulation may also be limited by infrastructural constraints. There is considerable concern that deregulation will aggravate an already congested and intrinsically confusing air traffic control system (Vincent and Stasinopoulus, 1990). As has been documented in a report by the Association of European Airlines, there is no unified air traffic control system for Europe. The situation that existed in the late 1980s and early 1990s of 22 different systems and 44 operating centers based on political boundaries and not operational considerations seriously disrupts air travel and creates intolerable delays.

The outcome of the liberalization effort has not been all as planned. It has improved competition on some domestic routes but not across Europe. Price competition of international routes are limited and only 7% of international routes are operated by more than two carriers. These are reinforced by problems of airport capacity where inadequate landing and take off slots create barriers to entry by new competitors (Hotten, 1995). Proposals for changing slot allocation are often watered down providing no reprieve from the problem. Other competition hindering forces have been state aid and air traffic control problems; there are too many of the latter, often one for each sovereign state's air space, leading to delays and hence increases in annual cost of flights. Financial pressures from high cost of operation, including high navigational, airport take off and landing fees and 3% carbon tax, also stifle competition (*The Economist*, 1993).

That the "open skies" initiative has not produced much of a revolution has also been due to lack of compliance with the EU Commission's rules. For instance, the EU's effort to provide for competition in airport ground handling, which it believes to be 30% too high at many airports, by ordering airlines to handle their own effects in large airports has met with resistance. Lufthansa does not find the directive appealing because costs for handling at Frankfurt are twice those of other airports, and more than three times those at London Gatwick and Manchester. German airports also find this rule objectionable because ground handling generates around 40% of revenues. In addition, the Commission's attempts at reducing state aid to airlines has had similar difficulties. Airlines have disregarded these rules and some, such as Iberia, have requested repeated help by claiming a presence of "durable adverse condition" (*The Economist*, 1993).

3.3 DATA

Before we turn attention to our structural model of cartel behavior we will discuss in some detail the data on which is based the structural model's empirical implementation. We also discuss some characteristics of the European carriers in terms of partial factor productivities and how these differ from those of carriers in the U.S. where deregulation has had some twenty years to sort itself out. We also examine patterns of radial measures of technical inefficiency that have existed over the period based on a simple Cobb-Douglas form for the production function using the Cornwell et al. (1990) time-varying inefficiency model. Differences in partial factor productivities are significant for some inputs while the technical inefficiency gap appears to have closed considerably in the late 1980s and early 1990s.

Our supply data set consists of a panel of the eight air carriers from Europe that were used in Captain and Sickles (1997). A number of data series used therein were extrapolated between 1985-1990. Results presented here are based on a newly constructed and complete data set of 37 international airlines from 1976 to 1994 (Good, et al., 1997). A list of these carriers are presented in Table 1.1. These carriers and countries are followed with annual observations from 1976 through 1994.

The primary sources for the supply data is the Digest of Statistics for Commercial Air Carriers from the International Civil Aviation Organization and the Penn World

Table [Mark 5.6] (Summers and Heston, 1994). There are frequent instances where this source is not complete. Consequently, data is supplemented from other sources such as the International Air Transport Association's World Air Transport Statistics and Federal Express Aviation Service's Commercial Jet Fleets. Using these sources, we construct a set of three airline inputs: Labor, Materials, and Aircraft Fleet. In addition we construct an aggregate airline output variable along with some output characteristics. Descriptive statistics for our data set can be found in Table 1.3.

Table 1.1 List of Carriers and Countries

Sabena (Belgium)	Air France (France)
Lufthansa (Germany)	Alitalia (Italy)
KLM (Netherlands)	SAS (Sweden, Norway, Denmark)
Iberia (Spain)	British Air (United Kingdom)

The materials index is based on the financial data from ICAO. It uses total operating expenses minus the amounts spent on aircraft rental, depreciation and labor (from ICAO Fleet and Personnel). Since our data are in different currencies we need to put amounts in common terms. Simply using exchange rates does not adequately make expenditures comparable across countries as exchange rates are heavily influenced by the narrower sets of goods which are imported and exported. Instead, we use purchasing power parities. We do not have much detail about subcomponents. While expenses are broken up along functional lines (ticketing, passenger services, etc.) we generally do not have adequate information to remove other physical inputs (primarily labor) from these categories and do not have separate price indices for them, even in those cases where we can. This leaves our materials index with a single subcomponent.

Inconsistencies in the definition of labor categories, differences in aggregation and missing data (primarily expenditure data) demand that our labor index is also constructed from a single subcomponent. Our labor index uses the number of employees at mid-year as the measure of quantity. Prices are calculated by dividing expenditures by this quantity.

Because of the importance of flying capital in our model, we have described this input in considerably more detail: providing several characteristics of the fleet in addition to its quantity and user price. We use an inventory of aircraft fleets provided by ICAO to determine the number of aircraft in over 80 separate aircraft types. For each aircraft type, we construct a user price, roughly comparable to an annual rental price. Total expenses are then the sum of these user prices, weighted by the number of aircraft in a carrier's fleet in each category. We considered several alternatives in constructing these user prices. We rejected the traditional approach of basing cost on book value since this is not responsive to changing demands for different types of aircraft at different points in time. For example, following deregulation in the US, the demand for small aircraft increased dramatically (along with their selling price) while wide bodied aircraft had a dramatic decrease in price. Our valuation of individual aircraft types is based on the average of Avmark's January and July subjective valuations of each type of aircraft for every year. These valuations are based on recent sales and perceptions of changing market conditions for aircraft in half-time condition. The primary liability of this approach, is that it does not capture benefits (for example reduced maintenance) for newer rather than older aircraft within a particular type. This approach also poses some problems for aircraft which are not widely traded or for aircraft which are not jets. For aircraft which are not widely traded, we used the most comparable aircraft which was traded in order to get a market value. For the BAC/SUD Concorde, we used the Boeing 747-200. While the 747 is a much larger aircraft, because of its speed, the revenue generating capability of these two aircraft are roughly comparable.

Table 1.2 List of Countries and Financial Instruments Used to Find Short-Term Interest Rates

Country	*Instrument*
Belgium	Three Month Treasury Certificates
Denmark	Three Month Interbank Rate
France	Three Month Pibor
Germany	Three Month Fibor
Italy	Interbank Sight Deposits
Netherlands	Three Month Aibor
Norway	Three Month Nibor
Spain	Three Month Interbank Rate
Sweden	Three Month Treasury Discount Notes
United Kingdom	Three Month Interbank Loans

Table 1.3 Descriptive Statistics for Data Set

Variable	n	μ	σ
P	141	1.12	0.29
Q	141	2304691.91	1601575.90
p_L	141	31.91	14.37
p_M	141	138.88	28.92
p_K	141	1900.78	942.63
C	141	2786113.99	2054086.57
Pindex	152	1.13	0.22
Prail	152	0.05	0.02
Gasp	152	0.71	0.21
GDP	152	670.24	450.14

Avmark also provides some limited information about turbo-prop aircraft. We divided turbo-prop aircraft into six categories (YS-11, Lockheed Electra, Lockheed Hercules, Fairchild F-227, Fokker 27, and Saab 340) and allocated different types to these categories based on age and size (for example, we allocated the Fokker 50 into the Saab 340 category since they are both relatively new design commuter aircraft. We allocated the HS-748 to the YS-11 category since they are both 1960s design 50 passenger aircraft). We had a final residual type of aircraft which could not conveniently be categorized this way. Some carriers for example, operate a small fleet of single engine aircraft. Others operate one or two helicopters. We valued single engine piston aircraft at 100,000 and helicopters at 400,000. These residual aircraft are so small (in terms of the number of seats of capacity) which our cost per seat user price is insensitive to whatever decisions we make about their valuation.

Because we value aircraft in half time condition, we assume that their remaining useful life is 14 years and use a 1.5 declining balance method to calculate economic depreciation. Under the assumption that marginal decisions about fleet size were based on the international leasing market, and that the leasing market was dominated by US carriers and US prices, we used rates based on Moody's Baa rate for 6 month commercial paper.

An alternative to using the depreciation method described above is to construct the depreciation portion by viewing an aircraft as both a financial and economic asset. Under this approach, the cost of holding and using the aircraft would be the difference in market value at the end of the year compared to the beginning of the year plus the nominal interest rate. We ultimately rejected this approach because it lead to several instances where the capital price fluctuated dramatically near periods when the price for a particular aircraft was depressed due to random events (such as the DC-10 grounding in 1979, or the bankruptcy of a carrier leading to a particular aircraft type flooding the market). In addition to constructing price and quantity measures, we also generate two characteristics of the capital stock: a classification of the aircraft as turbo-prop or wide bodied jet.

This classification is expressed as the percentage of aircraft in the two categories: turbo-prop and wide bodied jet (determined by having two aisles in the main cabin). These categories roughly provide measures of the potential productivity of capital as well as its heterogeneity. As more wide bodied aircraft are used, resources for flight crews, passenger and aircraft handlers, landing slots, etc. do not increase proportionately. The percent turbo-props also provide a measure of aircraft speed. This type of aircraft flies at approximately one third of the speed of jet equipment. Consequently, providing service in these types of equipment requires proportionately more flight crew resources than with jets.

Scheduled passenger output is measured in revenue ton kilometers. This is calculated under the assumption that a passenger, along with checked baggage constitutes 200 pounds in weight. Our non-scheduled output measure combines charter, mail and cargo operations. Charter passenger traffic again assumes 200 pounds per passenger. For our scheduled and non-scheduled outputs, both quantity and expense information are available. We convert these two measures of output into one output by taking the share-weighted average of the two output measures.

Finally, we construct three measures of the carrier's output: stage length, load factor and network size. Load factor provides a measure of service quality and is often used as a proxy for service competition. Stage length provides a measure of the length of individual route segments in the carrier's network. The number of route kilometers provide a measure of the total network size.

The demand data was collected for the European countries shown in Table 1.1. The demand data for Denmark, Sweden and Norway are used to create as single data series for Scandinavia by weighting by their respective GDPs. The GDP series was obtained from the *Main Economic Indicators*, a publication of the Economics and Statistics Department of the Organization for Economic Cooperation and

Development (OECD). The GDP figures are reported in billions of dollars. The series on private consumption expenditure growth is taken from the publication *Historical Statistics*, which is published by the OECD. These data are an implicit price index with year to year percentage changes. The annual short-term interest rates are also taken from *Historical Statistics*. Table 1.2 lists the financial instruments that are the basis for the series for the respective countries. The rail data is from *Jane's World Railways*. The rail price was calculated as the ratio of passenger and baggage revenue to passenger tone-kilometers. This is consistent with the price of air travel. The OECD International Energy Agency's publication *Energy Prices and Taxes* is the source for the gasoline price data. The gasoline prices include all taxes.

3.4 COMPARISON OF US AND EUROPEAN CARRIERS

As was pointed out earlier, European airlines' inefficiencies relative to U.S. airlines is one possible explanation of high prices of air travel in Europe since excess costs need to be recouped as direct subsidies are under increased scrutiny. A possible explanation for the difference in efficient scores is that that European airline industry make poor use of labor (McGowan and Seabright, (1989)). It is also possible that labor is being paid a wage that is too high (Captain and Sickles (1997)).

In earlier work utilizing data predominately based on the late 1970s and early 1980s, Good et al. (1993a,b, 1994, 1995) noted differences in technical efficiency between Europe and post-regulatory U.S. of between 10 and 15 percent. We can use our newly extended data set to examine whether or not the general trends which manifested themselves as we found them to in the decade following the U.S. experiment with deregulation while Europe was still strongly entrenched in its rich regulatory traditions have continued into the second half of the 1980s and into the 1990s. To that end we construct several series of partial productivity indexes and examine their temporal pattern during the 1970s through the 1990s. The U.S. firms used in this comparison are drawn from the same newly created international carrier data set (Good, et al., 1997) and comprise the vast majority of the total U.S. industry. The firms are American, Continental, Delta, Eastern, Northwest, Pan Am, Trans World, United, USAir, and Western. Figure 1.1 displays the partial productivity index for labor. We can see a substantial disparity when our sample period begins in 1976 that has narrowed substantially by 1994. Although a similar convergence does not appear in the simple partial productivity measure for the residual materials input (Figure 1.2), the capital input series for Europe and the U.S. are indistinguishable by 1994 (Figure 1.3).

Since it would appear that substantial convergence has occurred in the partial productivities of the factor inputs we next ask if a similar convergence has occurred with regard to radial technical efficiency measures. We have estimated a simple Cobb-Douglas model and have constructed time-varying relative technical efficiency measures using the Cornwell, et al. (1990) within estimator and a pooled regression of European and U.S. firms. We them have weighted the relative efficiencies by the output share of the particular carrier in the European or U.S. industry to construct the differential between Europe and U.S. over the 1976-1994 period. These are displayed in Figure 1.4.

Figure 1.1 Ratio of Labor Quantity to Scheduled Output for Both US and European Airlines

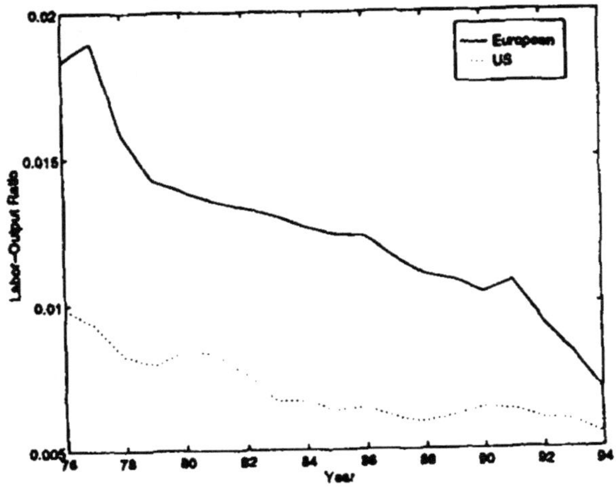

Figure 1.2 Ratio of Materials Quantity to Scheduled Output for Both US and European Airlines

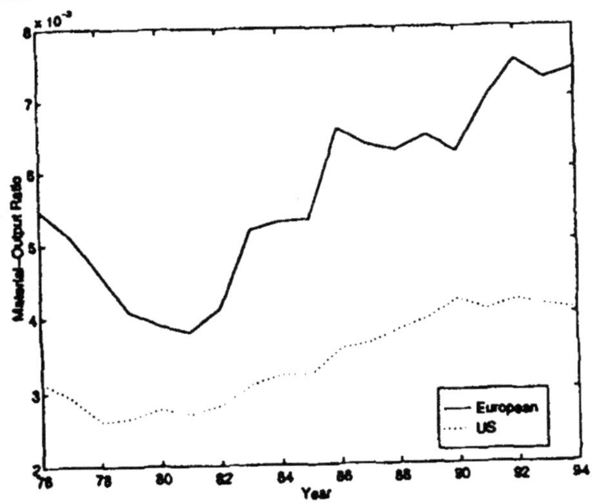

Figure 1.3 Ratio of Capital Quantity to Scheduled Output for Both US and European Airlines

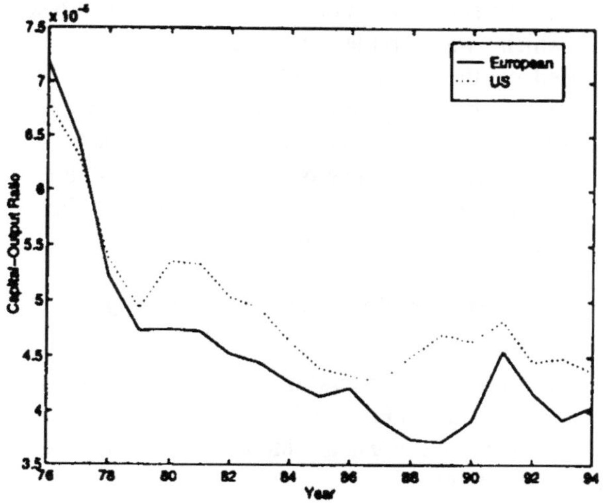

Figure 1.4 Differences in Average Efficiency Scores Between the US and European Airlines

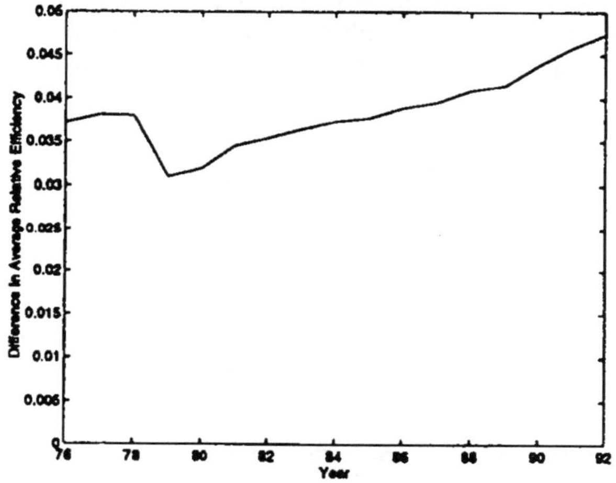

It is clear that with the addition of data from the mid-1980 through 1994 the story about inefficiency patterns between Europe and the U.S. that is presented in Good, et al. (1993a,b, 1995) and based on the decade earlier appears to have changed. Although there still exists an efficiency difference of about 5% in favor of the U.S., this difference is substantially lower than the average of 10%-15% that appeared to exist in the decade following U.S. deregulation. The remarkable progress of British Air after privatization (and its large share of European total revenue passenger miles) and the steady progress of Lufthansa, KLM and Air France from the mid-

1980s through the present also has appeared to have flattened the temporal pattern over the entire period 1976-1994.

In the next section we consider a more structured argument based on a model of cartel behavior which was applied to the European industry using data predominantly based on the period 1976-1985 (Captain and Sickles, 1997). A number of data series in that study were not available for later periods through the end of the study period (1990) and were interpolated and/or forecasted using time-series methods. The model will explore whether or not there is evidence of noncompetitive pricing or whether competitive pressures in Europe have also had their way in reducing price/marginal cost markups.

3.5 ECONOMETRIC MODEL OF CARTEL BEHAVIOR

We will study the European carriers in an oligopoly structure with product differentiation.[1] Consider an industry with N firms that produce a differentiated output q. The output is produced using n inputs $x = (x_1, x_2, ..., x_n)$. Market demand for firm k at time t is given by

$$q_{kt} = q_k(p_t, p_{mt}, Y_t, \psi, \epsilon_{dt}), \tag{1.1}$$

where p_t is the average price charged by firm k, p_{mt} is an index of all other firms' prices, Y_t are other variables that shift demand, ψ are unknown parameters of the demand function, and ϵ_{dt} are the random errors. The "perceived" marginal revenue function is

$$\text{PMR} = p_t + D_1 q_{kt}, \tag{1.2}$$

where $D_1 = \partial p_{kt} / \partial q_{kt}$.

The cost function for firm k is

$$C_{kt} = C_k(q_{kt}, W_{kt}, Z_t, \omega, \epsilon_{ct}), \tag{1.3}$$

where W_{kt} is a vector of input prices that firm k pays at time t, Z_t are industry variables that shift cost, ω are the unknown parameters in the cost function, and ϵ_{ct} are the random errors. Marginal cost is

$$\text{MC} = C_1(q_{kt}, W_t, Z_t, \gamma). \tag{1.4}$$

In an oligopolistic industry, a firm chooses output where marginal cost is equal to "perceived" marginal revenue (in a perfectly competitive industry, MC = p). We

---

[1] This section is based on Captain and Sickles (1997).

equate marginal cost and "perceived" marginal revenue to get the quantity setting condition

$$C_1(q_{kt}, W_t, Z_t, \gamma) = p_t + D_1 q_{kt}\theta, \tag{1.5}$$

where θ is an index of the competitive nature of the firm. That is, when θ = 0, the industry is perfectly competitive since marginal cost equals price. A θ value of unity is consistent with Nash behavior. Thus, 1.5 is referred to as the behavioral equation.

The profit function for airline k at time t is

$$\Pi_{kt} = q_{kt}(p_{kt}; p_{1t}, \ldots, p_{k-1,t}, p_{k+1,t}, \ldots, p_{Nt}) \cdot p_{kt} - C_{kt}(q_{kt}(\cdot)). \tag{1.6}$$

Taking the derivative of this function with respect to p_{kt} and holding all other prices constant, we have the first order conditions for profit maximization in a price setting game:

$$\frac{\partial q_{kt}}{\partial p_{kt}} p_{kt} + q_{kt} - \frac{\partial C_{kt}}{\partial q_{kt}} \frac{\partial q_{kt}}{\partial p_{kt}} = 0. \tag{1.7}$$

By summing over the N firms, we have

$$\frac{\partial Q_t}{\partial p_t} p_t + Q_t - \sum_k \frac{\partial C_{kt}}{\partial q_{kt}} \frac{\partial q_{kt}}{\partial p_{kt}} = 0, \tag{1.8}$$

where $Q_t = \Sigma_k q_{kt}$. Assuming symmetry in cost, (1.5) reduces to

$$p_t = \frac{\partial C_{kt}}{\partial q_{kt}} - \frac{Q_t}{\frac{\partial Q_t}{\partial p_t}} \theta. \tag{1.9}$$

With this, we can estimate θ by specifying a demand and a cost equation.

For the market demand equation, we specify a semi-logarithmic function:

$$\begin{aligned} \log q_{kt} &= \delta + \delta_P P_{kt} + \delta_{P_i} P_{ikt} + \delta_{GDP} GDP_{kt} \\ &\quad + \delta_{GASP} GASP_{kt} + \delta_{GCONS} GCONS_{kt} \\ &\quad + \delta_{RAILP} RAILP_{kt} + \epsilon_d, \end{aligned} \tag{1.10}$$

where q_{kt} is the output of firm k at time t, P_{kt} is the price charged by firm k, P_{ikt} is an index of the price charged by the other $N - 1$ firms, *GDP* is the gross domestic product, *GASP* is the retail price of gas including taxes, *GCONS* is the growth in consumer expenditures and *RAILP* is the price of rail travel.

For the cost function, we use a trans-logarithmic specification. After we impose symmetry, the cost function is given by

$$\begin{aligned}\log C &= \alpha + \sum_{i=1}^{3} \beta_i \log p_i + \sum_{j>i}^{3} \sum_{i=1}^{2} \beta_{ij} \log p_i \log p_j + \frac{1}{2} \sum_{i=1}^{3} \beta_{ii} \log^2 p_i \\ &+ \gamma_q \log q + \frac{1}{2} \gamma_{q^2} \log^2 q + \sum_{i=1}^{3} \gamma_{qi} \log q \log p_i \\ &+ \beta_{TP} TP + \beta_{WB} WP + \beta_{SL} \log SL + \beta_{LF} \log LF \\ &+ \beta_{Netsize} \log Netsize + \sum_{i=1}^{7} \alpha_i AIR_i + \epsilon_c \qquad (1.11)\end{aligned}$$

where p_i is the ith input price, q is output, PT is the percentage of the fleet which are turbo-prop aircraft, WB is the percentage of the fleet which are wide-body aircraft, SL is the stage length, LF is the load factor, and *Netsize* is the size of the network.

The $\alpha_i AIR_i$ represent fixed firm effects in the cost equation. These firm effects can be given the reduced form interpretation of omitted variables which are specific to the firm and display little variability over the sample period, or can be given a more structural interpretation as time-invariant technical inefficiencies from a stochastic frontier cost function (Schmidt and Sickles, 1984; Cornwell, et al., 1990).

The cost shares must add to unity and we must have linear homogeneity in input prices. The following restrictions are thus applied on the cost function:

$$\begin{aligned}\beta_K + \beta_L + \beta_M &= 1 \\ \beta_{Ki} + \beta_{Li} + \beta_{Mi} &= 0, \qquad \text{for all } i \in \{K, L, M\} \\ \gamma_{qK} + \gamma_{qL} + \gamma_{qM} &= 0.\end{aligned}$$

Summary statistics based on the translog and its associated share equations are provided by the Allen-Uzawa, Morishima and own- and cross-price substitution elasticities, and a measure of returns to scale. The Allen-Uzawa elasticities of substitution and own-price elasticities are given by

$$\begin{aligned}\zeta_{ij} &= \frac{\beta_{ij} + S_i S_j}{S_i S_j} \\ \zeta_{ii} &= \frac{\beta_{ii} + S_i(1 - S_i)}{S_i^2}, \qquad (1.12)\end{aligned}$$

where S_i is the fitted share for input i. Morishima elasticities are given by

$$\sigma_{ij} = (\zeta_{ji} - \zeta_{ii}) S_i, i \neq j. \qquad (1.13)$$

The own- and cross-price elasticities are

$$\begin{aligned} \nu_{ii} &= \zeta_{ii} S_i \\ \nu_{ij} &= \zeta_{ij} S_j, i \neq j \\ \nu_{ji} &= \zeta_{ij} S_i, i \neq j. \end{aligned} \tag{1.14}$$

Returns to scale are computed as the inverse of the cost elasticity of output. This is give by

$$\mu = [\beta_q + \beta_{qq} \log q + \beta q L \log p_L + \beta q M \log p_M + \beta q K \log p_K]^{-1}. \tag{1.15}$$

The behavioral equation we estimate is

$$P = \mathrm{MC} - \frac{\theta}{\delta} + \epsilon_b. \tag{1.16}$$

We then estimate a system of five equations using iterated non-linear three-stage least squares (ITNL3SLS). The five equations are the demand, cost, labor share, capital share and the behavioral equation. We treat the price of air travel, quantity, total cost, labor share, capital share, and labor price as endogenous variables. All other variables are treated as exogenous.

3.6 EMPIRICAL RESULTS

The parameter estimates for the system of equations given in Section 1 can be found in Table 1.4. Fitted share values, returns to scale, and various elasticities calculated from these estimates are in Tables 1.5 through 1.9.

We identify the market structure by testing the null hypothesis that $\theta = 1$ versus the alternative that $\theta < 1$. The null hypothesis is rejected at the 95% level of significance. The European airlines industry does not behave consistently with Nash behavior.

In the demand equation, all the parameters (with the possible exception of gas price) have the expected sign and are significant. The output price elasticity of -0.55 means that demand for air travel is inelastic and consumers will decrease air travel demand proportionally less with price increases. However, the elasticity of the price index is positive and quite large (1.98), so airlines in Europe are thought of as substitutes and any product differentiation is quite small. The rail price cross-price elasticity is positive so rail travel is also a substitute for air travel. The output GDP elasticity is also positive, so countries with higher GDPs have a larger demand for air travel, which is expected. The gas price output elasticity is negative. This may be due to a link between gas price and aircraft fuel price.

Table 1.4 Nonlinear IT3SLS Parameter Estimates

Cost Equation					
Variable	*Parameter Estimate*	*T-Ratio*	*Variable*	*Parameter Estimate*	*T-Ratio*
$\log p_K$	0.044	2.30	$\log p_L$	1.163	14.35
$\log p_M$	-0.207	-2.38	$\log Q$	-2.174	-27.31
$\log^2 Q$	0.198	27.62	$\log Q \log p_K$	-0.007	-5.36
$\log Q \log p_L$	-0.043	-7.70	$\log Q \log p_M$	0.050	8.42
$\log^2 p_L$	0.117	17.47	$\log^2 p_K$	0.041	21.49
$\log^2 p_M$	0.158	60.41	$\log p_K \log p_L$	-0.016	-8.28
$\log p_K \log p_M$	-0.025	-13.52	$\log p_L \log p_M$	-0.133	-21.17
$\log SL$	0.309	6.19	LF	0.514	1.82
$\log Netsize$	0.036	0.72	PWB	-1.247	-6.16
PT	0.004	0.66	Iberia	20.628	23.63
Air France	20.590	22.98	Lufthansa	20.689	23.53
Alitalia	20.438	23.52	KLM	20.420	23.63
British Airways	20.499	23.32	SAS	20.620	23.93
Sabena	19.929	23.12			

Demand Equation					
Variable	*Parameter Estimate*	*T-Ratio*	*Variable*	*Parameter Estimate*	*T-Ratio*
Intercept	12.726	78.94	P	-0.490	-3.70
$Pindex$	0.249	9.44	$Gasp$	-0.822	-4.22
GDP	0.001	10.25	$Prail$	9.265	7.80

Behavioral Equation		
Variable	*Parameter Estimate*	*T-Ratio*
θ	0.112	3.58

Table 1.5 Fitted Share Values and Returns to Scale at Data Mean

Labor	0.32224
Capital	0.06921
Materials	0.60855
Returns to scale	
1.29449	

Table 1.6 Output Price Elasticities at Data Mean

Price	-0.55067
Price Index	1.97558
Gas Price	-0.58783
GDP	0.39114
Rail Price	0.49357

Table 1.7 Allen-Uzawa Elasticities of Substitution at Data Mean

	Labor	Materials	Capital
Labor	-0.97450	×	×
Materials	0.48524	-0.30367	×
Capital	0.27067	0.41079	-4.87196

Table 1.8 Morishima Elasticities of Substitution at Data Mean

	Labor	*Materials*	*Capital*
Labor	×	0.47039	0.40124
Materials	0.48008	×	0.43478
Capital	0.35594	0.36563	×

Table 1.9 Input Price Elasticities at Data Means

	Labor	*Materials*	*Capital*
Labor	-0.31402	0.29529	0.01873
Materials	0.15636	-0.18480	0.02843
Capital	0.08722	0.24998	-0.33720

The cost function estimates produce fitted share values that are positive at all the observations. The estimated cost function is concave in input prices at the data mean and at 60% of the data points. The estimated returns to scale at the data mean is 1.29. Of the five airline specific variables included in the cost function, only stage length and percentage of wide bodied aircraft are significant. The parameter estimates for both stage length and load factor do not have their expected signs.

Labor, capital and materials are all substitutable inputs as measured with the Allen-Uzawa elasticities of substitution (see Table 1.7). Likewise, the Morishima elasticities of substitution (see Table 1.8) show that capital, labor and materials are all substitutable inputs.

Finally, we compute the average θ values and mark-ups over the sample, by year, and airline in Tables 1.10 through 1.12. Over the entire period, mark-ups averaged 22.8%. For the years 1976-86, mark-ups averaged 23.1%. Mark-ups started the period at near 25% level and only declined slightly over the period. In 1987, when the European market was opening to a more competitive environment, mark-ups started to increase (this trend actually starts in 1986). However, after three years, this trend stops, and mark-ups start to decline to levels lower than before 1986. The average mark-up for the years 1989-93 is 17.8%. Despite inelastic demand, with other airlines and railroads as close substitutes, high mark-ups in the European market could not be sustained.

Table 1.10 Competition Variable (θ) Estimates, Average Prices, Mark-Ups and Marginal Costs

θ	P	*Mark-up*	MC
0.11198	1.12295	0.22835	0.89460

Table 1.11 Competition Variable (θ) Estimates by Year with Average Prices, Mark-Ups and Marginal Costs

Year	θ	P	*Mark-up*	MC
76	0.11958	0.75462	0.24386	0.51076
77	0.12485	0.81495	0.25459	0.56035
78	0.12161	0.86208	0.24799	0.61409
79	0.11786	0.97906	0.24035	0.73871
80	0.12027	1.13539	0.24526	0.89013
81	0.10594	1.06049	0.21604	0.84444
82	0.10968	1.03702	0.22367	0.81335
83	0.10229	1.00239	0.20860	0.79379
84	0.09707	0.96881	0.19796	0.77085
85	0.09512	0.98858	0.19397	0.79461
86	0.13280	1.14232	0.27082	0.87150
87	0.14922	1.30037	0.30429	0.99607
88	0.14874	1.31317	0.30332	1.00984
89	0.12856	1.31988	0.26216	1.05772
90	0.13472	1.41744	0.27473	1.14271
91	0.09476	1.57249	0.19324	1.37925
92	0.05523	1.44570	0.11263	1.33308
93	0.02271	1.25186	0.04631	1.20555

Table 1.12 Competition Variable (θ) Estimates by Airline with Average Prices, Mark-Ups and Marginal Costs

Airline	θ	P	*Mark-up*	MC
Air France	0.08590	1.11060	0.17518	0.93542
Alitalia	0.14489	1.11382	0.29546	0.81836
British Airways	0.05254	0.97647	0.10713	0.86933
Iberia	0.10450	0.97410	0.21309	0.76101
KLM	0.07348	0.87520	0.14983	0.72536
Lufthansa	0.07336	1.32840	0.14961	1.17879
SAS	0.18205	1.43472	0.37124	1.06348
Sabena	0.18460	1.12909	0.37645	0.75264

3.7 CONCLUSIONS

In this paper, we have examined the productivities, efficiencies, and market conduct of firms in the European airline industry. We have found what appears to be convergence in several of the major sources of factor productivity to the standard of the unregulated industry in the U.S., inefficiency differentials that are substantially moderated by the competitive pressures induced by measures put in place through the European Union, and little evidence that competitive pricing is violated on average. Whether or not selected firms in the industry are candidates for takeover or what potential exists for selected firms to join in strategic alliances, mergers, and/or simple code-sharing arrangements is not explored in this paper. It would appear, however, that a combination of aggressive cost-cutting, exploitation of the production capacity of lower-cost U.S. carriers and marketing alliances will continue to drive the European industry as the dynamic of the competitive market continues to rationalize airline firm decision-making.

Acknowledgments

The authors would like to thank Lullit Getachew for her able research assistance. The authors also would like to thank Purvez F. Captain, David Good and Patrik T. Hultberg for helpful comments on this paper. Sickles acknowledges support from the Logistics Management Institute and the National Aeronautics and Space Administration. The usual caveats apply.

References

Agence Europe, (April 5, 1994). "EU: Europe Documents; No 1878-Main Conclusions of the 'Committee of Wisemen' for Air Transport."

Avmark, Inc., (1992). "The Competitiveness of the European Community's Air Transport Industry," prepared for the Commission of the European Communities.

Barla, P. and S. Perelman, (1989). "Technical Efficiency in Airlines Under Regulated and Deregulated Environments," in *Productivity Studies of Public Transport Companies*, edited by S. Perelman and B. Thirty, from *Annals of Public and Cooperative Economics*, 60: 103-124.

Borenstein, S., (1990). "Airline Mergers, Airport Dominance and Market Power," *American Economic Review*, 80: 400-404.

Borenstein, S., (1992). "The Evolution of U.S. Airline Competition," *Journal of Economic Perspectives*, 6: 45-73.

Borenstein, S., and N.L. Rose, (1992), "Competition and Price Dispersion in the U.S. Airline Industry," mimeo.

Brander, J.A. and A. Zhang, (1990). "Market Conduct in the Airline Industry: An Empirical Investigation," *The RAND Journal of Economics*, 21: 567-583.

Bresnahan, T.F., (1990). ``Empirical Studies in Industries with Market Power," in *Handbook of Industrial Organization*, Vol. II: 1011-1058.

Bruckner, J.K. and P. Spiller, (1991). "Competition and Mergers in Airline Networks," *International Journal of Industrial Organization*, 9: 323-342.

Button, K., (1991). *Airline Deregulation: International Experiences*, New York: New York University Press.

Captain, P., (1993). *Competition and Efficiency in the European Airline Industry*, Unpublished Ph.D. Dissertation, Rice University, Houston, Texas.

Captain, P. and R.C. Sickles, (1997). "Competition and Market Power in the European Airline Industry: 1976-1990," *Managerial and Decision Economics*, 18: 209-225.

Caves, D., L. Christensen, and E. Diewert, (1982). "Multilateral Comparisons of Output, Input, and Productivity Using Superlative Index Numbers," *Economic Journal*, 92: 73-96.

Christensen, L.R., D.W. Jorgenson and L.J. Lau, (1973). "Transcendental Logarithmic Production Function Frontiers," *Review of Economics and Statistics*, 55: 29-45.

Cornwell, C., P. Schmidt, and R.C. Sickles, (1990). "Production Frontiers with Cross-Sectional and Time-Series Variation in Efficiency Levels," *Journal of Econometrics*, 46: 185-200.

The Economist, (June 12, 1993). "Europe: Airlines Survey--Cartels Start to Crack."

Emerson, M., M. Aujean, M. Catinat, P. Goylet, and A. Jacquemin, (1988). *The Economics of 1992*, Oxford: Oxford University Press.

Europe 2000, (August 1, 1992). "EC: Air Transport Agreement Reached on 'Open Skies' Package."

Feldman, J.M., (1997). ``For 1997, the Big Fizz," *Air Transport World*, April 1, 1997.

Fiorino, F., (1997). "Growth Pattern," *Aviation Week and Space Technology*, February 17, 1997.

Good, D., M.I. Nadiri, and R.C. Sickles, (1992). "The Structure of Production, Technical Change and Efficiency in a Multiproduct Industry: An Application to U.S. Airlines," NBER Working Paper No. 3939.

Good, D., I. Nadiri, L.-H. Roeller, and R.C. Sickles, (1993a). "Efficiency and Productivity Growth Comparisons of European and U.S. Air Carriers: A First Look at the Data," *Journal of Productivity Analysis*, special issue edited by J. Mairesse and Z. Griliches, 4: 115-125.

Good, D., L.-H. Roeller, and R.C. Sickles, (1993b). "U.S. Airline Deregulation: Implications for European Transport," *Economic Journal*, 103: 1028-1041.

Good, D., L.-H. Roeller, and R.C. Sickles, (1994). "EC Integration and the Structure of the Franco-American Airline Industries: Implications for Efficiency and Welfare," in *Models and Measurement of Welfare and Inequity*, edited by W. Eichhorn, Heidelburg: Physica-Verlag.

Good, D., L.-H. Roeller, and R.C. Sickles, (1995). "Airline Efficiency Differences between Europe and the U.S.: Implications for the Pace of EC Integration and Domestic Regulation," *European Journal of Operational Research*, 80: 508-518.

Good, D.H., A.K. Postert, and R.C. Sickles, (1997). "A Model of World Aircraft Demand," Rice University, mimeo.

Greene, W.H., (1993). *Econometric Analysis, Third Edition*, New Jersey: Prentice Hall.

Hotten, R., (1995). "UK: Air Competition Slow to Take Off," *Reuter Textline*, September 20, 1995.

Johnson, J., M. Etheridge, D. Lee, E. Roberts, J. Villani, E. Wingrove, and E. Narragon, (1997). *Advanced Systems and Resource Analysis, Technology*

Assessment: Program and Capabilities, McLean, Virginia: Logistics Management Institute.

Kaplan, B.J., D.A. Lee, N. Retina, E.R. Wingrove III, B. Malone, S.G. Hall, and S.A. Houser, (1997). *The ASAC Flight Segment and Network Cost Models*, Hampton, Virginia: National Aeronautics and Space Administration.

Kravis, I., A. Heston, and R. Summers, (1988). *World Product and Income: International Comparisons of Real Product and Purchasing Power Phase III*, Baltimore: Johns Hopkins University Press.

Lowden, I.J., (1996). "Pushy Upstarts," *International Business*, October 1996.

McGowan, F. and P. Seabright, (1989). "Deregulatory European Airlines," *Economic Policy*, 9: 284-294.

Roeller, L.-H. and R.C. Sickles, (1994). "Competition, Market Niches, and Efficiency in the European Airline Industry," mimeo.

Sampson, A., (1988). *Empires of the Sky*, New York: Random House.

Shapiro, C., (1989). "Theories of Oligopoly," in *Handbook of Industrial Organization, Vol. II*, 329-414.

Sickles, R.C., (1985). "A Nonlinear Multivariate Error Components Analysis of Technology Specific Factor Productivity Growth with an Application to the U.S. Airlines," *Journal of Econometrics*, 27: 61-78.

Sickles, R.C., D. Good, and R. Johnson, (1986). "Allocative Distortions and the Regulatory Transition of the U.S. Airline Industry," *Journal of Econometrics*, 33: 143-163.

Sparaco, P., (1995). "Europe Faces Tense Social Disputes," *Aviation Week and Space Technology*, November 20, 1995.

Summers, R. and A. Heston, (1991). "The Penn World Table (Mark 5.0): An Expanded Set of International Comparisons, 1950--1988," *Quarterly Journal of Economics*, 106: 327-368.

Torres, A., (1995). "Belgium: Commission to Adopt Guidelines on Aid to Airlines," *Reuter Textline*, November 15, 1995.

Vincent, D. and D. Stasinopoulos, (1990). "The Aviation Policy of the European Community," *Journal of Transportation Economics and Policy*, 24: 95-110, 1990.

Wingrove III, E.R., P.F. Kostiuk, R.C. Sickles, and D. Good, (1996). *The ASAC Air Carrier Investment Model (Revised)*, McLean, Virginia: Logistics Management Institute.

4 PRICING AND DEREGULATION IN THE AIRLINE INDUSTRY

Philippe Barla

4.1 INTRODUCTION

Structural shifts are an important source of knowledge for economists, though unfortunately they are relatively rare. It is therefore no surprise that an event such as deregulation in the airline industry has given rise to literally hundreds of studies. Much has been learned about how airline markets and markets in general work. Studies have looked at the impact of deregulation on various aspects of airline strategies. Pricing is probably the aspect that has been most studied. In this paper, we review some of the evidence on the impact of deregulation on fares. We also review what has been learned about pricing in a deregulated environment. Given the volume of papers on the subject, this review can only be partial. Since there is no obvious or unique way to limit the scope of such a review, our choices are therefore subjective and thus contestable.

The U.S. experience has been the first, most dramatic and best documented example of airline deregulation. Most of the evidence we review here concerns the U.S. domestic market. In the last section, however, we examine some studies of deregulation in the airline industry in other countries.

The structure of this paper is as follows. First, we tackle the question of the effect of deregulation on fares. We show that most of the evidence suggests that deregulation has lowered fares. One study, however, (Dempsey, 1990) found that deregulation lowered fares initially but that with time this effect phased out. This would mean that today's fares could actually be higher than what regulated fares would have been. We reexamine this result and show how it depends very much on the functional form used. Using a more flexible form, we show that the gap between regulated and deregulated fares may in fact have increased over time. Second, we examine what has been learned about pricing in a deregulated environment. The existence of market power and the identification of its sources have been major topics of research. We review some of this work and then provide some new results for old questions. Most notably, we show that the impact of a route competitive structure on prices may be stronger than usually thought. Third, we discuss questions and problems that remain to be answered or addressed by economists. The dynamic aspects of airline interactions and the implications of network structure are probably two dimensions where efforts should be directed. Fourth, we examine some of the evidence available on the impact of liberalization in Canada and Europe.

4.2 THE EFFECTS OF DEREGULATION ON FARES

Has deregulation led to lower or higher fares ? This question has received some attention following deregulation in the late seventies. In figure 1, we reproduce the industry average yield (fare-per-passenger-mile) over the period 1965 to 1995. With a few exceptions, real yield has been continuously decreasing over this period of time. The question is then what role has deregulation played in the decline of fares after 1978.[1]

Figure 1. Annual Real Yield (1995 U.S. $)

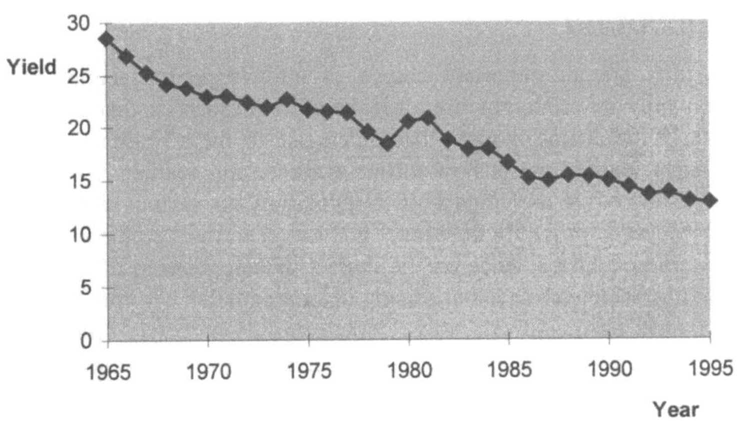

To test the specific effect of deregulation on fares, several methodologies have been proposed. Morrison and Winston (1986) try to estimate what deregulated fares would have been in 1977 and compared them to the actual regulated fares of 1977. To construct the deregulated fare, they obtain a deflator by estimating a fare equation based on data for the period 1980-1982 (they include factor prices, number of departures and distance as explanatory variables). They conclude that in 1977 actual fares were around 30% higher that what they would have been in a deregulated environment. One difficulty with this approach is that their fare equation does not include a time trend and thus does not allow for technological progress. This could overestimate the effect of deregulation.

[1] The exact time of deregulation is not as clear as one might think. The Deregulation Act was adopted in 1978. However, starting in the mid-seventies, the CAB (Civil Aeronautic Board) introduced some flexibility in the way airlines could set their prices.

More recently, Morrison and Winston (1995) try to predict how fares would have evolved had deregulation not taken place. They use the SIFL (Standard Industry Fare Level) fare formula that was used by the CAB in the last few years of the regulated area to determine regulated fares. Using this counterfactual methodology, they also find that the average fare was significantly lower as a result of deregulation (about 22%).

Dempsey (1990) looks at the changes in yield over the period 1970-1988. He adjusts yield to take into account fuel-price changes. He finds that fuel-adjusted fares (i.e., holding fuel price constant) are lower after deregulation. However, he also finds that fares were declining more rapidly in the regulated era than in the deregulated period. This means that the difference between projected regulated fares and deregulated fares becomes smaller over time and that the impact of deregulation on fares would only have been transitory. His projections suggest that in 1988, deregulated fares were at the same level as what (estimated) regulated fares would have been. He also obtains similar results when regressing real yield on labor and fuel price, a dummy variable for deregulation and a time trend that may be different in the regulated and deregulated period.

As the results of these studies are quite different (see table 1 for a summary), we look at this issue again. The type of analysis used by Dempsey is now used on European data to access the impact of deregulation and it is therefore important to examine the validity and robustness of such an approach.[2] Using ATA (Air Transport Association) aggregate annual data, we estimate the link between the average yield (on all traffic - domestic and international), fuel price, a time trend and a deregulation variable. The results are reported in table 2.

Table 1. Effect of Deregulation on the Average Price

Studies	*Methods*	*Results*
Morrison and Winston (1986)	Regulated 1977 fare vs. estimated deregulated fare	-30%
Morrison and Winston (1995)	Simulated regulated fare (SIFL) vs. deregulated fare 1979-1993	-22%
Dempsey (1990)	Regression of annual yield 1970-1988	•Deregulation lowers fare •Yield was declining more rapidly before deregulation

Using the same specifications as Dempsey[3], we arrive at very similar results. Deregulation has a one time negative impact on yield (the coefficient on the

[2] Dempsey's results have also been used recently as arguments against deregulation policies in other industries (see Business Week, March 17, 1997, p. 92).

[3] There are a few differences between the Dempsey model and the model estimated here. First, our time period is longer. So as to have more data before deregulation, we start the time series in 1965 (starting in 1967 as Dempsey has not changed the results). Second, we do not dispose of either fuel prices or labor costs before 1970. We replace the fuel price variable by a proxy - the producer price index for gasoline.

deregulation dummy is negative and significant). However, the yield was declining over time more rapidly in the regulated era.[4] This implies that deregulated yields were lower than what they would have been under regulation for the period 1977-1985, but that they were higher after this period (see figure 2).

Table 2. Regression Results (Endogenous Variable: Log(Yield))

Variables	*Dempsey specification*	*Non-linear trend*	*Non-linear trend*
	1965-1995	*1965-1978*	*1979-1995*
Intercept	3.32* (0.015)	3.3708* (0.0243)	3.1682* (0.1475)
Der	-0.2212* (0.0571)	--	--
Time	-0.0280* (0.0021)	-0.0472* (0.0095)	-0.0251" (0.0130)
Time-squared	--	0.0017" (0.0008)	0.0001 (0.0002)
Time x Der	0.0101* (0.003)	--	--
Log(Fuel)	0.1761* (0.0262)	0.0469 (0.4478)	0.1926* (0.0372)
R-square	0.988	0.963	0.970
# obs.	30	12	17

Der: is a dummy variable equal to zero before 1978 and one after.
Time: is the variable that captures the time trend.
Year x Der: is the interaction term between the time trend and the deregulation variable.
Fuel: a proxy for fuel price (i.e., the producer price index for gasoline)
*: significant at 0.01%
#: significant at 0.05%
": significant at 0.1%

As the labor cost price is never significant (even on regression using post 1970 data), we simply exclude this variable.

[4] Indeed, the coefficient on the time trend is -0.0280 in the regulated era, it is - 0.0179 in the deregulated period (that is -0.0280+0.0101).

Figure 2. Estimated Time Pattern - Dempsey Specification

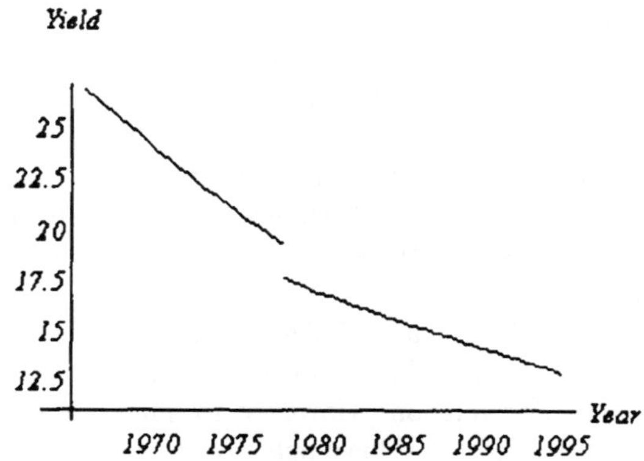

One problem with this result is that the slowdown in the yield decline may have started before deregulation and that the functional form used does not allow this decline to be captured. This would be consistent with the general slowdown in productivity gains for the whole U.S. economy in the seventies. We test for this possibility, by introducing a non-linear relationship for the time trend in the regression of Log(Yield). Likewise, as there is no reason for the coefficients of the explanatory variables to be identical in the two periods, we test the relationship separately for the two periods (regulated and deregulated era). The results are reproduced in table 2. Figure 3 shows the estimated time pattern with this specification. The results confirm that the rate of fare decrease was already becoming smaller before deregulation. In fact, deregulation appears to have helped fares decline more rapidly. This means that the gap between regulated and deregulated fares may actually have increased.

Figure 3. Time Pattern with Time-Squared

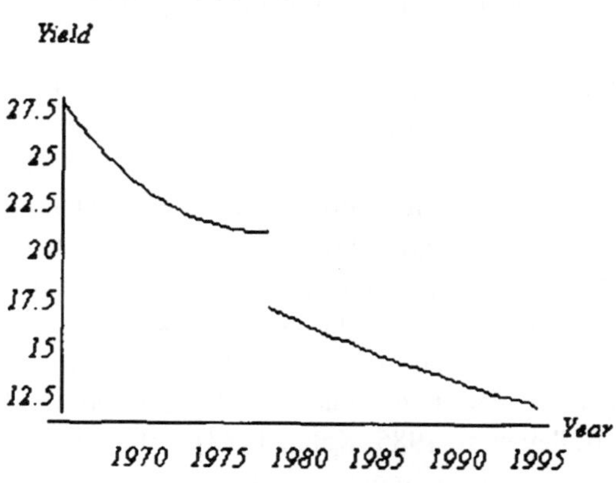

There are several limitations with such an approach: the data are too aggregate, the time series is very short and serial correlation could plague the results. This exercise, however, has two implications. First, it shows how the most critical views concerning the impact of deregulation have a weak empirical foundation. Second, it shows how careful one has to be when assessing the impact of deregulation using aggregate time series data.

If the effect of deregulation on the average yield is somewhat controversial, its impact on fare variability is not. Deregulation has given rise to a very complex fare structure and price discrimination among consumer types appears to be a major source of the fare dispersion. Borenstein and Rose (1994) calculate that for the second quarter of 1986, the average difference in the price paid by two passengers chosen at random (for a same route-carrier) was on average 35% of the average price on the route.

It also appears that the impact of deregulation has been quite different for different fare categories. Fare for the low-cost passengers (tourist) have clearly declined as a result of deregulation. However, for high-fare passengers (business), evidence suggests that prices may have actually increased following deregulation. Likewise, the impact of deregulation has been different depending on the route length. The decrease in prices following deregulation has been more pronounced for long haul routes.

The question of the impact of deregulation on fare cannot be separated from the effect of deregulation on service quality. Indeed, fares may be lower in deregulated markets but service quality may have declined as well. We will not go into detail here about all the changes in service quality since deregulation (see Morrison and Winston, 1995). Let us note, however, a few negative points: circuity (i.e., the distance actually flown compared to the direct distance) has increased (from about 3% to more than 4%); on average planes are more crowded; the load factor has increased from an average of 53.8% for the period 1970-1978 to 62% for the period 1979-1995. Positive points includes: the development of hub-and-spoke networks which has given rise to a dramatic increase in flight frequency and a sharp decline in interline connection (change of airline on a route). The issue of safety is tackled elsewhere in this book.

4.3 PRICING IN A DEREGULATED ENVIRONMENT

Following deregulation, researchers have tried to determine what factors may explain differences in fares across airlines and routes. A first step has been to test whether contestability applies to the airline industry. The general idea of contestability is that the actual competitive structure of a market should not matter if there are no barriers to entry or exit. Indeed, if there is no sunk cost to entry or exit, the simple threat of entry should be enough to discipline the price to a competitive level. Before deregulation, the airline industry was believed to respect these conditions (for example, capital in this industry is highly mobile, "capital on wings"). Following deregulation, economists have therefore tried to test the validity of this hypothesis (Bailey et al. 1985, Kahn, 1988). If contestability applies, prices should be independent of the number and size of competitors on a route. Very rapidly, it was clearly established that market structure matters in the airline industry. Fares are lower on routes where market concentration is lower. In table 3, we show the impact of concentration on fares for a few selected studies.

Table 3. The Effect of Route Concentration on Prices

Studies	*Sample*	*Effect on prices of a change in market structure (*)*
Bailey et al. 1985	5053 routes 2nd quarter 1981	+ 4.49%
Borenstein 1989	3591 routes 3rd quarter 1987	+ 2.86% - 3.36%
Evans et Kessides 1992	1000 routes 4th quarter 1988	+ 1.7%

(*) The Herfindahl index (HERF) is used to characterize the route competitive structure. The Herfindahl is defined as the sum of squared market shares of airlines on a route. A low HERF means a competitive structure while HERF equals 1 implies a monopoly situation. We look at the estimated price change when HERF increases from 0.375 to 0.625. This would correspond to a situation where, starting with three firms having 50%, 25% and 25% of the market respectively (so that HERF=0.375), the first two merge giving market shares of 75% and 25% (HERF=0.625).

Other studies have directly examined the impact of potential entrants on fares. Several definitions of potential entrant have been proposed, but they usually involve airlines that are present at both endpoints of the route but do not serve the route itself. The impact of the number and size of these potential entrants has been shown to be very limited (see Morrison and Winston, 1987, Hurdle et al., 1989, Evans and Kessides, 1991) . This suggests that potential competition does not replace actual competition. However, an interesting observation is provided by Peteraf and Reed (1994). They show that on monopoly routes, the average cost of a potential entrant significantly affects prices. Facing Southwest (a low-cost carrier) rather than USAir (a high-cost carrier) as a potential competitor actually does matter. This may suggest some form of limit pricing.

The next step has been to identify other sources of market power. To begin with, airport dominance ("hub effect") has been shown to be an important source of market power (see Borenstein, 1989, Evans and Kessides, 1993). An airline that dominates an airport enjoys a price premium of about 5 to 15%. Loyalty inducing marketing strategies like frequent flyer programs or travel-agent commission structures would favor major airlines at a hub (for an empirical test, see Borenstein 1991).

Another source of market power is multimarket contacts (MMC). Firms that compete in several markets may be more likely to recognize their interdependence. This may help them to collude and develop "live and let live strategies". Evans and Kessides (1994) and Singal (1993) show that prices are significantly higher in markets where competitors meet in many other markets. Morrison and Winston (1995) investigate how the multimarket effect varies over time. They find high

MMC increases prices in periods of high demand, whereas it appears that high MMC lowers prices in periods of low demand.

A general conclusion that emerges from these studies (see, for example, Evans and Kessides, 1991) is that if route structure (notably concentration) has an effect on prices, this effect is relatively small compared to the effect of airport dominance, which would be the main source of market distortion. In the following pages, we present some results that seem to contradict this general conclusion.

Using the Origin and Destination Survey data bank 1A for the second quarter of the years 1987-1993, we estimate the following reduced-form price equation:[5]

$$Log(P_{irt}) = \alpha_i + \alpha_r + \alpha_t + X_{irt}\beta + \varepsilon_{irt} \qquad [1]$$

(with i the airline, r the route and t the time)

The endogenous variable (Pirt) is the average price charged by an airline on a route over a specific quarter. This represents a measure of the pricing policy of the firm. The explanatory variables (Xirt) includes factors that capture demand, cost and structure changes. We have adopted this methodology of estimating a reduced-form price equation as it is the methodology usually used to study airline pricing. Note that the panel structure of our data allows us to introduce route (αr), airline (αi) and time (αt) specific effects. These three effects control for all the factors at the route, airline and time level that we do not observe but that affect prices. For example, the route-fixed effect will control for such things as the type of clientele on the route (leisure or business) or the distance between the two endpoint airports; the carrier-specific effect will control for the carrier reputation or the network structure (assuming these factors are relatively stable over time); and the time-effect will control notably for the general economic conditions.[6]

To capture the effect of the competitive structure, we include the route Herfindahl (ROUTE-HERF) and the airline market share of traffic on the route (ROUTE-MS). To capture the effect of the endpoint-airport competitive structure, we include the airline's average market share of total traffic at the two endpoint airports (AIRPORT-MS) and the average concentration at the two endpoint airports measured by the Herfindahl (AIRPORT-HERF). We also include two variables to control for cost; the average operating cost-per-passenger-mile of the airline (COST) computed over its whole network since route specific cost information is not available and the operating cost-per-passenger-mile of the airline on the route with the lowest cost (LOW-COST). Finally, we include the degree of circuity (CIRC, which is the ratio of the distance flown divided by the direct distance) and the total number of destinations offered by the airline at the two endpoints airports (# DEST).

---

[5] The O&D data represent a 10% random sample of all the tickets used on U.S. carriers. They are gathered by the U.S. Department of Transport.

[6] These effects are allowed to be correlated with the other exogenous variables and thus are treated as being fixed (see Baltagi, 1995). This is important, since ignoring these effects appears to lead to significant bias in the coefficient estimate of some of the included variables (see Barla, 1994).

We estimate the price equation on three different samples: (1) the 1,000 largest routes, which represent about 75% of all the traffic, (2) the 500 largest routes, which account for about 60% of the total traffic, and (3) the 100 largest routes (35% of the total traffic). We proceed in this way since there is no assurance that airlines behave in the same way in large dense markets, like New York-Boston as they do in smaller markets like Boise (Idaho)-Portland (Oregon).

The results are reproduced in table 4.[7] It would appear that the effect of the route and airport competitive structure are quite different for the three samples.[8]

The effect of ROUTE-HERF appears to be more important in dense markets. To appreciate the difference, we present, in table 5, the estimated impact on prices of a change in route and airport competitive structure. First, we examine the effect of a change in route concentration on the average price. An increase in ROUTE-HERF (from 0.375 to 0.625 corresponding to a one standard deviation increase from the mean) has a much higher effect on dense routes than on thin markets. On the other hand, the effect of airport control by a firm appears much smaller for large, dense markets. We compare the average price in a market where no airline dominates the endpoint airports (10 firms have each 10% of the traffic so that AIRPORT-MS=0.1 and AIRPORT-HERF=0.1) with a situation where one firm controls 50% of the endpoint airport traffic while 5 other firms have each 10% of market share (AIRPORT-MS=0.5 and AIRPORT-HERF=0.3). Based on these results, it therefore appears that the main source of market power on dense market is route concentration rather than airport control.[9]

---

[7] Note that we assume that the error term ε has the usual properties (iid normal with finite variance). This is clearly restrictive since we may expect serial correlation for an airline on a route and correlation across carriers on the same route at a specific time. Ignoring this will still give us unbiased estimators though they will not be efficient and the estimated standard error will be biased. This may potentially lead to wrong inferences. However, Evans and Kessides (1994), Brueckner et al. (1992) and Barla (1997) have all shown, that in the airline context, ignoring these correlations does not lead to major bias in the estimated standard errors and thus do not have any major impact on the inference.

[8] Note that these differences are significant; indeed, estimating the model on the large sample and allowing the coefficients of the variables of the route and airport structures variables to vary with market size indicates that these coefficients are significantly dependent on market size.

[9] Also note the negative coefficient on AIRPORT-HERF which seems to suggest that if the market share of the dominant airline is held constant (AIRPORT-MS), then as concentration at the endpoint airports increases, the prices decrease. This would suggest that prices are higher if the dominant airline faces small carriers rather than large ones.

Table 4. Regression Results for Average Airline Price (Endogenous Variable Log(Pirt))

VARIABLES	*SAMPLE 1* *1,000 largest routes*	*SAMPLE 2* *500 largest routes*	*SAMPLE 3* *100 largest routes*
ROUTE-HERF	0.186* (0.014)	0.235* (0.023)	0.328* (0.058)
ROUTE-MS	0.081* (0.007)	0.089* (0.011)	0.199* (0.030)
AIRPORT-MS	0.341* (0.015)	0.465* (0.024)	0.419* (0.067)
AIRPORT-HERF	-0.155* (0.035)	-0.323* (0.056)	-0.651* (0.165)
Log(COST)	0.354* (0.018)	0.350* (0.025)	0.424* (0.059)
Log(LOW-COST)	0.231* (0.014)	0.256* (0.020)	0.308* (0.049)
Log(CIRC)	-0.073* (0.013)	-0.089* (0.023)	-0.228# (0.102)
Log(# DEST)	0.063* (0.004)	0.045* (0.007)	0.067* (0.015)
R—SQUARE	0.801	0.825	0.884
# obs.	26,906	13,627	2,793

*: significant at 0.01%
#: significant at 0.05%
": significant at 0.1%
Fixed effects not reported

Table 5. Estimated Effect of Route and Airport Structure

SAMPLE	*ROUTE CONCENTRATION* *(1)*	*AIRPORT DOMINANCE* *(2)*
1,000 largest routes	+4.7%	+11%
500 largest routes	+6%	+13%
100 largest routes	+8.5%	+3.8%

(1) We look at an increase in ROUTE-HERF from 0.375 to 0.625
(2) We look at a change in AIRPORT-MS from 0.10 to 0.50 and AIRPORT-HERF from 0.1 to 0.3

One explanation for these results is that airlines behave differently in different types of markets. Another possible explanation of the smaller effect of ROUTE-HERF in thin markets is that this variable may be capturing economies of density. A high ROUTE-HERF means that a small number of firms share the market or that a few airlines dominate the route and thus are better able to exploit economies of traffic density. ROUTE-HERF would capture part of the efficiency gains due to the exploitation of economies of traffic density. In dense routes, it may be that even airlines with a small market share are able to exploit most of the economies of traffic density. ROUTE-HERF would then only capture the existence of market power. Results on large markets would give a better idea of the effect of route concentration on prices. On the other hand, the smaller effect of airport dominance may be due to the fact that dense routes involve large airports that are less concentrated on average.

When we use the equation [1], we try to explain variation in prices across markets, airlines and time. For example, the variable AIRPORT-MS primarily helps to explain price differences among airlines on the same route. Based on the results above, it appears that the dominant airline at an airport enjoys a price premium over its competitors. What is, however, the effect of the presence of a dominant airline at the endpoint airports on the average price paid by consumers on this route ? We address this question by attempting to explain the average market price on a route at a particular time. The estimated equation is now:

$$Log(P_{rt}) = \lambda_r + \lambda_t + Y_{rt}\delta + \eta_{rt}$$

Prt is the average price paid by travelers on route r at time t. The explanatory variables are the route Herfindahl (ROUTE-HERF), the endpoint airports Herfindahl (AIRPORT-HERF), the market share of the dominant airline at the endpoint airports (DOMINANT-MS), the average operating cost of the airlines on the route (COST), the operating cost of the lowest cost competitor on the route (LOW-COST), the average circuity (CIRC) and the number of destinations offered (#DEST).

The results are reported in table 6. Based on these results, if the ROUTE-HERF increases from 0.375 to 0.625, the average market price would increase by 6.8%. On the other hand, a market in which a firm controls 50% of the traffic at the endpoints while 5 other firms share the rest of the market will have an average price 0.8% higher than a market in which all the firms at the endpoint airports have 10% market share. The major source of price variation across markets therefore appears to be route concentration rather than airport control.

We have looked, up until now, at determinants of the average price. However, as we mentioned in section 1, price dispersion has greatly increased since deregulation. Few papers have looked at this issue (Borenstein and Rose, 1994 and Morrison and Winston, 1995). Price differences may reflect differences in cost structure or price discrimination. Borenstein and Rose find that price dispersion in 1986 was significantly higher in concentrated markets. More competition would yield lower price dispersion. However, Morrison and Winston (1995) show that the sign of the correlation competition - price dispersion changes over time and becomes positive in the late eighties.

Table 6. Regression Results for the Average Market Price (Endogenous Variable Log(Prt))

VARIABLES	*SAMPLE 1* *1,000 largest routes*
ROUTE-HERF	0.2635* (0.0204)
AIRPORT-HERF	0.3003* (0.0739)
DOMINANT-MS	-0.1295* (0.0427)
Log(COST)	0.6007* (0.0303)
Log(LOW-COST)	0.1571* (0.0215)
Log(CIRC)	0.8417* (0.0946)
Log(#DEST)	0.1361* (0.0112)
R-Square	0.905
# obs.	6,940

*: significant at 0.01%
#: significant at 0.05%
": significant at 0.1%
Fixed effects not reported

4.4 OPEN QUESTIONS

Though we have learned much about airline pricing since deregulation, many questions still remain unanswered. A question that has received relatively little attention in relation to its importance is the impact of networks on pricing on a particular route. Network structure may affect prices in several ways. First, it affects cost through economies of traffic density (this has been shown by Brueckner, Dyer and Spiller, 1992). Second, demand in a network may also be related (notably because of the use of frequent-flyer programs). This has implications on pricing that have not received much empirical investigation. Finally, network structure and interconnection among firms may affect the intensity of rivalry. While a few papers have looked at the impact of multimarket contact on pricing (Evans and Kessides 1994, Singal 1993) much remains to be studied. For example, what is the effect of multimarket contact on entry and exit decision ? Is a firm more likely to enter in price war with a competitor if it has a monopoly position on many routes?

A second issue that needs more investigation is the dynamic aspect of pricing in the airline industry. For example, what are the causes and consequences of periodic price wars ?[10] Are they really price wars or simply adjustments to new demand conditions ? What is the effect of the state of demand on firm strategies? Some of the results reviewed earlier suggest that airline strategies may change with demand conditions. For example, the link between price and multimarket contact or the link between price dispersion and concentration have been shown to vary with time (Morrison and Winston 1995). The answers to these questions are important in that they may provide clues to a question that is still controversial namely is competition really viable in the airline industry? One argument against deregulation was that a "laisser faire" policy would lead to cutthroat competition and instability in the industry. Indeed, the cost structure in this industry is characterized by a low short-run marginal cost (the cost for an extra passenger) compared to the average cost. This means that airlines have an incentive to cut prices to fill up their planes. This incentive is particularly important in the presence of excess capacity. Excess capacity has indeed been blamed for the poor financial results of the industry in the early nineties. The question that arises then is what explains the existence of excess capacity ? Is it error in forecasting demand conditions or is there something in the structure of the industry that leads periodically to excess capacity ? [11] Theoretical work suggests that strategic considerations may lead to excess capacities (for example Bulow et al., 1985). Competition could lead itself to excess capacities.

4.5 INTERNATIONAL EXPERIENCES

In this section, we will review rapidly the small amount of evidence available on the deregulation experience in other countries. Unfortunately, the lack of good data (primarily for prices) has made it difficult for researchers to access the impact of regulatory changes outside the U.S. This is, however, an area of intense research activity and this short section will discuss just a few examples of this research. Canada initiated deregulation in its domestic market just after the United-States. Contrary to its neighbor's "big bang" approach, Canadian deregulation was phased in over a period of almost ten years. Complete deregulation of prices was achieved in 1988 when the National Transport Act came into effect.[12] However, flexibility was already introduced as far back as 1979. For the most part, the structure of the domestic market has been characterized by a duopoly situation between Air Canada and Canadian Airline previously CP Air. This situation is evolving with the recent entry of new low cost carriers like West Jet, mostly in the West. Oum et al. (1991) show that aggregate yield in constant dollars declined by 18% over the period 1978-1988. Over the same period the U.S. domestic yield declined by 22%. The percentage of discount fares increased from 15% in 1980 to 60% in 1988, while the average discount, over the regular unrestricted fares, climbed from 25% in 1983 to

[10] See Morrison and Winston (1995) for some an analysis of price wars.

[11] Morrison and Winston (1995) provide some indirect support for the forecasting error hypothesis.

[12] Note that the Northern part of the country is still regulated.

45% in 1988. Unfortunately, due to lack of detailed data, it is difficult to know the exact role played by deregulation in these changes.

Europe has also adopted a step-by-step approach to deregulation of the intra-European market. This process was phased in over the 1988-1997 period. This period corresponds to the adoption of three packages (i.e., three sets of new rules). However, some European countries had adopted bilateral agreements prior to the Europe-wide deregulation (for example, the UK and the Netherlands). The little empirical evidence available suggests that so far deregulation of the European markets has had little impact. Concentration appears to have increased. Monopoly routes on intra-European markets have increased from 56% in 1992 to 64% in 1996, the number of duopoly routes have declined from 40% to 30%, while routes with more than two competitors have slightly increased from 4% to 6% (see Morrell, 1997). Comparison of actual yield with projected trends (using 1970-1989 data), reveals that fares were 4% below trends in 1992 and 13% below trends in 1994. There is no evidence for the role of deregulation in explaining these results. It is probably too early to truly assess the impact of the European deregulation process. However, bilateral agreements that were signed well before the European-wide deregulation provide some insight into what to expect. Uittenbogaart (1997) looks at the changes that occurred on the Amsterdam-London route which was deregulated in 1984 when the UK and the Netherlands signed a bilateral agreement. With respect to market structure, the number of active competitors has climbed from 5 in 1987 to 8 in 1997. Flight frequency has doubled over this period. There is no evidence for the average price on the route. However, the standard economy fare has been stable, while capacity allocated to first class passengers has declined and the discount fare capacity has increased. This would suggest that the average fare has probably declined.

4.6 CONCLUSIONS

The airline industry has been one of the first to go through a major deregulation process. Evaluation of this experience is thus capital to understanding the potential difficulties of liberalization in other industries. Much has been learned over the past two decades about how airlines compete and what affects their prices, and this knowledge should help policy makers. There is now clear evidence that every effort should be made to stimulate real competition at the route and airport level. This may be achieved by assuring a fair access to airports and gates and by actively limiting non-competitive practices.

There are, however, still many unknowns. The difficulties in forecasting the future of the airline industry emphasize the fact that there are still many aspects to be studied. One question that we believe remains crucial is to know whether or not competition in this sector is really viable in the long run.

Reference

Bailey E., D. Graham and D. Kaplan (1985), *Deregulating the Airlines*, MIT Press.

Barla, P. (1994), "Multimarket Contact and Pricing Strategy in the U.S. Domestic Airline Sector," *Ph.D. Dissertation*, Cornell University.

Barla, P. (1997), "Firm Size Inequality and Market power," *First Conference of the ATRG proceeding*, forthcoming.

Baltagi B. (1995), *Econometric Analysis of Panel Data*, Wiley.

Berry S. (1990), "Airport Presence as Product Differentiation," *American Economic Review*, vol. 80, No. 2, 394-399.

Borenstein, S. (1989), "Hubs and High Fares: Dominance and Market Power in the U.S. Airline Industry," *RAND Journal of Economics*, Vol. 20, No. 3, Autumn, 344-365.

Borenstein, S. (1991), "The Dominant-Firm Advantage in Multiproduct Industries: Evidence from the U.S. Airlines," *The Quarterly Journal of Economics*, 106, 1237-66.

Borenstein, S. (1992), "The Evolution of the U.S. Airline Competition," *Journal of Economic Perspectives*, Vol. 6, No. 2, 45-73.

Borenstein S. and N. Rose (1994), "Competition and Price Dispersion in the U.S. Airline Industry," *Journal of Political Economy*, 102(4), 653-83.

Brander J. and A. Zhang (1990), "Market Conduct in the Airline Industry," *RAND Journal of Economics*, Vol. 21, No. 4, 567-583.

Brueckner J., N. Dyers and P. Spiller (1992), "Fare Determination in Airline Hub-and-Spoke Networks," *RAND Journal of Economics*, Vol. 23, No 3, 309-333.

Bulow J., J. Geanakoplos and P. Klemperer (1985). "Holding Idle Capacity to Deter Entry," *The Economic Journal*, 95, 178-382.

Dempsey P. (1990), *Flying Blind: The Failure of Airline Deregulation*, Washington, DC: Economic Policy Institute.

Evans W. and I. Kessides (1991), "Structure, Conduct, and Performance in the Deregulated Airline Industry," *Symposium: The Deregulated Airline Industry.*

Evans W. and I. Kessides (1993), "Localized Market Power in the U.S. Airline Industry," *Review of Economics and Statistics*, Vol. 75 (1), 66-75.

Evans W. and I. Kessides (1994), "Living by the "Golden Rule": Multimarket Contact in the U.S. Airline Industry," *The Quarterly Journal of Economics*, 341-366.

Kahn A. (1988), "Surprise from Airline Deregulation," *American Economic Review*, Vol. 78, No 2, 316-322.

Green W. (1994), *Econometric Analysis*, Prentice Hall.

Hurdle G., R. Johnson, A. Joskow, G. Werden and M. Williams (1989), "Concentration, Potential Entry, and Performance in the Airline Industry," *Journal of Industrial Economics*, 38, 119-39.

Morrell P. (1997), "Air Transport Liberalization in Europe: the Progress so far," First Conference of the ATRG proceeding, forthcoming.

Morrison S. and C. Winston (1986), *The Economic Effect of Airline Deregulation*, Washington D.C: Brookings Institutions.

Morrison S. and C. Winston (1987), "Empirical Implications and Tests of the Contestability Hypothesis," *Journal of Laws and Economics,* 30, 53-66.

Morrison S. and C. Winston (1995), *The Evolution of the Airline Industry,* Washington D.C: Brookings Institutions.

Singal V. (1993), "Interdependence among Firms that Compete in many Markets: the Airline Industry and its Mergers," mimeo., Virginia Polytechnic Institute.

Oum T., W.T. Stanbury and M.W. Tretheway (1991), "Airline Deregulation in Canada and its Economic Effects," Transport Journal, Vol. 30, No 4, 4-22.

Peteraf M., R. Reed (1994), "Pricing and Performance on Monopoly Airline Markets," Journal of Law and Economics, Vol. 37, 193-213.

Uittenbogaart P. (1997), " Airline Competition on the route between Amsterdam and London," First Conference of the ATRG proceeding, forthcoming

5 THE IMPACT OF AIRLINE DEREGULATION ON COSTS AND EFFICIENCY

Randal Reed

In assessing the impact of deregulation on costs and efficiency in the airline industry it is necessary to analyze what airline costs look like. In this short paper a brief analysis of airline costs will be presented and the effects of deregulation on these costs assessed. The analysis will be broad, rather than specific, and thus the conclusions will be merely predictive and suggestive of the effects of deregulation on an individual firm. The goal of this paper is to present general trends in airline costs and efficiency. As such, cost study methodology is not presented and exact comparisons of airlines (or groups of airlines) are not carried out.

Perhaps the most famous study of airline costs is that of Caves, Christensen, and Tretheway (1984). In their study CCT found that both trunk and local airlines had economies of scale (at roughly the same level) and that the costs differed between these two groups primarily due to the difference in output levels (with a secondary effect from network composition). In this work, the results of CCT will be compared with two studies that include post-deregulation data. In addition, a new means of evaluating changes in costs will be presented and the resulting figures examined.

The presentation is in four sections. The first section summarizes the results of CCT and other cost studies that use data (primarily) from the regulated time period. In this section a few results about post deregulation costs are presented. The second section explores the implications of CCT's results and analyzes whether or not the results make sense in a post-regulatory environment. The third section looks at the changes in costs arising from deregulation while keeping in mind the change in technology that occurred with deregulation.

5.1 COST ESTIMATES

CCT estimated a translog cost function over a panel of 18 firms and 12 years. The results obtained have been used in merger hearings as well as by economists as a benchmark. Other studies have followed and the some of the key results have not changed. The primary result, economies of density but not of network size, has not always been obtained in these other studies. Table 1 below presents results from three studies, CCT, Kumbakhar (1990) and Reed (1994). The latter two studies have data from the post-regulatory era. The studies varied in included variables and methodology but the results on returns to density are similar and Kumbakhar and Reed are similar in their results on returns to network size. Reed includes more variables and has more detailed measures of returns to scale while Kumbakhar utilizes a symmetric generalized McFadden cost function that enforces global concavity of the cost function in the factor prices. Both Kumbakhar and Reed find that returns to density are lower after deregulation. Table 1 contains the estimates of Returns to Scale from these three studies.

Table 1

Cost Function Estimates - Returns to Scale

	CCT	Kumbakhar	Reed
Returns to Density (pre-deregulation	1.25	1.35	1.52
Returns to Network Size (pre-deregulation)	1.00	1.23	1.42
Returns to Density (post-deregulation)		1.20	1.46
Returns to Network Size (post-deregulation)		1.09	1.44

It can be seen that the estimates for each of the various measures differs from study to study. The most important result for this paper is the fact that there are economies of traffic density. This means that as an airline increases its output on a fixed network, the average costs of producing the output fall. All three studies find this in the pre-deregulation environment and the two studies that include post-deregulation data find this for the post-deregulation environment as well. In this paper, it will be assumed that there are increasing returns to traffic density in both periods for this work. The minor differences in levels are relatively unimportant for this work. The figures used in the last section will most closely match those of Reed.

Note that there are differences in the qualitative results on returns to network size. CCT find constant returns to network size while both Kumbakhar and Reed find increasing returns to network size (in both time periods). For the purposes of this paper, I will use the results of Kumbakhar and Reed and assume that there are increasing returns to network size. This is unimportant to the results presented here.

5.1.1 Changes in Firm Size Distribution

Leaving aside the issue of economies of density and network size, CCT present some other noteworthy results. For our purposes the most important is the result that small and large firms have roughly the same level of economies of scale and thus differences in output levels are the principle reason for differing unit costs across firm types. I break firms into three groups (roughly equivalent to national, large regional, and small regional carriers). Movement between groups is possible and several carriers did move between groups. Most notably were the carriers like Continental and USAir which moved from Group 2 to Group 1 during the time period in question. Table 2 defines the groups exactly.

Table 2

Definition of Groups

Name of Group	Output in Revenue Passenger Miles
Group 1	> 3,000,000,000
Group 2	> 1,000,000,000 but ≤ 3,000,000,000
Group 3	≤ 1,000,000,000

Table 3 presents the distribution of firms by firm size and year. It is important to note that these percentages reflect only the firms that reported cost data to the DOT. All the data for this paper are drawn from Form 41 traffic and financial reports made to the DOT. If a firm did not report data to DOT it is not counted at all in these figures.

Table 3

Firm Size Distribution by Year

Year	Group 1	Group 2	Group 3
1974	18.2%	13.1%	68.7%
1975	17.6%	14.0%	68.4%
1976	18.1%	13.8%	68.1%
1977	18.4%	14.7%	66.9%
	Beginning of Deregulation		
1978	19.1%	14.7%	66.2%
1979	14.6%	8.5%	77.0%
1980	12.4%	6.8%	80.9%
1981	9.5%	8.5%	82.0%
	End of Deregulation		
1982	9.4%	7.4%	83.2%
1983	11.1%	10.3%	78.6%
1984	10.9%	12.4%	76.6%
1985	11.8%	10.8%	77.4%
1986	13.4%	10.4%	76.2%
1987	17.0%	9.4%	73.6%
1988	20.2%	7.8%	72.0%
1989	17.3%	8.2%	74.5%
1990	18.3%	9.1%	72.6%
1991	17.9%	7.1%	75.0%
1992	18.2%	5.9%	75.9%
1993	18.6%	6.8%	74.6%
1994	17.7%	6.8%	75.5%

The important dates in the industry are quite obvious just from looking at Table 3. The large entry wave precipitated by deregulation is evidenced by the drop in percentage of firms who are Group 1 beginning in 1978. This trend turns around in the mid-1980's when the percentage of Group 2 firms decreases. Though this is partially the result of growth, a far more important contribution to this redistribution of firm sizes is the merger wave in the industry. Even the firms that moved from Group 2 to Group 1 through growth also participated in the massive merger wave.[1] Since the merger wave in the 1980's the distribution of firm sizes has been relatively stable.

5.1.2 Change in Costs

One of the key questions addressed in this paper is: Is knowledge of the three cost studies sufficient to understand the change in airline costs since deregulation? If the answer were yes, that would imply that changes in output levels would dominate any other contributions to lowered costs. Also, if economies of density explained the differences in costs, the differences in costs between the groups would remain large throughout the entire time period (for this work 1974-1994). As can be seen from Table 3, if economies of density alone were responsible for the dropping of costs we could expect to see a reduction of costs overall (due to the increase in size of the Group 1 firms and the percentage of Group 1 firms) but Groups 2 and 3 should have relatively stable costs over the time in question (since the average size of these firms does not change greatly from year to year.[2]

We look at changes in unit costs to see if knowledge of economies of scale are enough to explain the differences in costs over time. The outputs of the firms are shown for pre- and post-deregulation periods in Table 4.

Table 4

Output Levels by Firm Group

	Output (Millions RPM)
pre-deregulation	1,401
post-deregulation	1,704
Group 1	
pre-deregulation	5,621
post-deregulation	9,587
Group 2	
pre-deregulation	1,852
post-deregulation	1,840
Group 3	
pre-deregulation	187
post-deregulation	201

[1] Most notably, Continental acquired PeoplExpress, New York Air, and eventually Eastern while USAir formed from Alleghany, Piedmont, Mohawk, etc.

[2] Obviously, individual firms can have large changes in their sizes. However, if firms grow too much they move to the next group and are often replaced by new firms that offset individual growth within the group. Table 4 and Figure 1 below show this relationship more exactly.

Note that while the overall average output level rose, this was primarily driven by the nearly doubling of the size of the Group 1 firms. Group 2 firms actually became slightly smaller after deregulation (due primarily to the loss of several of the largest Group 2 firms to mergers or other exits). Figure 1 contains slightly more detailed data on outputs for each Group. In the figure it is quite obvious that the trend upward in output for Group 1 firms was strengthened by both deregulation and the merger wave of the 1980's. It is also fairly obvious that the Group 2 output levels did not change very much over time.

We now turn our attention to average costs in the industry. The costs are presented in real normalized terms. The average cost of a passenger mile is normalized to 1.00 for Group 1 firms in 1974. Costs are deflated using CPI figures. Thus, any figure greater than 1 is the percentage premium (in real terms) in costs for the Group-Year relative to 1974 Group 1 firms. Any figure less than 1 is the percentage cost savings for that Group-Year relative to 1974 Group 1 firms.

Again, just from a simple table such as Table 5, we can learn much about the costs in the industry. First, we note that average costs fell by over 40% for Group 1 and Group 2 firms and by over 50% for Group 3 firms. It also appears, though this is less obvious from just these numbers, that cyclical shocks affect the costs of smaller firms more than larger firms. The evidence of this is that in 1989-1990, the costs of the Group 1 firms rose about 2.5% while the costs of Group 2 firms rose about 12% and the costs of Group 3 firms rose about 24%. Though this is not proof that smaller firms face larger cost shocks during a recession, it is evidence that this may be the case.

Figure 1

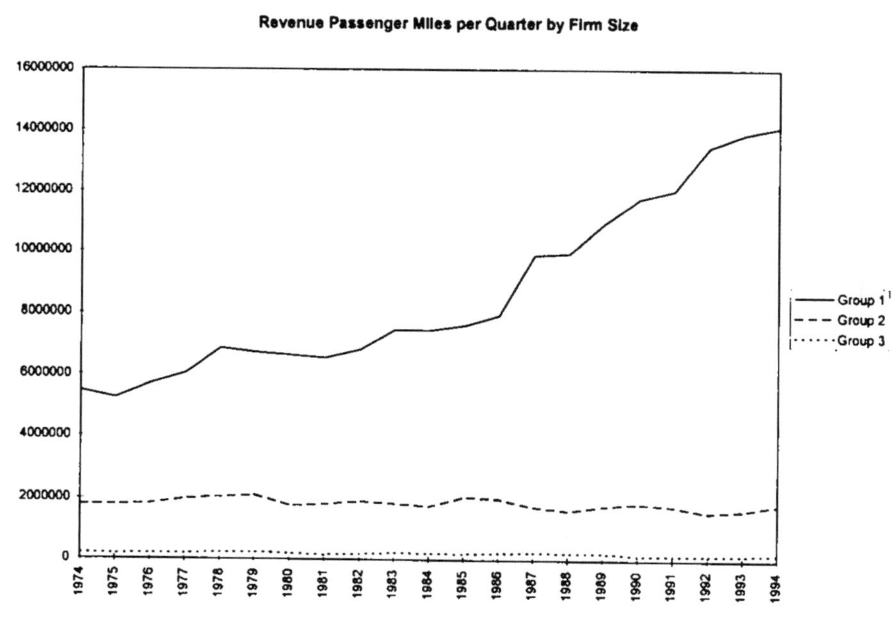

Table 5

Normalized Real Average Unit Costs by Firm Size

	Group 1	Group 2	Group 3
1974	1.0000	1.1925	3.0753
1975	1.0190	.9194	2.6529
1976	.9380	.9118	2.8347
1977	.9373	.9042	2.6235
Beginning of Deregulation			
1978	.8474	.8910	2.3250
1979	.8563	.8640	2.0212
1980	.9382	1.0870	2.0991
1981	.9524	.9765	2.0475
End of Deregulation			
1982	.8848	.9263	1.6983
1983	.8222	.8820	1.2705
1984	.7888	.7796	1.3158
1985	.7284	.7568	1.2596
1986	.6946	.7401	1.4899
1987	.6813	.6680	1.4145
1988	.7012	.5653	1.3807
1989	.7217	.6312	1.3619
1990	.7259	.6198	1.6985
1991	.6792	.6154	1.6174
1992	.6390	.5792	1.5222
1993	.6265	.5135	1.2853
1994	.5885	.5424	1.2277

The same data is presented in Figure 2.

Figure 2

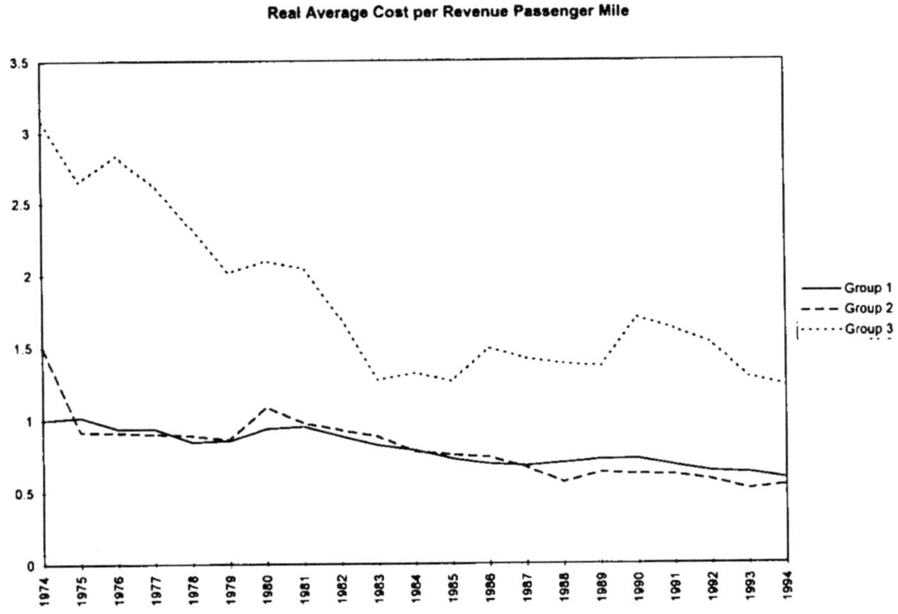

More important for the subject of costs, it is evident that there is no real cost advantage for Group 1 firms compared with Group 2 firms. This is surprising, especially given the results of CCT. This implies that the reduction in costs is not solely driven by economies of scale. A comparison of normalized real costs and outputs makes this point even stronger. Restricting our attention to just Group 1 firms we see that outputs rise and costs fall. This is consistent with the story that economies of scale are responsible for the majority of the cost savings. However, examining Group 2 leads to a different conclusion. Output was relatively stable for Group 2 firms (on average) yet the costs fell by more than for the Group 1 firms. Obviously this drop in average costs was not generated by an increase in output and economies of scale.

By observing that the drop in costs seems more steep after 1980, it appears evident that deregulation was linked to the drop in costs since the fall in average costs begins with the deregulation of the industry. It may be true that the merger craze actually caused a rise in average costs, though this is less sure. The other notable conclusion from these figures is that the small carriers have come the furthest in efficiency gains in both absolute and relative terms. The relative efficiency of these small carriers has gone from an average cost 2.5-3 times that of the other groups to an average cost about double the larger firms. In fact, the smaller carriers have a real average cost in 1994 that is only about 25% higher than the largest carriers in 1974. Clearly, average costs have fallen dramatically in real terms and deregulation seems to have played a role.

Using only economies of scale and increases in output, it is not possible to understand the change in costs from deregulation. This is not to say that economies of scale and increased output were not important in the overall reduction of costs since deregulation. Particularly for the large carriers this plays an important role in cost reduction.

5.2 NETWORK CHARACTERISTICS AND COSTS

Since economies of scale and output increases alone do not explain the drop in costs after deregulation, it is necessary to look at other factors. The obvious starting point is the network characteristics that are known to affect costs. For example, it is known that an increase in load factor lowers average costs. If load factors rose after deregulation then this can help explain some of the drop in costs. Several network characteristics will be looked at here. The network characteristics that are examined are: load factor, points served, density of service, traffic configurations, and network configuration.

Figure 3

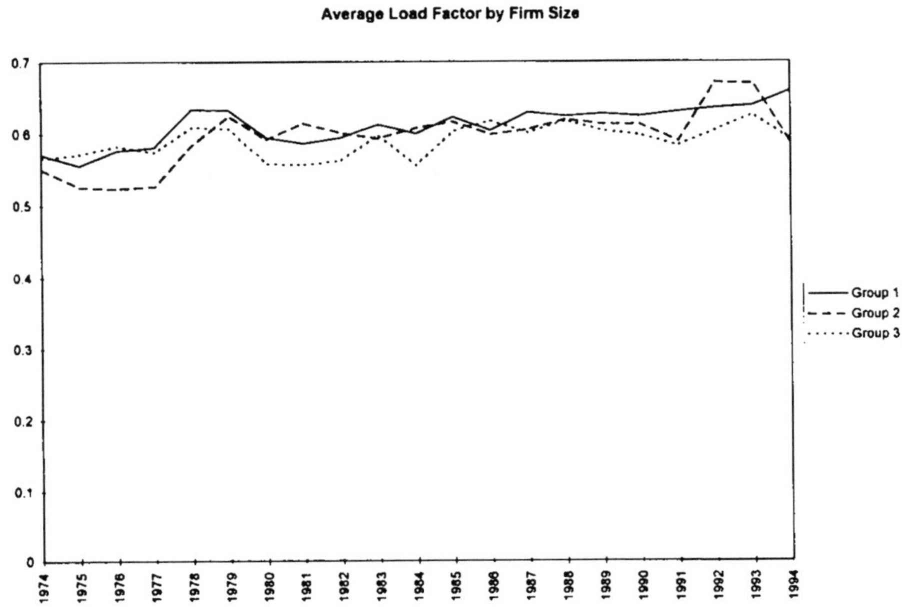

Figure 4

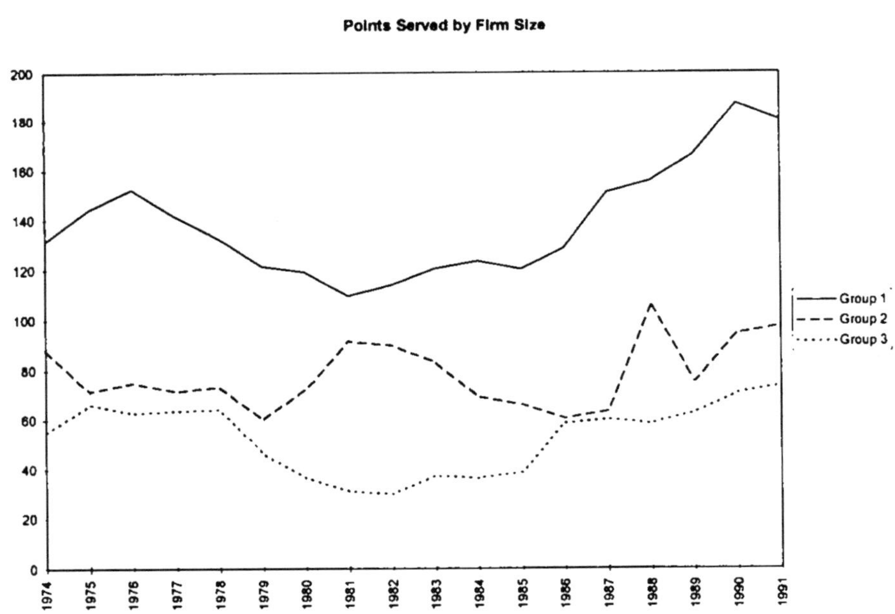

5.2.1 Hedonic Variable Effects

The first set of effects examined are the direct effects of variables normally included in cost estimations as control variables. The variables that all three studies include as control variables[3]: load factor and points served. Figures 3 and 4 show the changes in these variables over time for the three groups of firms.

We can see several things immediately. The first is that, while load factors rose for all three groups since the 1970's, this rise in load factors was very small. This implies that while contributing to the fall in costs since deregulation, load factor changes were not a very large contributor to the cost savings.

It can be seen from Figure 4 that the number of points served by the carriers rose over time. This is a cost *increasing* activity. As the number of points served rises (holding output constant) the density of service falls initiating the opposite process that an increase in output creates. The lowered density, coupled with economies of density, leads to higher average costs. Obviously, this affect is dominated by something else. Since the output levels rose and the number of points served also rose, it is necessary to look at the actual densities to determine what really happened.

5.2.2 Traffic Densities

The first type of density to be examined is the traditional form of density as defined by CCT. CCT define density of traffic as revenue passenger miles per point served. Figure 5 shows traffic densities of this type for the three types of firms.

It is readily seen that densities increased dramatically for the largest carriers. Group 2 and Group 3 carriers did not have as drastic a change in density of service after deregulation. If an arithmetic mean of the density figures is taken, all three groups experienced an increase in traffic density. This tells us that while increased density might explain part of the fall in costs for the largest firms, it is not a viable story for the other two groups of firms.

5.2.3 Traffic Configurations

Obviously, airlines are concerned with many variables other than output and points served when constructing their networks in an optimal fashion. These other variables include the number of departures and plane sizes utilized on the network. If large changes in the way airlines used departures and plane sizes led to a reduction of costs, this would not show up in the above figures. It is necessary to look at these separately.

---

[3] Reed includes two other variables: departures and routes served. These variables will be dealt with below. Also, in Reed, these variables are not treated as control variables but as essential to the analysis of returns to scale. See Reed (1994) for details. CCT and Kumbakhar include stage length which is not used here since it explains little of the cost difference.

Figure 5

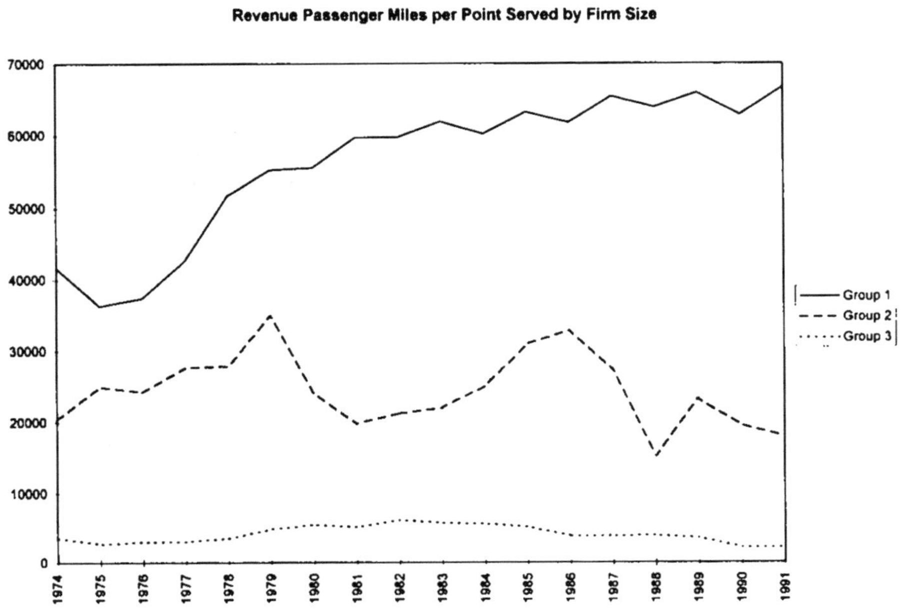

The number of departures plays an important role in airline costs. Integral to the decision about the number of departures used is the type of plane used. Most cost studies, including the three used as reference points in this paper, do not explicitly include plane size the estimation.[4] Plane size will be dealt with more explicitly in the next section. Several statistics relating to departures and traffic configuration are given in Table 6.

Both Group 1 and Group 2 firms increased their levels of departures along with their levels of output. Group 3 firms experienced a massive drop in the average level of departures. This was primarily due to a few firms dropping out of the group (through exit, merger, and growth). The Group 3 data is therefore difficult to analyze in this instance.

For the Group 1 firms it is evident that the average plane size (or distance flown) greatly increased after deregulation. In addition, the number of departures per point served increased. This is a potential measure of density (referred to here as departure density). Both of these are factors that contributed to the reduction in costs after deregulation. The Group 2 firms did not have the same pattern. Departure density increased quite a bit but output per departure fell. This is mostly due to attrition but is problematic for explaining a drop in costs. Nearly every variable that could explain a drop in costs from a traditional cost study point of view

---

[4] Reed implicitly controls for average plane size across the network but does not explicitly include a variable to control for it.

is absent in the Group 2 firms. The next section looks at what else could cause this drop in costs, for the Group 2 firms in particular.

Table 6

Departures and Traffic Configurations Relating to Departures

	Departures	1000 RPM per Departure	Departures per Point Served
pre-deregulation	37,623.4	22.84	433.2
post-deregulation	26,710.9	32.71	337.3
	Group 1		
pre-deregulation	94,989.5	59.15	665.5
post-deregulation	105,857.4	81.94	749.5
	Group 2		
pre-deregulation	42,653.8	44.23	563.2
post-deregulation	50,720.5	37.37	679.4
	Group 3		
pre-deregulation	21,337.7	8.79	344.8
post-deregulation	9,559.8	23.28	221.7

5.2.4 Network Configuration

The last piece of information easily imbedded in a cost function is the network configuration. Obviously a network is comprised of more than just a set of endpoints (points served). The network is defined by the connections between these points as well (routes served). CCT and Kumbakhar (indeed almost all cost studies) do not include a variable that controls for network configuration. Reed includes routes served which controls for this. For the purposes of analyzing the changes in network configuration a variable called the degree of connectivity will be introduced.[5] This variable represents how connected the points on the network are. If every point has a direct connection to every other point, the degree of connectivity is 1. If the network is very sparse (a perfect hub-and-spoke network for example) the degree of connectivity is very low (2/P in the perfect hub-and-spoke example).

Figure 6 shows the changes in this variable for a subset of firms. The subset is nearly all of the Group 1 firms and about half of the Group 2 firms.

Obviously, the degree of connectivity has fallen since deregulation. This is an extremely important factor in costs. As networks become less connected the airlines are better able to utilize departures and plane sizes to serve the entire network and thus reducing costs. While many economists have attributed some cost savings to the development of hub-and-spoke networks, a variable controlling for this is rarely included in cost studies.

[5] The formula is $DOC = 2R / P (P-1)$.

Figure 6

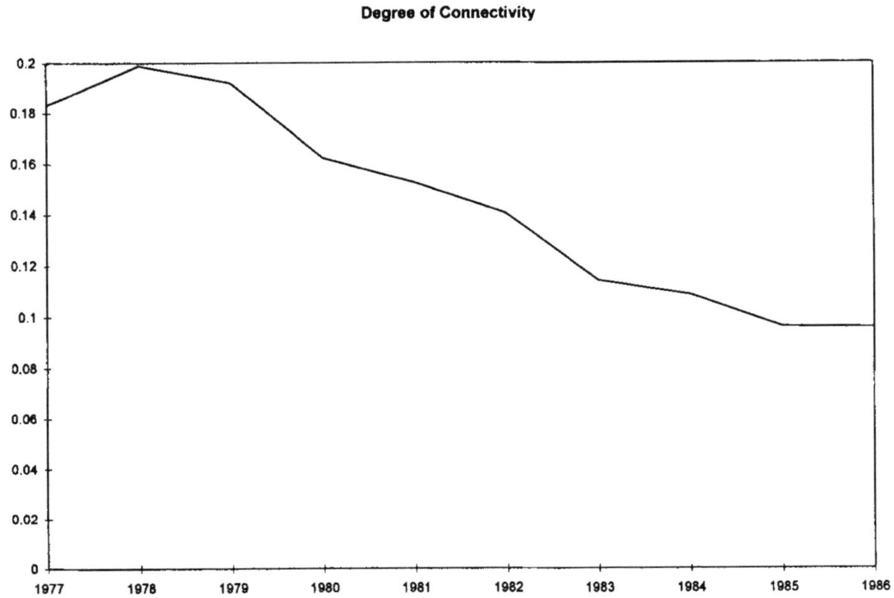

5.3 DEREGULATION AND TECHNOLOGICAL CHANGE

The last piece of the cost puzzle is technology. For the purposes of this paper we will define the technology of an airline as everything that is not included in the cost function as a variable. While this definition is not a problem theoretically, it does lead to some confusion in its application. To illustrate what is meant by technology for this paper, examples of what is and what is not included as technology are offered.

5.3.1 What is Technology?

Often when one talks about technology, they refer to the means of production of a good. While in some instances this will match the definition for this paper, there are others where this is not a good description. Things that are part of technology are: plane types flown, plane utilization, factor mix, and efficiency of engines. Things that are not part of technology are: type of network used, plane size (aggregate), and load factor.

To be sure that all of these are clear, brief definitions of each of the terms above are given here.[6] The plane types flown refers to the actual make of the planes used. Obviously, different planes are better suited for different uses. The matching of the

[6] For a more detailed description of technology and how it affects costs see Peteraf and Reed (1998).

fleet of an airline to its network is an important part of operating efficiently. Since there is no way to include this in a cost estimation this is part of what is referred to as technology. Plane utilization is very similar. Even if a firm has an optimal mix of planes in its fleet, it is still necessary to deploy these planes in an efficient manner. For example, large planes are more efficient on longer routes (in general). *Where* firms use their planes is also a part of technology.

The airlines use many inputs to produce their output (passenger-miles). Usually, economists boil these down to four: labor, fuel, capital (planes and engines), and materials (food, commissions, advertising, etc.). The mix of inputs (particularly the first three) is a choice of the firm. There are tradeoffs between capital investment and fuel consumption for example. The mix of factors is part of technology. The efficiency of engines is very similar to plane types and the mix of inputs. Obviously, the type of engine used can influence costs and is not included in the cost estimation. These are the principle components of what is termed technology in this paper. If these things changed due to deregulation, then the technology employed may be part of the reason for the decrease in costs.

The elements listed as not being part of technology are listed simply because there are variables in the cost function controlling for these. The most confusing of these is probably the type of network used. Many people refer to the use of hubs as a hub-and-spoke technology. While in some respects this may be correct, since the connectedness of the network is included in the cost function it is not a part of technology for the purposes of this study.

The question of whether or not the technology changed is answered by Peteraf and Reed. In their study they find that the technology employed by the airlines has undergone drastic changes since deregulation. The move toward a more rationalized (hub-and-spoke) network has allowed major changes in the way firms utilize their capital. The mix of plane types, and more specifically *how* the planes are used, has allowed a much more efficient use of airlines' resources. In addition, the mix of inputs has changed as well. Firms have moved away from labor and fuel intensive technology and have started to employ more efficient capital. This leads to increased capital costs but reduces the labor and fuel costs (and sometimes material costs as well).

Peteraf and Reed introduce a methodology for analyzing the impact of technological change on costs. The details of this methodology are not presented here. The results of their work are adapted to this study and presented below.

5.3.2 Implications of Technological Change

From Tables 5 and 6 it is obvious that the airlines have changed their structure since deregulation. The airlines have grown both in absolute size and in density. The results of CCT (as well as Kumbakhar and Reed) would predict that this would lead to a reduction in unit costs. However, the drop in costs for Group 2 firms remains an enigma using the standard cost analysis such as employed by CCT.

In addition, as firms move from Group 2 to Group 1 we see no reduction in their unit costs. This means that the reduction in unit costs attributable to deregulation can not be explained merely by the increased density. The density of the Group 2 carriers has remained about the same while unit costs have fallen about 40%. What has caused this? The rationalization of networks is part of the answer. This rationalization has come primarily through the reduction of direct routes flown (for a given network size) with the increased use of hub and spoke systems. The cost advantages of such a system are that increased load factors and plane sizes can be used. This change in network structure has not been achieved through a drop in routes served but rather through a rapid increase in points served with a much more modest increase in routes served. This has created much larger networks that are more sparsely connected.

In addition to the increased density and the rationalized network there is a third element in the cost savings that carriers have enjoyed since deregulation. This component is managerial flexibility in the production process. Though this is an amorphous term, it can be identified (see Peteraf and Reed) The airlines have produced the using a new "technology" since deregulation. The technology described here does not refer to new plane designs (though this may account for a small amount of the gain) but to a reorganization of capital and employees. The cost technology of the firm (after the network structure is accounted for) is determined by the relative mix of inputs and the deployment of capital. A restructuring of capital to use aircraft more efficiently has resulted in even further gains in costs.

It is this increased flexibility that the removal of route restrictions allowed. The removal of route restrictions allowed the rapid development of highly hubbed networks which allowed a redeployment of capital and employees that further reduced costs. The end of regulation allowed many changes to not only networks and their structures, but also to the way firms did business. The cost savings from deregulation can be attributed to many factors, but a change in the production technology is an important one.

The decomposition of cost savings in Peteraf and Reed is much more detailed than necessary for this work. Presented here is a summary of cost savings components for a typical Group 1 or Group 2 firm.

Table 7

Breakdown of Cost Savings from Deregulation

Component	Percent of Savings
Increased Density and Economies of Scale	50%
Rationalized Network and Hedonic Variables	20%
Technological Advance (Not Specific)	20%
Technological Change (Specific)	10%

As can be seen, 50% of the savings are from increased density and economies of density. This figure is an average over all medium and large carriers and is probably a bit larger for Group 1 carriers alone and quite a bit smaller for Group 2 carriers. 20% of the savings came from rationalized networks and changes in load factors. This is an important dividend of deregulation. Prior to deregulation it was extremely difficult to change network structures due to the approval process of the

CAB. Since deregulation carriers have added and dropped routes at a rapid rate and rationalized their networks to provide much more cost efficient service.

Another 20% of the savings came from technological progress that cannot be attributed directly to deregulation. This technological progress came in the form of improved engine efficiency among other improvements. Part of this 20% is probably a result of deregulation (since movement toward more efficient production methods was enhanced and sped up by deregulation) but it is not possible to directly attribute any part of it to the deregulation of the industry.[7] The last 10% of the savings came from the switch in the production process that was a direct result of deregulation. Again, this is an average over all medium and large carriers. Due to the fact that Group 2 carriers did not gain any density advantages it can be assumed that this component is more important for these carriers than for the larger Group 1 carriers.

5.4 CONCLUSIONS

The deregulation of the airline industry led to wholesale changes in the way the firms did business. Traffic densities rose, fares fell, firms entered and merged, network configurations changed drastically, and the production technology was altered. All of these changes led to large drops in average costs in the industry. Traditional cost analysis is not capable of picking up all of these savings, however slight modifications of the methodology allow a reasonable approximation of the true cost savings from deregulation.

Though increased density and load factors explain a bit over 50% of the cost savings for the larger firms, these factors contribute only marginally to the drop in costs for medium and small firms. The change in production technology accounts for about 10% of the savings in large firms and most likely a very large part of the savings for medium and small firms. Though not the focus of this work, this implies that the smaller firms reacted more strongly to the change in environment as far as network rationalization and technological change were concerned. In all, costs fell about 40% in real terms between 1974 and 1994 (with nearly all of these savings realized by 1987).

In closing it is important to note that these savings are in unit costs per revenue passenger mile across the industry. It has been noted by many researchers that the hub-and-spoke system actually increases the number of miles a passenger must fly to reach his destination. If the percentage increase in miles flown (to get to the same destination) has increased then these savings in costs are not representative of the costs of flying the passenger to his destination. The extra miles flown are not likely to be more than 40% so that implies that there are cost savings regardless of the circuitous routes required to reach destinations. In addition, if competitive changes

[7] For a detailed analysis of the technological progress of firms see Baltagi, Griffith and Rich (1995) and Gordon (1995).

in the industry lead to price increases then cost savings may not be passed on to the consumer in any event.[8]

The question of whether or not consumers are better off due to deregulation is left for another study. It is evident, however, that the real average unit cost of production has fallen drastically since the 1970's and that a large percentage of this drop is attributable to deregulation. The relaxation of economic constraints on the industry has allowed an adaptation of technology, pricing practices, and network configurations that has lowered costs.

References

Baltagi, Badi H., Griffith, James M., and Rich, Daniel P. "Airline Deregulation: The Cost Pieces of the Puzzle." *International Economic Review*, September-November 1975, pp. 937-57.

Caves, Douglas W., Christensen, Lauritz R., and Tretheway, Michael W. "Economies of Density versus Economies of Scale: Why Trunk and Local Service Airline Costs Differ." *RAND Journal of Economics*, Winter 1994, pp. 471-89.

Gordon, Robert J. "Productivity in the Transportation Sector." Working Paper, National Bureau of Economic Research, 1991.

Kumbhakar, S.C. "A Reexamination of Returns to Scale, Density and Technical Progress in U.S. Airlines." *Southern Journal of Economics*, April 1990, pp. 428-442.

Peteraf, Margaret and Reed, Randal. "Regulatory Reform and Technological Choice: An Analysis of Cost Savings from Airline Deregulation." CRT Working Paper, 1998.

Reed, Randal L. "Relevant Measures of Returns to Scale and Size in Multiproduct Network Technologies: An Application to the U.S. Domestic Airline Industry." Unpublished Ph.D. dissertation. Northwestern University, 1994.

[8] Though there has been evidence of price increases since the late 1980's, real prices have not increased from their pre-deregulation levels. In fact, there have been real price declines in the industry (at least through the early 1990's) to accompany the real cost savings.

6 AVIATION DEREGULATION AND SAFETY IN THE UNITED STATES: EVIDENCE AFTER TWENTY YEARS

Ian Savage

6.1 INTRODUCTION

Ten years ago myself and my colleagues at Northwestern University organized a conference to consider whether economic deregulation of the aviation (and trucking) industries in the United States had resulted in a diminution of safety performance (Northwestern University Transportation Center, 1987; Moses and Savage, 1989a, 1990).

At that time deregulation had occurred relatively recently having been phased in over the period 1978-83. The insights offered by time-series analyses of pre- and post-deregulation safety performance were therefore limited. A decade later much more data are available and it is now possible to observe where deregulation "fits" in the long-term history of safety in commercial aviation.

6.2 THE HISTORICAL PERSPECTIVE

Five-year moving averages of the number of commercial aviation passenger fatalities, and the number of revenue passenger miles from the early 1950s to the mid 1990s are shown in figure 1. Both series have been indexed to 100 for the period 1950-1954. Passenger miles have increased almost 35 fold since the early 1950s whereas the total number of annual fatalities have remained about the same. In the early 1950s about 110 passengers a year where killed in aviation crashes, which is about the same as it is nowadays. In between times the five-year moving average fatality count has been as high as 200 a year in the early 1960s, and as low as 60 a year in the early and late 1980s.

The implication is that the fatality rate must have fallen considerably over the period. The annual passenger fatality rate per billion passenger miles is shown as the symbols in figure 2, with a five year moving average plotted as the solid lines. The graph differentiates between the large carriers, regulated under Part 121 of the federal regulation, and the commuter airlines operating aircraft with 30 or less seats regulated under Part 135.

The most notable feature is the major improvement in the fatality risk for commuter airlines since 1975. Whereas the risks involved in 1975 were perhaps four times those of flying large airlines in the immediate post-war period, nowadays the risk is converging on that of the large Part 121 airlines. It is worth remembering that the Part 135 carriers still only account for 1.3% of the industry's passenger miles. Part 121 safety saw its most rapid improvement in the 1960s and 1970s. Since that time the fatality risk has remained at a very low level. A more detailed discussion of the Part 121 fatality rate is reserved for the next section of the paper.

Figures 3 and 4 present a similar analysis but this time using a more engineering based measures of accident rate. Accidents (in figure 3) and fatal accidents (in figure 4) are shown relative to the number of aircraft departures. This measure of aircraft activity is usually preferred as a measure of exposure as the vast majority of crashes occur during the takeoff and landing stages of flight. Changes in accident rates over time mirror the fatality-rate trends described in figure 2.

6.3 TIME TREND FOR PART 121 CARRIERS

Figure 5 is an enlargement of figure 2 showing the fatality risk for the Part 121 carriers since 1961. A visual inspection of this graph, and also the accident rates shown in figures 3 and 4, suggests a massive improvement in the 1960s which accompanied the technological improvements of air traffic control and the introduction of jet aircraft. The rate of improvement was much more modest in the 1970s, and then the accident rates in figures 3 and 4 appear to have levelled out since 1980. There has been an upswing in the fatality rate in the 1990s, but that may be an artifact of an highly unusual string of five crashes between 1994 and 1996 where aircraft in flight have crashed killing everyone (or almost everyone) aboard. Even including these crashes, the passenger risk is half that in 1980.

The changes in each decade for the three measures of safety are shown in table 1. The data are expressed as an average *annual* change in the decade. A five-year average using the years at turn of each decade as the midpoint are used for the calculations to try to avoid problems of unusual numbers of accidents or fatalities in any one year.

Figure 1. Five-Year Moving Average Passenger Miles and Fatalities

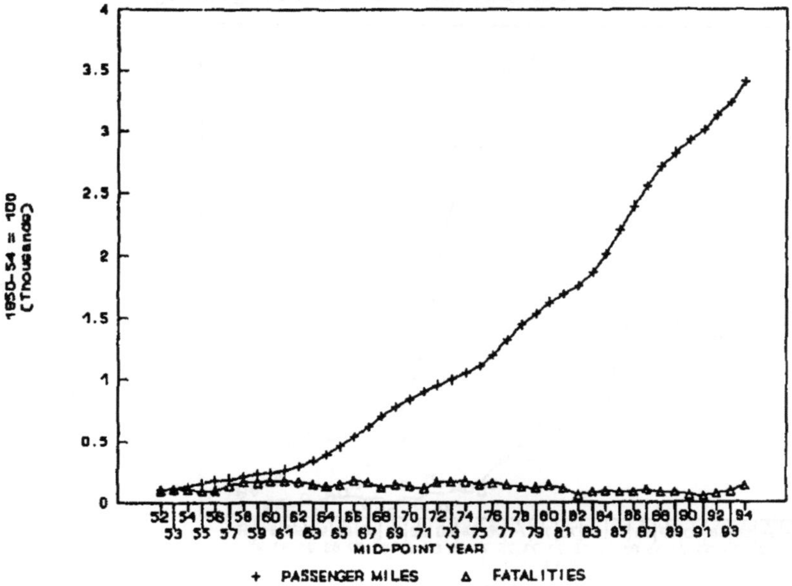

Figure 2. Fatalities Per Billion Passenger Miles with Five-Year Moving Average

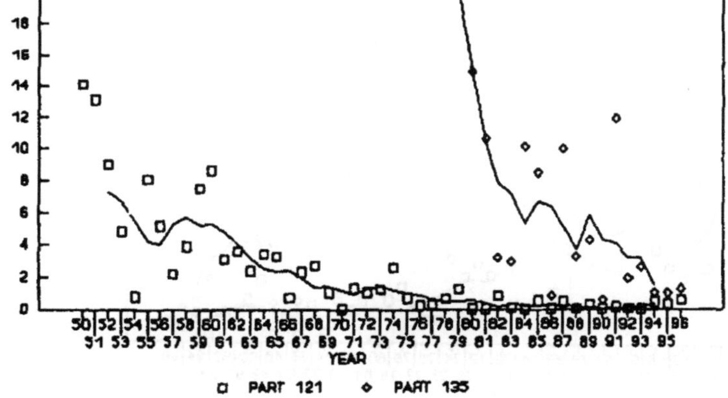

Figure 3. Accidents Per Million Departures with Five-Year Moving Average

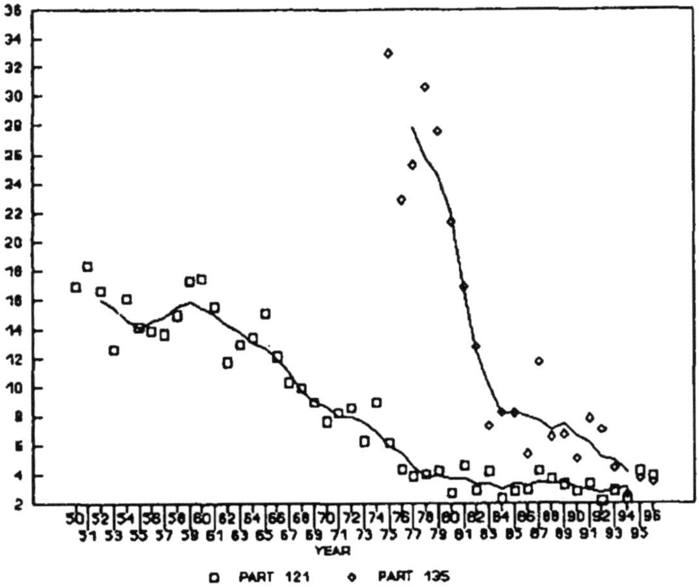

Figure 4. Fatal Accidents Per Million Departures with Five-Year Moving Average

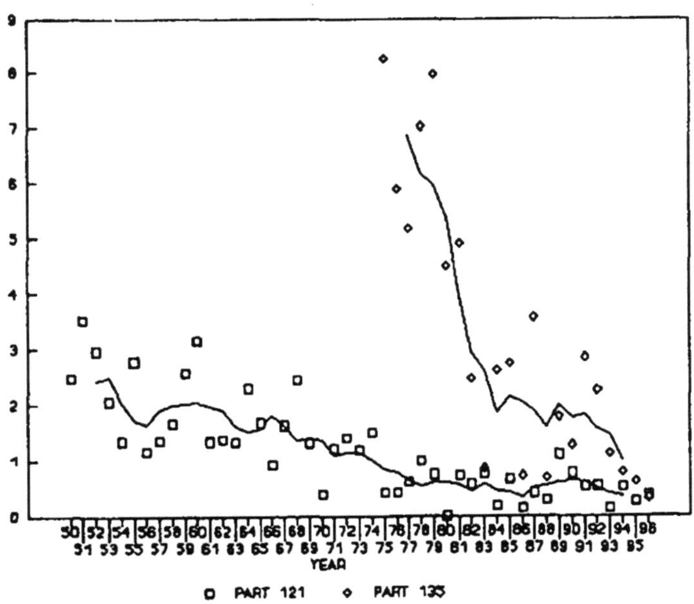

Figure 5. Part 121 Fatalities Per Million Passenger Miles

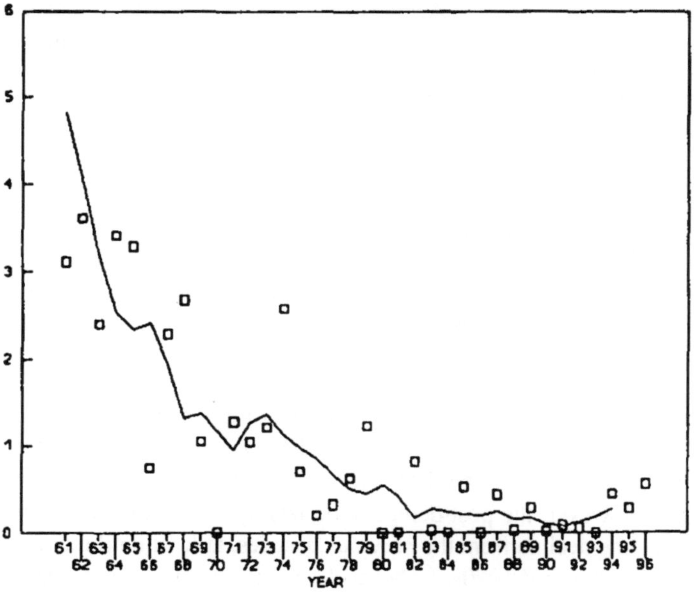

One will note that fatality risk has fallen much faster than the decline in accident rates. In part this is due to the considerable increase in average journey length (passenger miles divided by passenger enplanements) from just over 500 miles in 1950 to almost 1,000 miles today. This reduces the risk per passenger mile given that the majority of the risk is in the takeoff and landing stages of flight. Crashes have also become more survivable. In the 1950s an average accident killed 80% of the passengers aborad, while today that figure is less than 40%. In addition average aircraft size has increased from an average of 27 passengers per flight in 1950 to 102 today. In general, larger aircraft appear to be safer.

To determine statistically whether deregulation had changed the rate of improvement, Rose (1990) and Kanafani and Keeler (1990) fitted regressions to data on accidents per million departures and fatalities per ten million passenger miles respectively. Data from the mid-1950s or 1960s up until the late 1980s were used. Both regressed a time trend and a deregulation dummy combined with the time trend for the period after 1978 on the logarithm of accident rates. Neither found that deregulation had disturbed the long running trend. I came to the same conclusion by replicated both studies using data up to and including 1996.

However, one could take a different approach to the problem by fitting a time trend to the data for the period between 1960 and 1978 and then observing whether the actual data since 1978 is consistent with the extrapolated time trend. I did so for two measures of safety: accidents per million departures, and passenger fatalities per billion passenger miles. For the latter I used five-year moving averages for the base data so as to avoid the wild fluctuations from year to year, and the problem of taking logarithms of for years when there are no passenger fatalities.

Table 1. Annual Percentage Change in Each Decade

	Passenger Fatalities per Passenger Mile	Accidents per Departure	Fatal Accidents per Departure
1950s	-3.7%	-0.4%	-2.2%
1960s	-14.1%	-5.6%	-3.9%
1970s	-7.4%	-8.2%	-7.9%
1980s	-16.4%*	-2.1%	+0.6%
1990s	+32.8%*	+0.8%	-13.4%

*The 1990s figures are compromised by a string of five high fatality accidents in 1994-96. The annual percentage change for the 1980s and 1990s combined is -4.3%.

Figures 6 and 7 show the data as the symbols, and the extrapolated 1960-1978 time trend as the solid lines. In figure 6, one can immediately see that the number of accidents levelled off after 1978 and now lies considerably above the trend line from the 1960s and 1970s. However, the post-deregulation fatality rate, shown in figure 7, has continued to follow the decline from the previous decades, at least until the rash of high-fatality accidents in the mid-1990s. The declining fatality rate in the face of constant accident rates is explained in part by the increase in average journey length by 20%, from 825 to 990 miles, since 1978.

Critics of deregulation would look to the analysis in figure 6, and argue that deregulation has stalled the improvement in safety. They would argue that the aviation system in 1996 is quite similar to that in 1980. There have not been the dramatic changes in aviation technology similar to those in the 1960s and 1970s. The technology of air traffic control is unchanged in the past sixteen years, and the same Boeing 727s and DC9s form the backbone of the domestic fleet.

To support a hypothesis that deregulation has harmed safety, one would have to argue that deregulation has held back technological advances. Such an argument would be quite subjective and speculative. The second generation jets have been such a design success that it is quite likely that they would have persisted in service even if a cozy regulated environment had generated the cash to fund replacements. It is still argued in aviation circles whether the fly-by-wire third generation jets are safer than the second generation jets. Declining world fuel prices since 1980 would have justified retention of less fuel-efficient aircraft under any regulatory regime. One wonders whether the sad saga of the Federal Aviation Administration's (FAA) attempts to upgrade the air traffic control system would have been any more successful under continued regulation. To the extent that traffic growth since deregulation has increased the income of the Aviation Trust Fund, there should have greater funding available and political will to overhaul the system.

Figure 6. Part 121 Accidents Per Million Departures with 1960-78 Trend Line

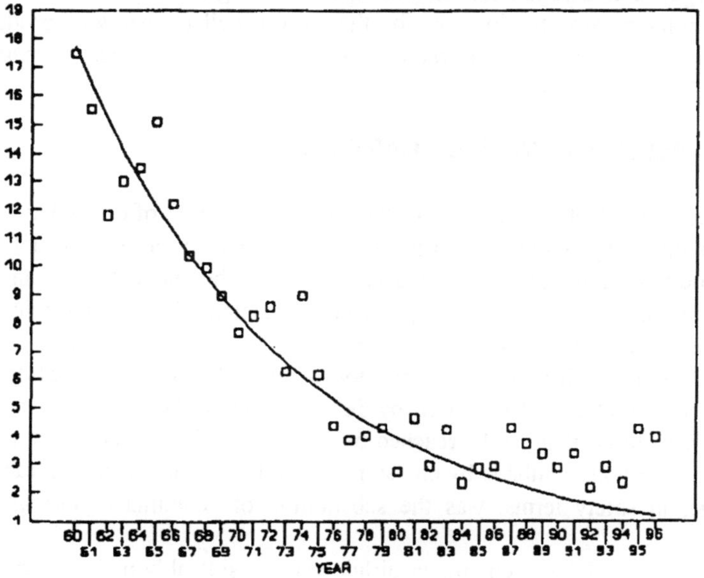

Figure 7. Part 121 Fatalities Per Billion Passenger Miles with 1960-78 Trend

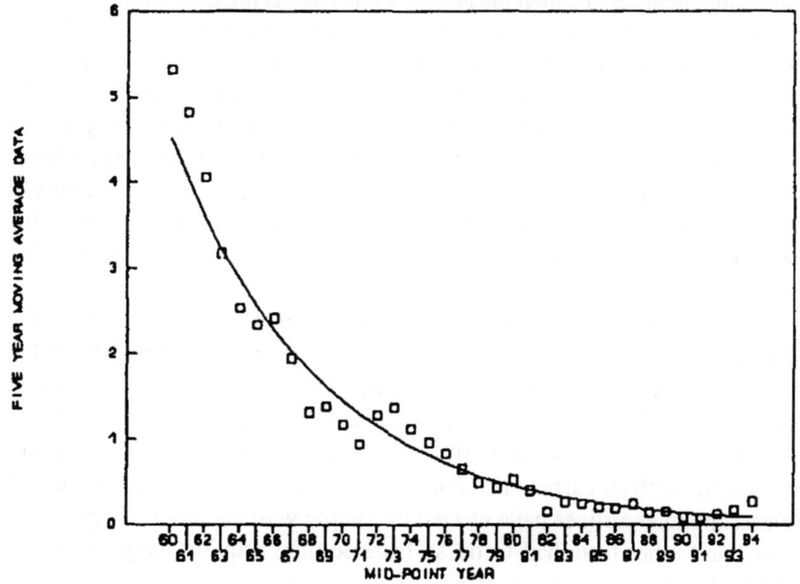

In conclusion, fatality rates have continued their long-run decline since deregulation. However, accident rates since 1980 have remained constant, primarily because the technology of aviation safety has stood still. However, I think it is a

stretch to argue that deregulation caused that technological standstill. I think the aviation community are still looking for the "silver bullet" that will produce the technological leap forward that will reduce accident rates by the orders of magnitudes seen in the 1960s and 1970s.

6.4 TIME TREND FOR PART 135 CARRIERS

One may well argue that this segment of the industry is a child of deregulation. Prior to deregulation many secondary airports were served by infrequent jet service providing multiple-stop point-to-point service. With the move to hub-and spoke operation many of these secondary airports saw an increased level of service to hub airports where there are convenient connections to many destinations. A recent General Accounting Office (GAO) report (1996a) found that the number of departures from small communities had increased by 50% between 1978 and 1995. While the number of destinations that can be reached by nonstop service has declined, the range of possible destinations available by one-stop service has expanded considerably. The disadvantage, in safety terms, was the substitution of "commuter" aircraft for jet aircraft.

In the late 1970s flying a commuter airline was considerably more hazardous that flying on a large jet airline. By any measure it was at least six times as risky. Then in 1978 there was a major overhaul of safety regulations including new pilot qualification and training requirements, new maintenance requirements, and an upgraded list of required safety equipment. Since then the accident rate has declined significantly.

The main explanation is that increased traffic required the deployment of larger aircraft with turboprop rather than piston engines, as vividly shown in table 2. In 1978 70% of the commuter airline fleet was powered by piston engines, and 80% of the passenger miles flown were in aircraft with less than 20 seats. By 1994 the proportions were almost exactly reversed. Seventy percent of the fleet were turboprop powered and 80% of passenger miles were on aircraft with larger than 20 seats, and almost a third of passenger miles on aircraft with more than 40 seats. Clearly the growth of this sector of the industry has led to kinds of technology-lead improvements in safety that were witnessed in the Part 121 carrier sector in the 1960s and 1970s.

With the rapid change in the technology of the commuter airline industry, the traditional dividing line between large jet and commuter carriers has become somewhat fuzzy. The dividing line between Part 121 and Part 135 safety regulations was set in 1978 at aircraft with 30 seats. At that time almost 90% of passenger miles on commuter airlines were on aircraft with 30 or fewer seats, so one could say that Part 121 was synonymous with jet carriers and Part 135 with commuter airlines. However, over time some commuter airlines have elected to comply with the more stringent Part 121 regulations, and other have had to do so because they acquired larger aircraft. Indeed by 1994 60% of commuter passenger miles were on aircraft with more than 30 seats. In 1997 the boundary between Part 121 and 135 operations was lowered to aircraft with 10 seats. Now more than 98% of the flying on commuter airlines will be done on aircraft certified under the Part 121 regulations.

Figures 1 through 4 differentiate between Part 121 and Part 135 carriers rather than between jet versus commuter carriers. This makes the improvement in accident rates for the Part 135 carriers even more remarkable given that, especially since 1990, most of the larger commuter carriers have transferred from the Part 135 category to the Part 121 category.

Table 2. Change in Composition of Commuter Airline Fleet

	1978	1994
Number of Aircraft	1195	2170
METHOD OF PROPULSION (as a proportion of the fleet)		
Single-engine piston	18%	12%
Multi-engine piston	56%	14%
Turboprop	23%	72%
Jet	3%	2%
SEATING CAPACITY (as a proportion of revenue passenger miles flown)		
1-9	22%	2%
10-19	58%	19%
20-30	9%	22%
31-40	5%	27%
41+	7%	31%

Source: Regional Airline Association *Annual Reports*

6.5 PUBLIC PERCEPTIONS

Despite the seemingly positive view contained in analysis of statistical risks, public perceptions of events are somewhat different. In general, I would suggest that public attitudes to aviation safety have not changed much in the past decade.

Ten years ago a particularly disastrous year for airline safety worldwide in 1985 led to considerably concern that economic deregulation had led to a decline in safety. The weekly news magazines presented tales of crashes, escalating numbers of near midair collisions, and allegations of improper maintenance. In the minds of the public, the latter was confirmed by the record fines for maintenance irregularities imposed on household name airlines. The popular belief, expressed for example by Nance (1986), was that deregulation had led to competitive pressures on air carriers to reduce expenditures on safety related items, allowed entry into the market by inexperienced new carriers, and led to the substitution of riskier commuter airlines in secondary markets. In addition many believe that the congestion caused by the greater number of airline flights, occasioned by the substantial rise in demand since deregulation, has led to an increased probability of collision.

These concerns were graphically illustrated by a *Time* magazine cover story on January 12, 1987. Ten years later *Time* ran another cover story (March 31, 1997). The story was not much different. The latter story reported on a book written by Mary Schiavo (1997), the former Inspector General of the Department of Transportation, which described the dangers caused by the entry of new inexperienced airlines, sloppy maintenance practices, and general failures by the FAA in certification of aircraft, new airlines, and requiring upgrades of existing equipment. Ten years ago the concerns led to the establishment of a Presidential Commission on Aviation Safety in 1987. A decade later the President established another commission under Vice-President Al Gore.

While the story may be the same, the details of the plot have changed in subtle ways. Commuter airlines no longer produce the same amount of concern, mostly likely due to the rapid improvement in their safety performance. Concern about financially stressed airlines skimping on safety has diminished as the weakest carriers have exited the market and buoyant business conditions in the mid 1990s have improved the fortunes of even the companies with traditionally poor financial performance. The concern about airport congestion and its relationship to an increased collisions also appears to have disappeared off the radar screen, although one still despairs that the same vacuum tube technology and elderly computers are used for air traffic control. Geriatric jets have become a much talked-about issue. Following the bombing of an Pan American aircraft over Scotland in 1988 security has become an increasing concern.

Most importantly the villain of the story has changed. Shiavo's book points the finger not at the curse of deregulation, as Nance had done ten years earlier, but rather at the failure of the FAA to carry out the duties assigned to it. Perhaps in the minds of the general public, as opposed to industrial organization economists, deregulation has faded into the realm of ancient history to be filed away along with leisure suits, high inflation, and disco records.

To a great extent the public's continued concerns about aviation safety are valid. For jet airlines accident rates have not changed substantially since the end of the 1970s. There continues to be spectacular crashes and exposés of errors and mismanagement which are guaranteed to be racy subjects for a press story. Barnett (1990) calculated the ratio of front-page stories in the *New York Times* to the fatality risk for six common mortality risks, and found that reports on aviation safety appeared 50 times more frequently than any other risk. One might conclude that aviation safety continues to provide a good story, albeit that the cast of characters and the villain keeps changing.

6.6 DEREGULATION AND NEW ENTRANT JET AIRLINES

The initial concern about inexperienced new entrant jet carriers stemmed from the 1982 crash of an Air Florida Boeing 737 at Washington National Airport due in part to poor certification of its pilots. Kanafani and Keeler (1989) used data for the period 1982-1985 to compare the records of 20 established carriers and 25 "new entrant" airlines. The two groups of carriers were compared on the basis of maintenance expenditures, the results of FAA inspections, near midair collisions, and accidents. The researchers were unable to establish that new entrants had an inferior safety record. Indeed there was weak statistical evidence that new entrants spent relatively more on aircraft maintenance and were involved in fewer near midair collisions. Classification of which firms were "established" and which were "new entrant" proved to be a bit of a problem. The reborn-out-of-bankruptcy Braniff and Continental Airlines were included as "new entrants" in this study, although their presence was recognized by firm-specific dummy variables. Two formerly-intrastate carriers were given different classifications. Pacific Southwest Airlines was classified as an established carrier whereas Southwest Airlines was classified as a new entrant.

While the names of the new entrant airlines have changed over time the concern about new entrant airlines has not disappeared. While Southwest and America West Airlines have become major airlines, other new entrant airlines such as Air Florida, the original Midway, New York Air and People Express exited the market to be replaced by the likes of American Trans Air, Western Pacific, Reno Air, Kiwi International, Vanguard and the infamous ValuJet. The 1996 inflight fire and subsequent crash of a ValuJet DC9 near Miami led to the well-reported public dispute between the aforementioned Mary Schiavo and David Hinson and Frederico Peña the heads of the FAA and the Department of Transportation respectively. Shocking stories of maintenance irregularities and in-flight problems led to the suspension of operations by ValuJet and the retirement or resignation of senior FAA officials.

Clearly Kanafani and Keeler's study could be repeated using data from the early 1990s. As I was limited for time I could not undertake a full econometric analysis, but I could calculate some mean values of three leading indicators of safety performance for the period between 1991 and 1995: accidents and incidents, near midair collisions, and pilot deviations, all measured as a rate per 100,000 departures. I grouped the Part 121 scheduled carriers into three: established jet airlines, commuter airlines operating under Part 121 regulations, and new entrant jet airlines.

Results of the analysis are shown in table 3. All the differences between the groups for each of the three measures are statistically significant. Surprisingly, the commuter airlines operating aircraft with 31 or more seats under the Part 121 regulations have the best safety performance. New entrant jet carriers have an accident and incident rate that is 50% higher than that of established jet airlines. Although their rate of pilot deviations is lower. Their higher rate of near midair collisions might be misleading if one does not take into account the areas in which the airlines are flying, and one should remember that involvement in a near midair collision does not imply blame. Based on this quick analysis, I think there is some evidence that a more careful study would reveal that recent new entrants do have less safe operations than established carriers. This view is supported by the analysis of the GAO (1996b) who found that jet carriers with less than five years experience had higher rates of incidents and also FAA enforcement actions taken against them than more established firms.

Table 3. Safety Performance 1991-1995

Rate per 100,000 departures	Accidents & Incidents	Near Midair Collisions	Pilot Deviations
Established	5.05	0.99	2.46
Part 121 Commuter	2.38	0.53	0.19
New Entrant	7.59	1.70	1.48

Established Carriers (5,800,000 annual departures): Alaska, Aloha, America West, American, Continental, Delta, Hawaiian, Midwest Express, Northwest, Southwest, TWA, United, USAirways, USAirways Shuttle.

Part 121 Commuter (840,000 annual departures): Air Wisconsin, Atlantic Southeast, Business Express, Continental Express, Executive, Horizon, Mesa, Trans States, Simmons, UFS.

New Entrant (145,000 annual departures): American Trans Air, Air South, AmeriJet, Carnival, Frontier, Kiwi, Morris, Midway, Reno, Spirit, Tower, ValuJet, Vanguard, Western Pacific.

Based on table 3 we can make some very crude estimates of the effect of new entrant carriers on annual aviation fatalities. That is, what would be the effect if the 145,000 departures each year operated by new entrant airlines were performed by established carriers. I will assume that new entrant carriers have an accident rate 50% higher than that of established firms. Given that the fatality rate for Part 121 carriers over the period 1992-1996 was 17.7 fatalities per million departures, the safety effect of new entrant carriers is 1.3 extra fatalities per year.

6.7 DEREGULATION AND FINANCIAL PRESSURE

In the years after deregulation unit costs fell, and poorly-managed or badly positioned carriers sort bankruptcy protection, and then either reemerged with different cost structures or exited the industry. In the early 1980s there was considerable concern that many airlines, and especially those near bankruptcy, were shaving costs in such a way that reduced safety.

While not an unbiased source of information, a survey of its members by the Air Line Pilots Association in 1986 (Fingerhut, 1986) describes the concerns. Half of the pilots surveyed felt that economic deregulation had greatly affected safety, with almost all acknowledging there had been some impact. In attributing the cause of this decline, nearly 70% felt that financial pressure on airlines was partly to blame, 40% felt inexperienced managers were partly the cause, and 60% said that the FAA was partly responsible. Evidence for the effect of financial pressure on safety can be detected elsewhere in the questionnaire. Ten percent of pilots said they were frequently pressured into flying aircraft in contravention of the "Minimum Equipment List," which specifies combinations of on-board equipment that can be inoperative without grounding the plane. Another 40% said that they were sometimes pressured. About half the pilots felt that the aircraft they flew had an excessive number of components whose maintenance had been deferred, with the same proportion believing that the airworthiness of their aircraft had declined since deregulation.

Moses and Savage (1989b) conducted an econometric investigation of the data and found that pilots who worked for airlines that had made financial losses in the period between 1980 and 1985 were statistically more likely to believe that deregulation had harmed safety. There was a very strong connection between financial condition and pilots' opinions on whether their initial training was inadequate, and whether the maintenance and airworthiness of their aircraft had declined.

There is some theoretical economic basis for believing the opinions of the pilots. Golbe (1981, 1988) and Bulow and Shoven (1978) demonstrate that firms close to bankruptcy might choose to select low safety levels because the downside risk of crashes would not be borne by stockholders if bankruptcy is declared. However, the effect on safety provision by firms whose financial position is declining, yet are not in danger of declaring bankruptcy, is theoretically indeterminate (Golbe, 1986). In other words, the safety-profitability issue is an empirical and not a theoretical one.

Rose (1990) conducted econometric investigations relating financial condition and accident experience. This work updated and expanded the analysis of Golbe (1986) who found a insignificant yet positive relationship (more profits equals more crashes) based on pre-deregulation data. Rose's work used data for 35 large scheduled air carriers over the period 1957 to 1986. A Poisson model is used with total accidents per departure as the dependent variable, and the previous year's operating margin (1 - operating expenses/operating revenue) as the primary financial measure. She found a negative relationship that was statistically significant at the 10% level: more profits implied lower accident rates. A decrease in financial performance from average to one standard deviation below average was estimated to increase the accident rate of the carrier by 7.5%. Models using firm fixed effects suggest that the effect may be larger and more robust in terms of statistical significance. When categorized by size of firm, it would appear that the profitability - safety relationship only holds for middle and small carriers. There was no statistical relationship for large carriers whatever the functional form.

Rose then estimated a similar model for 26 carriers over the period 1981-1986 using incidents, reported non-accident events involving actual or potential hazards to safety, as the dependent variable. Here there is a strong negative relationship between operating margin and incidents for small and medium sized carriers, but not for large carriers.

So, how do the findings of Rose and the survey of pilots square with the data shown at the beginning of the paper? The early 1980s were marked by a recession that hurt airline finances in general, and in addition certain carriers suffered severe financial difficulties. Those carriers included Eastern Air Lines which was classified by Rose as a large airline, and Pan American, Continental, Braniff, People Express and Frontier which were classified as medium-sized. Yet the early 1980s saw a continued improvement in accident rates, and some of the safest years on record with no passenger fatalities recorded in 1980 and 1986, and only one in each of 1982 and 1984.

One should remember that 75% of Rose's dataset is prior to deregulation. While bankruptcy was rare prior to deregulation, changes in profitability and variations in profitability between carriers were not. It is possible that Rose's results were driven by events in 1960s or 1970s when more financially-able firms invested in the safer second-generation jet aircraft.

However, Rose's analysis of incident rates in the early 1980s, coupled with Moses and Savage's (1989b) analysis of the pilots' survey and the anecdotal evidence of Nance (1986), do suggest that something untoward was going on at financially-stressed carriers, even those which were large household-name firms. Over the past ten years my own informal conversations with people in the industry have also provided me with anecdotal support for these assertions. It is my opinion that we were "lucky" that there were no major fatal crashes in the early 1980s involving firms that were just about to exit the market.

Alternatively, the dichotomy can be explained by the specification of the safety production function which describes how safety inputs (training, maintenance and so on) are transformed into actual safety performance. It is possible that safety could be seen as *partly* a type of stock variable. Airlines close to bankruptcy may have, in better financial days, invested in hiring highly qualified personnel, organized extensive training programs, and bought new aircraft which were carefully maintained at state-of-the-art maintenance bases with large inventories of parts. While, as an economist, I question the very concept of a "margin of safety," I can readily acknowledge that there may well be a time lag between reduction in maintenance and training programs and a resulting increase in accident rates.

Crude estimates can be made of the effect of financial pressure on safety. In recent years about 12% of, or 960,000, annual Part 121 departures have been operated by carriers that were recently in Chapter 11 bankruptcy protection. Rose calculates that firms that have operating margins two standard deviations below that of the mean for the industry have a 14.8% higher accident rate. Based on an average Part 121 fatality rate for 1992-1996 of 17.7 per million departures, financial stressed carriers may have led to 2.5 additional fatalities each year.

6.8 DEREGULATION AND THE GROWTH OF COMMUTER AIRLINES

Much of the debate concerning the impact of airline deregulation on safety has concerned the substitution of less safe Part 135 carriers on services previously operated by Part 121 jet carriers. However, the magnitude of the risk difference between the two types of service is the subject of some controversy. Table 4 presented calculations of a contemporary comparison of risks of flying Part 135 versus Part 121 carriers. Four measures of risk are shown: accidents per departure, fatal accidents per departure, fatalities per passenger mile, and fatalities per passenger enplaned. The data for exposure is 1995, while the count of fatalities and accidents is the annual average for the period 1992-1996.

Table 4. Comparison of Accident Rates 1992-1996

	Part 121	Part 135
Accidents per Million Departures	2.98	4.41
Fatal Accidents per Million Departures	0.34	1.06
Passenger Fatalities per Million Enplanements	0.26	0.38
Passenger Fatalities per Billion Passenger Miles	0.27	1.56

Measured in terms of aircraft departures, accidents occur 50% more frequently and fatal accidents 150% more frequently on Part 135 as compared with Part 121 aircraft. When measured from a consumer's point of view, the risk per passenger mile is almost six times higher on a Part 135 aircraft. However, this measure is misleading because average journey lengths vary so much. The average journey length on a Part 121 carrier is 990 miles while that on a Part 135 carrier is 240 miles. Given the high proportion of the risk of air travel is in takeoffs and landings, a more appropriate comparison is the risk per passenger enplaned. Here the risk is much closer, with Part 135 carriers having a fatality risk about 46% higher than Part 121 carriers.

Oster, Strong and Zorn (1992) argue that a further adjustment is necessary in the comparison. When Part 135 service was substituted for Part 121 service the number of intermediate stops (and hence takeoffs and landings) was reduced from an average of 0.59 to 0.30 per trip. The Part 121 accident rate should therefore be inflated by 22% to account for the additional takeoff and landing risk. The risk per enplanement on a Part 121 carrier should therefore be about 0.317 per million enplanements as compared with the 0.38 risk on a Part 135 carrier. The net result is that Part 135 carriers are about 20% riskier than Part 121 carriers. Of course, as can be seen from the figures presented earlier in the paper, the risk differential would have been much larger in the early 1980s when the accident rate on Part 135 carriers was much higher.

To calculate the net effect of the higher accident rate of Part 135 carriers it is necessary to speculate on the number of passenger enplanement who now travel on a Part 135 aircraft where previously they would have traveled on a Part 121 aircraft. I decided to try to calculate upper and lower bounds. The upper bound is based on the assumption that Part 135 carriers would have continued to hold their mid-1970s 0.5% share of the market, as opposed to the 1.3% to 1.5% share that they hold now. Of course, as the total market has grown over the years, this assumption implies that the number of passengers who have to substitute Part 135 for Part 121 service has also grown. A lower bound is based on the assumption that the number of annual passenger enplanements who had to substitute Part 135 for Part 121 service remained at the 8.5 million which was applicable to the early 1980s.

I divided up the post deregulation period in three (1980-1984, 1985-1989, and 1990-1996) to reflect the improved accident record of the Part 135 carriers over time. I calculated the number of passenger enplanements that would be made on Part 121 rather than Part 135 for an average year in each time period, and estimated the number of fatalities that be avoided by using the average fatality rate for both types of service.

The fatality rate for Part 121 carriers was inflated by 22% to represent the increased number of takeoffs and landings required for Part 121 service as discussed in a previous paragraph.

Table 5. Additional Fatalities Caused by Part 135 Substitution

Annual Averages		1980-84	1985-89	1990-96
Fatality Risk per 1,000 enplanements	Part 135	0.00115	0.00089	0.00062
	Part 121	0.00017	0.00027	0.00027
Enplanements Substituted (000s) per Year	Upper	8,510	14,187	20,214
	Lower	8,510	8,510	8,510
Additional Annual Fatalities	Upper	8	9	7
	Lower	8	5	3

The results of the analysis are shown in table 5. My estimate of the upper bound of the number of fatalities caused by a substitution of Part 135 for Part 121 service since 1980 is 136 passengers. The lower bound is 89. Therefore the substitution of Part 135 for Part 121 service has led to between 5.2 and 8 additional passenger fatalities per year.

Of course, the growth of the airline industry in general has had a spillover effect on that segment of the market what always was and still is served by commuter airlines. These markets may have seen the influx of new technology and new aircraft. It is possible that these passengers have witnessed an improvement in their safety that would not have occurred without the spur to aircraft design and construction caused by deregulation. However, one should remember that there are still markets served by piston-engine aircraft with 20 or fewer seats whose safety record is inferior to turbo-props.

6.9 DEREGULATION AND THE LEVEL OF SURVEILLANCE

Ten years ago there was considerable concern that the level of surveillance activity by the FAA had not responded to the changes caused by deregulation. The FAA's workload had increased dramatically compared with that needed to oversee the stable and predictable industry that existed in the days of entry control. The number of large jet air carriers increased from 60 in 1978 to 148 in 1985. FAA resources were needed to provide initial certification of these carriers. In addition, the new regulations for Part 135 carriers in 1978 required considerable time recertified airlines, pilots and aircraft. Despite the increase in workload, the decline in FAA staff numbers initiated in the early 1970s continued unchecked through January of 1984. O'Brien (1988) calculates that the net result was a decline in the number of inspectors per airline from 4 in 1978 to 1.5 in 1985. The FAA admitted that in order to carry out certification duties "routine operations and maintenance compliance (ie. inspection and surveillance) were mostly left undone" (Kern, 1988). The trend was only reversed in 1984 when the FAA conducted a number of major safety audits of the aviation industry resulting in large fines against household-name firms.

It is my opinion that in the period between 1978 to 1984 FAA surveillance activity was clearly out of line with the needs of the market. Yet analysis of overall accident data indicates nothing untoward during these years. How close, if at all, America came to an increased accident rate due to inadequate surveillance of new entrants and financially-stressed carriers is an issue we can probably never resolve.

But are things much different ten years later? The early 1990s saw another growth in the number of new airlines after a period of consolidation in the late 1980s. The ValuJet affair revealed deficiencies in the FAA oversight of the industry. A recent GAO report (1996b) is subtitled ".. long-standing problems in FAA's Inspection Problem." An appendix to this report lists 31 GAO reports written over the period 1985 to 1996 critical of the FAA's inspection programs. In the report the GAO writes "[o]n a broader scale, serious problems that hamper the effectiveness of FAA's aviation safety inspection program have remained unresolved for nearly a decade." Shiavo (1997) goes further alleging that the mission of the FAA to "promote" aviation, which was only rescinded in the light of the ValuJet affair, had led to a very cozy relationship between the FAA and the industry it was supposed to be overseeing. In writing this paper I reread the charter of the 1987 Presidential Commission and it is clear that the problems at the FAA were well known a decade ago.

6.10 DEREGULATION AND THE QUANTITY OF INFRASTRUCTURE

Ten years ago there was also concern that the infrastructure of the industry has been severely strained since deregulation. The number of departures by Part 121 and 135 scheduled carriers had increased by 44% from 1978 to 1987. In addition, flights had become concentrated at specific airports at certain times due to the adoption of hub-and-spoke operating practices. Yet, capacity has not increased. Prior to the opening of Denver in 1995, the last major new airport was Dallas-Fort Worth in 1973. In 1987 the number of air traffic controllers was still below what it was when most controllers were fired because of illegal strike action in 1981. Air traffic control reequipment programs were, on the evidence of the GAO, running years late. The system had in many ways been the victim of its own success.

Ten years later the increase in the number of departures has been much more modest at 12%. However, the reequipment of the air traffic control system is not much further forward. The grand National Airspace System Plan of 1981 was eventually canceled in 1994 when it was years late and considerably over budget. The FAA has been the butt of jokes about vacuum-tube technology and a series of embarrassing failures of aged computers at control towers in 1995 and 1996. Yet there have been some improvements. Doppler equipment to detect windshear has been deployed at some places, collision warning detection and avoidance equipment has been fitted to Part 121 aircraft; and small private aircraft have been required to be fitted with mode C transponders in certain areas so that they can be adequately monitored by air traffic control and other air traffic.

Many may remember that the most talked-about issue in 1987 was the congestion at major airports with the resultant well-publicized traffic delays, plus an increased rate of near midair collisions and runway incursions. Nowadays complaints about traffic delays and collisions are not as vociferous. It is possible that the 1990 requirement that airlines reveal the on-time ratio for individual flights has put an end to a practice from the 1980s when airlines were, to put it charitably, "optimistic" about the elapsed flight times shown in their public schedules. To the dismay of economists, pricing solutions to congestion are no nearer to fruition. Peak load pricing is not employed, and aircraft are still charged a landing fee on the basis of weight.

There would appear to be evidence that the dramatic increase in air travel in the early 1980s was imposed on an infrastructure system near technological capacity, becoming increasingly technologically outdated, and seriously impaired by the dismissing of air traffic controllers in 1981. Many people allege that the failure of the air traffic control system to respond to the increased demand was due to congressional intervention concerning the spending of the Aviation Trust Fund, and government procurement rules which delayed buying new equipment to update the system. There has been continual discussion over the past fifteen years of removing the air traffic control portion of the FAA from the aegis and budgetary control of the Department of Transportation. It would be made financially independent, and its funds provided entirely by existing user fees.

6.11 DEREGULATION AND REDUCED ROAD TRAFFIC

Deregulation has been attracted a large number of new customers to airlines. It is quite likely that some of these new airline trips are substitutes for trips previously taken by automobile. There could be direct substitution when, for example, a commuter airline trip was substituted for driving to the nearest hub airport, or an indirect substitution when the increasing attractiveness of airline travel substitutes an aviation vacation for one that previous was made to another destination by automobile. Given that fatalities per billion passenger miles in the late 1980s were 12.8 for auto travel and 0.27 for airline travel, the nation would experience a substantial benefit from any diversion from the automobile.

Bylow and Savage (1991) estimated an aggregate time-series demand model for intercity auto travel which included variables representing the price and availability (number of flight departures) of airline service. Annual data was used for the period between 1965 and 1988. They then estimated reduced form equations for the combined Part 121 and 135 airline industry over the same period so as to calculate the changes in airline fares and departures occasioned by deregulation. Deregulation was found to have lowered real airfares by 8.6% and increased departures by 6.7%. Substitution these numbers into the automobile model predicted that deregulation led to a reduction in annual automobile miles by 2.2%

Translating the reduction in vehicle miles into reduced fatalities requires assumptions concerning the types of roads that the reduction occurs on, and also the types of drivers who shift from automobiles to air. The death rate on rural roads is 50% above the national average; for while congested urban streets result in a large number of crashes, the relatively low vehicle speeds reduce the probability that a fatality will occur. Evans, Frick and Schwing (1990) analyzed the sex and age of airline passengers and suggest that such people, when driving, have a 24.1% lower fatality rate than the average driver. Airline passengers are predominantly in the 30-50 age group, whereas the age group of auto drivers which have the highest fatality rates are young people under 25.

Based on these calculations, Bylow and Savage estimate that for each year between 1978 and 1988 between 200 or 300 road deaths were averted due to deregulation of the airlines. Even the lower bound of this range is much larger than the average number of deaths in commercial aviation each year.

6.12 SUMMARY AND CONCLUSIONS

Table 6 summarizes the calculations we have already made concerning the effect of the various facets of airline deregulation on annual fatalities. Deregulation is estimated to result in between 9 and 12 additional fatalities each year in the aviation sector. However, that number pales into insignificance compared with the number of lives saved because deregulation encouraged people out of their cars and onto the airlines. The net result is a saving of between 193 and 298 lives each year. Thus the policy debate on the impact of airline economic regulatory reform on safety should be focused on the mode shifting implications rather than concentrating on effects internal to the airline industry such as financial distress, new entry, and the substitution of turbo-prop aircraft for jets.

Even the decline in safety within the airline industry need not be seen as bad. The architect of deregulation Alfred Kahn hypothesized that quality was overprovided, or provided inefficiently, in the era of regulation. Therefore, an efficient market solution may entail reductions in overly large stocks of safety investments, and the excessive use of current safety inputs. Such reductions can lead to increases in accident rates. Nevertheless, the solution achieved can represent an increase in social welfare. Morrison and Winston (1986) calculated annual benefits from deregulation of about $22 billion at current prices. Empirical estimates of the value of life are controversial. Even if the extra 9-12 aviation fatalities per year are valued at a figure towards the top of the range, say $4 million, the disbenefits would amount to between $36 and $48 million, or at best about a fifth of one percent of the benefits.

Conversely, taking into account the reduced road traffic, and valuing life at a conservative $1.5 million, there would be safety benefits valued at between $0.3 billion to $0.5 billion to add to those calculated by Morrison and Winston.

Table 6. Summary of the Effect of Deregulation on Safety

Change in Annual Fatalities	High	Low
New Entrant Part 121 Airlines	+ 1.3	
Financially-Stressed Part 121 Airlines	+ 2.5	
Substitution of Part 135 Aircraft	+ 5.2	+ 8
Reduced Automobile Traffic	- 307	- 205
Net Effect	- 298	- 193

Notes

Data for large aircraft cover the whole period from 1950 to the present. Data for small aircraft (under the Part 135 regulations) start in 1975. Throughout this paper, we will only be considering scheduled service, and do not consider charter or on-demand air taxi operations. Sabotage and terrorism accidents have been excluded.

Number of Accidents, Fatal Accidents and Passenger Fatalities. Since 1966 these data have been collected by the National Transportation Safety Board (NTSB). Previously, they were collected by the Civil Aeronautics Board (CAB). Historical information back to the early days of commercial flight in 1938 are published on the web site of the Air Transport Association of America. An aviation accident is defined as "an occurrence associated with the operation of an aircraft which takes place between the time any person boards the aircraft with the intention of flight until such time as all persons have disembarked, in which any person suffers death or serious injury as a result of being in or upon the aircraft or by direct contact with the aircraft or anything attached thereto, or in which the aircraft receives substantial damage."

Number of Incidents, Near Midair Collisions and Pilot Deviations. These data are collected by the FAA. An incident is "an occurrence other than an accident associated with the operation of an aircraft that could affect the safety of operation." Near midair collisions are when aircraft come with 500 feet. A pilot deviation is "the actions of a pilot that result in the violation of a Federal Aviation Regulation."

Number of Aircraft Departures. Since 1983 these data are collected by the Department of Transportation (DOT). Previously, they were collected by the CAB.

Number of Passengers Enplaned, and Revenue Passenger Miles on Large Aircraft. Since 1983 these data are collected by the DOT. Previously, they were collected by the CAB. They are published in the monthly *Air Carrier Traffic Statistics*, of which the December editions reports annual totals.

Number of Passengers Enplaned, and Revenue Passenger Miles on Small Aircraft. Total industry data are reported in the *Annual Report* of the Regional Airline Association (previously the Commuter Airline Association) and are based on data collected by the DOT, and previously the CAB. Since some members of the Regional Airline Association operate large aircraft, it was necessary to subtract from these figures the data for those airlines that appear in the publication described in the previous paragraph.

References

Barnett, Arnold (1990). "Air safety: end of the golden age." *Chance: New Directions for Statistics and Computing* 3:8-12.

Bulow, Jeremy, and John Shoven (1978). "The bankruptcy decision." *Bell Journal of Economics* 9(2):437-456.

Bylow, Lance F., and Ian Savage (1991). "The effect of airline deregulation on automobile fatalities." *Accident Analysis and Prevention* 23(5):443-452.

Evans, Leonard, Michael C. Frick and Richard C. Schwing (1990). "Is it safer to fly or drive?" *Risk Analysis* 10(2):239-246.

Fingerhut, Vic (1986). "The pilots view of air safety." *Air Line Pilot* 55:17-22.

General Accounting Office (1996a). *Airline Deregulation: Changes in Airfares, Service , and Safety at Small, Medium-Sized, and Large Communities.* Report GAO/RCED-96-79. Washington D.C.: U.S. Government Printing Office.

General Accounting Office (1996b). *Aviation Safety: New Airlines Illustrate Long-Standing Problems in FAA's Inspection Problem.* Report GAO/RCED-97-2. Washington D.C.: U.S. Government Printing Office.

Golbe, Devra L. (1981). "The effects of imminent bankruptcy on stockholder risk preferences and behavior." *Bell Journal of Economics* 12(1):321-328.

Golbe, Devra L. (1986). "Safety and profits in the airline industry." *Journal of Industrial Economics* 34(3):305-318.

Golbe, Devra L. (1988). "Risk-taking by firms near bankruptcy." *Economics Letters* 28(1):75-79.

Kahn, Alfred E. (1988). "Surprises of airline deregulation." *American Economic Review Papers and Proceedings* 78(2):316-322.

Kanafani, Adib, and Theodore E. Keeler (1989). "New entrants and safety." In Leon N. Moses and Ian Savage (eds.) *Transportation Safety in an Age of Deregulation.* New York: Oxford University Press.

Kanafani, Adib, and Theodore E. Keeler (1990). "Air deregulation and safety: some econometric evidence from time series." *Logistics and Transportation Review* 26(3):203-209.

Kern, John S. (1988). "Effect of deregulation on the Federal Aviation Administration's inspection and surveillance efforts." *Proceedings of the Transportation Deregulation and Safety Conference.* Evanston, Ill.: Northwestern University Transportation Center.

Morrison, Steven A., and Clifford Winston (1986). *The Economic Effects of Airline Deregulation.* Washington, D.C.: Brookings Institution.

Moses, Leon N., and Ian Savage (1989a). *Transportation Safety in an Age of Deregulation.* New York: Oxford University Press.

Moses, Leon N., and Ian Savage (1989b). "The effect of airline pilot characteristics on perceptions of job safety risks." *Journal of Risk and Uncertainty* 2(4):335-351.

Moses, Leon N., and Ian Savage (1990). "Aviation deregulation and safety: theory and evidence." *Journal of Transport Economics and Policy* 24(2):171-188.

Nance, John J. (1986). *Blind Trust.* New York: William Morrow.

Northwestern University Transportation Center (1987). *Proceedings of the Transportation Deregulation and Safety Conference.* Evanston, Ill: Northwestern University Transportation Center.

O'Brien, John E. (1988). "Deregulation and safety: an airline pilot's view." *Proceedings of the Transportation Deregulation and Safety Conference.* Evanston, Ill.: Northwestern University Transportation Center.

Oster, Clinton V., John S. Strong and C. Kurt Zorn (1992). *Why Planes Crash: Aviation Safety in a Changing World.* New York: Oxford University Press.

Rose, Nancy L. (1990). "Profitability and product quality: economic determinants of airline safety performance." *Journal of Political Economy* 98(5):944-964.

Schiavo, Mary (1997). *Flying Blind, Flying Safe.* New York: Avon Books.

7 EARNINGS, EMPLOYMENT AND THE ECONOMICS OF AIRLINE LABOUR COSTS

Daniel P. Rich

7.1 INTRODUCTION

There is an old Irish story about a man who visits a nearby town. As he walks down the street he comes upon a dog attacking a child. The man acts without hesitation, kicking the dog until it is dead. The local newspaper editor is a witness to the event and prepares a banner headline, *Neighbor Saves Child from Vicious Dog*. The editor asks the man for his address only to discover that the hero is just passing through. Headlines in the next morning's newspaper proclaim *Stranger Murders Family Pet*.

The labour market impact of airline industry deregulation also makes a compelling narrative with seemingly incompatible headlines. The impact of nonunion subsidiaries and other low cost entrants, unilateral revision of labour contracts through bankruptcy, diverse wage and work rule concessions throughout the industry, and worker displacement with the demise of several carriers all indicate a turbulent transition. A sense of stability is projected with greater emphasis on the market share of three dominant firms, industry employment growth, persistent degree of unionization, and continuing wage advantage relative to workers in other industries. Events of the past twenty years have provided a wealth of anecdotes but have not resolved conflicting perspectives.

Our initial goal is to derive a consensus from the literature on deregulation and labour earnings. Three essential findings emerge. First, real earnings of airline industry workers and earnings relative to similar workers in other industries declined from the early 1980's through the early 1990's. Second, both earnings and employment patterns have been notably asymmetric across occupations since deregulation. Third, labour costs have grown more diverse across individual carriers.

The decline in relative earnings is commonly attributed to elimination of noncompetitive rents as a consequence of the market presence of new entrants and increased competition among incumbents. Earnings losses observed in the labour market would then represent consumer and product market efficiency gains. The diversity of wage levels, work rules and labour costs may increase initially; however, rents associated with regulation should dissipate after a period of transition. This perspective appears to dominate the ex ante predictions of economists and continues to guide ex post analysis.

Traditional economic models of production and price competition in their simplest form are not always sufficient for meaningful applied analysis. Network aspects of production, multiple products, technical change, and non-price competition are pervasive issues in air transportation (Winston 1985). In this discussion we promote consideration of several contemporary themes in labour economics that influence interpretation of airline labour market outcomes.

Relative earnings tend to be measured in a single period context despite exceptionally steep tenure-earnings profiles for airline occupations. A multi-period perspective on earnings emerges when we consider internal labour markets, implicit contracts, and returns to career investments. The observed relative earnings advantage may be a meaningful outcome of a mutually beneficial arrangement between labour and the firm. Do relative earnings declines represent a deterioration of conditions for these productivity-enhancing arrangements?

Another set of considerations relates to non-price competition. Deregulation opens the door to pricing innovations and the roster of relatively successful firms indicates that there are alternative paths to profitability. Do labour cost differences simply reflect strategic choices with regard to pricing and quality of service? An appreciation for labour's role in service quality explains a portion of the relative wage premium and leads to a prediction of sustainable labour cost differences within the airline industry.

7.2 DEREGULATION AND LABOUR EARNINGS

To what extent have the real earnings of labour in the U.S. airline industry been affected by deregulation? This deceptively simple question is the subject of numerous empirical studies. Real earnings effects range from zero to a decline of nearly forty percent in recent contributions by Johnson (1991), Hendricks (1994), Hirsch and Macpherson (1995), Cremieux (1996) and Card (1996). At first glance, the labour market impact attributable to deregulation appears quite elusive.[1]

Our initial goal is to reconcile seemingly incompatible research findings on labour earnings. We begin with a summary of the issues which complicate measurement and account for the significantly different outcomes presented in the literature.

[1] Cappelli (1992) offers a comprehensive review of airline labour relations issues.

7.2.1 Overview of Measurement Issues

Timing. Average real earnings of airline industry workers exhibit a clear positive trend in the years leading up to 1978. The rate of real earnings growth somewhat exceeds that for workers across other U.S. industries. One of the difficulties in assessing the impact of deregulation on real and relative earnings arises because 1978 serves as a turning point for real earnings in the economy as a whole. Real earnings growth, in general, becomes stagnant at the outset of the time period over which we are hoping to measure real and relative earnings changes specific to the airline industry.

Real earnings for most airline occupations continue to rise immediately following deregulation, peak around 1983 and experience an extended period of real decline thereafter. Under these circumstances, findings with respect to both real and relative earnings are quite sensitive to choice of endpoints. A relatively small and variable impact is found in analyses of data starting in the middle to late 1970's and ending at various points in the middle to late 1980's (Johnson 1991, Hendricks 1994). More robust findings of moderate decline are evident when data from the early 1990's are included (Hirsch and Macpherson 1995, Cremieux 1996, Card 1996).

Data Source. Labour economists have approached this research question using information from an unusually diverse array of sources. These include household surveys, detailed cost reports from individual airline firms and collective bargaining agreements. All of these sources yield a similar pattern of real earnings growth until the early 1980's and decline through the early 1990's. The most recent studies, such as Card (1996), have grounded their analysis using more than one source. This is a commendable practice as each data source presents a unique combination of inherent advantages and limitations.

The Current Population Survey (CPS) represents an accessible source of data on earnings and a host of other individual characteristics. The CPS provides a timely and extensive cross-section of individuals across industries. Hirsch and Macpherson (1995), using CPS data, identify an 11 percent real decline in mean weekly earnings for airline industry workers from the early 1980's through the early 1990's. The primary shortcoming of CPS data is the relatively small sample of airline workers, an especially troubling issue for analyses of wage dispersion or specific occupations. Truncation of high earnings levels presents an additional liability.

Census data also provide a match of individual earnings with an extensive set of individual characteristics. The primary advantage of the Census is a more comprehensive sample with several thousand individual airline employees observed in each survey year. Card (1996) compares Census data from 1980 and 1990 which support a 7 percent real decline in weekly earnings for airline workers. The obvious liability of the dicennial Census is a severe lack of frequency. Both household survey sources, Census and CPS, share an imprecise definition of the airline industry and fail to provide information on relevant firm-specific elements.

Form 41 reports filed quarterly with the Department of Transportation provide detailed information on airline costs and operating characteristics for an almost comprehensive set of individual airline firms. Employment by occupational category is reported annually. Hirsch and Macpherson (1995), as well as our own analysis, indicate an 11 to 16 percent real decline in annual earnings across all workers and firms from 1983 through the early 1990's. Form 41 data have proven especially useful for evaluation of inter-firm wage dispersion and inclusion of non-wage employment costs. The primary liability of this source is the absence of information on the intra-firm distribution of individual characteristics and earnings. Cremieux (1996) also notes sample selection problems in response to inconsistent reporting across firms.

Collective bargaining agreements on file with the National Mediation Board offer a unique perspective on wages and conditions associated with a particular job category and seniority level. Card (1996) presents real declines over 1980 to 1995 of 14 percent for selected pilot hourly rates and 40 percent for flight attendant monthly earnings. Cappelli (1992) also reviews negotiated changes in work rules and the evolution of two-tier wage scales. With contract data we tend to exclude new entrants and cannot directly observe wage patterns associated with changes in union certification. Collective bargaining agreements remain a valuable source of detailed wage rate changes due to persistent union coverage across most of the largest employers in the industry.

Empirical Specification. Research on the earnings impact of deregulation has not been guided by a common empirical framework. Many of the published studies develop ad hoc specifications with unique sets of control variables. The wide range of conclusions found in the literature arise, in part, from diverse choices with respect to empirical approach as opposed to inconsistencies in the raw data.

Johnson (1991), for example, imposes a highly restrictive pattern on the timing of deregulation effects while product market conditions and the firm's financial position are treated as exogenous controls. Consequently, deregulation does not appear to have a significant impact on earnings. On the other hand, Cremieux (1996) contends that the impact of deregulation has been substantial. He incorporates an extensive set of controls, including earnings in related occupations and a continuous trend over the entire 1959 to 1992 sample. In this study, the impact of deregulation is best understood as unexplained deviations from the long term trend in relative earnings.[2]

What is the appropriate comparison for relative earnings? It is tempting to compare average earnings for airline workers with readily available aggregates, such as hourly wages in manufacturing or weekly earnings for all private sector workers. The relevance of these wage series as a counterfactual for airline earnings is questioned convincingly by Cappelli (1992) and Cremieux (1996).

Several recent efforts rely on measurement of industry wage premiums in the context of a human capital empirical framework. The appropriate comparison group for relative earnings is defined by a set of observed characteristics for each

---

[2] This measure may overstate the role of deregulation to the extent that the pace of aircraft innovations is independent of air transport market structure and has contributed to a decline in relative productivity growth (Gordon 1992).

individual. The standard specification controls for age or experience, education, occupation, veteran status, marital status, gender, race and region. An extensive cross-section of individual data is clearly required.

The range of findings within this approach is consistent with our discussion of timing. Hendricks (1994) finds no conclusive evidence of relative earnings decline from the early 1970's through 1988. Card (1996), with data from the 1980 and 1990 Census, establishes a 10 percent decline in relative earnings. Hirsch and Macpherson (1995) include more detailed controls for occupational classification and job characteristics. They present a reduction of 17 percent in the airline industry wage premium from 1983 through 1993.

A concern worth noting is the imposition of similar returns to human capital and demographic characteristics across industries. Industry-specific changes in either tenure distribution or returns could be a source of bias when evaluating changes in the industry wage premium. Hirsch and Macpherson (1995) indicate that tenure-earnings profiles for pilots, flight attendants and passenger service agents are exceptionally steep and have grown even steeper relative to those in other industries. A comprehensive analysis of earnings profiles implied in collective bargaining agreements would be a valuable contribution.

7.2.2 Occupations and Relative Earnings

The recent literature highlights meaningful differences in the real and relative earnings experiences of different occupations. Hirsch and Macpherson (1995), Cremieux (1996) and Card (1996) all find substantial earnings losses for flight attendants and negligible declines for mechanics. Pilots and other workers tend to fall at various points in between. With the complications discussed above in mind, we are prepared to examine representative Form 41 data series on labour earnings by occupation.

Real earnings for pilots, flight attendants and maintenance workers are presented in Figure 1.1 for the years 1971 through 1996. Index values are based on the 1976 to 1978 mean of real earnings for each series. The sample is restricted to domestic operations of carriers engaged primarily in scheduled passenger service. The unbalanced panel includes a total of thirty-eight firms. There are twenty-one incumbents in 1971 with seventeen new entrants joining the sample in various years after 1978. The final period sample in 1996 consists of ten incumbents and ten entrants.

Real earnings growth for all occupations is evident prior to 1978. An era of stagnant earnings for mechanics is introduced with a temporary decline in the early 1980's and periodic fluctuations around the base value which persist through 1996. Real earnings for flight attendants and pilots, on the other hand, continue to rise through 1983 then decline sharply. The real earnings decline for flight attendants reaches 36 percent from the peak through 1991 while the corresponding maximum decline for pilots is 21 percent. Despite a few consecutive growth years of late, real earnings for most airline occupations remain below their levels of almost twenty years ago.

Figure 1.1: Real Earnings for Airline Occupations, 1971-1996

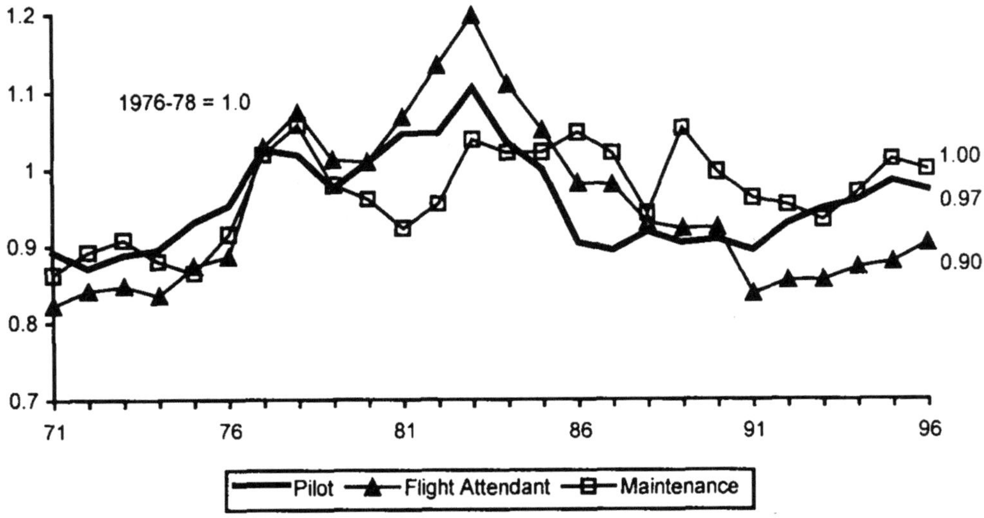

Table 1.1 offers a summary of these observations. Timing clearly matters. It would have been difficult to achieve any consensus on occupational impact until data from the early 1990's became available. Even then, should earnings changes be measured from a pre-deregulation base (Hendricks 1994) or from the early 1980's peak (Hirsch and Macpherson 1995, Cremieux 1996)? This choice alone has profound impact on measured earnings loss. What conclusions will be warranted as real earnings growth resumes and eventually surpasses the pre-deregulation standard?

Rough measures of relative earnings can be constructed using median earnings data by occupation from the household survey. Consistent occupational classifications are available from 1983 to present. Consequently, we adapt the relative earnings indices to equal one over the 1983 to 1985 period. Table 1.1 offers a summary of relative earnings results that reflect similar findings throughout the recent literature.

Earnings of airline mechanics are evaluated relative to precision production, craft and repair occupations. The stagnant real earnings series for airline mechanics compares favorably to more substantial declines for similar workers spanning a variety of industries. Service occupations, excluding household and protective service, represent a meaningful comparison for flight attendants. Hirsch and Macpherson (1995) expand the definition of this group to include administrative support and sales workers. Cremieux (1996) argues that engineers are an appropriate occupation for evaluation of airline pilots. Flight attendants and pilots lost ground relative to earnings in related occupations from the early 1980's through the early 1990's.

Table 1.1: Real and Relative Labour Earnings, 1971-1996

	1971-1973	*1976-1978*	*1983-1985*	*1989-1992*	*1994-1996*
Pilots					
real earnings	0.88	1.00	1.05	0.91	0.97
relative to engineering occupations			1.00	0.85	0.93
Flight Attendants					
real earnings	0.84	1.00	1.12	0.88	0.88
relative to service occupations			1.00	0.80	0.83
Maintenance					
real earnings	0.89	1.00	1.03	0.99	0.99
relative to craft occupations			1.00	1.00	1.05

Notes:

Annual labour earnings represent an employment-weighted average across individual airline firms. Wage and employment data obtained from Form 41 reports. Each real earnings series is presented as an index with the 1976-1978 mean equal to one.
Median weekly earnings for full-time workers in selected occupations are used to construct a relative earnings index. Consistent household survey data series for occupational earnings are only available from 1983 to present. The mean of relative earnings over 1983-1985 serves as the base value.

The recent trend toward stock-based compensation plays a role in the observed earnings patterns at the very end of the sample period. Substantial equity transfers at Northwest Airlines and United Airlines and a portion of stock-based compensation arrangements at other firms appear as wage and salary on Form 41. These arrangements may be treated differently by household survey respondents. Stock-based compensation accounts for approximately 5 percent of reported labour earnings across all firms in our sample from 1994 through 1996 and is not distributed equally across occupations.[3] General participation by pilots and resistance by flight attendants coincide with the propensity to accommodate deferred compensation as a function of income level.

Employee benefits and other nonwage labour costs are excluded from our analysis to maintain comparability with the emphasis in the literature. Nonwage

[3] Annual reports filed with the Securities and Exchange Commission and direct contact with airline firms are used to supplement Form 41 information.

costs include employee benefits, employer pension contributions, payroll taxes and other costs of employment. These components have risen as a share of airline labour costs from thirteen percent in 1971, to seventeen percent in 1978 to over twenty-five percent by the 1990's. A somewhat different perspective is achieved when these costs are included. Real labour costs per employee have continued to rise despite the decline in real labour earnings.

7.3 OCCUPATIONAL LABOUR DEMAND

Airline industry employment has grown at a more positive but also more variable pace from 1978 to present as compared to the preceding decade (Card 1996). Employment variation at the firm level has been considerably more pronounced with deregulation. Flight attendants and other selected occupations have enjoyed employment growth above the economy-wide average while maintenance workers have lost ground as a proportion of industry employment.

The impact of deregulation is difficult to infer due to the number of potential influences on employment. Labour demand offers a structural econometric framework for evaluating these diverse influences. We provide an overview of labour demand estimates. Specific elements of deregulation have contributed to overall employment growth and promoted a redistribution of employment among occupations.

7.3.1 Sources of Employment Variation

The opportunity for firm level labour demand estimation is exceptional in this industry because Form 41 data provide detailed information on airline employment, production and costs. We have evaluated occupational labour demand functions for pilots, flight attendants, mechanics and other categories of airline employees (Rich 1990 and 1996). The underlying elasticities are consistent with estimates in other industries (Hamermesh 1993) and have proven robust to variations in the sample and estimation methods. The specific empirical findings selected for discussion have particular relevance to employment outcomes in response to global air liberalization.

Competition and elasticity of labour demand. Rising wages, with all else held constant, encourage the firm to substitute away from labour as a factor of production. Substitution takes many forms such as outsourcing of aircraft maintenance, baggage handling or ticketing procedures that reduce staffing requirements and fleet choices that alter the number of pilots per available seat mile. Substitution elasticities range from -.20 to -.80 for airline occupations in the U.S. and have remained reasonably consistent over time. Gillen, Oum and Tretheway (1985) find similar elasticities for airline labour in Canada.

Employment also tends to decline as the firm responds to increased costs associated with wages. Consumer behavior will determine whether this scale response leads primarily to higher prices or mostly reduced output and employment. Airline firms exhibit more elastic labour demand when consumers enjoy a greater number of air travel alternatives. Deregulation has created a more competitive environment with the presence of new entrants and increased rivalry among incumbents throughout a typical firm's domestic route system.[4]

The most basic element of observed earnings patterns is found in this scale response. As a consequence of increased competition, output and employment levels are more sensitive to wage and other input price changes (Rich 1990). The firm's employment response presents a tradeoff in wage bargaining and this tradeoff has grown more severe due to deregulation.

Airline costs, pricing innovations and output growth. The firm's response to a decline in production costs leads to employment gains. Historically, advances in aircraft technology have been a significant source of cost savings and output growth. Baltagi, Griffin and Rich (1995a) find that adoption of aircraft innovations continues to be a source of cost efficiency gains for the industry. Price fluctuations for fuel and existing flight equipment contribute substantially to year-to-year employment variations. These influences are largely independent of deregulation.[5]

Labour costs represent a declining portion of total operating costs through the early 1990's (Cappelli 1992). It is tempting to attribute observed labour productivity gains, in terms of revenue passenger miles per employee, to work rule revisions achieved in a new labour relations climate; however, it is difficult to identify empirical support for this claim. Labour productivity growth at U.S. airlines since deregulation has not matched growth observed prior to deregulation nor has it outpaced gains at major international carriers (Card 1996).[6] Merz (1995) cautions that labour costs and productivity are influenced by a host of factors, including fleet characteristics, market density and route system attributes, that outweigh marginal differences in labour utilization.

Regulatory reform, including selected policy experiments prior to 1978, opened the door to pricing innovations. Promotional price reductions, restricted fares and frequent flyer programs are relatively new practices. Equipped with a greater variety of revenue management instruments, airline firms have been able to increase overall capacity utilization. Load factors have risen and carriers have enjoyed cost savings from expansion of output along existing routes (Baltagi, Griffin and Rich 1995b). Occupations directly related to passenger flows, such as flight attendants and passenger service personnel, have experienced particularly strong employment growth.

---

[4] Increased competition is observed at the city-pair level. Aggregate measures of concentration may reflect conditions for collusive pricing behavior but must be viewed with an appreciation for the regional character of route systems under Civil Aeronautics Board authority.

[5] There is some evidence that aircraft innovations are not entirely exogenous to airline firm choices (Gordon 1992) and that competition promotes adoption of available aircraft technologies (Goel and Rich 1997).

[6] Total factor productivity growth has also slowed (Gordon 1992) although the impact of deregulation appears to be positive (Baltagi, Griffin and Rich 1995a).

Nonneutral technical change and route system choices. Technical change does not simply reduce costs but may also have unequal effects across occupations. Card (1986) and Rich (1996) find employment reductions for airline mechanics associated with a long term pattern of nonneutral technical change. New maintenance technologies, the evolution of maintenance shop processes, advanced materials used in aircraft manufacturing, and increased reliance on outsourcing are potential sources. The role of deregulation in promoting these innovations has not been empirically assessed.

With the removal of regulatory barriers to market entry and exit choices, airline firms have dramatically redefined their route systems. Hub and spoke operations combine passenger flows, improve capacity utilization, and may confer some degree of market power on selected routes. Increased hub concentration permits greater centralization of maintenance operations and may increase requirements for managerial coordination. Rich (1996) finds occupation-specific responses to increased hub concentration, including decreased employment for mechanics.

7.3.2 Occupational Employment and Labour Earnings

From a labour demand perspective, it is difficult to make sense of changes in labour earnings without reference to employment patterns. The industry as a whole posted its most positive job gains from 1983 through the early 1990's, a period of real earnings decline. Pilots and flight attendants appear to have achieved a wage premium under regulation. Relative earnings losses and employment gains attributable to deregulation have been most substantial for flight attendants. If an inherent tradeoff exists between employment and wages then deregulation has served to make this tradeoff more severe.

Mechanics have been least affected on wages but have not participated in industry employment gains. Their firm level bargaining faces a relatively elastic labour demand response due to outsourcing, automation and other substitution options. The apparent lack of wage flexibility may reflect the absence of a substantial industry wage premium. Hirsch and Macpherson (1995) find a relatively small wage decline for mechanics who leave the industry. Employment adjustments have been the primary response to nonneutral technical change and hubbing which reduced labour demand for mechanics.

A critical element of perspectives on the labour market impact of deregulation is the distinction between average outcomes and individual experiences. Industry-wide employment growth offers only limited comfort for employees subject to mass layoff at a particular firm. Eastern Airlines, for example, employed more than 40,000 domestic workers in 1988 and was liquidated in 1991. Card (1996) finds that displaced airline workers enjoyed superior reemployment odds to displaced workers in other industries but experienced similar unemployment spells and earnings losses.

Senior flight attendants at Continental Airlines and Trans World Airlines suffered real earnings losses in the mid 1980's that greatly exceed the estimates presented in the literature. On the other hand, two-tier agreements throughout the industry concentrated much of the observed wage decline on new workers who were hired at lower real wages than previous cohorts. In the dispute at American Airlines in 1997 pilots pointed to real declines in contract wage rates over several years while the firm emphasized the absence of "in-pocket" losses for individuals due to wage patterns associated with career progression.[7]

7.4 THINKING ABOUT LABOUR COSTS

Earnings differences across individuals and patterns over time reflect several fundamental themes in labour economics and present some of the most challenging questions as well. Real and relative earnings of airline industry workers have declined while labour costs have become more diverse across individual carriers. Why have airline workers enjoyed wage advantages and what are the implications of reduced relative earnings? What are the determinants of airline labour costs and are firm-specific differences sustainable? In this section we discuss conventional interpretations of airline labour market outcomes and consider alternatives derived from contemporary themes in labour economics.

7.4.1 Noncompetitive Rents and Union Behavior

In the textbook monopoly union scenario, labour pursues a wage increase and may address potential employment loss through restrictive work rules. With Civil Aeronautics Board regulation of the early 1970's, an industry-wide pattern of labour cost increase would yield an increase in the regulated price. Consumer alternatives are limited by barriers to entry, a separate regulatory instrument. Increased prices, reduced consumer welfare and loss of allocative efficiency are all reminiscent of monopoly firm behavior. Labour in this case, not the firm, enjoys earnings above competitive market alternatives. Regulation is the source of inefficiency and unionized labour is in the best position to capture the noncompetitive rents.

Observed wage premiums under regulation tend to be interpreted in this context. Subsequent earnings declines relative to comparable workers in other industries are generally viewed as a measure of noncompetitive rents. With deregulation, according to Kahn (1988), "competition has exerted powerful downward pressure on egregiously inflated wages - painful for the workers affected but healthy for the economy at large." Evidence linking increased competition to greater elasticity of labour demand establishes a primary mechanism through which changes in the regulatory environment induce earnings declines.

With increased competition among incumbents and the emergence of nonunion entrants, cost minimization becomes a matter of survival. Asset transfers to nonunion subsidiaries or bargaining approaches which yield labour concessions represent prudent management responses. The actions of Texas Air holding company in the early 1980's are consistent with this perspective. New York Air was formed with Texas International's assets but without their labour contracts (Cappelli 1992). Wage reductions of up to 50 percent were imposed unilaterally at

[7] Presidential Emergency Board report of March 19, 1997.

Continental Airlines following abrogation of labour contracts through bankruptcy. New entrants made up a growing share of the industry at the time while collective bargaining concessions on wages and work rules at incumbent firms became a widespread occurrence.

For the next ten years Continental survived as a highly unprofitable carrier while several entrants with the lowest labour costs failed or were acquired. The Texas Air experiments, in particular, could be viewed more as influential aberrations rather than representative best practices. American, Delta, United and Southwest achieved cost efficiencies while generally refraining from wage reductions for experienced workers. These firms steadily increased their share of industry output and employment through the early 1990's.

An extensive degree of unionization and significant labour cost differences across firms remain. Earnings relative to workers in other industries have declined for both union and nonunion employees; however, airline workers continue to enjoy a substantial earnings premium (Card 1996). It would appear that the airline industry has either not yet achieved the competitive ideal or that observed earnings advantages are not simply a measure of noncompetitive rents.[8]

7.4.2 Competitive Quasi-rents and Investment

There are several different types of rents in economics including some that occur in competitive environments. Quasi-rents describe earnings in excess of current opportunity cost which are part of a stream of anticipated competitive returns to durable resources (Alchian 1991). Investments in physical capital, research and development, brand recognition and human capital all involve initial period deficits with subsequent period returns. Throughout the payoff period the earnings stream may vary considerably without affecting the current flow of services from the resource.

Consumer alternatives in a competitive product market environment make it difficult for an individual firm to accommodate union relative wage gains with an increase in price. Quasi-rents to capital and other factors of production are reduced. Relative wage premiums impose a tax on normal returns to long term investments. Abowd (1989) finds that unanticipated union wage gains are associated with a decline in shareholder value. Examination of U.S. and Canadian manufacturing reveals significant quasi-rent sharing in response to product market disturbances (Hirsch 1991, Abowd and Lemieux 1993).

There is a gap between current opportunity cost and the earnings level that produces a competitive long run return for the durable resource; however, these circumstances are only temporary. Expropriation of quasi-rents in the short run discourages similar long term investments. Hirsch (1991) finds that highly unionized manufacturing firms in the U.S. exhibit "lower rates of profit, market value, capital investment, and R&D investment" when compared to less unionized

---

[8] Hendricks (1994) argues that service rivalry may have dissipated rents under regulation while industry concentration and hub dominance may perpetuate rents.

firms. In the absence of noncompetitive rents, union quasi-rent sharing has real consequences that restrain long run output and employment growth.

Quasi-rents offer a useful framework for viewing the eventual demise of Eastern Airlines and other incumbent carriers after several years of below normal returns. Capital and other durable resources are not likely to be replenished if labour cost flexibility is only forthcoming with a hostile takeover or credible threat of liquidation. There is a continuing potential for conflict between the interests of labour and equity shareholders at even the least troubled airline firms.

The evolution of stock-based compensation and employee ownership in the industry merits consideration in this context. Equity compensation in exchange for a temporary wage reduction provides an internal source of capital investment despite a firm's history of below market returns for external investors. The priorities of median union voters may adjust as returns on equity become a more significant portion of labour earnings. Labour may be less likely to expropriate competitive quasi-rents if equity ownership enhances the weight of long run interests in union objectives.[9]

7.4.3 Implicit Contracts and Human Capital

Workers make career investments. Market earnings provide incentives for individual investments in general skills. Pilots, mechanics and management personnel bear costs to satisfy minimum qualifications for entry positions. Firm-specific skill development presents opportunities for workers and firms to share investments. Firm-specific information gains are one of the conditions which explain shared participation in general training.

The implicit contract for a shared investment is likely to include earnings that rise with tenure. As an employee's career progresses, their productivity at the firm exceeds earnings and earnings exceed the value of market alternatives. Both the worker and the firm enjoy quasi-rents in the form of anticipated returns to human capital investment. Several airline occupations exhibit unusually long term commitments to a particular firm. Internal labour market arrangements reduce information costs, facilitate shared training investments, elicit effort and may lead to an increase in average earnings.

Labour's quasi-rents are a tempting target for capture by equity shareholders or management. However, an unanticipated reduction in career investment returns may be considered a breach of the implicit contract (Schleifer and Summers 1988). In the short run, workers might respond with diminished effort and discretionary behavior not consistent with service quality. From 1983 through 1986 flight attendants at Continental Airlines and Trans World Airlines were presented with no collective bargaining agreement, wage reductions of nearly 50 percent, and permanent replacements in response to strikes. Both firms experienced inferior service quality, loss of corporate clients and nonexistent profitability for several years thereafter (Flint 1997).

---

[9] National carriers in an era of global air liberalization face a comparable dilemma and employee ownership may represent a meaningful policy option.

In the long run, human capital is likely to adjust in much the same manner as other durable resources. Expropriation of labour's anticipated quasi-rents serves as a direct disincentive to engage in continued skill development, long term commitment to a particular firm, early career shared investments in training, and even occupational choices of young adults. Flight attendants hired under two-tier wage scales have exhibited higher turnover rates while negotiated entry level wages for pilots were abandoned in the face of hiring difficulties which persist to the present day (Cappelli 1992, Nelms 1997).

As real earnings decline toward labour's opportunity costs we may be witnessing expropriation of labour's quasi-rents as opposed to the elimination of noncompetitive rents. Evidence from job changers and displaced workers indicates earnings losses for individuals that are substantially less than average earnings level estimates (Hirsch and Macpherson 1995, Card 1996). The career investments of airline workers include transferable skills and the relative earnings decline for airline employees who have not changed jobs would seem to include an element of quasi-rent expropriation.

From this perspective, relative earnings effects of deregulation represent a deterioration of conditions for productivity-enhancing shared investment arrangements. Reluctant wage adjustments in response to hiring failures are unlikely to restore the credibility required for implicit contracts. The persistent degree of unionization in the airline industry may reflect the value of explicit contracts in facilitating shared investments. Equity ownership and participation in corporate governance might be considered in terms of additional steps by employees to restore an environment conducive to longer term implicit contracts.

It is essential to view airline labour costs in terms of career paths as opposed to single period measurements. Hirsch and Macpherson (1995) indicate that tenure-earnings profiles for pilots, flight attendants and passenger service agents are exceptionally steep.[10] The airline industry offers exceptional returns to tenure; therefore, the relative wage advantage measured in a general human capital framework overstates the degree of noncompetitive rents.

Marginal wages are substantially lower for the expanding firm and employment growth tends to lower the average wage. Marginal labour costs for the expanding firm include early career hiring and training investments. During the mid to late 1980's two-tier provisions were prevalent while industry employment growth exhibited unprecedented variance at the firm level. Year-to-year and firm-to-firm comparisons of average compensation are sensitive to the tenure distribution of the airline workforce.

7.4.4 Non-price Competition and Labour Costs

Profit-maximization does not always require cost-minimization. With non-price competition a wide range of quality-price combinations may be observed. Like, for

---

[10] Career earnings progressions have grown even steeper relative to those in other industries. Contributing factors include two-tier wage provisions and deferred payment aspects of revised compensation plans.

example, enjoys sustained profits without matching the low price, advertising costs, research investments, or quality of materials of generic tennis shoe producers. Emphasis on the gains to price-sensitive consumers has perhaps distracted the attention of many economists from non-price attributes of air transportation service.

Consider the role of labour in airline product quality. Thousands of passenger service and flight crew employees, largely unsupervised, engage in direct contact with customers. Employees accept responsibility for the timely transport, safety, comfort and convenience of each customer throughout a few hours of service for which several hundred dollars has already been paid. Advertising campaigns continue to emphasize airline workforce experience, dedication to service quality, and remarkable friendliness. Firms that succeed in this industry maintain exceptionally high minimum standards of excellence.

Hiring and promotion decisions are affected by technical competence, demonstrated knowledge, personal integrity, customer service abilities, physical appearance, dedication to quality standards, anticipated performance in team settings and decision-making under pressure. Extensive testing, probationary periods of evaluation, and other methods of screening are employed by firms throughout the industry (Nelms 1997). These traits and practices which determine an individual employee's contribution to service quality are generally unobservable in the data sources used in research to assess wages.

The appearance of industry-specific wage advantages may be a reflection of returns to unmeasured traits as opposed to noncompetitive rents. Steep tenure-earnings profiles are consistent with hiring strategies that invest in identifying exceptional individuals. Evidence from displaced workers and job changers who leave the industry is consistent with positive unmeasured skills (Hirsch and Macpherson 1995, Card 1996). Inclusion of skill, training and work condition variables significantly reduces the measured wage premium (Hirsch and Macpherson 1995). The apparent decline in relative earnings and increased dispersion of wages within the industry may simply indicate greater diversity of firm strategies with respect to service quality.

Labour cost differences across firms have been described as an unsustainable feature of the transition from a regulated environment. Merz (1995) emphasizes the complexity of labour costs and explains how measures such as labour cost per available seat mile are influenced by route, fleet, service quality and other strategic choices. The advent of deregulation permits heterogeneous pricing strategies and facilitates consumer response to price and service quality dimensions. American Airlines, Southwest Airlines and a handful of smaller carriers have derived profitability relative to industry peers from successful implementation of very different sets of service quality goals, route networks, revenue choices and labour costs. The success of diverse product market strategies implies that diverse labour cost outcomes are also sustainable.

7.5 CONCLUDING OBSERVATIONS

Airline industry workers in the U.S. are now fully immersed in the turmoil associated with private sector labour markets. Airline labour relations of the past twenty years have left their own imprint on the general landscape with a variety of innovative strategies. The transition from a regulated environment has extended over a remarkably long period of time with real earnings changes and diverse compensation initiatives continuing into the early 1990's. Airline industry employees worldwide should anticipate a similar transition and would be wise to consider the implications of comparative advantage for their firm's role and their individual role in the emerging global industry.

Twenty years have passed and several unique features of airline labour markets have endured, including a high degree of unionization and a compensation structure which reflects career investments. Alternative interpretations of the observed decline in real and relative earnings hold meaningful implications for efficiency, investment behavior, labour quality and other related outcomes. Empirical research on labour earnings and occupational labour demand has assigned low priority to these issues. For airline management, employees and investors today the enduring features are of much greater importance than the elusive impact of deregulation. Airline labour markets offer a sufficiently complex and data-rich environment for exploration of several contemporary labour economics themes.

References

John Abowd, "The Effect of Wage Bargains on the Stock Market Value of the Firm," *American Economic Review*, 79 (4), September 1989.

John Abowd and Thomas Lemieux, "The Effects of Product Market Competition on Collective Bargaining Agreements: The Case of Foreign Competition in Canada," *Quarterly Journal of Economics*, 108 (4), November 1993.

Armen Alchian, "Rent," in *The New Palgrave: A Dictionary of Economics*, ed. Eatwell et al, The Macmillan Press Limited, 1987.

Badi Baltagi, James Griffin and Daniel Rich, "Airline Deregulation: The Cost Pieces of the Puzzle," *International Economic Review*, 36 (1), February 1995a.

Badi Baltagi, James Griffin and Daniel Rich, "The Measurement of Firm-Specific Indexes of Technical Change," *Review of Economics and Statistics*, 77 (4), November 1995b.

Peter Cappelli, *Labor Relations and Labor Costs in the Airline Industry: Contemporary Issues*, U.S. Department of Transportation, Office of the Secretary, 1992.

David Card, "Deregulation and Labor Earnings in the Airline Industry," Working Paper 5687, National Bureau of Economic Research, July 1996.

David Card, "The Impact of Deregulation on the Employment and Wages of Airline Mechanics," *Industrial and Labor Relations Review*, 39 (4), July 1986.

Pierre-Yves Cremieux, "The Effect of Deregulation on Employee Earnings: Pilots, Flight Attendants, and Mechanics, 1959-1992," *Industrial and Labor Relations Review*, 49 (2), January 1996.

Perry Flint, "Speed Racer: Gordon Bethune has Continental Airlines on the Fast Track to Success," Air Transport World, 34 (4), April 1997.

David Gillen, Tae Oum and Michael Tretheway, *Airline Cost and Performance: Implications for Public and Industry Policies*, Centre for Transportation Studies, University of British Columbia, Vancouver, 1985.

Rajeev Goel and Daniel Rich, "On the Adoption of New Technologies," *Applied Economics*, 29 (4), April 1997.

Robert Gordon, "Productivity in the Transportation Sector," in *Output Measurement in the Service Sectors*, ed. Zvi Griliches, National Bureau of Economic Research, 1992.

Daniel Hamermesh, *Labor Demand*, Princeton University Press, 1993.

Wallace Hendricks, "Deregulation and Labor Earnings," *Journal of Labor Research*, 15 (3), Summer 1994.

Barry Hirsch, *Labor Unions and the Economic Performance of Firms*, W.E. Upjohn Institute for Employment Research, 1991.

Barry Hirsch and David Macpherson, "Earnings, Rents and Competition in the Airline Labor Market," Working Paper, Florida State University, December 1995.

Nancy Brown Johnson, "Airline Workers' Earnings and Union Expenditures under Deregulation," *Industrial and Labor Relations Review*, 45 (1), October 1991.

Alfred E. Kahn, *The Economics of Regulation: Principles and Institutions*, Cambridge: MIT Press, 1988.

K. Manfred Merz, "Labor Costs around the World," in *Airline Labor Relations in the Global Era: The New Frontier*, ed. Peter Cappelli, ILR Press, 1995.

Douglas Nelms, "Picking Perfect Pilots: Changing Needs and Conditions are Raising Controversial Issues in Cockpit Hiring," Air Transport World, 34 (3), March 1997.

Daniel Rich, "On the Elasticity of Labor Demand," *Quarterly Review of Economics and Business*, 30 (4), Winter 1990.

Daniel Rich, "Occupational Labor Demand and Technical Change: An Exploratory Analysis," Western Economic Association International Annual Conference, San Francisco, July 1996.

Andrei Schleifer and Lawrence Summers, "Breach of Trust in Hostile Takeovers," in *Corporate Takeovers: Causes and Consequences*, ed. Alan J. Auerbach, National Bureau of Economic Research, 1988.

Clifford Winston, "Conceptual Developments in the Economics of Transportation: An Interpretive Survey," *Journal of Economic Literature*, 23 (1), March 1985.

8 THE OECD PROJECT ON INTERNATIONAL AIR TRANSPORT

Dr. Wolfgang Michalski

International air transport is a driving force in the world economy, both as a major industry in its own right, and as a provider of vital services for a wide range of economic activities. The sector has played an important role in the globalisation of production and distribution systems, and without extensive air transport networks major service industries such as tourism would not have expanded to today's levels. As the world continues to change rapidly, the international aviation sector is confronted by a wide variety of new challenges. There is therefore a need to deepen the understanding of the role of air transport in the international economy and to review the regulatory structure which governs civil aviation.

This is the background against which the Organisation for Economic Co-operation and Development (OECD) embarked on a major project on the key policy challenges facing international air transport. The resulting report, which was released in 1997, takes as its point of departure an in-depth description of the role of international aviation in the globalisation process. In particular, it shows how developments in the world economy will change the nature of uncertainties in tomorrow's world and force all players to forge new degrees of flexibility and competitiveness to face the evolving economic environment. The report analyses the difficult issues of market entry and exit, and the complexities of competition within the market -- alliances, subsidisation, privatisation, foreign ownership -- focusing throughout on the role of policy-makers in helping or hindering the efficient functioning of international markets for air transport. It argues for further liberalisation, and makes recommendations to help decision-makers shape the regulatory framework of the future.

What follows is a synthesis of the above report under the specific aspect of policy requirements in the field of international air transport against the background of a globalising economy. To set the institutional and political context for the analytical conclusions and the policy recommendations, this paper starts with a few words on the OECD. Thereafter, it summarises some of the current quantitative forecasts for international aviation. Following this, attention is drawn to some fundamental qualitative trends and their implications for air transport. The fourth part focuses on major uncertainties surrounding the future of aviation. And the final section deals with present and foreseeable policy challenges as well as with the OECD recommendations for international air transport policy.

8.1 THE ORGANISATION FOR ECONOMIC CO-OPERATION AND DEVELOPMENT

The Organisation for Economic Co-operation and Development, whose roots go back to the implementation of the Marshall Plan after the Second World War, is an international intergovernmental organisation working in the field of economic and social policy. Compared to ICAO, WTO or the IMF, the OECD has a smaller membership consisting of 29 industrialised countries which are all market economies and pluralistic democracies. But the policy remit of the OECD is much broader than that of the other organisations mentioned.

In fact the Organisation's activities cover all dimensions of economic and social policy ranging from macro-economic assessments and policies through all areas of structural and sectoral policies to the issues of international trade and investment. The strengths of the OECD are its ability to offer independent economic analysis and policy advice, its close contacts and interactions with Member governments and the fact that it is a forum for enhancing international policy dialogue rather than negotiation.

The Organisation has a long track record of effectively shaping international policy. There is room here for only a few illustrations:

- First, the OECD pioneered work in the late 1970s and early 1980s on the links between economic performance and structural change. This has provided the underpinning of OECD policy advice to governments over the last decade or so, resulting in a fundamental shift in the approach to economic and social policy. Today, the importance for a high performance economy of the capacity for continual and rapid structural adjustment - supported by efficient product, capital and labour markets - is widely recognised.

- Second, in the fight against unemployment, the OECD was entrusted by Heads of State of the G7 Summit and OECD Ministers more generally to advance the analysis of the causes of joblessness, to design the strategy for addressing the problem, and critically monitor the implementation of this strategy by our member governments.

- Third, the OECD has traditionally served to provide analysis and conceptual policy development for the further evolution of the multilateral system of trade and investment in the framework of GATT. For instance, only until the OECD had sufficiently advanced its work on the basic concepts for international trade in services, such as the right of establishment or national treatment, was the issue of trade in services moved on the agenda of the Uruguay Round.

This leads immediately to the subject matter of international air transport.

Despite its importance as an international service provider, the international aviation sector is *de facto* excluded from the General Agreement on Trade in Services. It is covered only in an annex with three doing-business issues, namely: (1) air craft repair and maintenance services; (2) the selling and marketing of air transport services; and (3) the CRS, the computer reservation systems. All hard rights regarding international air transport are escaping, as before, the general multilateral rules and disciplines for international trade.

In the light of this, and recognizing that the international aviation industry is an integral part of the modern global economy, the objective of the OECD project and the resultant report, was to provide governments and major players in the industry with both a comprehensive picture of the possible future development in the field of international civil aviation and a common assessment of the policies needed to ensure that air transport can contribute fully to the sound evolution of the world economy.

8.2 CURRENT FORECASTS FOR INTERNATIONAL AVIATION

By any standard, international air transport is a large industry which has grown prodigiously over the past thirty years. International airlines now account for over 1,350 billion passenger kilometres of traffic a year, and freight and mail transported by air make up for well over a third of the value of the world's manufactured exports. Without extensive air transport networks, major service industries such as international tourism would not have expanded to today's levels. International air transport has also been a major driving force behind the globalisation of economic activities.

Economic growth, higher disposable incomes and increased leisure time on the demand side, combined with falling real airline tariffs and technical change on the supply side, have been important driving forces behind the long-term growth of international air transport. Indeed, air traffic has doubled in each of the past three decades, growing consistently at about twice the rate of global GDP growth. This evolution is expected to continue in the future. Most available forecasts, including in particular those of ICAO and IATA, foresee an increase in world passenger traffic until the end of this decade at an annual rate of around 5% and between 2000 and 2010 even slightly higher. All these projections are primarily based on the longer-term outlook for world GDP growth.

Regarding air freight, ICAO has developed a simple model of forecasting taking into account two major parameters : world trade instead of GDP, and the level of freight rates. According to this projection, international air freight will increase by 7 per cent a year from 1992 to 2003 and domestic air freight will increase by 3.5 per cent a year over the same period. The total market increase is forecast to be 6.5 per cent annually, which is slightly lower than the growth rate achieved in the 1982-1992 period.

One has to note, however, that all these forecasts rely upon more or less sophisticated extrapolations of past trends. Where they go beyond this, they frequently face the danger of allowing current events, particularly booms and slumps, to have undue influence on views about the future. Furthermore, one also observes the problem of a 'gregariousness syndrome' which leads to a fairly close community of forecasters being unduly influenced by the conclusions of other members of their fraternity. The most serious limitation of all these approaches, however, lies in the evolving nature of the global economy. The globalisation of production and distribution structures as well as the increasing maturity of the air transport market in some regions and the emergence of new markets in others, are radically changing the relation between the growth of income and trade on one hand and air transport activity on the other.

In addition, fundamental shifts in driving forces and trends are set to have a substantial impact on uncertainties in the years ahead. There are new products and services coming on-line. Methods of production, distribution and communication are changing. New markets for goods and services are emerging and the role of old markets is changing. Foreseeing the role of air transport, both as a carrier of passengers and of freight, is therefore particularly challenging. In the light of accelerating change and an increasing degree of complexity in underlying relationships, one can conclude that it is more complicated and more challenging today than ever before to attempt to forecast the future.

8.3 QUALITATIVE TRENDS AND THEIR IMPLICATIONS FOR AIR TRANSPORT

It is certainly still safe to say that income and trade will remain important determinants of overall air traffic growth, but the structure of the industry will also be influenced by a variety of other political, economic, social and technological factors. A consideration of the longer-term development of international aviation thus requires an understanding of the complex set of variables which influence its scale and structure, together with projections of future trends in key determinants. One likely fundamental trend in this context is the continuation of the rapid process of internationalisation of economic activities.

On a micro level, the internationalisation process is reflected in a profound transformation of corporate strategies. International sourcing of intermediate inputs and components is rapidly expanding, while corporate activity in the advanced industrialised countries increasingly tends to concentrate on higher-value segments of the production chain. World-wide interaction of corporate activity is being organised through networks of affiliates and through non-equity arrangements such as subcontracting, franchising, joint ventures and alliances. Modern transport and information technologies play a crucial role in these developments, providing the means to synchronise and co-ordinate geographically dispersed activities.

On a macro level, owing to far-reaching liberalisation measures and technological developments, strong growth of international transactions of goods, services and capital is being observed. The implementation of the Uruguay Round is expected to provide additional impetus to the internationalisation of economic activities by further reducing traditional trade barriers and introducing important new disciplines in the areas of services, investment, intellectual property rights, technical and safety standards and public procurement. Similarly, the Multilateral Investment Agreement which is under negotiation at the OECD, is likely to accelerate the international deployment of productive assets. Also the on-going integration into the world economy of countries that are distant from the old industrial centres will enhance the demand for air transport.

In parallel to the geographical widening and the extension in scope of trade within a global multilateral framework, countries in Europe, North-America and Asia are seeking even closer economic ties via regional agreements. Though it is sometimes claimed that there is a risk of these agreements turning into protectionist trading blocs, the dominant view is that regional arrangements lend support to the multilateral system by acting as way-stations to a more globalised economy. International civil aviation, while only marginally impacted by the Uruguay Round, is part of several regional agreements, the most noteworthy being the internal market programme of the European Union.

As production continuously shifts towards goods with higher value content, the use of new and lighter materials, and the miniaturisation of components, the material intensity of production is expected to decline. Indeed, over the last two decades, the material intensity has fallen at a rate of 0.6 per cent per year in the OECD countries. The share of transport costs in the overall value of internationally traded products is therefore diminishing. For high-value-added industries such as electronics, technical instruments and electrical machinery, transport costs already play only a minor role in the overall cost of the products. As a consequence, there will be a shift towards low bulk/high value products in the volume of overall trade. And these are the types of goods where international aviation often has a comparative advantage.

Growing pressure for rapid and reliable delivery is another evolution which favours the development of air transport. With the advent of lean production methods, economising on time and inventory holding is often more important than direct cost savings. Time precision will, therefore, become increasingly important for international trade, in particular for intermediate goods, which form part of just-in-time production chains, and for spare parts. Suitable access to air transport services is thus an important consideration for many industries when deciding upon the details of suitable production sites. In the case of electronics, for example, where overall transport costs amount to only 3-4 per cent of production costs, immediate proximity to an airport is a key factor in plant location.

A further aspect of deepening in the division of labour is the increasing services-content of production. Due to the rapidly growing importance both of knowledge and technology, and of the expanding possibilities of outsourcing services-related activities, a progressive dematerialisation of production is taking place. In addition, modern information and communication technologies have led to an increased tradability of services. It can be expected that, with the coming into force of more extensive liberalisation measures for trade in services in the framework of the GATS and within regional markets, such as the European Union and NAFTA, the current trend will become more accentuated. As services industries also tend to be travel intensive, the growth in international provision of services may have a significant positive impact on the demand for air services.

Finally, a key dynamic factor which will continue to stimulate future air passenger transport will be rapidly rising levels of international tourist travel. Forecasts by the World Tourism Organisation, taking into account the forecasts of several other bodies, suggest that tourism arrivals will almost double between 1990 and 2010, corresponding to an annual average growth rate of 3.5 to 4 per cent. As travel account receipts represent about 5 per cent of the OECD countries' exports of goods and services and as this share is even higher for a number of developing countries, the expected developments in tourism will have a major impact on the demand for air services in the coming years.

Long-haul tourist travel, in particular, is a rapidly growing industry involving an ever greater number of countries. The increasing freedom to travel to and from countries formerly subject to important restrictions, the creation of a seamless global transport system, the decline in air fares and the continuing forces of demographic change are expected to lead to increased demand for exotic, cultural and other newer forms of tourist travel. It is also expected for many OECD countries that the more traditional annual vacation trip is being supplemented by more trips of a shorter average duration. Taken all together, these factors suggest that, in the coming years, tourism will be a rapidly expanding industry for which aviation will be an important transport mode.

8.4 PERVASIVE UNCERTAINTIES

Unfortunately, the fundamental trends and driving forces which appear so reassuring for the future of international air transport, are surrounded by pervasive uncertainties. In a rapidly evolving world, the likelihood of new developments, new dynamic driving forces, trend breaks and other discontinuities will definitely also affect the longer-term outlook for civil aviation.

As was stated earlier, the availability of air transport has been a significant contributor to the rapid growth in leisure travel and tourism, and rising incomes are virtually certain to underpin continued strong growth in the demand for such travel overall. But higher incomes do not only provide the finance for more leisure related travel, they are also generally associated with more choice in leisure destinations, greater opportunities to visit friends and relatives and enhanced flexibility in the timing of tourist travel. This poses new additional challenges to the aviation industry which has to match its supply of services more than ever before to new and perhaps rapidly-changing consumer preferences. Important to note in the context is the fact that even in the scheduled market around 55 per cent of air travel is estimated to be for leisure purposes, three quarters of which is between OECD countries.

As concerns business travel, the geographical widening of manufacturing and distribution activities entails more and longer trips for managers and for technical liaison purposes. Set against this, however, are new developments in management philosophy which have resulted in major uncertainties about the role of travel intensive middle management. Another factor which will influence the longer term growth of business travel will be the development of business service activities. It cannot be ignored, however, that these industries tend to be relatively footloose, which means that they can change their geographic location quickly, and their overall growth is also highly sensitive to the business cycle.

When cargo is carried in belly-holds or on combi aircraft, air cargo markets become entwined with scheduled passenger operations. On many long-haul routes, carriers such as KLM, Northwest and Lufthansa earn a significant part of their revenue from cargo traffic. The demand for cargo space is determined by the geographical distribution of production and consumption, by the nature of goods traded and by the importance of attributes (such as speed) which air transport can offer. All these determinants may change more often and more quickly in the future than they have done in the past.

Air cargo provides an important service not only for low bulk/high value products, but also for perishable goods, such as flowers, fruits and vegetables. These are markets which are susceptible not only to changes in consumer tastes, but also to changes in production technology. The introduction of new horticultural methods, for instance, has in recent years permitted the growth of some tropical fruits and other exotic plants in temperate climates, reducing the demand for air transportation. New products from different regions, however, have also emerged as market widening has taken place; and of course, the longer the distance the products are transported, the greater the likelihood of the role of civil aviation as a transport mode.

Finally one has to pay attention to the development of alternative modes of transport and even to alternatives to transport. In Europe, for example, high-speed rail has taken traffic from aviation on some domestic routes (e.g. Paris-Lyon) and internationally across the English Channel. Whether, however, this reflects a genuine advantage is still an open question, given the capital subsidies injected into high-speed rail and the regulated environment in which aviation still operates. Further, whether such services will in the future simply meet demand in selected niche markets or prove a major competitor to air transport is hard to predict.

While the fare costs of business travel have fallen in real terms, the overall opportunity costs of attending business meetings (e.g. including travel time costs) have tended to rise. New communication technologies such as videoconferencing are now emerging as a direct response to this rise in opportunity cost. Although to date, the impact of such alternatives has been relatively small, the longer term implications for international aviation are not at all clear, neither in terms of magnitude nor of direction of impact. In terms of the potential order of magnitude, a range of studies suggest that telecommunications could technically replace up to 25 per cent of business travel. Potential, however, is not the same as actual and complementary effects might well outweigh substitution effects. Combining electronic and face-to-face communications could allow individuals to maintain a larger network of contacts and to intensify links with existing networks. Thus, it is also possible that developments in telecommunications may even encourage air travel.

8.5 THE CHALLENGES FOR INTERNATIONAL AIR TRANSPORT POLICY

Notwithstanding the positive overall outlook, the more detailed analysis shows clearly that the aviation sector will be confronted with a wide variety of challenges resulting from new economic and social developments, breaks in old trends, and new technologies. New markets are emerging and the requirements of established ones are changing. It is also a time of fresh ideas in regulatory policy and, partly related to this, the structure of the airline industry is itself undergoing important change. Given the industry's position in the national and international economy, it is vital that the civil aviation sector be enabled to respond effectively to the challenges of rapid political, economic, social and technological change. And ultimately the key to coping with related uncertainties is through greater flexibility in the way the industry operates, and to make this possible is the challenge for civil aviation policy.

In response to this challenge and based on the analysis of the role of efficient air transport for the wider economy at domestic and international level, the OECD report and especially its policy recommendations, sharpen the increasingly widespread recognition, particularly in OECD countries, that the focus of aviation policy must shift from protecting existing airlines to enhancing efficiency, facilitating structural adjustment, responding to consumer interests, and as a result, establishing aviation markets that are more firmly anchored in competitive processes. This entails a wide embrace of market forces, not least the provision of appropriate incentive structures and flexibility.

It is therefore important that governments aim at creating markets where competition prevails, allowing the benefits of market forces to operate within a relatively liberal regulatory regime. There is a need for both more liberal international agreements at the bilateral levels, and progress within regional plurilateral and multilateral frameworks which ultimately could evolve into a liberal multilateral regime. In the short term, this may be achieved through the granting of more extensive freedoms regarding capacity, fares and market access but in the longer term it will also require more flexible fifth and sixth freedom rights, and finally, the introduction of cabotage rights.

The market-oriented liberal approach should not be restricted to the provision of air services but should also extend to matters of investment, ownership and control. The OECD is convinced that, in general, privatisation enhances the efficiency with which air transport is provided and also offers more flexible mechanisms of finance. Liberal regimes allowing greater foreign participation in ownership, permit easier access to international capital. Indeed, during the recession in the late 1980s and early 1990s, a number of airlines only managed to survive due to foreign investments in them.

Subsidies to airlines, in contrast, lead to inefficiencies and act to distort competition between carriers. This also applies to those cases where an airline is maintained on the basis of government support as a national flag carrier. While there may be a political necessity for transitional subsidies to allow phased industrial restructuring, the general rule should be that subsidies and similar forms of financial assistance be removed as rapidly as possible. Only in a very few instances, there may be justification for subsidising an international route for social service reasons. In such exceptional circumstances, the subsidies should be designed to maximise the efficiency of the services offered and be transparent and rigorously controlled.

International air transport infrastructure poses both short-term problems of ensuring the current system is used optimally and longer-term problems of ensuring adequate investment in additional and improved facilities. There, too, greater use could be made of market forces. This means that appropriate economic pricing of infrastructure should be employed with the aim of signalling commercial needs and priorities to market participants. Together with this, it is important that all forms of discrimination and anti-competitive practices in the use of airport infrastructure be discontinued. In addition, the OECD Report requests that a clear distinction be made between user charges and indirect taxation.

For liberal markets to work effectively, efforts need to be made to ensure that consumers can easily acquire clear and full information, and that they are protected against delays, baggage losses and, in particular, accidents. The move towards a more competitive environment must not imply any reduction in safety and security. Air transport has an excellent record in these fields, and it is in the interest of all that this be maintained.

The elaboration of the OECD report benefited greatly from the advice of a high-level Steering Group representing governments, airlines, aircraft producers, airports and consumer groups. Needless to say that not all members of the Steering Group were able to agree on all points of the Report. In one particular case, however, this went far beyond details or nuances. In fact, the Report carries in an Annex, a dissenting opinion of the Government of Japan saying that the views expressed in the study on the deficiencies of the bilateral system, on the advantages of liberalisation, on the need for relaxing foreign ownership restrictions and on the application of general competition laws are "based not upon the reality of today's international air services but upon misconceptions". Nevertheless, both the analysis and the policy recommendations carried the support of the overwhelming majority of the Group, and the OECD Secretariat is grateful to the Japanese that, despite their very strong objections, they did not choose to prevent the Report's publication. It remains to be seen whose concepts and/or misconceptions better reflect the future reality of international air transport.

9 THE EU/US RELATIONSHIP

Ludolf van Hasselt

From a European perspective this symposium takes place at an interesting moment. It is only a few weeks ago, on 25 March last, that we in the Community have celebrated the 40th anniversary of the signature of the Treaty of Rome. With so many ambitious goals ahead, such as the introduction of the common currency, the revision of the Treat and the enlargement to Central Europe, it is good to reflect for a moment on the successes of the Community so far, since in the heat of the debate these are often overlooked. The main objectives of establishing peace, and stability in Western Europe have been achieved. Disputes are settled in meeting rooms in Brussels and not on battlefields and we have not needed the help of Canadian soldiers in the last 40 years to resolve our conflicts. This achievement has given Europe a period of unprecedented economic progress.

The fact that bridging the different interest in 15 Member States sometimes requires lengthy negotiations is a small price to pay, although the complicated decision making process and carefully crafted compromises do not always make our life easy.

Aviation legislation has not escaped these complications. Not only the third package, but almost all legislation is full of phasing-in periods, transition measures, safeguard clauses and so forth. One such compromise concerned the gradual liberalization of the internal aviation market. This process was completed only less than a month ago Since 1 April of this year Community carriers can operate on any Community route. In the press this has been presented as a major achievement which will lead to something of a revolution in civil aviation, with more competition, better service and lower prices.

In my view, however, the passing of the April 1, 1997 date is relatively insignificant. At the time of the adoption of the third package the Council entered into a heated debate on the liberalization of cabotage rights. Referring to the Chicago convention, most of the larger Member States of the Community argued against any liberalization of cabotage. The smaller Member States, which have little to lose and much to gain from cabotage, were strongly in favor of the inclusion of cabotage in the 3rd package. As usual the Council eventually came up with the compromise formula to phase in cabotage. In the first phase only so-called consecutive cabotage is permitted, which means that the service has to be an extension of a service from, or is a preliminary of a service to, the State of registration of the carrier. In addition to that, a capacity restriction applies.

The introduction of full cabotage, or stand-alone cabotage, was delayed until 1 April 1997. From that date onward, Community carriers are allowed to exercise cabotage rights without any limitation. It seems to me that for three reasons this will not have any further significant effect.

1. Carriers have only made limited use of the opportunities which were already available to operate consecutive cabotage on routes in other Member States.

   [Between 1993 and 1995 some 20 cabotage routes were operated by non-national carriers, which in 1996 this number was 22. In that same period the use of code sharing flights increased significantly, which leads me to the conclusion that carriers, rather than operating themselves, opt for using a domestic partner for the operation of cabotage services. For example, British Midland operates a large number of domestic routes in the UK, with flight numbers of Alitalia, Iberia and Air Portugal, while Tyrolian Airways operates domestic routes in Austria on behalf of Air France and KLM.]

2. The profit margin from the operation of cabotage routes has decreased due to increased competition among domestic carriers.

   [At the time of the conclusion of the third package there were many domestic routes which were operated by the national carrier in monopoly. These carriers could charge extravagant prices and offer low service levels, because they did not face any competition. Since 1993, however, much has changed on the domestic scene and the traditional carriers now face competition on domestic routes from aggressive new entrants who have successfully challenged these monopolies on the basis of the third package. Examples are Air One in Italy and Spanair in Spain. These carriers have, of course, concentrated on the most promising domestic routes, thus bringing down prices and leaving little opportunity for carriers from other Community Member States to enter their domestic market.]

3. Finally, in those cases where there were attractive opportunities to enter the domestic market of another Member State, the third package already permitted a Community carrier to establish itself in that State, or to take a share in a domestic operator prior to 1 April 1997.

   [These opportunities have been used particularly by BA. Through investments in Deutsche BA in Germany and in Air Liberté in France this company has been able to take part in domestic operations well before that date.]

For all these reasons I do not believe that the completion of the internal market on 1 April will lead to important new developments, but that does not mean that we have not seen remarkable develpments since the entry into force of the third package in January 1993. The Community aviation market has developed from a market dominated by State airlines, heavily subsidized and operating in a strictly regulated environment to an open market where most carriers are privately owned and are free to react to changing circumstances. This led to more competition, more passenger choice and prices have come down, most significantly in the area of promotional fares. The Commission published a full report on the impact of the third package of air transport liberalization measures last October and yesterday Mr. Sickles has given you an update of the European developments so far. Therefore, instead of looking back at the achievements so far, I should like to look forward and identify three main trends which will give direction to the policy developments in the Community in the next decade and explain what has already been done to address these issues.

9.1 THREE TRENDS

9.1.1 Growth Related Problems

The very substantial growth in air transport is increasingly creating problems. With an annual growth rate of air traffic of more than 7%, much of runway and terminal capacity, but also of ATC capability is clearly under strain and delays have become a common feature in Europe.

[Without better use of present capacity on the ground and in the air, without significant investments in airport runway capacity and without a fundamental restructuring of Europe's Air Traffic Control system, those delays will continue and intensify. At the same time the environmental impact of air transport is a matter of grave concern. While at the international level not much progress is made to strengthen the standards for noise and emissions, the pressure on many local, reginal and national authorities to take measures against the further growth of air transport, increases.]

As a result of the increasing congestion at some of the major Community airports the issue of **slot allocation** is quickly becomine one of the most sensitive subjects in the internal market. The common rules for the allocation of slots at Community airports, establish some basic principles and give rules for the airport co-ordinators.

However, the real problem remains. The Regulation gives no answer to the increasing difficulty of obtaining suitable slots to expand air services and the resulting mounting barriers to market entry. By protecting incumbent carriers which currently benefit from unrestricted 'grandfather' rights to hold the slots they currently use indefinitely, the current slot allocation system prevents the full benefits of liberalisation of air transport being achieved.

It is therefore necessary to create a means to facilitate the transfer of slots, to improve the efficiency of the market and to avoid a static and inflexible situation developing congested airports which prevents airlines entering the market or increasing frequencies to meet customer demand. We have to recognise in that respect that air carriers will only give up slots when they are legally obliged to do so, or when there is a clear incentive to do so.

[In our discussions to find solutions to these problems, interested parties stress that we must respect a number of basic principles:

- Grandfather rights should be respected
- There must be room for new competition
- Fragmentation must be avoided
- New entrants should get a chance
- Big carriers must be able to develop their hubs
- Airports must be able to attract new business
- Feeder traffic is necessary
- The average aircraft size should be increased

Clearly some of these principles are in conflict and cannot all be met at the same time.]

One of the key objectives of the Commission is that the dynamics of market forces must be allowed to play their part and competition must not be eliminated, even at the most congested airports. We are considering, therefore, ways and means to introduce a market mechanism in the slot allocation process, but with adequate safeguards to avoid that only carriers with deep pockets can expand and thus develop dominant positions at the key European airports.

[It is very important for the Commission to have a Regulation in place which is widely accepted as a reasonable way of dealing with this extremely difficult subject. With the liberalisation of bilateral air services agreements, the regulatory barriers to market access disappear more and more and the lack of available slots will become the last remaining barrier to market access. Without a widely accepted system of slot allocation, we risk that governments will no longer be required to negotiate on traffic rights but, instead, will have to negotiate on access to airports.]

In responding to the challenge posed by the increasing congestion problems, the Community has also considered ways and means to improve the **efficient use of the available airport infrastructure**. In this context a Directive on Groundhandling, was introduced to promote efficiency and cost-effectiveness of groundhandling services at airports. The gradual introduction of more competition in this area should give air carriers a choice in handlers, including handling for themselves, rather than just having to accept the price and service of a monopoly handler.

The other initiative concerns the issue of airport charges. They vary considerably across the EU and there is, as yet, no comparable basis of calculation from one airport to another. Proposals to introduce principles of transparency, non-discrimination and cost-relatedness in this area were adopted by the Commission this week and they give airports the possibility to fight congestion by introducing peak hour pricing.

Capacity problems have also been at the basis of the Commission proposals for reforming and strengthening **Air Traffic Management**. These proposals pragmatically build on existing structures and in particular aim to give EUROCONTROL a more effective role in this area. The discussions on this subject in the Council are far from easy, because they involve the sovereignty of States and the role of the military, but the basic aim of simplifying what is currently an inefficient and complicated system of air space management is generally shared by Member States.

We cannot discuss the enormous growth in demand without also taking account of the **environmental aspects** of air transportation. There is growing concern that, under the pressure of local communities, politicians will be forced to take unilateral measures reducing the adverse effects of expanding air traffic, whereas everybody agrees that such measures can best be taken at the international level of ICAO. Unfortunately building an international concensus on strengthening the standards on NOx emissions (Nitrogen Oxides) and noise takes very long and in Europe public acceptance of air transport is crumbling, despite all scientific evidence that the environmental impact of aviation should not be exaggerated when compared with other modes of transport. Therefore pro-active responses are urgently needed.

The Commission has published a consultation paper on the limitation of the impact of noise from air transport. It is expected that later this year proposals will be made on a non-addition rule for hush-kitted aircraft. Conscious of the fact that air transport growth can best be controlled by economic penalties the Community also considers the implications for the environment of the exemption of taxation on aircraft fuel. From an environmental point of view this exemption cannot be justified.

There can be no doubt that despite all these measures being taken the problems related to growth will determine much of our policies in the years to come and that more legislative measures will be needed to ensure a balanced development of air transport.

9.1.2 Restructuring

The second trend I should like to identify concerns the effects of the restructuring process. Since 1990 all major European carriers have undergone often dramatic and painful restructuring processes and they have managed to reduce their **costs**. Despite a reduction of the labor force in the order of tens of thousands of employees, the productivity per employee is, on average, still considerably lower in Europe than in the US, or the Far East.

A popular way for airlines to reduce their labor costs is by outsourcing part of their activities. Maintenance, computing services, invoices and revenue accounting are activities which are increasingly taking place in countries with lower wages. Obviously this trend raises concerns among some Member States and the Community has yet to decide how it should respond to these social implications of increased competition. This will most certainly become a major subject in the policy development of the Community in the coming decade.

Made possible by the more liberal operating environment route restructuring and changes in aircraft size have also contributed to a reduction of the unit **costs**, but many other cost factors are outside the direct control of airlines and it is understandable that the industry uses every opportunity to argue for a reduction of landing charges, ATC costs and other external costs, which are considerably higher in Europe than in other parts of the world and which affect their competitive position in the global marketplace. It is increasingly important, therefore, that the cost impact of new policy measures is carefully considered and that additional burdens on the industry are avoided as much as possible. This limits the policy options for the future.

[Ideally the restructuring process would have taken place for all European carriers broadly at the same time, that would have been best for competition. In reality, however, the required adjustments have, in some cases, been introduced by airlines and national authorities only in the last few years and that leads to an unbalanced situation. In many cases new capital is required for the restructuring of state owned companies.]

Therefore, in any discussion about the restructuring of the European air transport industry the issue of **State aids** comes up. Since 1993, the Commission has followed increasingly strict rules on State aid in this sector and in November 1994, it established new Guidelines for State Aid to the aviation sector with the basic objective of ensuring rigorous enforcement of the Treaty's ban on aids which distort competition. Any request for an aid now has to be assessed on the basis of these guidelines and on the one time, last time principle by which the Commission will not approve a second request, unless it is linked to factors which are exceptional, cannot be foreseeen and are external to the company.

[It is clear, however, that the Guidelines do not, and cannot, start from the assumption that every capital injection made by any public owner into any public company is a subsidy which distorts competition. Nor does Community law allow us to treat public and private companies differently, although it is clear that privatized carriers have done much better in recent years than publicly owned carriers.]

This leads to the situation where the Commission has to examine each and every case on the basis of two tests:

- Would a private investor make the investment, given the expected returns and risks involved, if not, then it is an aid

- If a capital injection is a state aid, would it distort competition

I am afraid that we have not yet seen the end of the state aid procedures. Not only has the Commission still a number of difficult cases under consideration, but it can also be expected that as a consequence of the negotiations with the 10 associated countries in Central Europe on the conclusion of an aviation agreement which will bring these countries within the scope of Community law, a number of new cases will have to be considered. It is a big challenge for the Commission to give airlines from Central Europe, which are in most cases publicly owned, undercapitalized and under the direct influence of politicians the possibility to restructure, without disturbing the competitive environment.

9.1.3 Liberalization

Thirdly there is the trend towards **liberalization** world wide, coupled with **consolidation**, and aviation is not insulated from this movement.

The gradual liberalization of the air transport market gives not only quality carriers more easy access to foreign markets, but also so-called **risky carriers** benefit from the abolishment of operating restrictions. Consequently the responsibility of governments to ensure that safety oversight is guaranteed throughout the world also increases. ICAO has responded to this problem with its successful safety oversight program and also in the Community rules have been developed for a safety assessment of third country aircraft using Community airports and for the creation of a single European Safety Authority. I have little doubt that a further strengthening of the rules will be needed in the years to come, preferably at the international level, but if needed at the Community level.

For airlines to respond to the demand of passengers in the so-called global market place, they need a liberal regulatory regime, with capacity freedom, with fare freedom, with market access freedom and with the opportunity to cooperate with partners elsewhere in the world. This was recognized at an early stage in the US, but today it is also accepted in Europe that liberalization is needed, not only in the internal market, but also externally.

Consequently in recent years a series of so-called 'open skies' agreements have been concluded between the US and individual European countries which eliminate many of the restrictions commonly used to regulate international civil aviation. These agreements do not stand on their own, but they are closely related to the development of alliances between a number of EC- and US carriers. With these alliances air carriers are able to overcome regulatory barriers and to offer their customers better service and a much larger network. Their downside is that they lead to concentration in the market and to a reduction of competition. Potentially, therefore, alliances may undermine the positive effects of liberalization.

For that reason the US administration examines the alliances closely before it grants them an anti-trust exemption and also the European Commission has expressed its concerns about the effects of large scale alliances on competition and it has started an investigation into all recently concluded alliance agreements. In the forefront is the AA/BA alliance and the Commission is presently considering if, and under what conditions that alliance can be accepted under the competition rules of the Treaty.

In the meantime the Commission has started negotiations with the US government on the conclusion of an aviation agreement which goes beyond an 'open skies' agreement and has as its ultimate objective the creation of an integrated EC-US aviation area. Why are we keen to enter into a new type of agreement with the US and why do we suggest that it is also in the US interest to consider such a novel approach?

First we believe that the integration of the industry raises issues which are not adequately addressed in the existing bilateral framework where each side designates its 'own' carriers, where traffic rights exchanged can be used and are not limited by airport - or airspace congestion and where governments control the commercial behavior of airlines.

Various forms of co-operation between carriers on both sides of the Atlantic make it increasingly difficult to distinguish between EU and US carriers; they are becoming global service providers and are, as such, subject to our legislative systems. Their interest is to have a more global regulatory regime which is predictable and as uniform as possible. They want a more global approach and not a mercantilist bilateral one.

The role of governments in our view should no longer be primarily to negotiate reciprocal beneficial traffic rights, since in a genuine market these rights should be freely available to all qualified operators. The emphasis today should be on creating a stable framework ensuring fair market conditions; on finding the right balance between traffic growth and the environmental impact of aviation; on ensuring safety and security; on providing the necessary infrastructure. These functions cannot be exercised in isolation, they require co-operation. The EU and the US administrations should act as guarantors of free and fair competition, not as contenders for mercantilist advantages.

Our objective in these discussions is certainly not to impose new limitations upon air carriers, but rather to go beyond the bilateral structure and follow-up at the government level what is already taking place in the industry. We would like to see if we cannot work closer together at government level and thus develop common responses to the challenges of the future. We have gained some experience from discussing these matters with the countries in Central and Eastern Europe and these experiences have demonstrated that under such conditions even these countries are prepared to abolish market restrictions. This gives us the hope that if between the EU and the US an adequate framework can be developed, many other countries in the world will be attracted to it.

A key area for such an integration of government policies concerns the application of **competition and anti-trust rules**. While we recognize, of course, that each side has its own responsibilities in this area, recent developments have demonstrated that it becomes very complicated for both EC and US airlines if two, or even three, different authorities apply different rules. If it is possible to intensify the already existing close co-operation between the two sides, we will have made an important first step towards genuine market integration.

Also a common approach in such areas as **leasing, computer reservation systems, code sharing,** etc. will certainly help to develop a framework where similar rules will be applied to the operations of air carriers in the different markets. This will facilitate the operations of EU and US carriers in the respective markets.

On the issue of the **ownership and control** our view is that a gradual liberalization of the restrictions in this area is the logical complement of the abolition of market access restrictions and of the on-going restructuring processes taking place both in the EU and in the US markets. European carriers have been actively investing in the US and we expect to see an increase of investments by US carriers in Community undertakings. After all, there are some interesting opportunities in the Community and only 8 airlines remain majority owned by Member States. Also this is a good example of how the rules of the classical post-war system are now operating as a brake on the development of carriers. They cannot adopt capital structures appropriate to their more global roles and have to find complex and sometimes doubtful devices to circumvent the system.

Finally we have suggested that it would be sensible to discuss at an early stage the subject of **dispute settlement**. The reason for this urgency is that we believe that the traditional consultation mechanisms do not lend themselves to the situation we envisage. Existing conflict resolution mechanisms are based on the assumption that Governments act on behalf of 'their' interests. It is, however, increasingly unclear where these interests are. Therefore, it is in the interest of our airline industry to seek the development of a speedy and easy to use procedure to resolve potential conflicts without putting the market structure at risk.

In short, we are offering the prospect of negotiating a total US/EU agreement on air transport which will provide the greatest possible operational clarity and certainty for our air carriers. A modern agreement which takes into account the developments towards globalisation of the industry and which should build a partnership rather than traditional bilateral rules.

These subjects have been discussed in two meetings, in October 1996 and on 3 April last and we have reached a stage where we can draw some initial conclusions. These conclusions will be presented to the Council of Ministers in June and after that we expect to be able to move to a second phase where also the subject of traffic rights will be on the table. I have no illusions as to the timeframe for the completion of the negotiations, since this may require some major concessions on both sides, but the prospect of creating a Transatlantic common aviation area is definitely challenging and is worth fighting for.

In our efforts to have a regulatory structure which is better adapted to the needs of civil aviation of today we welcome any multilateral initiative, be it in ICAO, or in WTO, or in OECD and in the long term such a multilateral solution may have some chance of success. In the shorter term, however, an agreement between two aviation blocs of equivalent size, both internally liberalized and with a well developed competition, or anti-trust policy has the best prospect of success. It is our ambition, however, that if and when an agreement can be reached between the EU and the US, other countries will be able to join. For that reason we welcome the presence of observers from Canada n the talks and we hope that your country will be among the first to join in such a future arrangement.

I believe that these three trends, the continued growth of air transport, the effects of the restructuring and the liberalization will determine the future policy making in the Community. A number of measures have already been taken to address the effects of these trends, but more will follow in the years to come.

10 THE CANADA-U.S. AIR AGREEMENT

Louis Ranger

10.1 INTRODUCTION

The Canada-U.S. air market has always been an important source of revenues for the Canadian airline industry. In fact, Air Canada's very first service, about 60 years ago, was between Victoria and Seattle.

To give you some appreciation of the size of the market, about 17 million passengers travelled between the two country air last year. We believe this to be the single largest international air market in the world. It is also over ten times the size as our next largest international market the United Kingdom.

So I can assure you that our decision in the early nineties to pursue a liberalized regime with the United States was not taken lightly. This was a much more important decision for Canada than for the United States. The transborder market represents 24% of our international operations while it represents only 1% of the international operations of U.S. carriers.

Canada had to convince itself that the liberalization of air routes with the United States was a good thing. This idea was counter-intuitive to most Canadians considering that our industry would be competing against another industry 15 times its size.

So we were very cautious. We did our homework. And, as many of you know, it took four years to negotiate a new agreement despite both countries sharing the same final objective, that is, an "open skies" regime. In additional, it took some 12 to 15 months of informal bilateral discussions at senior official and ministerial levels before the launching of formal negotiations.

What I would like to do in the next 15 to 20 minutes is to briefly review the reasons why the previous agreement had become unacceptable and summarize the findings of our analysis and the main features of the new air agreement. I will then share with you the results that we achieved over the last two years and compare these results with our initial expectations. Finally, I will conclude with some personal reflections on some of the lessons we have learned.

10.2 THE REGIME BEFORE 1995

It should like to take a few moments to explain the reasons why Canada wanted to change the old air transport regime.

The original agreement drawn up in 1966 and revised in 1974 was a conventional one: airlines were limited to serving only the markets covered by the agreement, and most routes were served by a single carrier per country.

This agreement proved very effective when the domestic markets in both Canada and the U.S. were regulated by the governments. This situation began to change, however, with the revision of the agreement in 1974 or thereabouts. The deregulation of these markets, first in the U.S. in 1978 and then in Canada 10 years later, entirely changed how the airlines conducted their operations.

In Canada, deregulation was accompanied by the privatization of Air Canada. From then on, the airlines needed more flexibility to adapt their networks to market conditions. In short, the industry should no longer be expected to be content to serve a set of government-assigned routes.

A more discreet change was also taking place among consumers. The North American economy was turning towards the service sector. And the economic development of both countries was also becoming dependent on international trade. Consequently, business travellers began to demand more frequent, direct air services for same-day return trips.

Unfortunately, because of the rigidity of the Canada-U.S. agreement, some destinations were left unserved, and many communities on both sides of the border were becoming aware of the impact of this situation. In their view, the agreement hurt tourism, and hence regional economic development.

In the middle of the eighties, therefore, Canada and the U.S. felt obliged to find a more comprehensive solution and tried repeatedly to negotiate a new agreement. All these attempts proved fruitless, the main reason being that the Canadian and American governments did not share the same vision of what an agreement for the liberalization of air services should be.

The main obstacle with which we were confronted was stagnation of the transborder market after the early eighties. We had to strike the right balance between the needs of consumers and the needs of airlines.

10.3 OUR ANALYSIS

Fortunately, 1988 was a record year for many airlines and this created the right climate for bilateral discussions.

While we wanted to create growth opportunities for Canadian carriers, our first priority was to ensure that a liberalized air agreement would not undermine the financial viability of our domestic industry.

As I mentioned earlier, a major concern was the size of the American industry compared to ours. In terms of revenues, seven of the twenty largest airlines in the world are based in the United States. Air Canada and Canadian Airlines rank 23rd and 33rd, respectively. A combined Air Canada and Canadian Airlines would still rank behind the seventh largest U.S. carrier, Continental Airlines.

The size of the U.S. industry, coupled with the need to effectively compete in the transborder market, convinced us that there had to be safeguards for the Canadian industry, at least during a transition phase.

The difficulty of competing in the U.S. was demonstrated by the declining market share of the Canadian industry. By 1993, our industry' share of the scheduled transborder market stood at 32%. Although the share was 41% of the total market when charter traffic was factored in, the prospects for recovery were poor.

U.S. airlines, even though they enjoyed less than open access to transborder markets, nonetheless had access to all of the major Canadian air travel markets. For instance, U.S. airlines could route passengers destined to Atlanta over a gateway like Buffalo or over a hub like Detroit. In contract, the only access that the Canadian industry had to Atlanta was through interlines. This example could be repeated in what seemed an endless list of U.S. destinations: Washington, Denver and Orlando among others.

It was clear that something had to be done.

One of the first steps we took was to develop a model on how an "open skies" regime would affect the airline industry and how it would benefit communities. The results convinced us that the Canadian industry did complete effectively in many but not all markets. Canadian carriers did well serving markets that were not dominated by a U.S. hub carrier or in markets with a strong southbound tourist component.

Our analysis did conclude that the overall market share would not change significantly. There would be of course winners and losers but our analysis showed that all parties involved should be able to live with the results. It showed in particular that communities would benefit from the start-up of around 40 new services.

The economists in the audience will no doubt point out the limitations of our approach. First of all, we never clearly established the general impacts on the economy or the costs of transition towards an open regime. Other issues such as the effect of lower air fares were examined but never quantified. Our model also struggled with assumptions on competitive response and with the concept of induced traffic. These limitations do underscore the need for continued research in this area. However, we felt our analysis of these issues was sufficiently advanced to allow us to develop the conditions that would lead to a "win-win" scenario for the industry and communities.

10.4 THE NEW AIR AGREEMENT

The main aim of the new agreement, needless to say, is to open up all transborder markets to the airlines of both countries. Except for Montreal, Toronto and Vancouver, where new American services will gradually be introduced over a three-year transition period, there is no restriction on the number of flights, seats or designations.

The restrictions applicable to Montreal and Vancouver have already been lifted, and those applying to Toronto will go this coming February. Then, any airline based in Canada and the U.S. will be free to serve any transborder market it wishes.

Access to airports whose time slots are controlled was also central to our negotiations. It was scarcely logical for Canada to negotiate an open transborder regime if it could not obtain access rights to main markets like New York, Chicago and Washington.

Canada negotiated favourable terms in this regard: time slots were assigned to it free (14 for New York's LaGuardia Airport and 10 for Chicago's O'Hare). Our carriers can of course obtain others under the buy-and-sell rules on the American market.

The new agreement also provides direct access to Washington's National Airport, to all intents and purposes a domestic airport, from a number of airports in Canada with pre-clearance facilities.

The agreement is very open as regards fares. An air fare can be rejected only if both countries agree.

The new agreement also authorizes freedom of code-sharing between Canadian and U.S. carriers.

Further, it permits the use of a new dispute resolution process.

Note that the changes that we have been talking about affect only access to transborder markets. The new regime does not grant any rights such as cabotage, the right of establishment or access to third-country markets.

In this sense, the new agreement is not an American-style "open skies" agreement and does create a common market along European lines. It is nevertheless open where it serves our interests, that is, in the operation of transborder services.

10.5 THE RESULTS SO FAR

It has now been a little over two years since Canada signed the new agreement. Although there are still ten months remaining in the transition towards an open transborder regime, Canada views the agreement as an unqualified success. It has gained wide acceptance by airlines, airports, communities and travellers and I trust that this positive outlook is hared by our friends south of the border.

I would like to show you three slides which provide a good summary of results to date.

This first chart shows the number of new scheduled routes started since the agreement was signed in February, 1995. At last count, there will be 77 new services this summer which were not operated prior to the new agreement. It is encouraging that about half of these new routes, 36 of them to be exact, have been started up by the Canadian industry. These figures do not include former charter routes that are now operated as scheduled services.

The other interesting point about this chart is that the new services extend across all regions of Canada. Although smaller sites have fewer new services, the impact is proportionally the same as for major cities. For instance, a new Ottawa-Chicago service vastly improved the quality of transborder air service to Canada's capital.

The next figure tracks the total number of seats, both scheduled and charter, supplied in the Canada-U.S. market for the past eight years. It is evident from the right-hand side of the graph that the new agreement sparked a renewed interest by the airlines. We estimate that capacity is now running about 18% above pre-agreement levels. It is interesting to note that the gap between Canadian and U.S. capacity has narrowed considerably since the new agreement was signed. The Canadian share of capacity now stands at 43% compared to a figure of 40% in 1994.

This is not to say that the U.S. industry did not benefit as much a from a liberalized regime. In many cases, U.S. airlines were able to eliminate many of the unprofitable stops on the way to their hubs. In effect, these carriers are now providing better service to their customers even though they might have not increased their capacity.

The third chart shows the changes in transborder traffic levels since the new agreement was signed. About 1.8 million more travellers arrived in Canada by air from the United States in 1996 than in 1994 - an impressive 24% increase considering that the market had not grown appreciably in the years prior to the new agreement.

An obvious question is how do these results compare to those we expected when we were negotiating the new agreement. Although our general predictions were correct, we had misjudged the timing and extent of the benefits of an open regime. We are now seeing twice as much new service and induced traffic than we expected. Any analysis of this nature is sensitive to service and demand assumptions. For instance, we did foresee the use of regional jets in many transborder markets but we did not appreciate the extent to which they would be used in low-volume or highly competitive markets.

Another factor that we overestimated was the stability of our competitors. Our analysis had assumed that the U.S. airlines would use their hub and spoke networks to compete for transborder traffic. Since then, U.S. airlines have reduced or shut down many of their domestic hubs such as Nashville or Washington Dulles.

The benefits of an open transborder regime go far beyond the simple measures that I have shown you. For instance, I would like to comment on the profitability of transborder services but solid statistics of this nature are simply unavailable. We know that there has been a short-term decline in profitability. Average fares dropped by 10% and load factors declined by 5 percentage points during the first year of transition. But we are encouraged by the fact that both of Canada's major airlines have made the transborder market a key part of their future plans.

Consumers have obviously benefited form the greater choice of carriers and destinations. Canadian cities now enjoy new or improved access to major U.S. destinations like Atlanta, Denver, or St. Louis. Same-day, return travel is now possible in many more markets. Our analysis indicates that the new agreement has resulted in about 700,000 new business trips per year thus solidifying that is already the largest trading relationship in the world.

As you are doubtless aware, Canadian airports are in the process of being transferred to local authorities. These airports are free to market their services across North America or around the world if they wish. For example, Vancouver is now positioning itself as a gateway to North America for Asia—in part because of its free access to several transborder services. Generally speaking, the growth in traffic that has followed the signing of the agreement has generated significant inflows of funds in various forms for our airports—inflows that are now enabling them to consider long-term expansion plans without calling on the government for funding.

Of course, the agreement also benefits the economy as a whole, It contributes to creating jobs not only at airports but also at airlines. For example, Air Canada has announced the hiring of 1,100 new employees this year, in part to meet the demand for transborder services. Additionally, as we know, several new services are being operated with Bombardier's Regional Jet aeroplane, which is build right here in Montreal. All these benefits have not been quantified, but they are very real.

10.6 CONCLUSIONS

To conclude, I would like to share with you some of the lessons we have learned.

First, a rigorous analysis proved to be absolutely essential, of course, to understand the market, to identify the carriers' strengths and weaknesses in both countries, to assess the competitive environment, to develop our negotiating position and to decide where concessions were possible.

Second, we felt it was important to consult with all stakeholders, not just the airlines. During our negotiations, we had mounted a very elaborate consultation mechanism including provinces, airport communities, labour representatives, airlines as well as several federal government departments and agencies. Although consultations were difficult to manage at times, all parties clearly understood each other's position and this, I believe, helped us adopt a much broader view of the issues.

Third, no matter how robust your analysis is and how convincing you can be with stakeholders, governments have to wait for a "window" to undertake such major restructuring efforts. These efforts cannot be done at any time during an economic cycle. Airlines are prepared to take more risks during a period of growth than during an economic downturn. Our success in 1995 was partly due to the fact that the North American economies were just entering in a period of growth.

Fourth, we started to see the light at the end of the tunnel the day both countries recognized that some complex issues could be taken off the table without jeopardizing the main objective of the agreement. This was the case, for example, for the discussion on "intransit preclearance" issues which were resolved only a few weeks ago.

Lastly, it was important for us to recognize the strengths of our own airline industry and its critical role in supporting Canadian trade requirements. We had the conviction that Canadian carriers were capable of playing a significant role in the transborder market and that an open regime would give them new opportunities to strengthen their position. But we also had to recognize that the Canadian industry could not compete in each and every market and that denying U.S. airlines new access to transborder markets meant that we would also be denying the Canadian economy some of the tools needed to compete internationally.

It is clear from the results I have presented to you this morning that the new Canada-U.S. air agreement has struck the right balance between industry and other economic interests.

The new agreement is helping our industry to solidify its participation in global alliances and we think that, in the long-term, it will help our airlines to compete more effectively in international markets.

11 POLICY FORMULATION: THE IATA POSITION

Geo Besse

I am, in effect, asked to identify the IATA position on air transport liberalisation.

That is a quick and easy task. We don't have one.

Firstly because we don't *need* to have a position - and life is complicated enough these days without trying to do things we don't need to do.

Secondly because, even if there *were* a perceived need, it would be impossible to achieve a consensus among 250-plus air carriers, of whom the biggest performs 25,000 times the passenger traffic of the smallest. And where the per capita GDP of the richest state of registration is perhaps 40 or 50 times that of the poorest.

I think it is fair to say that IATA's position - or, rather, *lack* of a position - on liberalisation, has not always been as it is now.

Certainly, at the time of IATA's creation more than 50 years ago, then during the 1950s and 60s, and perhaps right up to the time of the CABs - remember that - "Show Cause Order" of the late 1970s, there was a strong identity between IATA Members and their governments. And, *ipso facto*, between IATA and governments.

Governments were in favour of the status quo of pre-assignation of two government-owned carriers on each international route; they specified the frequencies to be flown, and generally favoured a revenue or profit pool, so that if one carrier proved to be less efficient, it would not suffer any penalty.

The rubber-stamped the tariffs coming out of IATA - and they endorsed the carrier-given authority of IATA to fine its Members for contravening the level or conditions of any tariff.

So in those days, you could say that we - IATA, airlines, governments together - certainly had *attitude*. Those days were a bit like some peoples' view of Switzerland, where, if anything is not illegal it is compulsory.

We certainly - all of us - had a view on liberalisation. It was the same view that Senator Joseph McCarthy had of communism.

But note - that does not imply unique bigotry or a uniquely closed mind, on the part of aviation. Most international trade in goods and services was very far from being liberalised in the early post-way years. The road from the formation of GATT to the "Uruguay Round" and the transformation of GATT in WTO has been long and hard.

But, that road has been travelled and, for both trade in goods and services and international aviation - times *change and we change with them.*

Perhaps one key indication of this is the fact that the last time we fined any airline for failing to apply an IATA tariff was in 1979. It was one of those defining moments similar to the date on which any Western European country last carried out a judicial execution - which was also during the 1970s.

IATA tariff coordination is now one of the large range of products and services offered *à la carte*. Governments have widely differing views of its relevance and effectiveness. Airlines have widely varying rates of participation and adherence. In the meantime, about one in every six airline consumers on international scheduled services - that's still nearly 60 million a year - interlines. And the integrity of the interlining system is underwritten through IATA tariff coordination.

We state that. It's nothing to get excited about. If it ceases to be true and/or if our Members don't want it - we merely seek cheaper office space, with less meeting rooms. Or - we will do a bit more of what we have been doing, very successfully, over the past 10 years. Organising other conferences - on anything from the carriage of aardvarks to the development of yield management.

On one level, to have an attitude to liberalisation is to have an attitude to whether or not the tide should come in, or go out. King Canute of England is held to be the greatest exponent of this. Although, some people may find it significant that he himself remained an agnostic on the matter. It was his courtiers who insisted on the abortive attempts to prevent them all getting their feet wet, on the coast of Kent.

Such thinking - that there is an inevitability about today's economic and social tides, as immutable as the tide which washed over Canute - is strengthened by the apparent triumph of western liberal capitalism over state bureaucratism, at the end of the 1980s. The notion which was encapsulated in Francis Fukuyama's "The End of History".

But, of course, *nothing* is inevitable - except our two old favourites, death and taxes.

To assert that there is *one* unique model of liberal economic development, to be applied everywhere, for everyone, covering everything, to be applied at the same rate - "take three spoonfuls a day, after meals" - is as mistaken as the very determinism which provided the philosophical underpinning of soviet-type regimes.

If this is true of economic development as a whole, it must certainly be true of air transport!

But this is not universally self-evident. It occurs to me that, for some people - and perhaps some governments - their view of air transport is completely driven by technology.

Aircraft technology, together with telecommunications technology, has made Marshal Mcluhan's "global village" a reality. Or, as the environmentalist David Bellamy said at one of our many seminars, last year "...honey, we've shrunk the world."

Now, if identical units of the very latest, sophisticated aircraft technology are delivered daily from Seattle or Toulouse, to country X and country Y, the laws of aerodynamics are the same for both, the fuel consumption is the same, the range and carrying capacity are the same...etc., etc. For some people, it is but a small step, from that point, to thinking that these aircraft *must* be used in the same way everywhere - economically, commercially, culturally.

In IATA, we take a thoroughly pragmatic view of all this. For the most part, we view it at the level of individual governments. Where governments have gathered in a larger grouping and have an established policy towards the industry - we relate to that group. ICAO is the largest and oldest such group - and *the* logical group for much of our work.

But - with the best will in the world, and even with much greater resources - ICAO cannot be all things to all men, and everywhere at once. It cannot insist that a new radar set or a UHF radio net be available in state X, in three months' time, in order to maintain safety standards. It cannot insist that the depreciation policy of airport A in state Y be modified, in order to prevent crippling user chargers for our Members.

IATA cannot insist on such things either! But issues such as these are typical of what IATA has to deal with, on a daily basis. And we do not hesitate to use the Chicago Convention and its Annexes, and ICAO Resolutions, as the practical and moral underpinning of our work.

Since so much of what the industry, for which read our Members, does - and what it will be trying to do in the future, is bound up with governments - the attitude of governments will always be crucial.

Governments have the power to help us achieve our growth potential by:

- Encouraging industry profits - which result in faster acquisition of newest aircraft.

- Encouraging coordinated infrastructure development - including supra-national initiatives such as "FANS" and the work of the CFMU of Eurocontrol.

- Investing both in infrastructure and research.

- Refraining from self-defeating economic penalties on the industry, such as fuel taxes or kerosene used for international aviation.

Even all this will not be enough. Air transport *itself* will have to think seriously about how it copes with the relative gigantism of the year 2010 - being twice as big. And - about how it will then be perceived.

*****

One problem is that the sum of little decisions made - or not made - at the micro level, the level of the individual corporation, can represent an untenable whole which is somehow less than the sum of its parts. An accidental - and accident-prone - industry.

Let's start with airline finances.

Our Director General once likened international civil aviation to a roller-coaster. In so doing, he was referring to its profit record - not its airworthiness or the skill of the people who work for it!

In the four years 1990-93 the IATA airlines lost USD 15.6 billion net, on their international scheduled services.

With three years net profits already earned since then, it now seems probable that they will have *made* USD 15.2 billion in the four years 1994-97. That figure includes USD 4.4 billion, anticipated for the current year.

Even if that comes about - what all these figures show is a very exciting way to *lose* USD 400 million, during a period of *eight* years!

As they continue their re-structuring, preparing themselves for an ever more competitive, globalised, future - the airlines can do without such excitement. They need steady profits year after year, for fleet renewal and to satisfy the evident demand which, fortunately for all of us, continues out there in the marketplace.

As it continues its restructuring, in response to the inexorable pressure to reduce costs, the air transport industry remains in constant danger of being side-lined by the cyclical collapse of its yields.

However impeccable the logic of a particular cost-cutting measure - bit it down-sizing, outsourcing, or whatever...

However well thought out a particular alliance may be - and many of them are not well thought out...

However new - or old - an airline's fleet may be...

However well-tailored its products are, to the perceived needs of its customers...

However good - or bad - its route structure is ... one can go on adding "howevers" until the cows come home - there is no guarantee that any or all of these things will produce a decent profitability *unless* the balance between total market supply - capacity - and total market demand - traffic - is the *right* one.

But successful future growth will involve much more than the airlines getting their traffic/capacity sums right.

In fact, sustainable aviation growth needs to involve much more than the airlines themselves. It will need the involvement of airports, national and local governments, land-use planners, public transport authorities, aircraft manufacturers, and supplies of air traffic control and management systems.

To be sustainable, air transport has to grow in coordinated fashion, ensuring that the supply of the necessary infrastructure is not outstripped by the demand for air traffic movements, that maximum use of public transport to/from airports is built into the planning process, that *intermodality* of transport systems is actively encouraged, *and* that the application of sensible zoning laws around airports is an integral part of the process.

I quote our Director General, on the question of how our industry might be perceived.

"Our longer-term credibility could be substantially enhanced...if as an industry...we were to set ourselves some bold targets...to be achieved over the next 10 years.

Targets such as:

- Reducing the accident rate by half.

- Reducing the delays at airport entry/exit formalities...that is...the so-called facilitation delays...by half.

And...

- Developing clear targets for reducing the unit rate of *noxious* engine emissions...based on what technology can deliver...and working with regulators...manufacturers...airports...to ensure that regulations do not "second guess" scientific progress.

Such targets...in my view...clearly indicate...that we are determined to be a positive force on some of the key factors affecting us...and that we are acting as a responsible industry.

They suggest...that we are determined to achieve the growth promises of our industry...in an environmentally sustainable fashion...and at the same time improving safety...and service to the consumer.

Although demanding...it is my belief that these targets are achievable...but let me suggest that they can be achieved *only*...if we have a financially healthy and profitable airline industry."

*****

I have tried, so far, to give you the day-to-day flavour of an industry which is highly developed, highly diverse, which has responded in varying ways and at varying rates to economic fashion, yet which *still* represents a world system - and which *still* has plenty of growth potential.

Let me go back to those financial figures, for a moment. They demonstrate that commercial wisdom is not as thickly spread among the nations of the so-called developed world as many people would believe! This is important for the less developed nations, for two reasons. The first one is a matter of general economic philosophy. The second is a matter of specific air transport regulation.

As I have said - only one viable model of economic life seems to be on offer. It is one of liberal capitalism - allied to increasing globalism and transnational ownership. Some people believe that it may not be delivering the sort of economic growth, nor as wide a distribution of growth, as it should.

However, if there are complaints - there are no serious competitors. And, no matter how one views the world economic system, one cannot insulate oneself from the realities of it. It strikes me, though, in looking at the diverse world pattern of economies - that, whilst it may be heresy to be against the general model, it cannot be heresy to move forward at different rates!

As with economies - so, with aviation. Since everyone is concerned with growth, one must begin with the fact that aviation has grown faster than other industries. And, the growth in productivity has been pretty spectacular, as well. Some people might say that the growth could have been even more spectacular and the gain in labour efficiency even greater *if* the aviation world had been organised on a more competitive basis, everywhere, right from the start. The multilateralist solution, if you will.

We will never know, of course.

Now, the days of spectacular productivity gains are over. But, at the same time, we are in a situation where they are needed as never before. Market maturity and low yields dictate that the only way to generate profit is by reducing cost.

This imperative has given strength to the view that, only through *multilateral, global* solutions, can future efficiencies be guaranteed and continual profitability be assured.

One might observe that the strongest advocates of this view are nations or airlines who have an absolute or comparative advantage - to use the jargon of international trade - in operating international commercial flights.

In that respect, nothing has changed since Chicago in 1944 - but other nations have joined the US club! Each will pursue its own interests and the need for compromise is as great as ever.

However, let me also stress that the terms bilateralism and multilateralism tend to obscure the real issues under debate. Bilateralism tends to be interpreted to mean protectionism and multilateralism equates with liberalization. This is not always true. We should also not forget that in recent years many bilateral air transport agreements could be primarily protectionist and, particularly if they include regional cabotage provisions, would be unwelcome to the proponents of liberal multilateralism. Regional multilateral agreements would in any event, involve the negotiation of new bilateral agreements between the regions and this could create new problems in reconciling the conflicting national interests of members of the blocks.

Some fifteen years ago, we talked within IATA about an evolving form of "splintered multilateralism". This describes a partial move from bilateralism towards multilateralism but falling short of globalism. It is the trend, initially defensive-oriented, where regional interests combine, within blocks, to promote jointly their common interests. Such a scenario may represent the worst of all worlds for the small countries.

On the broader trade front, Raymond Krommenacker of WTO, very rightly affirms that this state of affairs might be categorized by the term "interest-lateralism" which describes the processes of shared interest motivated economic actions of a national or a bilateral or lastly of a plurilateral nature. The challenge as described by Raymond Krommenacker is "to move progressively from this context of interest-lateralism to an interwoven network of rights and obligations symbolic of reasoned multilateralism". This trend should be possible in the field of international air transport. Let us be pragmatic and not dogmatic: a combination of existing arrangements updated and new initiatives is probably the best solution to enhance international trade in aviation service.

However, one new element in the discussion seems to be a belief that multilateralism is not only desirable, but inevitable.

It is strange to think, after the brinkmanship and the seven years involved in the successful negotiation of the "Uraguay Round" within the GATT, that anyone should regard even the progress to multilateralism in *physical* trade as inevitable - let alone, trade in services.

If true multilateralism is not only an ideal, but an outcome dictated by globalism and economic efficiency, one outcome has to be faced. The end of several "single flag" carriers. In multilateral trade, nations specialise in doing those things in which they have an absolute or comparative advantage - then trade those things for something they don't have, because someone else is producing it more efficiently and cheaply. For some nations, the list of "don't have" things should, logically, include aviation, and for them the concept of community of interests between states belonging to some geographic area proposed by ICAO several years ago could be a satisfactory solution.

And yet, I am reminded of some words written more than ten years ago, by the chairman of Alia... "...whilst cooperation amongst nations has been readily forthcoming in other fields of economic activity, there has always been reticence on the part of the airlines to come forward together because of what I may term as a 'built-in' constraint - the glamour individual nations attach to their flag carriers and, as a corollary, their reluctance to forego even the semblance of sovereignty."

What is a later view of this? In his introduction to the report of the European "Wise Men", Herman De Croo wrote... "...national transport systems emerged, causing fragmentation and many inefficiencies. In this general trend, Europe was no exception. It still suffers from this heritage."

"Some argue (for a unique regulatory framework for a unique industry)...and it is true that air transport is often subject to less than rational commercial decisions...based on tradition, national pride, or simply on fascination...with realising the dream of Icarus. This fascination is an asset. The crux of the problem is to reconcile this asset with rules ensuring that economically rational decision-making prevails."

Today, no one carrier - with the possible exception of those of the Former Soviet Union - is without choice in terms of joining a regional association.

Regional airline associations have tended, in many cases to achieve a level of cooperation which has been in advance of government aviation cooperation. One should not be surprised at this, since - as I have already suggested - operational and commercial needs are urgent and constant.

One of the ironies of the situation - certainly in Europe - is that, now that the government regional cooperation has "caught up" with the airlines' own efforts, the very economic viability and existence of some of those airlines is being called into question.

A leaner and potentially more hungry international aviation will emerge from today's Europe. As it will emerge from Asia and South America. As it *may* emerge from Africa. As it has *already* emerged from the United States.

Looking at this, I am reminded of the fact that *"variable geometry"* is not something confined to the design of aircraft! The concept can apply equally well to regions and to membership of institutions and alliances.

We all have our ideas as to what works and what does not work. What is outward-looking and what is parochial. The past provides many examples of how perceived self-interest, unrelated to aviation, can render aviation cooperation untenable.

Around the world, airlines are flying at different heights, at different speeds - both operationally *and* politically. *But*, they are flying in the same atmosphere of market forces and global regulatory pressure. And they are flying in the same general direction.

In this world environment, it seems to make eminent sense for the aviation regulatory framework to be entrusted to the only two international organisations with both the required expertise and the world-wide coverage. WTA and ICAO. To facilitate the transition to a more liberalized economic regulation in civil aviation, ICAO, as a follow up of the 1994 worldwide air transport conference, is now providing states with useful guidance on new regulatory arrangements that ensure progressive changes towards market access, effective and sustained participating, and fair competition in international air transport.

Incidentally, I sometimes hear views expressed that these worldwide international organisations are ineffective because they have no mandatory powers. This is nonsense. If they had these powers, many States, including some of the most industrialised, would withdraw when some regulations adopted would be contrary to their national rules or interests. Consequently, these international organisations would then lose all credibility.

By proposing, recommendations, policy principles, guidelines, manuals, codes of conduct etc., the effectiveness of which is, of course, much more limited, they nevertheless preserve the necessary ingredients for a worldwide system, albeit based on consensus.

IATA considers that the application of GATT trade principles per se - such as mfn and national treatment - to civil aviation would result in a fundamental change to the existing bilateral air transport system which serves well the development of international air transport. Should any initiative be agreed by State to examine whether some different trade concepts should be applied to international air transport, IATA believes that the industry's special legal, technical and commercial features would have to be taken into account and that ICAO could make a positive contribution in this regard.

The last ICAO Assembly in 1995, in its Resolution A31-12 has requested the Council to promote an effective cooperation and coordination among ICAO, the WTO and other inter governmental and non-governmental organisations dealing with trade in services. IATA strongly supports this course of action and hopes it will be implemented soon.

I would also highly recommend that WTA and ICAO, in their essential role of catalyst between the different levels of air liberalization in the world, take into consideration the recent OECD Report on the future of international air transport policy, in particular the chapter 6 - perhaps not sufficiently highlighted by the authors - which deals with transition options in international air transport.

*****

In conclusion, I don't think anyone is seriously suggesting that there should be *no* regulation. After all, I was reliably informed, the *de*-regulation bible in the US was thicker than the regulation bible that it replaced!

At the same time, few would suggest that revision is not needed.

Such revision would probably result in a cocktail of bilateral, regional and multilateral agreements in the years ahead, as the aviation world continues its transition to true multilateralism. What should be avoided is any initiative which would increase the divisions between the developed and developing countries and create protectionist reflexes from the smallest countries or group of countries and therefore impair the prospects for liberalization in air transport. Finally, some elements, not unique but peculiar to the air transport industry (defense, safety/security, tourism, social services), should be given appropriate consideration.

Therefore what we need is a cocktail. A fruit salad. Something made up. Something messy. Not quite one thing or the other in order to ensure the coexistence of different regulatory regimes. Certainly. In fact, something very like the real world of continuing liberalisation and global competition!

Such revision would need to encompass, at the very least, as recommended by the OECD:

- Consistent application of competition policy to air transport.
- Encouragement of airline privatisation
- Gradual reduction of restrictions on foreign ownership of airlines.
- Efficient management of air transport infrastructure - with encouragement of private funding, but with safeguards against abuse of monopoly positions.

This sort of thing may be rather more prosaic than the grand vision attempted in Chicago in 1944 and at various other locations since. But it does have the virtue of practical relevance to a mature worldwide industry, embarked on its second fifty years of growth, but with its true potential and destiny unfulfilled in many parts of the world.

As you have seen, my approach is product-oriented rather than region-oriented, because a region-oriented system could result in blocks. Blocks imply an advance of that very protectionism which everyone wishes to avoid.

Paul Henri Spaak, a former Belgian Prime Minister used to say "we all live under the same sky - it is just our horizons that are different". As far as air liberalization is concerned, we should endeavour to bring those horizons a little closer together.

12 ARE FIXED-FORM REGRESSION MODELS EVER CREDIBLE ? SOME EVIDENCE FROM TRANSPORTATION STUDIES

Marc Gaudry

12.1 INTRODUCTION : TWO-STAGE DEMAND MODELLING AS A FRAMEWORK

We need a convenient framework to discuss the importance of functional form considerations in regression models, particularly those used in transport demand analysis, and provide a background for the presentation of advances in this area and demonstrations of their relevance. Two-stage demand models provide it because their key distinct components, models of levels and probabilistic or share models, cover much of the practical regression field in Economics and Transportation.

12.2 MAKING TOTAL DEMAND RESPONSIVE TO NETWORK CONDITIONS

Until the early 1960's, it was the practice to explain modal trip demand between any two points by breaking up the problem among at least 3 different steps : if we neglect the problem of service or path choice by mode, the steps involved the successive explanation of (i) total trips produced (T_i) or attracted (T_j) at a point, (ii) the total interzonal flow (T_{ij}) and (iii) the demand by mode ($T_{ij\ m}$). Although these steps were linked in the sense that the result from each became an input to the next one, they « could not reflect the fact that improved transportation performance by one mode or the introduction of a new mode would induce increased total demand for transportation between the two points » (Crow *et al.*, 1971). Two streams of models arose in order to obtain more reasonable overall properties.

12.2.1 Fixed-Form Single-Stage or Direct Models : 1963-1969

Utility is not separable. One-step models attempted to explain the demand by mode (T_{ijm}) directly, that is by writing a single equation where appear, denoted by A_i and A_j, various activities at the origin or destination (usually functions of Population and Employment or Output) and the U_{ijm}, or Generalized costs of the modes (usually functions of modal characteristics such as fares, travel time or frequency, and sometimes of socio-economic factors like income) :

$$T_{ijm} = f\,(A_i, A_j, U_{ij1}, \ldots, U_{ijM}) \quad , \mathrm{m}=1, \ldots, \mathrm{M} \qquad (1)$$

These models, such as Kraft (1963), were in the spirit of microeconomic demand models, attempting to make the demand for one good depend on the prices of all goods, or at least of prices of close substitutes. A branch developed to forecast the demand for « new modes » and included the famous Quandt and Baumol (1966) « abstract mode » model and its successors (Young, 1969), obtained by imposing « genericity » constraints on the money and time coefficients of the modes.

Generalized costs and mode-abstractness. Two specificities of transportation had to be incorporated. Firstly, the fact that money costs (prices) must be complemented by time costs (service levels) to obtain credible results, a requirement that often increased colinearity and probably also covered (Dagenais and Gaudry, 1986) still unresolved specification issues related to time variables, forced many modelers to use restrictions on signs in estimation procedures. Secondly, the resilience of « mode specificity », easily established by relaxing the genericity coefficient constraints embodying « abstractness ».

12.2.2 Fixed-Form Two-Stage or Quasi-Direct Models : 1968-1971

Breaking up the problem—in effect a 3-component structure. The second stream formulated two-step three-component models, namely products of two coupled models where the first one explains the total demand for all modes but includes a measure of the utility of all modes, U_{ij}, and the second one « splits » this demand with a mode choice model. The coupling arises from the fact that the overall utility measure is the denominator of the mode split model :

$$T_{ijm} = T_{ij} \bullet p_{ijm}. \qquad (2)$$

or, more explicitly :

$$T_{ijm} = f\,(A_i, A_j, U_{ij}) \bullet \left\{U_{ijm} \Big/ \sum_m U_{ijm}\right\}, \text{ m= 1, ..., M} \quad (3)$$

with

$$U_{ij} = \sum_m U_{ijm} . \quad (4)$$

These models rapidly produced results that were reasonable without resorting to constraints on regression signs. They were estimated in two separate steps for practical reasons, a situation that has not changed due to computing costs : the only known exception is Laferrière's (1988, 1998) demonstration of statistical gains from joint estimation in his quasi-direct model of the demand for air travel by itinerary, where the total demand for air travel is multiplied by an itinerary choice model.

Multiplicative throughout. The series of two-step models that starts with McLynn *et al.* (1968), used multiplicative forms in all functions of (3). Dropping *ij* subscripts, neglecting both constants and errors, these models can be written less abstractly if we denote any activity variable by A_a, any socio-economic variable by S_s and any modal network characteristic by N_n :

$$T = \prod_a A_a^{\beta_a} \; U^{\beta_U} \qquad \text{a = 1, ..., F} \quad (5)$$

$$U = \sum_m U_m \qquad \text{m = 1, ..., M} \quad (6)$$

$$U_m = \prod_n N_n^{\beta_{mn}} \prod_s S_s^{\beta_{ms}} . \qquad \text{n = 1, ..., G} \quad (7)$$

In spirit and form, these models, such as those by McLynn and Woronka (1969) are quite close to the contemporaneous quasi-direct multiplicative model written by Armington (1969) to explain international trade flows : the trade flow literature had to specify forms in which each commodity (like a modal flow) was traded everywhere and in both directions (in spite of the theory of comparative advantage) in quantities that depended on all individual commodity prices. To achieve these ends, the trade literature used *a priori* restrictions on the coefficients (written as elasticities of substitution) and extremely simple specifications, typically collapsing all characteristics of goods into a single variable (price) in (7) and the whole structure of the economy into a single activity (GNP) in (5). A recent application of such a quasi-direct multiplicative trade model to the demand for air travel—requiring the inclusion of other network variables than price—is that by Gillen *et al.* (1998).

The linear Logit as a component. The only exception to the use of a multiplicative form within a recognisable quasi-direct model is Blackburn who, in the most tractable version of his model (1969), made use of a linear-in-variables exponential form of (7), effectively writing a linear Logit model :

$$U_m = exp(V_m) \tag{8}$$

$$V_m = \beta_{m0} + \sum_n \beta_{mn} N_{mn} + \sum_s \beta_{ms} S_s . \tag{9}$$

This classical linear Logit model had been used first by Warner (1962) as a binary mode choice model using individual (discrete or disaggregate) observations, studied by Cox (1970) and Ellis and Rassam (1970) and first linked to utility theory by Rassam *et al.* (1970, 1971) in a multinomial application with share (aggregate) data, a linkage later completed by Domencich and McFadden (1975). The model can also be obtained from other random processes : as a by-product of Wilson's (1967) derivation of the Gravity model as most likely arrangement under a total cost constraint ; from the asymptotic theory of extremes (Leonardi, 1982) ; by rearrangement of Theil's « rational random demand » (1975)—as pointed out by Truong (1981)—or for that matter from any process where maximisation involves taking the derivative of natural logarithms , such as entropy maximisation or information minimisation !

We will limit our discussion to the multinomial Logit model and neglect more complicated nested constructs because they are not central to our purpose here. Also, applications of the disaggregate Logit model to frequency and destination choice were late in coming and much more difficult than applications to the choice of mode : in that sense, the Logit model has become the workhorse of mode choice analysis but has yet to demonstrate its advantages over aggregate models in generation-distribution models—were that ever to be the case, it will be our implicit point that such a demonstration would not be credible without due consideration of functional forms.

12.2.3 Unification of Quasi-Direct Models—The Power of Flexible Forms : 1976-1981

Nesting previous models in a general form. These various models were compared as nested special cases of a quasi-direct model by Gaudry and Wills (1977, 1978) through the use of Box-Tukey and Box-Cox (1964) direct power transformations, defined with parameters λ_κ and μ_k on the positive variable X_k as in Table 1.

Although both the BC and BT forms are found in that 1964 paper, the expression « Box-Cox transformation » had come to denote only the BC form in common parlance, because Box and Cox had not found the shift parameter μ_k to be statistically significant : this limited its role to that of insuring that the variable considered becomes strictly positive before being raised to the power λ_κ . The absence of any other interpretation of this shift parameter also contributed to its falling into disuse and to the BC form progressively becoming the most widely used monotonic transformation of variables in applied work (Davidson and MacKinnon, 1993). The Gaudry and Wills paper demonstrated that the shift parameter, reintroduced under the name « Box-Tukey », could be statistically significant when applied to *variables* of the 4 time-series and cross-sectional models considered. The paper did not yet provide for the Tukey shift parameter the new behavioural interpretation that was to come later (Gaudry, 1981) by considering the BCG and BTG inverse forms and applying them to complete *functions* U_m or V_m in (8). This application was conceived from the realization that one could not directly transform the dependent variable of a Logit model and easily maintain the requirement that the choice probabilities sum to one, but that one could achieve this result indirectly by using inverse transformations on the right-hand side U_m functions of this model. However, the paper showed in a number of ways the decisive practical importance of Box-Cox transformations in terms of model properties, data fit, parameter signs and values, to be summarised and elaborated on presently. Some questions pertaining to the numerical and statistical costs of form estimation will be addressed in a later section.

Table 1. Transformations defined by Box, Cox and Gaudry

Ref.	Box and Cox (1964)		Gaudry (1981)		
Def.	Direct Power Transformation (DPT) of X_k		Inverse Power Transformation (IPT) of Z_k		
Code	$X_k^{(\lambda_k, \mu_k)}$	Condition	$Z_k^{(\phi_k, \mu_k)^{-1}}$	Conditions	Code
BC	$\dfrac{X_k^{\lambda_k} - 1}{\lambda_k}$	$\lambda_k \neq 0,\ X_k > 0$	$(\phi_k Z_k + 1)^{1/\phi_k}$	$\phi_k \neq 0,\ (\phi_k Z_k + 1) > 0)$	BCG
	$\ln X_k$	$\lambda_k = 0,\ X_k > 0$	$\exp(Z_k)$	$\phi_k = 0,\ (Z_k > 0)$	
BT	$\dfrac{(X_k + \mu_k)^{\lambda_k} - 1}{\lambda_k}$	$\lambda_k \neq 0,\ (X_k + \mu_k) > 0)$	$(\phi_k Z_k + 1)^{1/\phi_k} - \mu_k$	$\phi_k \neq 0,\ (\phi_k Z_k + 1) > 0)$	BTG
	$\ln(X_k + \mu_k)$	$\lambda_k = 0,\ (X_k + \mu_k) > 0)$	$\exp(Z_k) - \mu_k$	$\phi_k = 0,\ (Z_k > 0)$	

<u>*Model specification and meaning*</u>. Quite naturally, using BC on variables will change the meaning or properties of models of all types. Interesting differences arise with respect to common practice.

« Models of levels ». In Economics, the BC had been used previously in « models of levels » — where the dependent variable y is strictly positive but otherwise unrestricted—precisely because it includes both linear ($\lambda_y = 1$) and logarithmic ($\lambda_y = 0$) cases in nested fashion, and one is often interested in testing whether the effects are additive, multiplicative or other in the following, where the observation indices are introduced and denoted by t :

$$y_t^{(\lambda_y)} = \sum_{k=1}^{K} \beta_k \cdot X_{kt}^{(\lambda_{X_k})} + u_t \,. \tag{10}$$

In our case, there is a particular interest in the utility term U in (5) because the index (11-A)

$$\left.\begin{aligned} &(A)\quad U^{(\lambda_U)} = \frac{(\sum_m e^{V_m})^{\lambda_U} - 1}{\lambda_U}\,, \\ &(B)\quad V_m = \beta_{m0} + \sum_n \beta_{mn} X_n^{(\lambda_{X_n})} + \sum_s \beta_{ms} X_s^{(\lambda_{X_s})} \end{aligned}\right\} \tag{11}$$

yields the Williams-McFadden (1977) log sum term as a special case if the Box-Cox transformation is such that $\lambda_U \to 0$ in (10) :

$$U^{\beta_U} \equiv \left\{\beta_U \, ln \, (\sum_m e^{V_m})\right\} . \tag{12}$$

As a matter of fact, the results obtained for 1972 intercity Canadian flows were extremely close to the natural logarithm of the U variable constructed from 4 modal utility functions with 3 network variables, each having its own λ_k (and also sharing a μ_k not shown in (11-B)) ; for the other activity variables, they were different from both 0 and 1 and amply justified the general specification (10). This demonstration was useful because of the prevalence, in transportation, of multiplicative forms for generation-distribution models. Kau and Sirmans (1979) worked at the same time on a more limited application to a gravity model. In split models, the term (12) becomes the key coupling mechanism in the hierarchical logit model and advanced models even weigh its components (Mandel, 1998).

Outside of transportation, *a priori* multiplicative forms continue to be used without further testing, even in areas like trade modelling where gravity models (with a U term reduced to a simplistic distance proxy measure) are prevalent : Gaudry *et al.* (1996) appear to provide the first challenge to these practices, using intra-European and intra-North American trade flows.

« Probabilistic and Share models ». The BC had not been used previously in Logit models. The so-called « standard Box-Cox Logit » used in the Gaudry and Wills paper was shown to be a powerful general form naturally including both the standard linear Logit model and the multiplicative form (7) of the classical marketing and of the mode split literatures, where it was used simply or with additional restrictions on the β_{mn} in many quasi-direct models. In addition to this classification role, the « standard Box-Cox Logit » also possesses more reasonable properties than the popular linear form. Indeed, the non-linear Box-Cox form (i) makes the effect of a network improvement depend on the level of the characteristic, as shown in Table 2 : this means that the impact of a 10 minute change in travel time is not the same for a short and for a long trip...; (ii) makes derived marginal rates of substitution between time and money (values of time) vary both across modes (due at least to different sample levels of the characteristics) and with the amount of time saved. The standard Box-Cox Logit therefore avoids much market segmentation used to obtain reasonable and variable trade-offs by distance, income, etc.

Table 2. Non Constant Returns in a Box-Cox Logit Model

	$\frac{\partial U_m}{\partial X_{mk}} = \beta_{mk} X_{mk}^{(\lambda_{mk}-1)}$	$\frac{\partial U_m^2}{\partial X_{mk}^2} = \beta_{mk}(\lambda_{mk}-1) X_{mk}^{(\lambda_{mk}-2)}$	Returns
$\lambda=-1$	β_{mk}/X_{mk}^2	$-2\beta_{mk}/X_{mk}^3$	Decreasing
$\lambda=0$	β_{mk}/X_{mk}	β_{mk}/X_{mk}^2	Decreasing
$\lambda=1$	β_{mk}	0	Constant
$\lambda=2$	$\beta_{mk}X_{mk}$	β_{mk}	Increasing

In retrospect, it is amazing that a model with constant marginal effects and additive utility would establish itself as a reference model anywhere and come to supersede more credible non-additive utility forms, e. g. the multiplicative one, without notice being taken of test results—that invariably lead to rejection of the linear Logit in favor of a form like the square root or the multiplicative, as one would expect on the basis of classical utility theory. Indeed, in passenger studies, Koppelman (1980), Hensher and Johnson (1981), Mandel (1992, 1998) and Mandel *et al.* (1997) have clearly shown the superiority of the Box-Cox Logit over the linear Logit in passenger studies. Applications to freight are extremely recent (Fridström and Madslien ,1995 ; Picard and Gaudry, 1998).

If more reasonable properties and meanings cannot change the habit of presenting models of untested form, what of other motivations concerning data fit and elasticities ?

Model fit and results in general. By definition, the relaxation of constraints in a model must improve the fit and likelihood ratio tests can be used to determine how significant these gains are. The best way to understand model fit is to graph the curves that are drawn by the estimation procedures as these can always be thought of as summarising the information by « fitting » a curve of some shape through the data. This is true in all models and can easily be illustrated in graphs showing the value of the dependent variable y against an explanatory variable X_k. We shall first discuss the issue of form by assuming that a BC is used on the dependent variable y and/or one or more independent variables X_k either in models of levels or in split models of the Logit type. In these cases, it is used as a monotonic transformation. We shall also say a few words about the use of BC to detect quadratic effects.

Form in models of levels. The many models that are special cases of the Box-Cox model of levels are defined in Figure 1 and shown in Figure 2 for these convenient homely forms. The linear form is used because of the convenient statistical properties derivable under linearity assumptions, despite the often heroic assumption that a consequence can be decomposed into linearly additive causes and the bother of calculating elasticities that depend on where the change is considered. The log-log form is used because it implies interaction among causes and constant elasticities. Naturally, the « cross » forms, the log-inverse (exponential) and the semi-log, are less used because they involve more work on the part of the researcher, due to the somewhat more complicated elasticity calculations : they are only worthwhile if the combinatorial game played by the analyst yields desired results only with this form.

There is in general no good reason to expect these pure cases to give the best adjustments to the data : as in Figures 3-4, « true » shapes may be anywhere between the linear and the semi-log case, or between the latter and the log-log case. There are now many sound examples demonstrating that the best fit is indeed often between the linear and log cases in a variety of transportation demand models.

Form in Logit models. It can be pointed out that, as shown[1] in Figure 5, the linear Logit model is symmetric with an inflexion point at probability equal to ½ : by contrast, the presence of non-linearity implies asymmetry of the response curve. Mandel *et al.* (1997) demonstrated how much impact this could have on market share gains following an improvement in a mode—in that case the German ICE network. Intuitively, a response curve is not likely to be symmetric : <u>a utility function cannot be credible without being demonstrated to be so !</u> For instance, using an excellent data set on mode choice in Santiago de Chile, Gaudry *et al.* (1989) find that, in linear form, the models has elasticities of in-vehicle time greater than elasticities of wait time, and values of time that fall as incomes rise ! These results correct themselves as soon as a BC is applied to all variables. Fiogures 6 to 8 show further form issues that can be addressed by other generalisations of the Logit model obtained by the application of the BCG or the BTG to this model.

Further unpublished work on these data (Pong, 1991) also showed that the Train-McFadden (1978) goods/leisure trade-off assumed in this model, represented by the ratio of modal cost to income, is easily rejected for a more general specification, where each term is self-standing, for all functional forms except the linear—itself completely dominated by more general BC forms that also imply more reasonable

---

[1] Figures 1-4 are minor reeditions of overhead sheets drawn from A. Blanquier's presentation « Using the TRIO Level 1.4 Algorithm at *SETEC-économie*», Ecole Nationale des Ponts et Chaussées (ENPC), Paris, October 25, 1993.

trade-offs (marginal rates of substitution) between time and money, so-called values of time.

Asymmetric quadratic effects on form. We note that if, in a model of the level class such as (13), a variable X is used both linearly and with a BC, $\lambda_X = 2$ yields the normal symmetric (integer=2) quadratic form and any other value (except 1) yields an asymmetric U-shaped form (see Figure 9) independently from the value of λ_y, if the two regression coefficients are of opposite signs (with the conditions for a maximum or minimum reversed depending on whether the BC on X is smaller or greater than 1)—a result (Gaudry, 1996), that should also hold *mutatis mutandis* in a Logit model :

$$y^{(\lambda_y)} = \beta_0 + \beta_1 X + \beta_2 X^{(\lambda_X)} + u. \qquad (13)$$

Figure 1. Box-Cox Models of Levels: Four Nested Classical Models

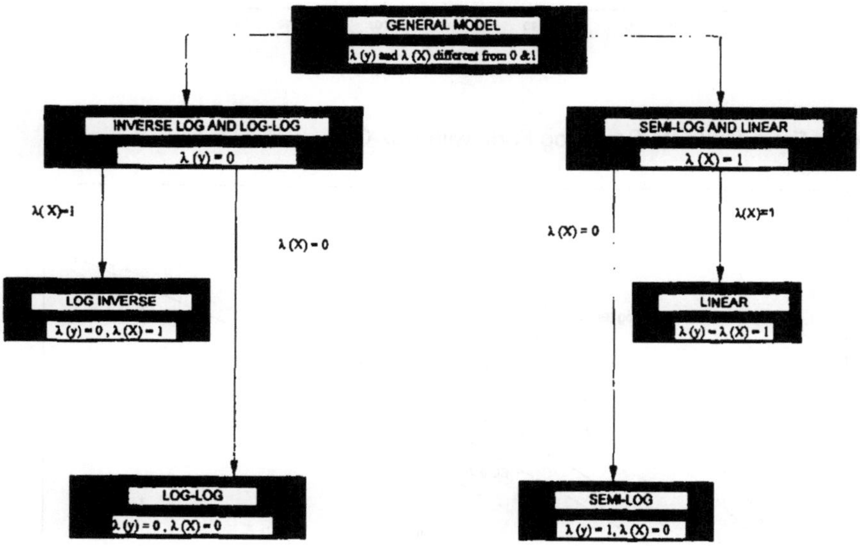

Figure 2. Four Classical Shapes in Linear Regression

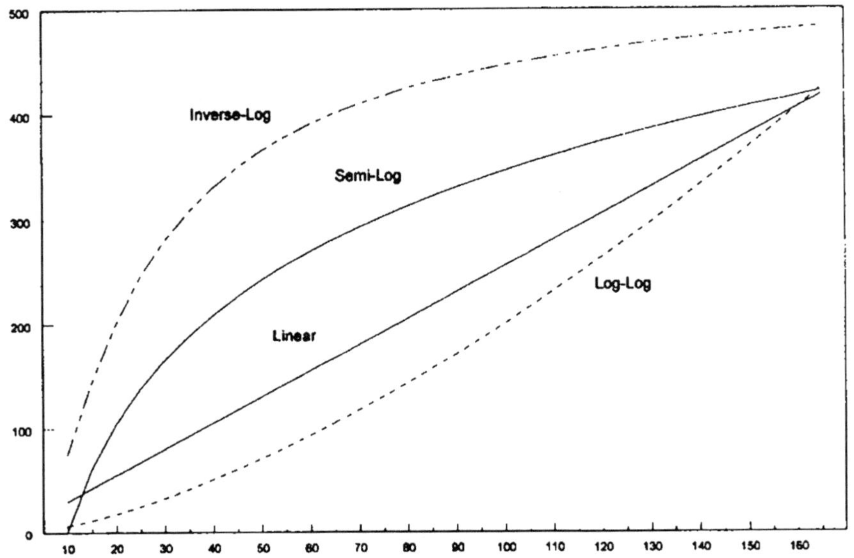

Figure 3. From Linear to Semi-Log Form with Box-Cox

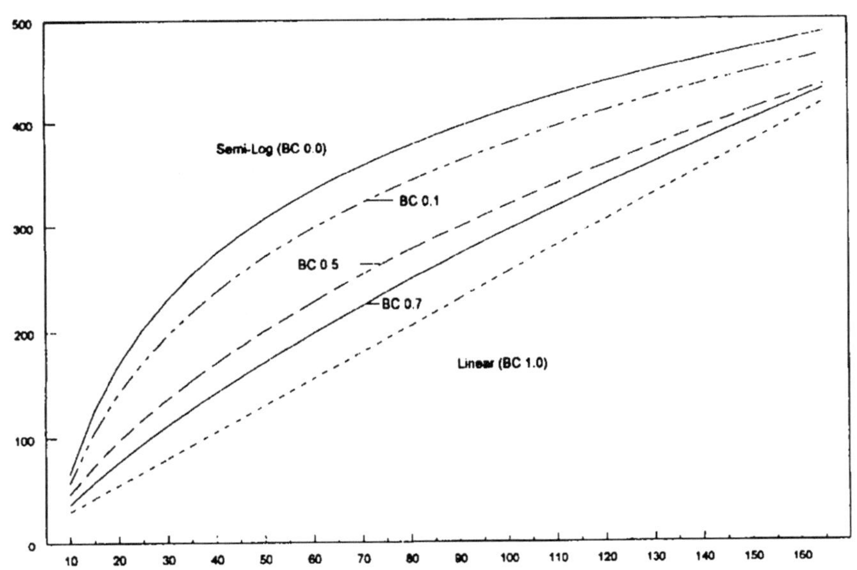

Figure 4. From Log-Log to Semi-Log Form with Box-Cox

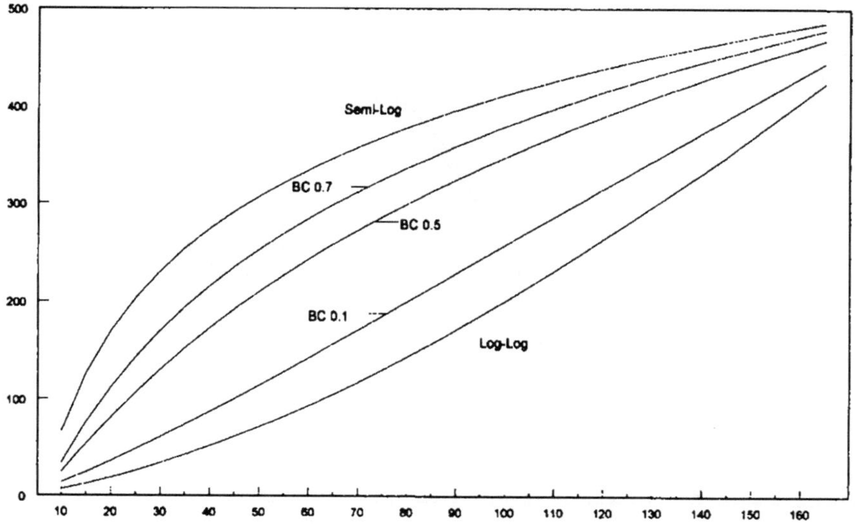

Figure 5. Linear-Logit vs Box-Cox-Logit

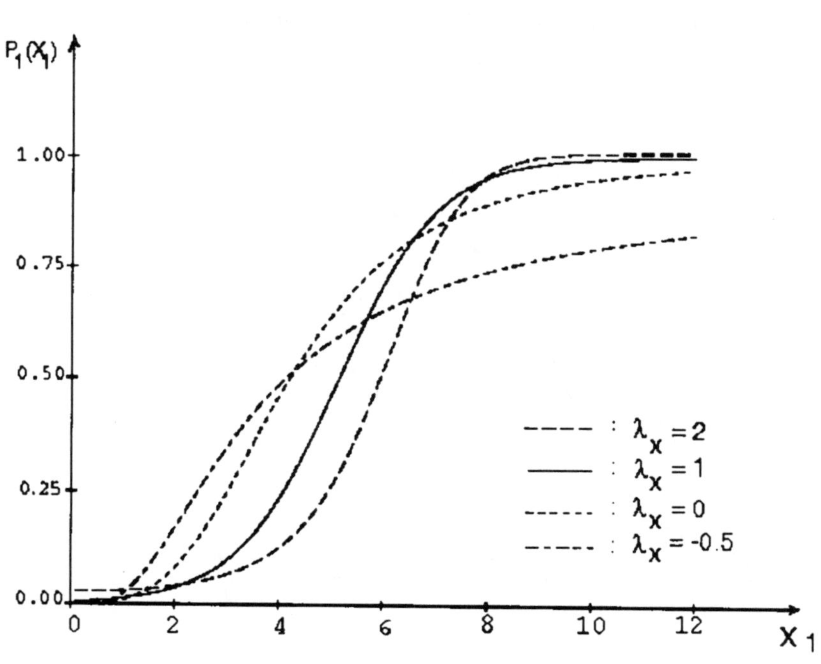

Figure 6. Linear-Logit vs Standard-Dogit

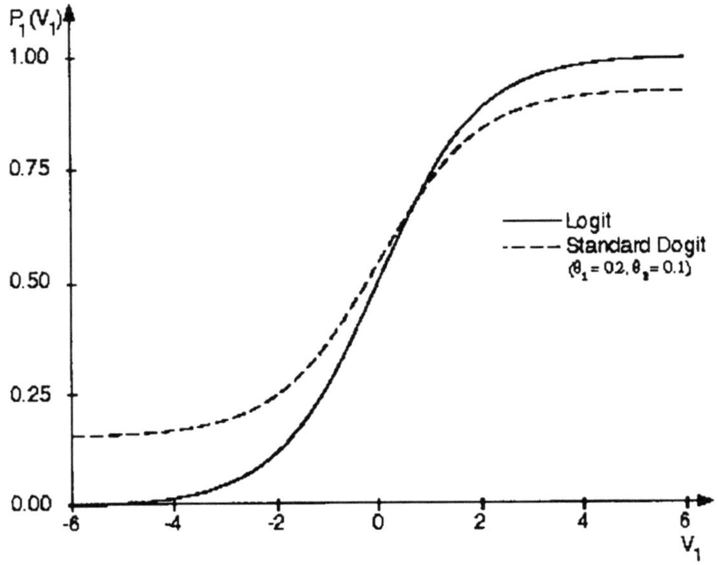

Figure 7. Linear-Logit vs Linear-Inverse-Power-Transformation-Logit

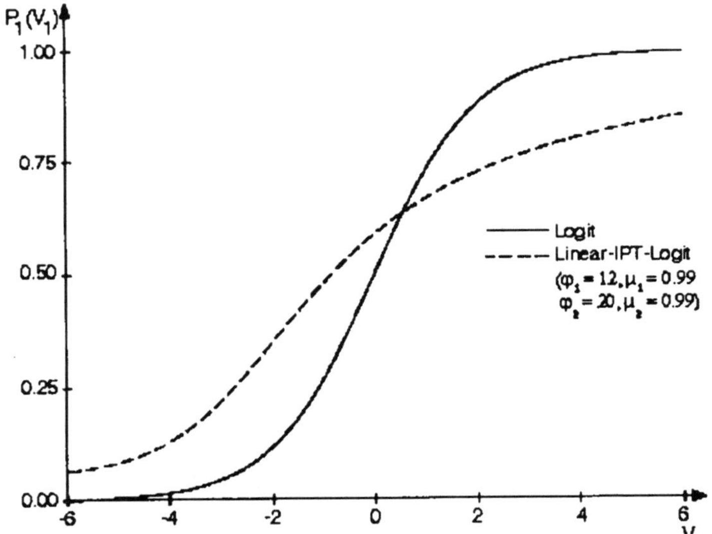

Figure 8. Linear-Logit vs Box-Tukey-Inverse-Power-Transformation-Logit

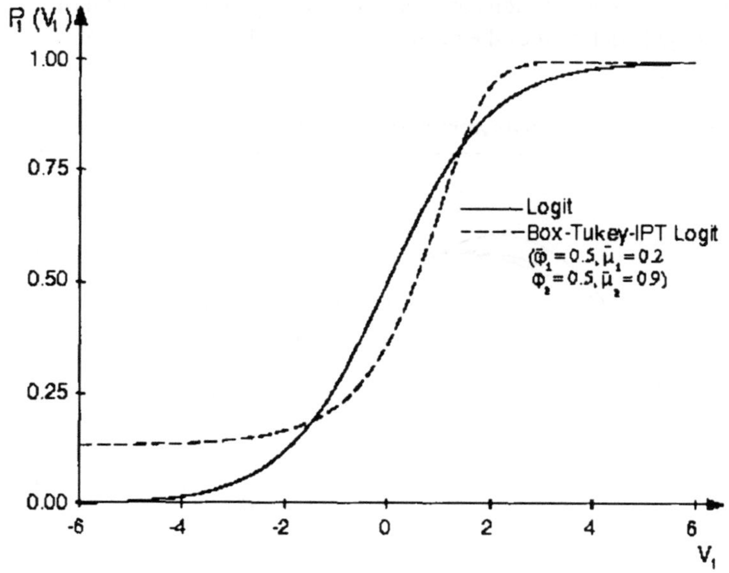

<u>*Changing form can change regression signs*</u>. As just implied by statements about results in general, elasticities will differ from what they would have been had a non-optimal form been used. The 1978 paper showed this with graphs of elasticities changing continuously with the BC parameters. But it also showed what practitioners had long known : changing the functional form can change *not only the size of coefficients, but also their sign* ! In multivariate models, because regressors are not generally orthogonal (uncorrelated) in any form, the sign obtained for a given variable depends on the covariances among regressors—depends on the functional form used. In the paper, this was demonstrated with models of levels but is also true of split models. There are many examples of such sign reversals even in published articles.

Signs in « Models of levels ». Despite this clear visual demonstration of signs changing with the functional form used, many papers have been written during the last 20 years after using a « by hand » search for the for the form that gives the *desired* results. For instance, in a recent study of the impact of competition on the dispersion of prices charged by airlines, the authors (Borenstein and Rose, 1994) obtain positive and significant signs for 3 of their crucial variables (pertaining to the degree of competition among airlines) when the model is linear, but negative and significant signs when the model is multiplicative (log-linear); they then accept the linear model without formal tests of the appropriate form, preferring to ignore that such tests might well invalidate their preferred finding, perhaps by revealing a point between the linear and logarithmic cases, and *insignificant* results , or even a point not too far from the log-linear point...and *contrary to their expectations*! Mind you, the same issues arise outside of transportation as well as in other domains of application : for instance, Blum and Gaudry (1990) show that, in the discussion on the impact of social security contributions on household savings, the very form of the savings function largely determines the results obtained and the *direction* of influence of the variables.

Figure 9. From Symmetric ($\lambda_x = 2$) to Asymmetric ($\lambda_x \neq 2$) Quadratic Forms

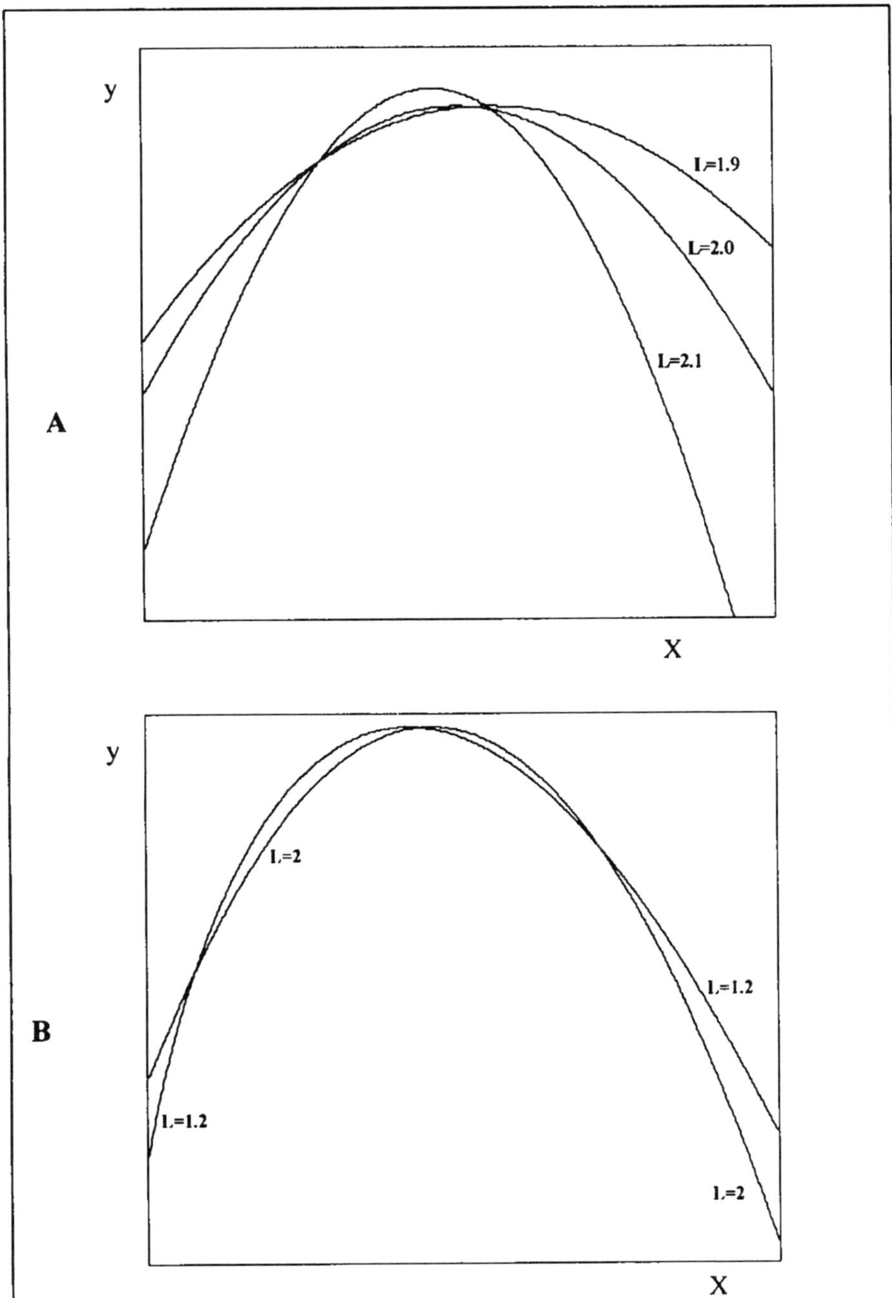

Signs in Logit models. The demonstration of robustness of regression signs is also crucial in Logit models. A few years ago, Gaudry (1985) reproduced the linear Logit results obtained by R.A.T.P. and Cambridge Systematics (1982) using a first rate data base on Paris work trips (Moïsi *et al.*, 1981) and easily showed, using only one BC transformation that dramatic gains in fit could be achieved with an optimal BC value at mid-point between 0 and 1 but that, at that point, the parking cost variables obtained an « incorrect » sign in the R.A.T.P.'s favourite model that had required two years of work....More recently, Fridström and Madslien (1995) obtain the correct sign on transport time in a Logit model as soon as they use BC transformations.

It is well known that practitioners arbitrarily play with the functional form until they obtain desired results. It is therefore hard to resist this recent « Proposition PF-1 on Form » :

PF-1 : Models of untested functional form are not credible, irrespective of the economic or other theory on which they are based. Such tests, applied to many current models using predetermined monotonic forms would show that the models are not robust. This is true irrespective of the kind of data used : revealed and stated preference data, experimental data...(Gaudry, 1998b)

References

Armington, P., « A Theory of Demand for Products Distinguished by Place of Production », International Monetary Fund Staff Papers, 159-176, 1969.

Blackburn, A.J., « Estimation of the Behavioral Model », in Studies in Travel Demand, Vol. V, Mathematica, March 1969.

Blum, U.C. and M. Gaudry, "The Impact of Social Security Contributions on Savings: an Analysis of German Households by Category Using Flexible Econometric Forms". Jahrbuch für Sozialwissenschaft 41, 2, 217-242, 1990.

Borenstein, S, and N.L. Rose, « Competition and Price Dispersion in the U.S. Airline Industry », Journal of Political Economy 102. 4, 653-683, 1994.

Box, G.P. and D.R. Cox, « An Analysis of Transformations », Journal of the Royal Statistical Society, Series B, 26, 211-243, 1964.

Cox, D.R., Analysis of Binary Data, Methuen's Monographs on Applied Probability and Statistics, Methuen, London, 1970.

Crow, R., Young, K.H. and T. Cooley, « Models of Intercity Travel Demand. Part I. Theoretical Aspects », Mathematica, Inc., Princeton, New Jersey, for the Northeast Corridor Transportation Project, Department of Transportation, Washington, D.C., NTIS PB 201 206, 86 p., June 1971.

Dagenais, M. and M. Gaudry, "Can Aggregate Direct Travel Demand Models Work?", Proceedings of the World Conference on Transport Research, The

Center for Transportation Studies, University of British Columbia, Vancouver, 1669-1676, 1986.

Davidson, R. and J.G. MacKinnon, «Transforming the Dependent Variable », Ch. 14 in Estimation and Inference in Econometrics , Oxford University Press, 1993.

Domencich, T. and D. McFadden, Urban Travel Demand : A Behavioral Analysis, North Holland, Amsterdam, 1975.

Ellis, R. H. and P.R. Rassam, « National Intercity Travel : Develoment and Implementation of a Demand Forecasting Framework » , U.S. Dept. of Transportation Contract T-8 542, Modification No. 1, National Technical Information Service PB 192 455, U. S. Dept. of Commerce, March 1970.

Fridström, L. and A. Madslien, « A Stated Preference Analysis of Wholesalers' Freight Choice », Institute of Transport Economics, Oslo, 35 p., 1995.

Gaudry, M. "The Inverse Power Transformation Logit and Dogit Mode Choice Models", Publication CRT-96, Centre de recherche sur les transports, Université de Montréal, and Transportation Research B 15, 2, 97-103, 1981.

Gaudry, M., "Modèles agrégés et désagrégés à forme variable: résultats sur Montréal et Paris", Transports 304, 288-293, 1985.

Gaudry, M., « FIQ : Fractional and Integer Quadratic Forms Estimated in TRIO », Manuscript, Centre de recherche sur les transports, Université de Montréal, 8 p., November 1996.

Gaudry, M. « Some Perspectives on the DRAG Approach and Family of National Road Safety Models », Publication CRT-98-07, Centre de recherche sur les transports, Université de Montréal. Also Working Paper N° 9808, Bureau d'économie théorique et appliquée (BETA), Université Louis Pasteur, 1998. Forthcoming in the Proceedings of The Third Annual Conference on Transportation, Traffic Safety and Health, 1998b.

Gaudry, M., Blum, U. and J. McCallum, "A First Gross Measure of Unexploited Single Market Integration Potential". In S. Urban, ed., Europe's Challenges, Gabler Verlag, 449-461, 1996.

Gaudry, M., Jara-Diaz, S.R. and J. de D. Ortuzar, "Value of Time Sensitivity to Model Specification", Transportation Research B 23, 2, 151-158, 1989.

Gaudry, M. and M.J. Wills, "Estimating the Functional Form of Travel Demand Models", Publication CRT-63, Centre de recherche sur les transports, et Cahier 7702, Département de sciences économiques, Université de Montréal, juin 1977, and Transportation Research 12, 4, 257-289, 1978.

Gillen, D., Harris, R. and T. Oum, « Evaluating Air Liberalization Agreements : An Integration of Demand Analysis and Trade Theory », Forthcoming in Gaudry, M. and R. Mayes, eds, Taking Stock of Air Liberalization, Kluwer Academic Press, 1998.

Hensher, D.A. and Johnson, L.W., « Behavioural response and form of the representative component of the indirect utility function in travel mode choice », Regional Science and Urban Economics, 11, 559-572, 1981.

Kau, J.B. and C.F. Sirmans, « The Functional Form of the Gravity Model », International Regional Science Review, 4, 127-136, 1979.

Koppelman, F.S., « Nonlinear Utility Functions in Models of Travel Choice Behavior », The Transportation Center, Northwestern University, 37 p., May 1980.

Kraft, G., « Demand for Intercity Passenger Travel in the Washington-Boston Corridor », Part V, Northeast Corridor Project, U.S. Department of Transportation, 1963.

Laferrière, R., « Une Agrégation Nouvelle des Itinéraires de Transport Aérien (ANITA) », Publication CRT-574, Centre de recherche sur les transports, Université de Montréal, 106 p., Février 1988.

Laferrière, R., «The Air Network Itinerary and Trip Aggregation (ANITA) Model », Forthcoming in Gaudry, M. and R. Mayes, eds, Taking Stock of Air Liberalization, Kluwer Academic Press, 1998.

Leonardi, G., « The Structure of Random Utility Models in the Light of the Asymptotic Theory of Extremes », WP-82-91, International Institute for Applied Systems Analysis, 45 p., September 1982.

Mandel, B., Schnellverkehr und ModalSplit, Nomos Verlag, Baden Baden, 1992.

Mandel, B., « The Interdependency of Airport Choice and Travel Demand », Forthcoming in Gaudry, M. and R. Mayes, eds, Taking Stock of Air Liberalization, Kluwer Academic Press, 1998.

Mandel, B., Gaudry, M. and W. Rothengatter, "A Disaggregate Box-Cox Logit Mode Choice of Intercity Passenger Travel in Germany and its Implications for High Speed Rail Demand Forecasts". The Annals of Regional Science 31, 2, 99-120, 1997.

McLynn, J.M., Goldman, A.J., Meyers, P.R. and R.H. Watkins, « Analysis of a Market Split Model », Journal of Research of the National Bureau of Standards, 72-B, #1, 1968.

McLynn, J.M., and T. Woronka, « A Family of Demand and Mode Split Models », Arthur Young and Co., April 1969.

Moïsi, F., Raison, M. and L. Silman, « A Mode-Split Model with Multiple Transit Modes », Proceedings of the PTRC Summer Annual Meeting, 1981.

Picard, G. and M. Gaudry, "Exploration of a Box-Cox Logit Model of Intercity Freight Mode Choice", Transportation Research E, 34, 1, 1-12, 1998.

Pong, S. « L'application du modèle probabiliste et la transformation de Box-Cox au choix du mode de transport au Chili », Thèse de Maîtrise, Département de sciences économiques, Université de Montréal, 1991.

R.A.T.P. et Cambridge Systematics, « Etudes de politiques de transport en région Ile-de-France. Mise au point et utilisation de modèles désagrégés de choix modal ». R.A.T.P., Direction des études générales, Service GL, 53ter Quai des Grands Augustins, Paris 6ème, juin 1982.

Quandt, R.E. and Baumol, W.J., « « The Demand for Abstract Transport Modes : Theory and Measurement », Journal of Regional Science, 6, 2, 13-26, 1966.

Rassam, P. R., Ellis, R.H. and J.C. Bennett, « The N-Dimensional Logit Model : Development and Application », Peat Marwick and Mitchell & Co, Washington, D.C., 42p., 1970. Also in Highway Research record, 369, 135-147, 1971.

Theil, H., « The Theory of Rational Random Behaviour and its Application to Demand Analysis », European Economic Review, 6, 217-226, 1975.

Train, K.E. and D. McFadden, « The Goods/Leisure Trade-Off and Disaggregate Work Trip Mode Choice Models », Transportation Research 12, 5, 349-353, 1978.

Truong, T. P., « A Theoretical Analysis of Choice Demand and Time Allocation : with Reference to Travel », Ph. D. Thesis, School of Economics and Financial Studies, Macquarie University, 282 p., December 1981.

Warner, S.L., Stochastic Choice of Mode in Urban Travel : A Study in Binary Choice, Northwestern University Press, Evanston, Ill., 1962.

Williams, H.C.W.L., « On the Formation of Travel Demand Models and Economic Evaluation Measures of User Benefit ». Environment and Planning, 9a(3), 285-344, 1977.

Wilson, A., « A Statistical Theory of Spatial Distribution Models », Transportation Research, 1, 253-269, 1967.

Young, K. H., « An Abstract Mode Approach to the Demand for Travel », Transportation Research, 3, 443-461, 1969.

13 THE INTERDEPENDENCY OF AIRPORT CHOICE AND TRAVEL DEMAND

Benedikt N. Mandel

13.1 INTRODUCTION

It is necessary to embed air forecasting in a in framework of relevant relationships that include and take into account the whole transport market as well as demographic, economic, political, spatial and technical components. Figure 1 gives an idea of the considered determinants.

Figure 1. System Approach

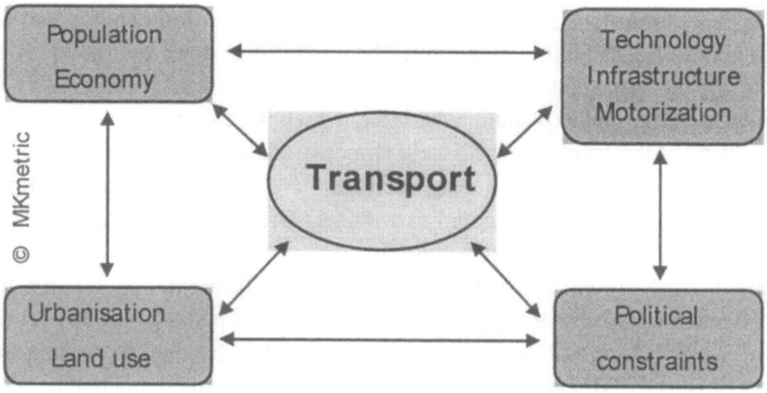

A modelling process based on these interrelationships explains the transport market by multimodal and multisectoral determinants. This form ensures the consistency of the whole model system in every step of the simulation process. Considering detailed exogenous impact factors as population, economic and political circumstances, technical development and spatial structures the models always process balanced figures of all endogenous measures. Hence, no transport activity appears or disappears unexplained within the system. Changes in the system's state are substitutive or complementary and synergetic effects, as well as competition, lead to new situations concerning diversion, accessibility or attractiveness. These effects can be analysed with respect to modes (e.g. road, rail, sea, air) and/or trip purposes (e.g. business, vacation, private).

13.2 SYSTEM APPROACH

In the light of the complex problems stated above it is obvious that the airport choice model has to be embedded in some sort of model explaining total trip making by all modes and a sort of model explaining the choice of mode for a trip. It is convenient to postulate, for the sake of discussion, the existence of an aggregate generation-distribution model: this corresponds to frequent practice and the points that should be made about an ideal specification also hold when disaggregate generation-distribution specifications are used. In addition the existence of an disaggregate mode choice model based on a logistic function, say a logit-model, has to be assumed so that the consumer elasticities in respect to the alternative modes can be identified. Some additional models are needed to face the problems of access/egress choice to the airports and slot choice to explain the consumers selection of departure time. Last but not least, assignment procedures are needed to compute based on the infrastructure networks of all modes, impedances which reflect the attractiveness of each alternative. Figure 2 shows the steps of air transport forecast and the context of the different models.

To encounter the effects from one decision level to the other, say from mode choice to generation-distribution or from airport choice to mode choice and further on to generation-distribution, one links the modelling steps by the quasi-direct format using the representative utility function of the lower level models in the upper ones as additional explanatory variable, which we call modal utility index *U*.

In addition at the level of the discrete choice models the explanatory impedance variables used in the model specifications are computed considering the probabilities of the lower level model as weights. The idea of linking the models in the forecasting system is shown in Figure 3.

Applying this system approach, a consistent instrument can be constructed which reflects the impacts of supply changes through all instances at any level. The effects of supply changes at an airport (e.g. a new O-D service, increasing aircraft fees, low cost tariffs) can be analysed in detail. No matter whether this are intramodal impacts, say the competition of airports about market shares as well as the competition of different levels of service (non-stop versus via connections), or multimodal impacts, say the substitution of air traffic by inter city high-speed trains or car but also the vice versa case is possible due to the offers of low cost carriers, or intermodal impacts, say the co-operation of air and rail services on the access/egress side to/from the airport (like a lot of tourist companies already include in their price offers in form of rail&fly tickets). Therefore the interdependency of airport choice and travel demand can be analysed out of different point of views.

Figure 2. Steps of Air Transport Forecast

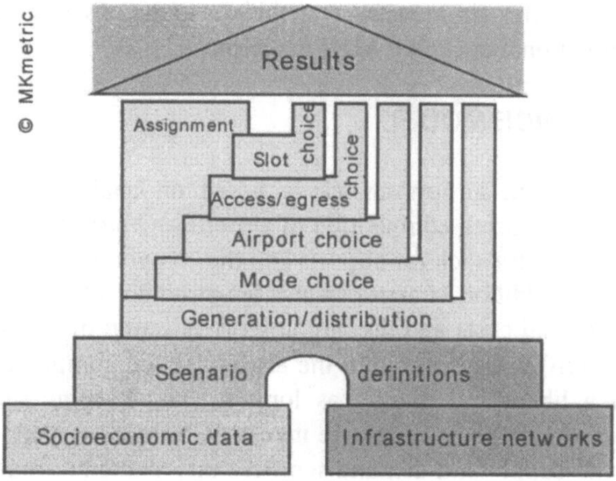

Figure 3. Linking the Models in the Forecasting System

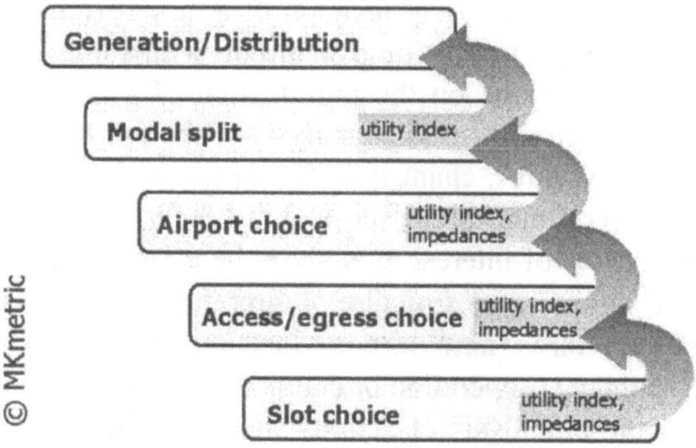

Instead of extending this paper by the theory of all modelling steps used in the system approach it is referred to various publications. A detailed theoretical background of the modelling steps is given by the following literature.

For the generation-distribution modelling it is referred to Gaudry-Mandel-Rothengatter 1994a, 1994b, Sen-Smith 1995 and Last 1997 and for the mode choice modelling see the publications of Mandel 1992, Mandel-Gaudry-Rothengatter 1991-1994-1997 and Mandel et al 1997. The more general focus of discrete choice modelling you'll find in Domencich-McFadden 1975, Manski-McFadden 1981 and

Ben-Akiva-Lerman 1985. The quasi-direct format is explained by Tran-Gaudry 1994. Concerning the assignment procedures there is a lot of literature therefore it is referred to a more general operations research summary of Neumann 1974 and a more transport oriented publication of Gallo-Pallottino-Florian 1984. For details of the assignment procedure used in the system approach see Last-Mandel 1997. As introduction an overview concerning all steps is given by Ortuzar-Willumsen 1990. Specific information concerning air transport is found in Doganis 1991-1992 and in several publications of the air industry and their associations like ICAO, IATA, CAC and ECAC or national ones like ADV in Germany.

13.3. AIRPORT CHOICE MODEL

The reason for modelling airport choice is based on analysing the consumer behaviour due to the increasing competition of airports and airlines in context to the ongoing liberalisation, bottlenecks at airports and the competing environment of the land based modes. In addition changes in the fee structure at airports due to the internalisation of external costs and the ongoing privatisation of airports as well as the changes in the tariff structure due to the already stated competition of airlines are of interest in a liberalised market as long as they become relevant to the consumer. The idea was to provide private investors, airlines, airports and political decision makers with supply and demand sensitive information to make the market more transparent to actions planned.

On the more political side the system can be used in the area of environmental policy (e.g. regulations), regional development and spatial planning. The latter encloses questions about the accessibility of single regions and its enhancement when improving the infrastructure (e.g. location of a new regional airport, build a new road link towards an airport or to equip an airport with a railway station).

For airlines the focus may be on the introduction of a new O-D service, the decrease or increase of tariffs, the market analysis of the existing air network or a future one considering new hubs, changes in the frequency of a service offered or the co-operation with other modes in the sense of rail & fly.

And for the airports it is of interest to analyse the effects of new O-D services, capacity constraints, changes in the structure of aircraft fees and passenger charges, investments in infrastructure (new airport location, high-speed train station, terminal or runway) and the co-operation or competition of airports.

Of course any of these analysis of actions stated can be used as input for an economic analysis.

13.3.1 Theory

On most flight journeys consumer have the opportunity to start their trip from more than just one single airport. Just in Germany - which fits into Quebec roughly 5 times - there are 16 international airports and several regional airports so that often the situation appears where the consumer can choose out of a whole bunch of alternatives all serving his needs in nearly the same way. So it often happens that there are more than four airports offering the same destination and in addition at each airport non-stop as well as via services are available. At least once the consumer evaluated the different opportunities he selects only one out of the available set of alternatives. This is a classical discrete choice problem. For details see the suggested literature about mode choice and discrete choice modelling in section 2 so that there is no need to go through the whole theory again.

Here the focus is on the differences of the chosen to the standard approach and the resulting advantages. To understand the issues in an easy way it will be referred to examples taken from the field of mode choice alternatives).

Properties of the linear standard model. The "classical" linear Logit model specification normally assumes (Gaudry 1992):

(i) linearity in variables;

(ii) the exclusion of characteristics of other alternatives $j \in C_n$ from the representative utility of the *i*-th one ($i \in C_n$, $i \neq j$);

(iii) equal "abstract" or "generic" coefficients for the network charac-teristics, a constraint that is not necessary but is frequently imposed.

These assumptions lead to unrealistic properties. Because of (ii), the standard model implies:

a) equal cross elasticities of demand: this means that setting up a bicycle path between two cities will draw the same percentage of travellers from the plane, car and train or in the sense of airport choice the same percentage of travellers will be drawn from all considered air services. Furthermore (iii) implies identical values of time across the alternatives: this means that representative train and plane users (mode choice) or non-stop and via flight passengers (airport choice) value time identically;

b) the exclusion of complementarity among alternatives;

c) that only differences in the level of characteristics matter, or that the function is not homogenous of degree 0: in consequence doubling all fares and income will change the market shares.

Because of (i) the standard model further implies that:

d) the effect of a given difference in transport conditions is independent of the service level characteristics so that the response curve to changes in service characteristics is symmetric with respect to its inflection point (see figure 4). For instance, a 30 min train service improvement has the same impact on choice probabilities for the Hamburg-Hannover origin-destination pair as for the Hamburg-Munich pair. Similarly increasing the air tariffs by 50 DM has the same impact on choice probabilities for the Hamburg-Frankfurt origin-destination pair as for the Hamburg-Paris pair. Furtheron adding an amount of 20 DM to the price of travelling by plane will have the same impact as adding 20 DM to the price of travelling by train. Generally speaking, symmetry, with respect to the inflection point, implies that potential asymmetry of behaviour, where consumers/travellers suddenly start to react and then change their behaviour, cannot be detected;

Figure 4. Linear Logit Versus Box-Cox Logit

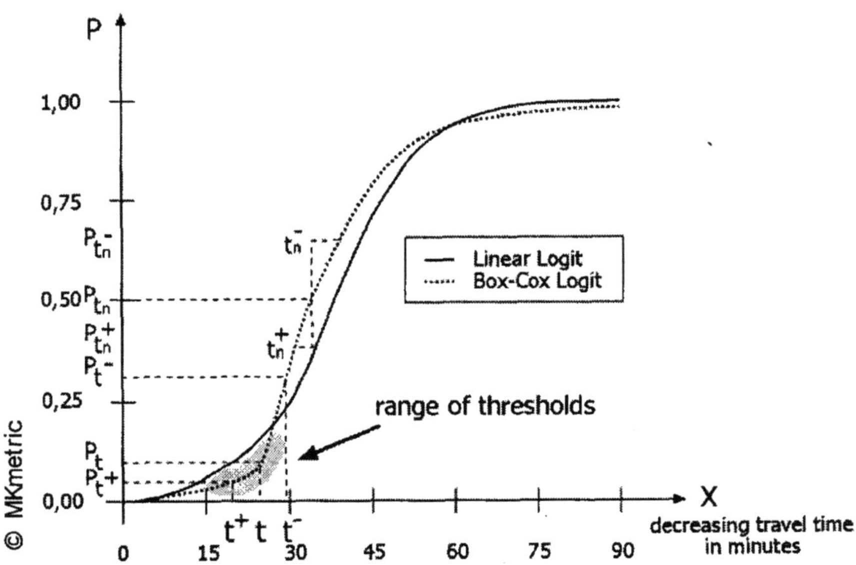

e) coefficients for the constants and for the variables common to all alternatives are underidentified, which means that, for these variables, only differences with respect to an arbitrarily chosen reference can be identified.

We also note in passing that the logit form requires that

f) the choice probabilities go to zero (one) when the representative utility V_i goes to $-\infty$ ($+\infty$) so that (see figure 4) one cannot model thick tails due to specification error, modeller ignorance, compulsive consumption or captivity to alternatives. The latter case includes the situation of business travellers which have to do a one day return trip and are therefore not elastic to price.

The Box-Cox device. To bypass most of these constraints (generally speaking, only (c) and (f) will remain), the Box-Cox transformation is used:

$$X_{kjn}^{(\lambda_{kj})} = \begin{cases} \dfrac{(X_{kjn}^{\lambda_{kj}} - 1)}{\lambda_{kj}} & \text{if } \lambda_{kj} \neq 0, \\ \ln X_{kjn} & \text{if } \lambda_{kj} = 0. \end{cases} \tag{1}$$

Hence, the choice model can be written as:

$$P(i)_n = \frac{\exp\left(\beta_i X_i + \sum_{k=1}^{K} \beta_{ki} X_{kin}^{(\lambda_{ki})}\right)}{\sum_{j \in C_n} \exp\left(\beta_j X_j + \sum_{k=1}^{K} \beta_{kj} X_{kjn}^{(\lambda_{kj})}\right)}, \tag{2}$$

where $X_i = X_j = 1$ are regression constants.

If λ_{kj} is equal to 1 (or zero), then the variable is entered in its linear (or logarithmic) form. Since the transformation is continuous for all possible values of the λ-parameter, but defined only for a positive variable, it is clearly understood that in above formulas some of the X_{kjn}'s cannot be transformed: the constant, the dummies and the ordinary variables that contain negative observations. Variables that contain positive and null values can be transformed as long as a compensating dummy variable is created (Gaudry et al. 1993).

Visual and economic significance. Figure 4 clearly shows the difference between the linearity and nonlinearity of a variable. The asymmetric curve (in respect to its inflexion point) given by Box-Cox transformation (Box et al. 1964) of the strictly positive variable X_t illustrates the error which will occur when a non-linear variable is forced to be linear. For example, assume X_t denotes total travel time: in the linear case, the value X_t equal to 30 is associated to the probability P equal to 0.25; in the non-linear case, the probability is higher if $\lambda < 1$ and smaller if $\lambda > 1$. Hence, if one forces a non-linear variable or in equality the utility function to be linear, this will result in an over- or underestimation of the probability related to this variable. In addition to asymmetry of the response function ($\lambda \neq 1$), reaction thresholds, defined in terms of acceleration of the rate of change of the probability, can be identified.

The Box-Cox transformation of the strictly positive variables of the linear Logit model leads to the Box-Cox Logit model with an asymmetry of response, as shown in figure 4, because the effect of a unit change in the service will depend on the levels of the variables X_{kj} for all values of λ_{kj} not equal 1. This can be seen by examining the partial derivatives of the representative utility function V_j of the j-th mode. It is obvious that the effect of additional service will be smaller at higher service levels than at lower ones if λ_{kj} is smaller than 1. These diminishing returns mean that given absolute reductions in total travel time have more impact when total travel times are low than high: a gain in travel time of 15 minutes means less on a long trip than on a short one. The same effects appear in the case of an increase of air tariffs. Conversely, increasing returns exist if λ_{kj} is larger than 1.

Clearly, if one is considering very small changes in the service levels of a mode, the mathematical form used does not matter very much because one is forecasting in the immediate neighbourhood of current sample values. However, if one is considering significant changes in service levels, such as increasing aircraft fees or decreasing air tariffs by a third or reducing train travel time by one half with high-speed trains, then curvature is decisive.

Asymmetry. To illustrate the asymmetry of the response functions due to the inflexion point of the curve and the threshold effect mentioned before, figure 4 shows a general example of a response curve for an alternative with respect to the variable travel time while all other conditions (characteristics and alternatives) remain unchanged. On the x-axis the change in travel time is displayed (t minutes decrease in travel time on the air service alternative) and on the y-axis the change of the probability choosing this alternative is given. Hence the interdependency of airport choice and travel demand is obvious when the probability is multiplied with the total demand of the origin-destination pair which will show you the demand for the alternative.

To describe asymmetry more formally one first has to define the inflexion point of the curve. At this point the curvature changes its functional shape from convex to concave and one can compute the value of the inflexion point (Pt_n, t_n) by equating to zero the second derivative of the alternative share in respect to the travel time. The response curve can be called asymmetric with respect to its reflection point if equidistant reductions and increments of travel time t_n by Δt [that is, $t_n^+ = t_n - \Delta t$ and $t_n^- = t_n + \Delta t$] will give different absolute values, namely $\Delta P^+ = | P_{t_n} - P_{t_n^+} |$ and $\Delta P^- = | P_{t_n} - P_{t_n^-} |$: otherwise the curve has to be called symmetric. More formally, one can define asymmetry, as in Laferrière and Gaudry (1993) in terms of the partial correlation ξ of $P_{t_n^+}$ and $(1 - P_{t_n^-})$: this yields an indicator that is necessarily between 0 and 1.

Threshold. A threshold effect occurs when the travel time reaches a critical value of t beyond which any further reduction of t to $t^- = t + \Delta t$ provokes a more substantial growth of the mode share P_t than an equidistant increment of t to $t^+ = t - \Delta t$, so that the absolute difference of the mode shares $| P_t - P_{t^-} |$ is higher than $| P_t - P_{t^+} |$.

The word threshold implicitly involves an individual evaluation of the perception of change; hence it is up to decision maker to define his threshold by exploring the percentage of alternative share increment which he will consider as a threshold i. e. which will satisfy his opinion about a threshold. More formally a critical value η has to be defined so that the absolute difference of $| P_t - P_{t^-} | = (1+\eta) | P_t - P_{t^+} |$. Alternatively, $\Delta P_{t^-} = (1+\eta)\, \Delta P_{t^+}$ and hence $\eta = (\Delta P_{t^-} / \Delta P_{t^+}) - 1$. From a visual point of view, one would intuitively expect to find the thresholds to be in the range given by the grey zone in figure 4, where a reduction of one unit would increase the probability of choosing the alternative by an additional 20% (η= 0.3), so that ΔP_{t^-} would be equal to 6 times ΔP_{t^+}.

It is obvious that the given results in figure 4 are based on a *ceteris paribus* assumption: consequently a variation of other mode specific characteristics like frequency and travel cost would imply a change of the location of the response curve so that the threshold would have to be relocated.

It has to be mentioned that in general by interpreting the results shown in figure 4 one has to take into account that the travel time represents the time of a door to door trip. Therefore a change of the access/egress services can have an important impact on the choice of an alternative.

Other considerations. The purpose of the latter example is to visualise the asymmetry of the response functions, the existence of the thresholds and the impact of travel distance on consumer behaviour: it is clear that for a detailed analysis of an investment or planned action it would of course be necessary to consider in addition the impact of travel cost, frequency, access/egress characteristics, etc.

The examination shown in figure 4 also can be done in reverse direction where one first defines the probability of choosing the mode and then computes the necessary characteristics which satisfy this condition. Different kinds of services, which are related to different actions can be represented by changes in the underlying characteristics. Implicitly there is the possibility to verify the optimal investment by relating it to the alternative specific characteristics that maximise revenue.

13.3.2 Database

The next question to answer is: What database made it possible to shed some light on this issue? The major source for the airport choice model presented in this paper is a disaggregate database based on air passenger surveys of all international airports of Germany. These data were checked and corrected by the DLR (German Aerospace Center - Cologne) and enriched by the access/egress mode characteristics based on the road and rail networks provided by MKmetric. To define the air alternatives the publicly available schedule information of some tourist offices, the OAG (Reed) and airport publications were implemented as air network.

How the network is implemented and which sources were used in detail you'll find in Mandel 1992 and Last et al. 1997. For further details of the survey all international airports of Germany or their association ADV (Arbeitsgemeinschaft Deutscher Flughaefen - Stuttgart) have to be ap-proached because unfortunately there is no public availability of these data.

13.3.3 Interdependency of Models

In this section the focus is on the question: How does airport choice influence travel demand? The principle how the models are linked and how the different effects are forwarded from airport choice passing mode choice to the generation-distribution of travel demand has to be explained to show the interdependency of airport choice and travel demand. Figure 3 in the section system approach already displayed the principle. The underlying theoretical background will not be stressed but the reasons will be outlined: Why this way of modelling was used.

Linking the models. Instead of nesting models in a hierarchical way where always problems of interpretation appear when moving from one level or segment to another the simultaneous approach was extended by including the denominator of the logit model (further on called utility index) as explanatory variable in the following model step. In addition the explanatory impedance variables used in the model specifications are computed considering the choice probabilities of the previous model as weights. Linking the models in such a way allows to pass the effects of changes on the supply side of access/egress to an airport directly to the airport choice model and moreover indirectly to the mode choice and generation-distribution model.

The utility index is treated like an additional variable in the representative utility function such as price, time, frequency, number of transfers to describe the attractiveness of an alternative. In the case of the airport choice model the emphasis is to enrich the model specification by the attractiveness to get to the airport represented by the utility index of the access/egress choice model. The same idea holds for the mode choice model where the utility index of the airport choice model can be interpreted as the attractivity of the air mode in form of the richness of air services. The enrichment of the model specification by the utility index allows to include the results of other models in a consistent way and helps to distinguish the different alternatives and to reduce the error term.

One should keep in mind that in all cases the utility index is a continuous variable which is computed O-D specific. Referring to the basic example in section 3.5 (figure 8) this will be explained. The utility index of the access/egress model which is used in the airport choice model as variable in each representative utility of the different air alternatives differs accordingly to the airport which is considered in the air alternative. Say the representative utility function of the air alternative Heidelberg - Rome via Stuttgart will include an access/egress utility index which considers the impedances of the land based modes to get to the airport Stuttgart. In the case of the air alternative via Frankfurt the access/egress utility index will be based on the impedances to the airport Frankfurt.

The mathematical form of this index is (like for any other variable) not restricted so that the estimation procedure allows this variable to become linear or non-linear (including logarithmic). This is necessary because if one forces a utility function to be linear, an error is introduced that cannot easily be compensated by an additional term in a linear utility function. It is known (Gaudry and Wills 1978) that an incorrect specification of functional form not only modifies elasticities - which are essential for any model - but can reverse regression signs - which will give you the reverse influence of a variable on the consumers behaviour (increasing the price of an alternative *ceteris paribus* will increase the probability of choosing this alternative).

Concerning the formal interpretation of the utility index it should be mentioned that the denominator of a logit model is a non-linear aggregator of utilities while the log denominator of a logit model is known to represent the expected value of the maximum utility available to the consumer over all alternatives which can be interpreted as the inclusive value or price of the alternatives.

Another problem one has to take care of concerns missing data. For example the basic transport surveys for mode choice cover all kind of transport modes but do not allow to extract the route choice within one mode so that one has to deal with a mis-specification problem. In the case of air transport on the one hand in the general transportation surveys one often has no information about the origin and destination airport but one knows the true origin and destination of the trip, on the other hand the airport surveys often concentrate on the route choice, namely the sequence of legs or airports used at a trip, but include no or no detailed information about the true origin and destination of the trip. Therefore it is obvious that the surveys or respectively the models based on the different surveys should be linked to combine both information. Partly this can be done by using the quasi-direct format as described above but still a mis-specification problem has to be solved when assigning the impedances to the modes.

Impedances like price or time are used in the model specifications as explanatory variables and where usually computed on the base of shortest path algorithms because the observed information in the survey, if there are any, are often biased due to travellers very subjective impression. But using the shortest path is not evident if no information of route choice is available. For example in the case of mode choice one would assign to an air trip from Heidelberg to Rome the time shortest path which will only consider Stuttgart as origin airport and one would neglect the existing alternatives at the airports Frankfurt, Strasbourg and Basel. As shown later on in a basic example (section 3.5, figure 8) this assumption is wrong.

To encounter the problem of missing information the time used for this air trip has to be computed in respect to the existing alternatives for the O-D pair in the air mode, which can be extracted from the airport surveys by a model dealing with the airport choice question. Therefore in the mode choice model the travel time for the alternative air is computed on the base of the probabilities for each considered alternative given by the airport choice model. Referring to our basic O-D example Heidelberg - Rome (section 3.5, figure 8) the travel time would be weighted by the probabilities the different air services are used where the travel time using Stuttgart would count by 30%, the one of Frankfurt by 66%, Strasbourg 2% and Basel 1%; e.g. in the mode choice model for vacation trips the travel time Heidelberg - Rome by air is equal to 0.3 times the travel time using the air alternative Stuttgart plus 0.66 times the travel time using Frankfurt plus 0.02 times the travel time using Strasbourg plus 0.01 times the travel time using Basel. The same procedure is used to calculate the variables cost and frequency. Of course if via and non-stop connections within the supply of one airport are used as alternatives one has to take this into account in the same way, which is easy because the airport choice model will compute the proportions. Applying the results of the airport choice model by the computation of the impedances of the air mode in the mode choice model one avoids the wrong hypotheses of time shortest path for the air mode. More simple one could say that for each O-D pair a kind of 'observed generalised cost function' is applied to compute the impedances used in the representative utility of the air mode.

As shown there are two ways how the models are linked and interact. On the more theoretical level the utility index is considered as variable in the specifications of the representative utility functions and on the more practical level the probabilities were used as filter to deal with the mis-specification of variables. The first case enriches the model specification by a general preference which influence the attractiveness of an alternative and the second case corrects the value of variables so that the elasticities are computed at the correct level. While the latter case just concerns the O-D specific impedance variables time, cost and frequency the first case considers with the O-D pair related utility index all variables used in all specifications of the representative utility functions.

Example. To ensure a consistent way of dealing with problems such as effects based on changes of air tariffs at one airport which will shift demand from one mode or airport to another and in some cases will induce air traffic (e.g. cheap ticket offers, new services) the system approach has to be applied. To explain the interdependency of airport choice and travel demand more practically the following example will help.

Lets assume *ceteris paribus* the supply side at an airport changes in the sense that tariffs due to a new structure of the aircraft fees increase for some services, new air services are offered and at the airport railway station new stops of high-speed trains are installed. Effects resulting out of these actions can be summarised as follows.

The attractiveness of the airport will decrease because of the higher tariffs which will be reflected in the model system by the competitive situation to other airports - taken into account by the intramodality in the airport choice model - and the land based modes - by the multimodality in the mode choice model. New air services as well as a high-speed access/egress train services to the airport will increase the attractiveness of the airport. Both actions will strengthen the competitive position of the airport in front of other airports and other modes. In addition a high-speed train service to/from the airport will push the intermodality and enlarge the catchment-area of the airport.

The link to the travel demand is given by the use of the utility index of the mode choice model, which incorporates already the effects captured by the airport choice model, as variable in the generation-distribution model. In addition the mode choice model incorporates already the new competitive situation of the airports because the characteristics / impedances of the mode air - which are competing with the ones from the other modes car and rail - are computed considering the new probabilities of the airport choice model as weights, whereby the probabilities just reflect the attractiveness of the airports (or alternative air services).

It has to be stated that this is only a general explanation of the actions effects on the airport, the system approach will analyse them specific for each origin-destination (O-D) pair.

13.3.4 Model Specification

The specification of the airport choice model touches two issues. First variables have to be defined which explain the decision process of the consumers and in this context one has to take care of the functional form which is decisive to represent the behaviour in a realistic manner. Second the definition of alternatives is essential because they restrict the set of possibilities a consumer has, e.g. they reflect the possible alternatives the consumer is aware of when taking the decision.

To define the alternatives of the choice set an air network was created which reflects the existing services at this time. To do this world airways guides, airport, airline and tourist office information were used. Flights of different airlines were considered as equal services as long as they did not differ in travel time significantly and type of connection. The survey did not allow to extract information on the real ticket price spend by the consumer so that average prices based on the published information have been used. Therefore it was not necessary to distinguish services at the level of tariffs, but it has to be stated that this would increase the quality of the models.

Analysing the network database by applying the route choice algorithms in different ways and comparing the results with the available ca. 238.000 observations it was found that there is a necessity to split the database by trip purpose. The reason for this was the high difference in the number of alternatives taken into account by the consumers. While vacationists consider up to eight alternatives the business travellers just take note of four. Within the choice sets it is clear that the highest preference is on the alternative which is closest to the starting point of the trip and offering a non-stop service. The preferences of the following alternatives are rapidly falling for business and slowly for vacation trips. Non-business trips with a total duration of four days are defined as trips with private purpose and they are somewhere within between the two other purposes due to their sensitivity to the price and their restricted time limit of four days. Anyhow out of the economic point of view the segmentation by trip purpose is sensitive due to the quite different priorities and elasticities on price and time. To be sure to capture all possibilities the set of alternatives was defined for all trip purposes by the maximum of eight alternatives for each origin-destination trip. But due to the very time consuming computational burden and the requested interactivity of a simulation tool one can restrict the set of choice to six alternatives in the case of vacation, to three for business and to four for private trips without a big loss of precision in the result.

Characteristics. The analysis of the available disaggregate information of the survey resulted in a set of characteristics which are determining the airport choice, namely:

- Access/egress to the airport - weighted travel time and travel costs of individual and public transport to/from an airport - and distance from origin to the airport

- Further attributes of public transportation to/from an airport - summarised in the denominator of the access/egress choice model

- Total travel times between origin and destination of passengers trip via several airports and/or air services, transfer and check in/out time inclusive

- Travel costs of each trip, including access and egress (average costs are used because the survey did not contain the real ticket price)

- Service attributes of the flight - e.g. frequency and type of connection (non-stop, via)

- Attractiveness indicator of an airport, e.g. number of destinations and non-stop flights offered in total.

Further socio-economic variables and characteristics of the land based modes were not considered because the generation-distribution and mode choice part of the system approach are already taking care of them. In addition the use of nonlinearity reduces the need for certain kinds of segmentation - e.g. by fare or distance classes - typically done in order to obtain adequate representation or fit in domains other than that of the sample mean. Of course it would be very useful to study the extent to which market segmentation is a partial substitute for nonlinearity, as it is clear that nonlinearity- whether applied to network variables or to socio-economic variables like income or age- is distinct from market heterogeneity.

Based on the listed characteristics for each trip purpose a model was developed to explain the airport choice. The specification of each model is shown in the following table.

As already indicated in the table the most variables are used in a generic way so that the β of this variable is common to all alternatives. Only the type of connection used in the private model is defined specific so that each alternative has its individual β. In general the specification focuses on robustness so that all variables have a t-student of at least 2.81 and sign conversions do not show up when setting variables to specific or adding other variables or exponents. Variables are only used as specific if the gain in likelihood justifies this. Of course the specifications were checked to avoid correlation and multicolinearity.

For example business travellers have a high time sensitivity and therefore prefer fast non-stop connections which are offered as close to the starting point of their trip (e.g. origin) as possible. This behaviour is already reflected in the number of alternatives considered as stated above. Therefore the variables non-stop and distance to the airport are indirectly captured by the travel time variable.

Table 1. Model Specification

Variable	Business	Private	Vacation
Travel cost	generic, λ-1	generic, λ-1	generic, λ-1
Travel time	generic, λ-1	generic	generic, λ-2
O-D frequency	generic	generic	generic
Non-stop connection*	---	specific	generic
Airport attractivity	generic	generic	generic
Distance to airport	---	generic	----
Access/egress utility index	generic	generic	generic

*for the last three alternatives

For the vacation model the travel price is the dominant variable and the distance to an airport is just a matter of time which is already captured in the travel time variable. Another variable which could be of redundancy to travel time is the type of connection. Clearly a non-stop flight is usually faster than a via flight and therefore this information should already be covered by the time variable. But the type of connection also mirrors the service quality, e.g. vacation travellers with a lot of luggage prefer to check in close to their home even if it is a via flight. In addition they often use as access/egress mode the kiss&fly service offered by relatives or friends. The alternatives four to seven seem only to be taken into account if this is a non-stop flight.

The latter argumentation concerning non-stop flights also holds for the consumers travelling on private purpose. Here it was even more interesting to find out that private travellers are so sensitive to this non-stop service that the variable could be set to specific. The variable distance to the airport is only taken into account by the model for trip purpose private. Due to the fact that no correlation to other variables of the specification was detected this information could be interpreted as a kind of familiarity to the air mode if an airport is close to the home. May be the offers for short trips are much more intensive in high populated areas where airports are located than elsewhere. Further analysis of the survey showed in addition that there is a correlation to the age classes 20 to 40 years. Therefore this variable might also capture socio-economic effects and is no redundant information to travel time.

Functional form. The next step to develop the models was the check on functional form, e.g. are the variables linear or non-linear. As stated in section 3.1 forcing variables to be linear is equal to accepting errors of mis-specification. Therefore it has to be analysed whether there is an asymmetry in the consumers behaviour or not and furtheron are there thresholds where consumer start to change their behaviour more rapidly.

Concerning the functional form several tests have been made. The sign of λ identifies in table 1 the variable as non-linear, where in the case of the same number the variables have a common transformation and elsewhere a different one. A λ in specific or generic form was only justified if there was a gain in the likelihood value and the t-student was at least 2.33. If there was more than one λ then a test was made to check whether one found a local or global maximum whereby only the latter was accepted.

Table 2. Selected Results for the Linear and Non-linear Airport Choice Models

Model	Business		Private		Vacation	
Characteristics	linear	non-linear	linear	non-linear	linear	non-linear
Final loglikelihood value	-45100070	-43334113	-8030071	-7663015	-73800195	-72697398
λ-1	1.000	0.399	1.000	0.694	1.000	0.010
λ-2	1.000	0.399	1.000	1.000	1.000	0.637
Rho-squared	0.251	0.281	0.301	0.333	0.147	0.160

In the case of the business model it was decided to use a common λ because in the specific case they were not quite different and the gain in likelihood was small. For the vacation model the contrary was the case. Here two different λ were necessary because λ-1 on travel cost indicated a logarithmic form which was quite different from λ-2 indicating a strong nonlinearity of travel time. For private trips the λ on travel time was not significant so that only one on travel cost was used. In all cases where the Box-Cox transformation was applied the gain in the final log-likelihood value was large and the rho-squared values improved.

Elasticity and value of time. Of practical importance are the elasticities of demand. In table 3 the elasticities of the Box-Cox estimates for the first six alternatives are given for the most interesting variables travel time and travel cost. A comparison of the linear and the Box-Cox estimates showed that there were strong differences to the linear ones. Generally in the linear case of the models the elasticities differed strongly; the ones for the cost variable were lower and the ones of time were higher.

Of course if one computes the values of time they will differ for each alternative in the non-linear case while they are equal for the linear models. It is important to note that values of time are, technically speaking, marginal rates of substitution between two variables - cost and time - holding the level of utility constant. As these marginal rates are simply ratios of partial derivatives, the Box-Cox logit results will have a significant built-in advantage over the linear logit results because they will vary not only with each mode (as the derivatives will not be evaluated at the same point for each alternative on average) but will also depend on how much time is saved, as the value of the marginal minute depends on trip length, e.g. trip time (Mandel et al. 1997). Therefore non-linear models imply that consumers using the first alternative (e.g. the fastest) are evaluating their time differently from the ones choosing the last alternative (e.g. slowest).

The computed elasticity of demand reflects a 1% change of the variable so that the values given in the table indicate a percentage. For the interpretation it has to be clear that the elasticities have to be evaluated only in context to the market share of the alternative. Therefore the low value of the elasticity of alternative one has a much higher impact on the market share of alternative one - which is big - than a high elasticity of alternative six - which has a small market share (Mandel 1992).

Table 3. Weighted Aggregate Elasticity of Choice Probability of the Non-linear Airport Choice Models

Model	Alternative	Business	Private	Vacation
Own clasticity travel cost	1	-0.233	-0.879	-1.219
	2	-1.696	-4.955	-3.846
	3	-2.464	-5.503	-4.879
	4	-2.881	-6.263	-4.928
	5	-3.156	-6.369	-5.043
	6	-3.292	-6.529	-5.162
Own elasticity travel time	1	-0.932	-0.480	-1.948
	2	-7.081	-3.195	-6.569
	3	-10.109	-5.649	-8.812
	4	-11.696	-5.727	-9.408
	5	-12.659	-6.312	-9.738
	6	-13.281	-6.312	-10.597

To demonstrate the practical relevance of the consumers elasticities the change of the market shares and travel demand of an alternative is computed in condition to an absolute change of the travel costs of this alternative whereby all other conditions remain *ceteris paribus* equal. As example the alternatives at the Hamburg airport in the year 1991 are used and displayed for three different market segments, namely domestic, european and intercontinental. The computed probabilities of the models will differ for each origin-destination pair as well as they depend on the specific trip purpose. The curvatures of elasticity are aggregated for each market segment based on the specific origin-destination (O-D) results.

The following figure 5 displays the change of passengers demand (y-axis) based on the year 1991 when tariffs change (x-axis). The zero-zero co-ordinates display the *status quo* at Hamburg in 1991. It can clearly be seen that the elasticity of business travellers is the smallest because changes of the tariffs have the smallest effect on their behaviour. Although increasing the tariff of domestic flights by 100 DM only 28% will skip the alternatives offered at Hamburg. At the same price change the share of vacationists will decrease by 37% and the private travellers by 51%. On the domestic market segment the air services have to face a strong competition to the land based modes and in addition there are a lot of other air alternatives around so that easily instead of Hamburg the airports Hannover or Bremen can be used.

The results at a 100 DM change of the tariff for European destinations give roughly the same picture just the losses of market shares are smaller (business 7%, vacation 25%, private 38%). Surprisingly the results for intercontinental destinations are different. While the vacationists react strongly (24%) followed by the business travellers (19%) the private travellers show the smallest effect (12%).

The strong reaction of private travellers has to be seen out of the point of view that the total length of the trip does not exceed four days and therefore the ticket takes over a major part of the total trip expenditures. This argumentation even holds if one has a look on their behaviour if the price decreases by 100 DM. The gain varies from 100% on domestic and 64% on European to 25% on intercontinental destinations.

The small reaction of business travellers is consistent with the idea of the high time sensitivity of these consumers and the fact that the ticket is usually paid by the company or the visited client.

The idea of price sensitivity of vacation travellers is reflected at least in the domestic and European cases while on intercontinental trips the change of the ticket price does only slightly increase the total expenditures of the trip, so that this is of minor relevance. Anyhow the high competition on the intercontinental market is ensuring a low price level.

By the way in an air demand forecast study for Hamburg (1996) it was found that holiday trips to the same destination, same hotel etc. in the same time period offered by Hamburg tourist offices differed in price by up to 1.000 DM to those offered in other German cities. The major difference was just the originating airport: instead of Hamburg airport the journeys started from Frankfurt or Dusseldorf airport.

To see the effects of consumer behaviour on travel demand the following figure 6 displays the results already explained on the market share level. The absolute passenger values (y-axis) refer directly to the market shares stated above so that the interpretation of the results is obvious. One remark should be made. Some changes of the travel shares seemed to be high or low but looking at the absolute number of travellers will adjust this objective.

Figure 5. Share of Travel Demand Depending on Cost Changes

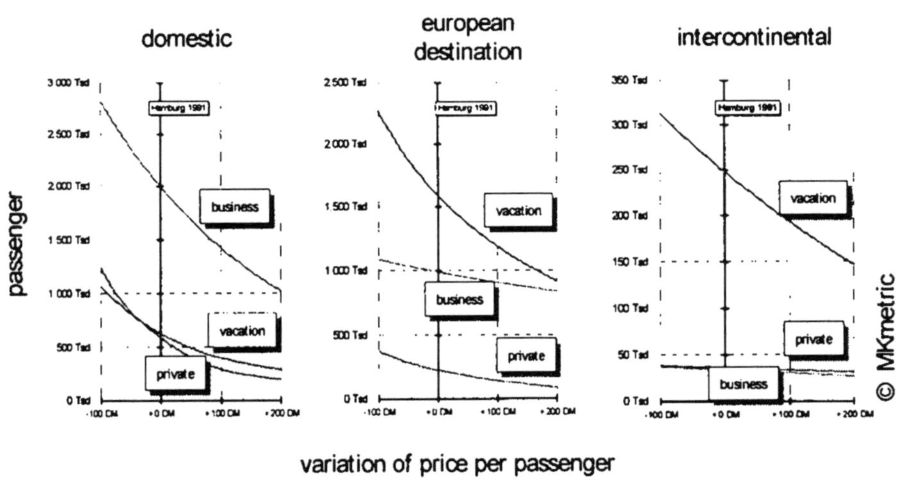

It should be kept in mind that the losses on the passenger side are not losses in total for the air market which will be shown later on in section 4 in more detail (see passenger shifts). A lot of travellers just choose another air alternative - intramodality - only on short distance flights the competing high-speed trains and the car mode - multimodality - will draw market shares and of course less attractive destinations will be substituted by other ones due to the generation-distribution approach used.

Generally it has to be stated that changes of tariffs higher than 150 DM are not covered by the database and therefore the precision of the results is decreasing. The models have to be updated when new observations are available which catch consumer behaviour due to such large changes.

But despite this fact to the real example of an unrestricted return business trip between Hamburg and Frankfurt should be referred to because the comparison of model results and the true observations was encouraging in the sense that nor large changes of air tariffs are unusual neither the elasticities found by the models can be neglected.

For example an increase of the tariff of about 50 DM within a year (9.96 to 8.97) or a drop of the price by 30% and more as soon as another airline offers their service (e.g. Frankfurt – Berlin, Hamburg - Munich or Munich - Ruhr area in 1997) or the anti trust office claims monopolistic behaviour of an airline are normal if one observes the market in detail. In the light of the ongoing liberalisation, deregulation and privatisation process and the very elastic pricing strategies of airlines the question is: How can airports participate at market procedures like airlines already do for some time? Due to the enlarging capacity constraints the growing air market is facing and the huge infrastructure investments airports have to undertake the airlines and respectively the consumers have to face higher charges and / or fees. It will be a matter of time that airports will be forced to turn to a more market oriented pricing strategy like peak & off peak pricing or the more general approach of slot trading to handle the spare capacity resources more efficient or say on the level of a real market price.

Figure 6. Travel Demand Depending on Cost Changes

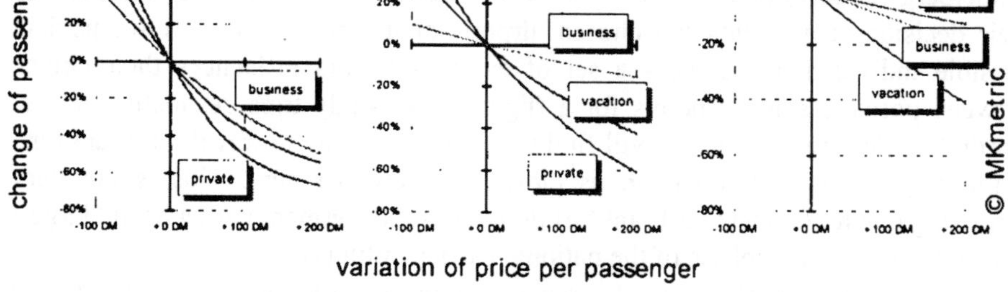

Concerning the elasticities it is refered to the example of the Frankfurt - Hamburg O-D passenger market which decreased by 4.8% from 1996 to 1997

stated by airport statistics Hamburg. Within this time period not only the air tariff increased also the service frequency on this O-D was reduced. Taking into account the average growth rate of about 7.4% in 1997 on the domestic German market the imaginable losses on this leg were 12.2% for the O-D traffic. Obviously the growth rates were induced by the additional competition of airlines on several markets in 1997 where the prices dropped significantly. Therefore considering all effects the elasticities of the models tend to be conservative. In this context the question rises: Who can benefit of consumer elasticity by applying a market oriented pricing strategy, exclusively airlines? More and more the airports view the travelers directly as clients and apply agressive marketing strategies to increase their attractivity (free or cheap parking and overnight stay, shops, play grounds, restaurants, high-speed rail access, etc.) to enlarge their catchment area. A new pricing strategy for the aviation side would be a natural enrichment of the existing marketing tools. In addition one could use a market oriented pricing as instrument to impose a price structure to meet political constraints like environmental benchmarks.

By the way by encreasing tariffs on an O-D the total demand on this leg need not necessarily decrease if one takes into account the transfer passengers, who usually pay different prices. In the case of the Hamburg - Frankfurt leg which is dominated by the origin-destination passenger market the losses on total demand were 1.8% to the demand in 1996 because the share of transfer passengers increased by ca. 2.3%.

Therefore to compute the effects on the leg level all itineraries on the total network have to be considered. Obviously it is wrong to concentrate on one airport and single services without considering the synergetic effects of a network and the competitive situation around. To face such and other complex problems the airport choice models have been embedded in the system approach.

13.3.5 Basic Example

Coming back to the roots of the original question why airport choice should be modelled a small example (basic year 1991) will demonstrate the decision problem a consumer faces and which even become more difficult in a liberalised air market with capacity constraints at different airports.

Comparing two German business travellers - e.g. one living in famous Heidelberg (county) and the other one in the neighbouring county of Karlsruhe - their decisions concerning the chosen airport for a trip will vary. If we neglect possible individual preferences a set of external factors influences their choice between possible starting points for a flight. If we study trips destinating in e.g. North America (see fig. 7) we will find that the probability to travel via Frankfurt-Main Airport for both travellers is close to ninety per cent. This is not very surprising due to the fact that Frankfurt dominates the German market as the largest hub and being the homebase of the national carrier Lufthansa.

Much more interesting are the remaining probabilities to choose alternative airport for business trips crossing the Atlantic. As described in the sections above the choice of airports is determinated by a set of factors including accessibility, offered frequencies and destinations. The figures above shows how the combination of these factors influences the probability to choose one of the remaining alternatives for such a trip. While the airport characteristics are equal in both cases the accessibility by private and public transport differs. In general it was found that business travellers prefer strongly the airport, which offers the highest flight frequencies and the shortest duration of the whole trip, including access and egress.

Figure 7. Airport Choice, Destination North America, Trip Purpose: Business

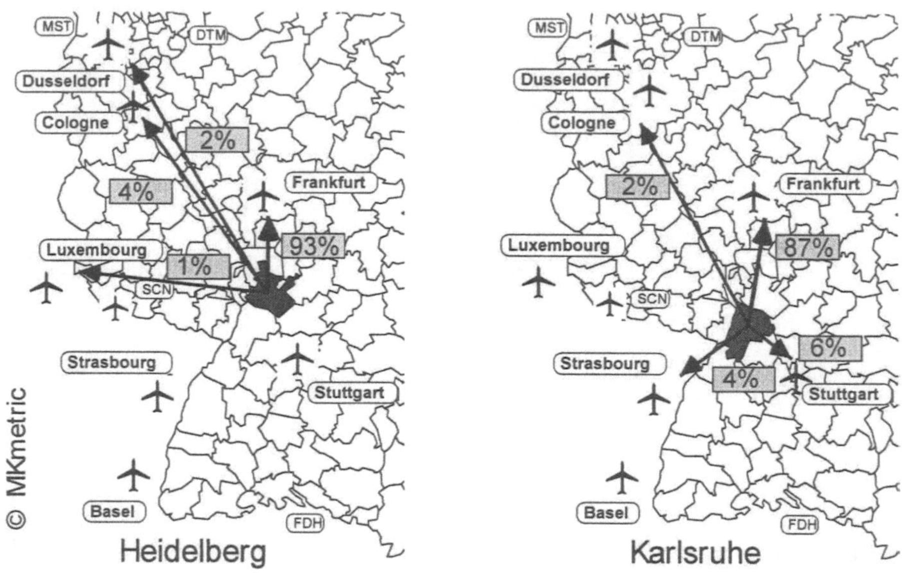

When analysing vacation trips one observes a completely different choice structure for the travellers in the example above. Due to less restrictions in time but higher price sensitivity vacationists prefer the most convenient kiss&fly access to possible airports offering non-stop or via flights to start their journeys but are open enough to choose other alternatives as long as the price differs significantly. Figure 8 depicts the choice probabilities for vacation travellers from Karlsruhe and Heidelberg, respectively, to an Italian destination.

Major differences rise from other characteristics, namely the distance between the origin and the airport or the availability of a non-stop flight (even if only once a week) or the accessibility by public transport. So travellers from Karlsruhe prefer strongly Stuttgart Airport. Frankfurt, which is situated additional 50 km away, can only attract a market share of 13%, although much more flights are offered than in Stuttgart. Due to a missing non-stop-flight to Rome, only 8% remain for Strasbourg Airport, despite the fact is it is the nearest one to the area of Karlsruhe county.

When starting a holiday trip from Heidelberg, Frankfurt is certainly the best choice for two third of all vacation travellers. But the second best alternative via

Stuttgart gets still 30%, while choosing other airports as e.g. Strasbourg or Basel will be an exception.

Figure 8. Airport Choice, Destination: Rome (Italy), Trip Purpose: Vacation

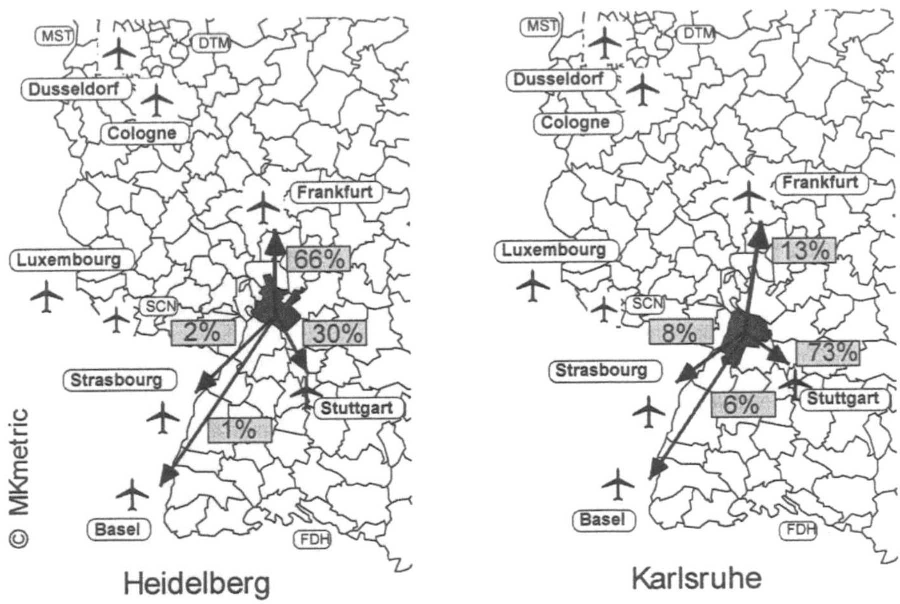

Such examples can be extended when ones moves to areas where a lot of services and airports are competing, like in the Rhein-Ruhr, Berlin, Paris or London area, and one analyses all possible destinations and alternatives. For the sake of understanding only this small example of Heidelberg and Karlsruhe was presented. By the way, in the meantime (1997) in the area of Karlsruhe a regional airport (Baden-Airport) opened and already offers interesting services to tourist centres which unfortunately could not be taken into account for these examples based on 1991.

13.4. SELECTED RESULTS

If we change our scope of analyses from the demand side to the fields of interest of the transport service suppliers, we might be interested in the question where our customers come from. If we ask e.g. for the market dominance of the Frankfurt Airport in Germany we obtain the catchment-areas by aggregation over regional and trip purpose specific transport flows using the considered airport. The resulting figures show us the realised market shares for this airport.

The figures 9 and 10 show that these spheres of influence vary according to the market studied. The primary figure gives an overall view taking all destinations into account. The latter depicts the market shares for intercontinental destinations.

Frankfurt as Germany's major hub is offering a large number of long-haul connections, so its market dominance covers a larger area in this market section than in total. Other international airports as Hamburg, Munich, Stuttgart or Dusseldorf are able to claim significant market shares in the domestic and charter segment as well as towards selected destinations abroad.

It is obvious that the hinterland of an airport cannot be described by one or several concentric circles. The shape rather depends on specific characteristics of the airport and its competitors, as number of destinations and flights offered or the accessibility by earthbound feeder systems. So the catchment-area (to all destinations and by more than 10% share) of Frankfurt extends to 600 km in the north-south direction, while in east-west direction only to 300 km. Of course the catchment-area exceeds the German borders but the main access lines by the land based modes are in north-south direction. For the sake of understanding all figures are restricted to the shape of the German borders.

If we substitute the regional market shares with the absolute number of passengers the spatial demand pattern for Frankfurt Airport gives deeper insight in the market potentials.

Beside the extended area of Frankfurt and the dense populated counties south of it, where most passengers are originating, a remarkable number of people are withdrawn from other metropolitan areas in Germany, although there are international airports in that counties (e. g. Cologne, Hannover) — even if some intercontinental flights are offered there (e. g. Munich).

Due to the linked models for access/egress one can analyse the number of passengers arriving at the airport by public transport. Compared to the previous figure one can see that the airport-railway station (high-speed intercity connections) has great impact on the access mode share.

Mode choice, airport choice and access/egress choice as a part of a traffic forecast can help to come to a decision where to place a new airport best. The comparison of five locations for a new airport near Berlin on several points of view will be shown in the following figures.

A set of locations has been evaluated with respect to different measures. All considered alternatives are located in the south respectively south-west of the German capital. The corresponding scenarios cover beneath the single airports also two airport systems that are combinations of Tegel and Schonefeld as well as Jueterbog-W. and Schoenefeld. The figure 12 depicts the different alternatives considered.

Various indicators could be assessed to evaluate the relevance of certain airport locations. Regarding to economic aspects decision makers are forced to compare the alternatives based on the number of passengers that are going to choose the airport when doing a journey.

Figure 9. Market Shares of Frankfurt 1991: All Destinations

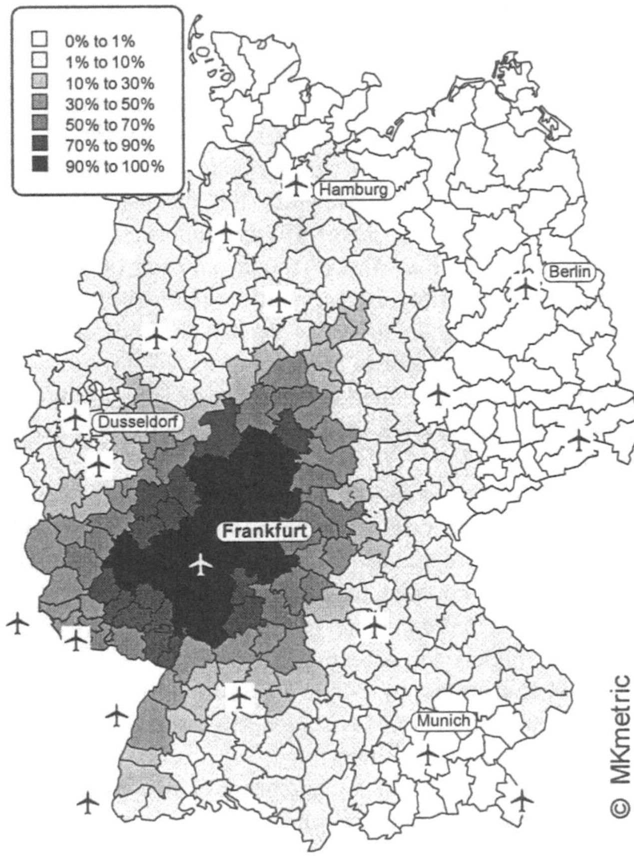

As travellers are making their choice not only between different airports but also are able to take a land-based transport mode the resulting demand figures could not be evaluated in the unimodal context of the air service system. Nevertheless the total passenger figures are essential indicators for economic evaluation.

Figure 13 shows the number of passengers forecasted for the year 2010 in seven scenarios. The highest number of passengers can be estimated, when a system of two airports will be operated: One close to the city, serving national short haul flights and routes to some important European capitals. The other is situated up to 60 km far away from Berlin's city centre. It is more assigned for long, especially intercontinental hauls. This covers also pure charter flights and direct flights to destinations, where the demand, originated at Berlin, has to be fed up by national commuter-flights to provide satisfactory load factors (hubbing).

Figure 10. Market Shares of Frankfurt 1991: Intercontinental Destinations

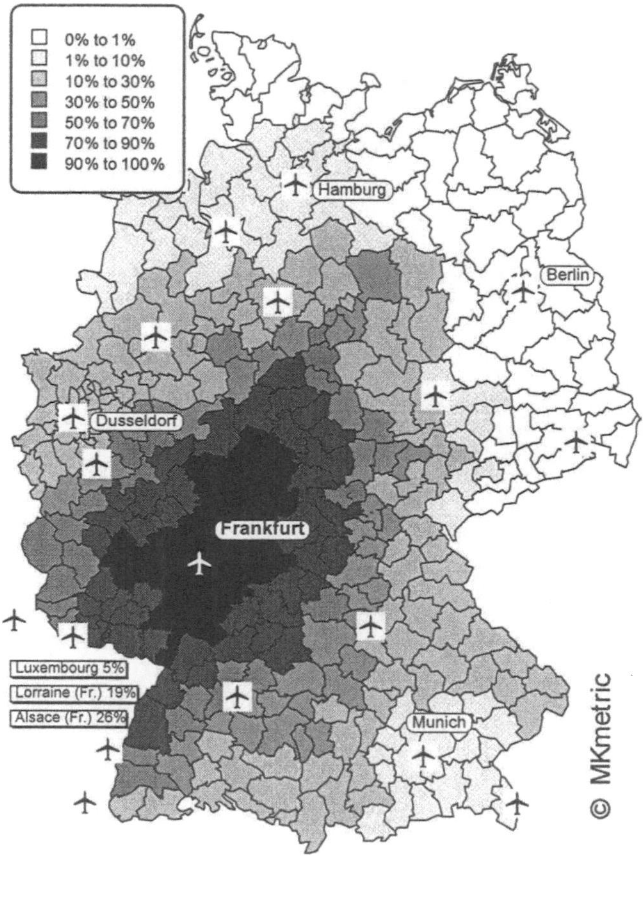

Regarding the environmental point of view decision makers will be also interested in the impact on natural and cultural resources. Measures for this field of interest could be derived e.g. from the modal split figures concerning the access and egress modes. Especially in dense populated areas as well as ecological sensitive areas the share of passengers using public transport for their ways from and to the airport are useful indicators. Pollution could be directly derived from the absolute demand figures when applying distance related emissions to it.

From a macroeconomic point of view the modal split is also an important measure. Infrastructure investments in Germany must be evaluated according to well-defined evaluation schemes. Herein the investor must apply cost benefit analyses beneath others. These processes requires very detailed figures to assess a set of related impacts. Figure 14 depicts as an example the resulting mode choice pattern on the relation Berlin-Munich in the year 2010 for the set of scenarios.

Figure 11. Passengers Frankfurt by Origin for Intercontinental Destinations 1991

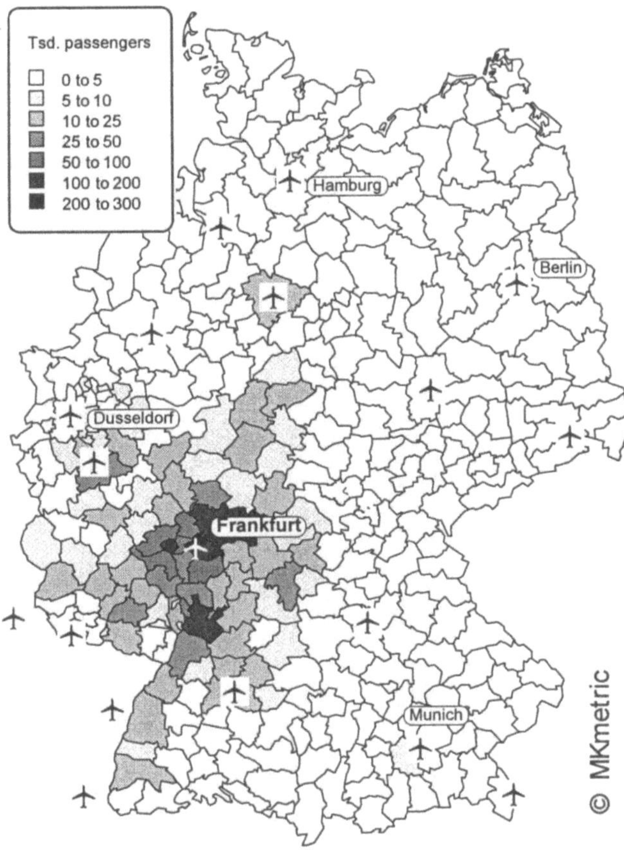

Figure 12. Comparing Locations for an International Airport for Berlin

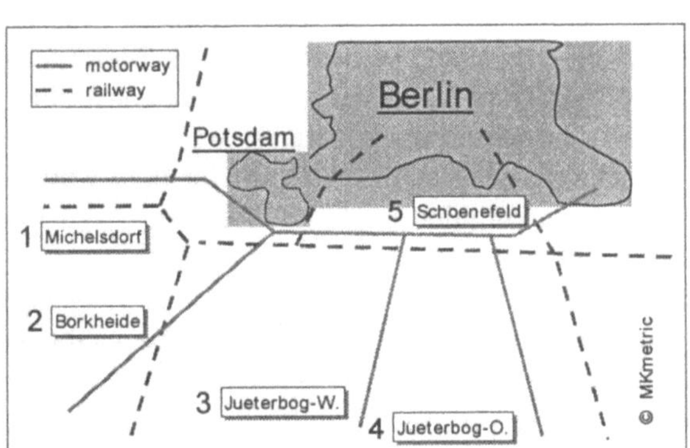

Figure 13. Passengers Berlin 2010 Depending on Airport's Location

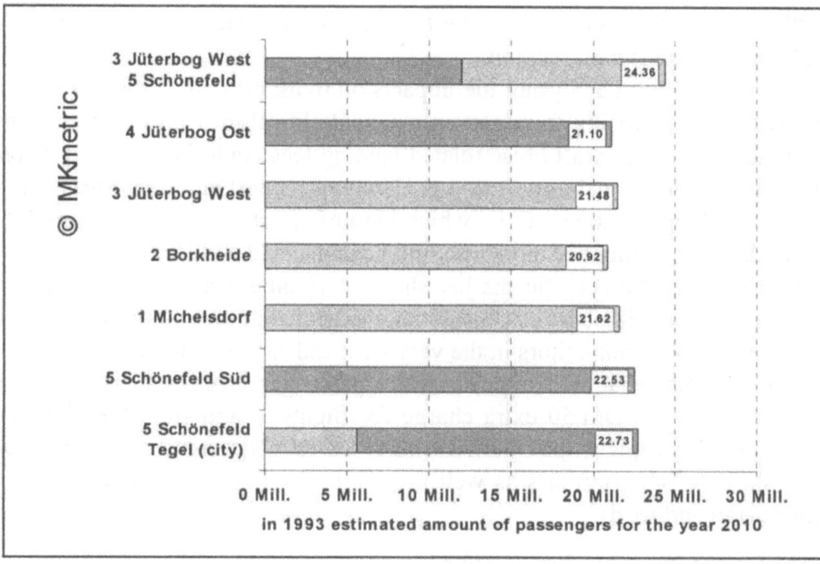

Figure 14. Modal Split Between Berlin and Munich 2010 Depending on the Location of an Airport

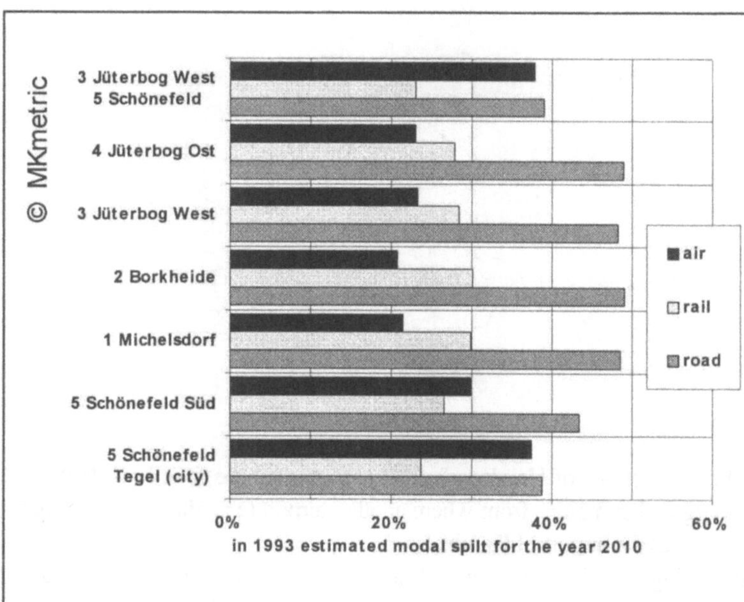

Highest mode choice for air transport is proved when there is an airport near Berlin's City centre, like Tegel or Schonefeld. Market shares up to almost 40% can

be estimated then. On the other hand, when Berlin's new airport is situated about 50 km far away, the share of travellers by plane between Berlin and Munich extends just a little beyond 20%. Obviously, the time needed to reach the airport plays a major role on such short haul relation.

Another possibility in analysing the impacts on transport demand is to focus on the intramodal effects arising from certain means. Political measures as constraints on airport capacities or aircraft noise related landing fees could be analysed. If one assumes that an international airport as e.g. Hamburg request additional fees and/or charges, the resulting question will be which kind of effects could be measured. Or one could ask which amount of money should be demanded and from whom.

Figure 15 shows the specific market share of Hamburg airport in 1991. The sphere of influence of Hamburg is considerably extended in the east-west-direction, as there are no serious competitors in the very west and east of Hamburg.

To give an idea what will happen, when passenger charges increases at an airport, we simulated a DM 50 extra charge for flights to and from the Hamburg airport. Figure 16 depicts the market share losses. The pattern results from passenger shifts to other airports as well as travellers taking other modes to their destinations (rail and road).

Figure 15. Market Shares Hamburg 1991: All Destinations

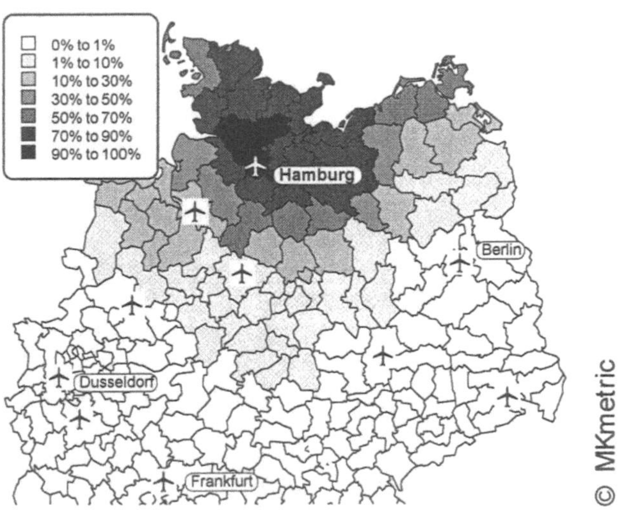

The highest reductions of Hamburg's market shares can be found inside the extended area of Hamburg and in regions from where another airport (e.g. Hannover) is reachable on similar conditions as the airport of Hamburg.

Still analysing the implications of a DM 50 extra charge at the airport of Hamburg, we can also have a look on other airports. Wondering if they are winners or losers of such a scenario. Figure 17 summarises the passenger shifts to other airports.

Figure 16. Market Share Losses Hamburg 1991: All Destinations

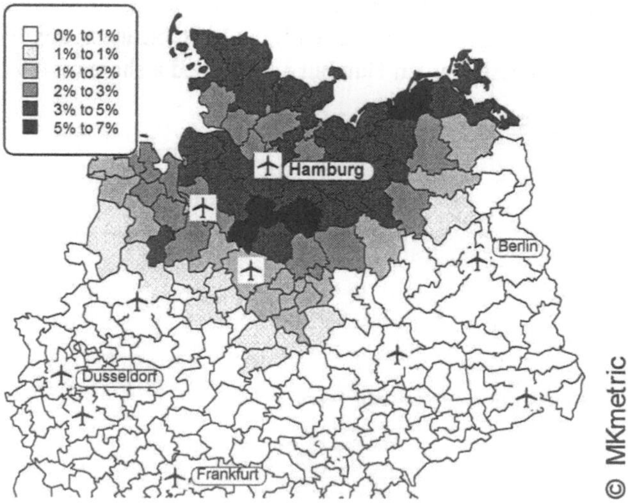

Those connected with Hamburg by short haul flights, like Frankfurt (FRA) and Dusseldorf (DUS) must be characterised as losers. Those connected with Hamburg by short haul flights, like Frankfurt (FRA) and Dusseldorf (DUS) must be characterised as losers. But the total number of passengers on these airports diminishes less than on the O-D flights because some of the travellers still reach these airports by plane just using a competitive airport like Hannover (HAJ) or Bremen (BRE) and some travellers just replaced their former connecting flight Hamburg - Frankfurt by car or rail trip to Frankfurt and therefore enlarge the catchment area of these airports.

Airports situated closer to Hamburg may be considered as winners in that situation, if they are not connected with Hamburg by plane and, in addition, provide a comparable number of destinations like Hamburg does. Here, Hannover (HAJ) and Bremen (BRE) win more than 50 Tsd. passengers each, while at Kiel (KEL), there is only a little increase in passengers amount, due to the very few destinations offered there. A special kind of winner, although the number of changing passengers is quite low, is the Copenhagen airport (CPH). Despite of losing passengers on the flights to and from Hamburg, the total number of people in Copenhagen raises. This result is caused by a combination of the two effects stated above for Frankfurt and Hannover.

When increasing airport fees at an airport, not only passenger's amount decreases, the number of aircraft movements diminishes, too as figure 18 shows. Here (DM 50 extra charge per passenger), we indicated the differences by type of aircraft. When regarding the reductions by percentage, the strongest effects are advised for the class of turbo prop (represented by ATR 72), which come into service on short hauls only. On long hauls, which are a domain of planes like the Airbus A340, the reduction of aircraft movements, caused by the lack of passengers, is almost of no account, as that DM 50 extra charge makes intercontinental flights only slightly dearer.

Having a look at the passenger figures of Hamburg, differentiated by trip purpose, you can see in figure 19 that already in 1991 business travellers were no longer the majority of passengers in Hamburg - they had a share of 48%.

Figure 17. Passenger Shifts

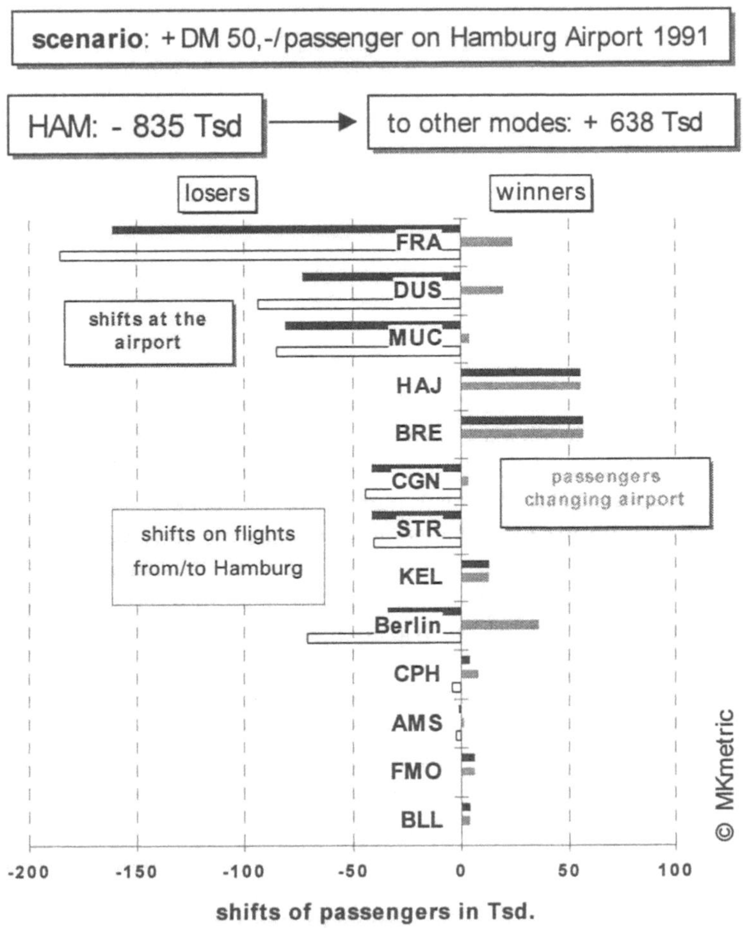

When simulating a DM 50 extra charge for travellers using the airport of Hamburg, the number of travellers there diminishes by 8% (resp. 835 Tsd.). While trips belonging to the purpose private (i. e. non business trips, up to a total duration of four days) are affected quite strongly of raising costs, the reaction of vacation or business travellers is quite meagre.

When simulating rising passenger charges, the changing economic situation of an airport is an important point of view. So figure 20 displays the development of aviation revenues. The actual revenues in 1991 at the airport of Hamburg were

DM 180 Mill. With an amount of 6.5 Mill. passengers, aviation revenues were DM 27.61 per passenger. When rising up passenger charges by DM 100, the aviation revenues will sum up to more than DM 300 Mill., although the number of passengers estimated at Hamburg decreases below 2.5 Mill. and there are less aircraft movements.

Figure 18. Aircraft Movements Hamburg Airport 1991 (Percentages)

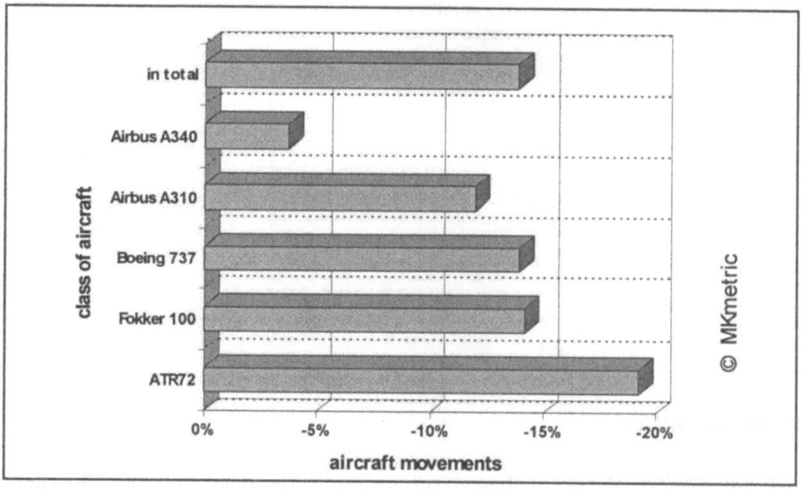

Figure 19. Passengers at Hamburg by Trip Purpose 1991

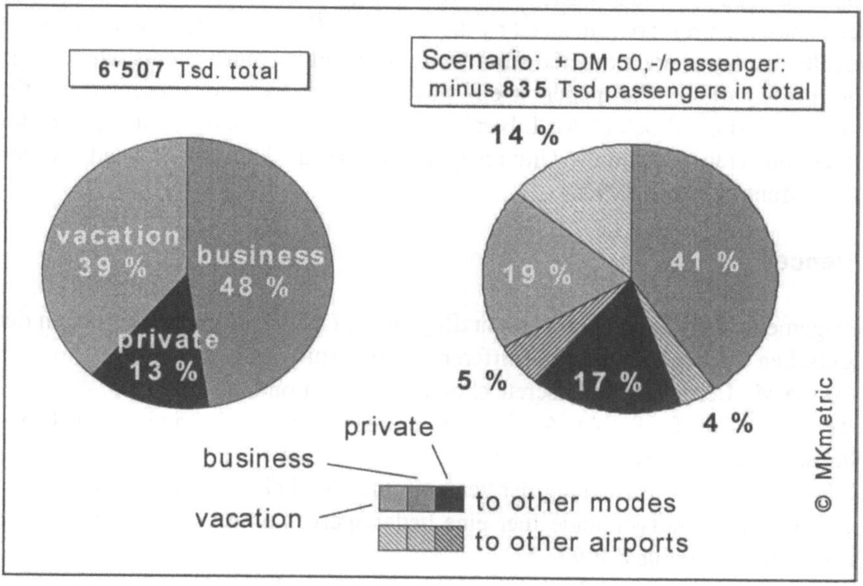

Figure 20. Aviation Revenues Depending on Passenger Charges

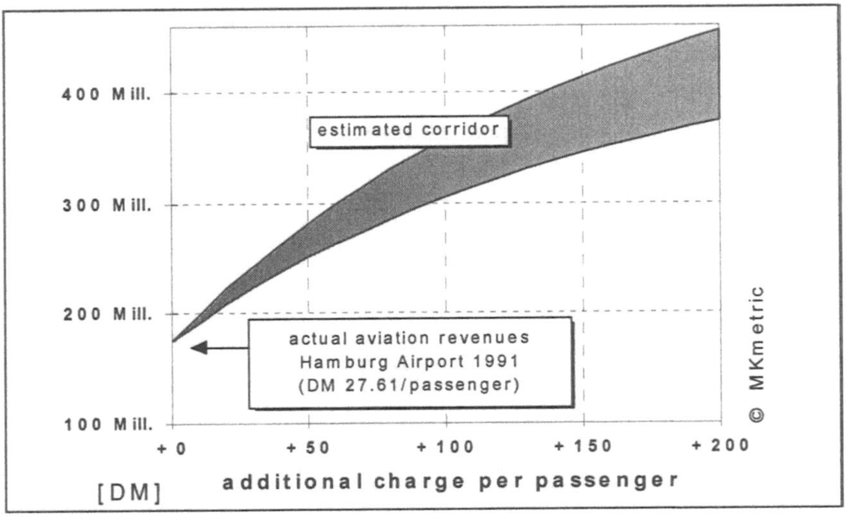

Acknowledgements

The work on airport choice is based on research financed by the Ministry for economics of the Free and Hanseatic City of Hamburg and benefited from survey data provided by all international airports of Germany which were checked by the German Aerospace Center (DLR). The work on generation-distribution and mode choice is based on research financed by the German Ministry of Transport. Some of the results displayed are extracted from work financed by other clients who agreed to the presentation. The paper itself was financed by and presented at the symposium 'Taking Stock of Air Liberalisation' organised jointly by the Centre for Research on Transportation - University of Montreal, Transport Canada at the ICAO in Montreal April 1997.

References

Arbeitsgemeinschaft Deutscher Verkehrsflughaefen (ADV): Verkehrsleistungen der deutschen Verkehrsflughaefen (different years); Stuttgart;

Ben-Akiva M., Lerman S.R.: Discrete choice analysis; London; 1985

Box G. E. P., Cox D. R.: An Analysis of Transformations; Journal of the Royal Statistical Society, Series B 26; 1964

CEC: Die kuenftige Entwicklung der gemeinsamen Verkehrspolitik. Globalkonzept einer Gemeinschaftsstrategie fuer eine bedarfsgerechte und auf Dauer tragbare Mobilitaet - Bruxelles; 1993

CEC: Impact of the Third Package of Air Transport Liberalisation Measures - Bruxelles; 10/96

CEC: EU-Leitschemata der Infrastrukturentwicklung fur Europa - Bruxelles; 1993

Civil Aviation Authority: The Economic Impact of New Air Services, CAP638; London;1994

Doganis, Rigas: Flying Off Course - The Economics of International Airlines; London; 1991

Doganis, Rigas: The Airport Business; London; 1992

Domencich T., McFadden D.: Urban travel demand - a behavioural analysis; North-Holland; Amsterdam; 1975

Gallo G., Pallottino S., Florian M.: Shortest Path Methods in Transportation Models, Transportation Planning Models; The International Center for Transportation Studies (ICTS); Amsterdam; 1984

Gaudry M.I.J., Mandel B., Rothengatter W.; Introducing Spatial Competition through an Autoregressive Continguous Distributed (AR-C-D) Process in Intercity Generation-Distribution Models with Quasi-Direct Format (QDF), Centre de recherche sur les transports, University of Montreal; CRT 971; 1994a

Gaudry M.I.J., Lestage P., Guélat J., Galvan P.: TRIO-Tutorial, Version 1.0; Centre de recherche sur les transports, University of Montreal; CRT-902; 1993

Gaudry M.I.J., Mandel B., Rothengatter W.: Entwicklung eines gekoppelten Verkehrserzeugungs- und -verteilungsmodells fuer den Personenfernverkehr; im Auftrag des Bundesministers fuer Verkehr, FENr.: 60307/92; Université de Montréal C. R. T., MKmetric GmbH - Karlsruhe, Institute of policy research (IWW) University of Karlsruhe; 1994b

Gaudry M.I.J.: Asymmetric shape and variable tail thickness in multinomial probabilistic responses to significant transport service level changes. Forthcoming paper in Transportation Research B; 1992

Gaudry M.I.J., Wills M.: Estimating the functional form of travel demand models; Transportation Research 12 (4), pp 257-289; 1978

Laferrière R. Gaudry M.I.J.: Testing the inverse power transformation logit mode choice model; Centre de recherche sur les transports, University of Montreal; CRT-892; 1993

Last J., Mandel, B.: VIA Systemkomponenten – software documentation; Karlsruhe; 1997

Last J.: Reisezweckspezifische Modellierung von Verkehrsverflechtungen; Institute of policy research - IWW, University of Karlsruhe; MKmetric GmbH; 1997

Mandel B., Gaudry M., Rothengatter W.: A disaggregate Box-Cox Logit mode choice model of intercity passenger travel in Germany; The Econometrics of Major Transport Infrastructures; editor Quinet E., Vickerman R., pp.19-44; MacMillian Press, London, 1997

Mandel B., Gaudry M., Rothengatter W.: Linear or nonlinear utility functions in Logit models? The impact on German high-speed rail demand forecasts; Transportation Research Part B, Volume 28B, No.2, pp. 91-101; 1994

Mandel B., Gaudry M.I.J., Rothengatter W.: Modell zur Abschatzung der modalen Wirkungen von Investitionen im spurgefuehrten Hochgeschwindigkeits-Personenfernverkehr, im Auftrag des Bundesministers fuer Verkehr, FENr.: 60284/89; Institute of policy and research (IWW) University of Karlsruhe (TH); 1991

Mandel, B., Gaudry M. I. J., Rothengatter, W.: A Disaggregate Box-Cox Logit Mode Choice Model of Intercity Passenger Travel in Germany and its Implications for High Speed Rail Demand Forecast; The Annuals of Regional Science, pp. 99 - 120; Springer Verlag; 1997

Mandel, B.: Schnellverkehr und Modal-Split; Nomos Verlag, Baden-Baden, 1992

Manski C. F., McFadden D.: Structural Analysis of discrete data with econometric applications; London; 1981

Neumann K.: Operations Research Verfahren Band I-III; Munich; 1974

Ortuzar, J. und Willumsen, L.: Modelling Transport; Chichester, UK; 1990

REED Travel Group (publisher): OAG World Airways Guide; Dunstable, UK; 1/87 - 5/97

Sen A., Smith T.E.: Gravity Models of Spatial Interaction Behaviour; Berlin; 1995

Tran L., Gaudry M.: QDF a Quasi-direct format Used to Combine Total and Mode Choice Results to Obtain Modal Elasticities and Diversion Rates; Centre de recherche sur les transports, University of Montreal; CRT-982; 4/1994

14 THE AIR NETWORK ITINERARY AND TRIP AGGREGATION (ANITA) MODEL

Richard Laferrière

14.1 INTRODUCTION

Many authors have used air travel demand analysis in several fields: regulation (Trapani and Olson , 1982; De Vany, 1975), demand analysis and forecasting (Lansig, 1961; Long, 1968; Ippolito, 1981; Brown and Watkins, 1968; Sobienak, 1972); values of travel time (De Vany, 1974; Gronau, 1970), etc. They estimated city pair aggregated demand by defining for each market one representative price, travel time or frequency.

One issue that the analyst must face when studying air travel demand concerns the aggregation of characteristics related to traveler's itinerary. For instance, there are several possibilities to do a trip from Montreal to Vancouver and the choice has to be made over fare class, departure time, carrier, etc. Usually, aggregated air travel demand is performed by defining a unique value for each market and for each characteristic assumed to influence trip making. However, measure of representativity is arbitrary and therefore changes from one author to another. For instance, representative price of one trip has been defined as: no restriction business class (Abrahams, 1980; Andrikopoulos, 1981; De Vany, 1974; Sobienak, 1972); weighted average with the number of trip (Brown Watkins, 1968); weighted average with the number of departure (Kanafani, 1975), etc.

This paper presents how the aggregation issue is treated within the Air Network Itinerary Trip Aggregation (ANITA) model. The ANITA model uses a meaningful set of itineraries in order to explain origin-destination aggregated air travel demand. The proposed method makes use of a full description of trips in opposition to defining representative value for each characteristic independently from other characteristic belonging to the itinerary. Thus, the ANITA model differs from the usual practice as it rests on the explicit recognition of the travelers' choice between several itineraries. The explicit formulation of travelers'choice among the itineraries of each origin-destination pair and the utilization of all of the observed characteristic of the itinerary set (or the level of service) to explain the level of the aggregated demand for a market.

14.2 AGGREGATION PROCEDURES

Let's illustrate with an example, the aggregation procedure retained in the ANITA model. Suppose that for a specific origin-destination market, there are 5 itineraries, or possibilities, to travel from the origin to the destination. Furthermore, let's assume that each itinerary is uniquely defined with only 5 characteristics, see Table 1.

Table 1 Example of Itineraries in an Origin-destination Market

Itinerary	Price	Travel time	Frequency	Carrier	Fare class
1)	120	60	50	1	1
2)	90	60	50	1	2
3)	50	60	20	1	3
4)	60	80	20	2	2
5)	30	80	10	2	3

It is common practice to define a representative value for each factor known to influence aggregated air travel demand. Frequently, a weighted average is retained as rule of aggregation. However, applying a weighted average, or any other rule of aggregation, may lead to representative value of a variable that does not necessarily reflect market conditions, see Table 2. Indeed, the representative itinerary does not correspond to any itinerary actually chosen by travelers. The reason for this result is due to the aggregation being "blindly" done for each characteristic separately. Furthermore, a single value for a variable may overly simplify a very complex reality.

Table 2 Simplistic Aggregation Procedure

	Price	Travel time	Frequency
aggregation method	weighted average	weighted average	sum
representative value	70	68	150

The ANITA model aggregates itineraries instead of characteristic. This is the main point of departure with the above approach. Aggregating itineraries ensures that market conditions are preserved with the aggregation process.

The aggregation procedure of the ANITA model proceeds from three steps:

1) the definition of an itinerary, i.e. a set of paths with similar values for some characteristic, namely travel time and fare. Thus we distinguish the paths with the dimensions most likely to influence total demand;

2) the computation of level of service for each itinerary (S_1 to S_5);

3) the computation of level of service (S) for the market, see Table 3.

Table 3 Aggregating Itineraries with the ANITA Model

Itinerary	Price	Travel time	Frequency	Carrier	Level of Service
1)	120	60	50	1	S_1
2)	90	60	50	1	S_2
3)	50	60	20	1	S_3
4)	60	80	20	2	S_4
5)	30	80	10	2	S_5
		Level of Service for the market =			S

In order to compute level of service for each itinerary, characteristics are multiplied by weights or parameters. Those parameters are not calibrated independently of the demand model. They are indeed estimated with other parameters of the model to explain origin destination air travel demand. Therefore, the aggregation procedure of the ANITA model is not another ad hoc procedure but really an integrated one aimed at explaining aggregated air travel demand.

14.3 DATA SET

The estimation of the ANITA model is done with a unique data set from the audit coupons (about 12 M) used by Air Canada and CP Air during 1983. This data set represents approximately 65% of the Canadian air travel demand in 1983. Both the confidentiality and the unavailability of similar data from other carriers have limited the number of carrier in the data set.

The following information appears on each coupon received from the carriers: ticket number, coupon number, traveling date, carrier code, flight number, fare, fare class, departure and arrival cities. The arrival and departure times associated to each coupon are obtained from the Official Airline Guide North American Edition (1983).

Two rules enable the gathering of coupons belonging to a same trip:

i) all the coupons (at most four) in a ticket have the same ticket number;

ii) if a trip requires many ticket, the tickets have consecutive numbers.

14.4 FORMULATION OF THE ANITA MODEL

The formulation of the ANITA model is expressed in equations (1) to (4). Round trips by plane from city i to city j (T_{iji}) are assumed to be explained by: level of service of market ij (S_{ij}) and ji (S_{ji}), car and bus attributes of a trip from i to j (M_{ij}), socioeconomic variables of cities i and j (X_i, X_j, X_{ij}), see eq. 1. One-way trips from city i to j are explained by similar variables, see eq. 2. The share of trips between origin i and destination j with itinerary t (O_{ijt}) over trips between origin i and destination j (O_{ij}) depends on the characteristic of itinerary t (Z_{ijt}), see eq. 3. The level of service of market ij (S_{ij}) includes the characteristic of all the itineraries in the market ij, see eq. 4. Each of the random variable ε_{iji}, ε_{ij}, u_{ijt} is assumed identical and independently distributed.

$$T_{iji} = \beta_0 + (S_{ij} + S_{ji})\beta_1 + X_i\beta_2 + X_j\beta_3 + (M_{ij} + M_{ji})\beta_4 + X_{ij}\beta_5 + \varepsilon_{iji} \quad (1)$$

$$T_{ij} = \gamma_0 + (S_{ij} + S_{ji})\gamma_1 + X_i\gamma_2 + X_j\gamma_3 + (M_{ij} + M_{ji})\gamma_4 + X_{ij}\gamma_5 + \varepsilon_{ij} \quad (2)$$

$$\frac{O_{ijt}}{O_{ij}} = \frac{[(\lambda \exp(Z_{ijt}\,\theta) + 1)^{1/\lambda} + \mu]\exp(u_{ijt})}{\sum_v [(\lambda \exp(Z_{ijv}\,\theta) + 1)^{1/\lambda} + \mu]\exp(u_{ijv})} \quad (3)$$

$$S_{ij} \equiv \log(\sum_v \exp(Z_{ijv}\theta)) \quad (4)$$

14.5 RESULTS

Estimated elasticities of round trips and one-way trips from the ANITA model are presented in Table 4. These results serve to illustrate that a consistent agregation procedure can be estimated and yield meaningful results.

A priori, travel time elasticity of the first and regular economy class demands should be higher than fare elasticity. The opposite relation is expected for other fare class demands. In Table 4, travel time elasticities and fare elasticities are similar. The grouping of the fare classes may have produced this result.

As expected, but to a smaller extent, travel time implies a greater utility than transfer time.

The demands are more sensitive to the presence of first class and second class services than the presence of third class service. The service on board may explain this result, but it could also reflect the presence of important markets (ex.:Toronto-Montreal, Toronto-Ottawa, etc.).

The fact of the presence of two itineraries is more important than the presence of more than two itineraries suggest that the network variables have a greater share of explanation for markets with more than two itineraries.

14.6 CONCLUSION

The agregation issue has not received much attention in the applied econometric litterature. Arbitrary agregation procedures are often proposed. For instance, representative price of one trip has been defined as: no restriction business class; weighted average with the number of trip; weighted average with the number of departure; etc. No consensus has been established.

Table 4 Estimation of the ANITA Model

	Round Trip Elasticity	One-Way Trip Elasticity
Air Network		
travel time	-1.14	-1.06
transfer time	-1.26	-1.17
price	-1.14	-1.06
number of departures	0.28	0.26
first class service	0.56	0.53
second class service	0.71	0.66
third class service	0.19	0.17
two itineraries	1.08	1.00
more than two itineraries	0.78	0.73
level of service	0.35	0.66
Network of substitute modes		
travel time by car * travel time by bus	0.08	0.16
number of departures by bus	-0.12	-0.15
bus fare	0.66	0.59
number of nights	0.07	0.07
number of departure of other air carrier	-0.11	-0.05
air distance	-0.53	-0.76
necessity of a ferry	-0.27	-0.10
Socioeconomic variables		
absence of cities near origin	0.11	0.13
O/D linguistic composition	0.24	0.31
in-migrants, origin (province)	0.11	0.11
population, origin	0.27	0.25
university students, origin	0.16	0.20
income, origin	2.04	2.21
out-migrants, destination (province)	0.16	0.29
population, destination	0.10	0.09
university students, destination	0.18	0.13
income, destination	1.93	2.91

This paper presents a new agregation procedure called ANITA. The aggregation procedure of the ANITA model is not another ad hoc procedure but really an integrated one aimed at explaining aggregated air travel demand. The ANITA model aggregates itineraries instead of characteristic. This is the main point of departure with the usual practice. Aggregating itineraries ensures that market conditions are preserved with the aggregation process.

Indeed, agregating characteristics may lead to representative value of a variable that does not necessarily reflect market conditions, representative itinerary does not correspond to any itinerary actually chosen by travelers. The reason for this result is due to the aggregation being "blindly" done for each characteristic separately. Furthermore, a single value for a variable may overly simplify a very complex reality.

References

ABRAHAMS, M.B., **A Simultaneous Equation Estimation of Air Travel Demand**, Ph.D. thesis, University of California, 1980, 91p.

ANDRIKOPOULOS, A.A. and T. BAXEVANIDIS, "Interurban Demand for Air Travel Services: the Case of Canada", **International Journal of Transport Economics**, vol. VIII(3), 1981.

BROWN, S.L., and S. WATKINS, "The Demand for Air Travel: A Regression Study of Time Series and Cross-Sectional Data in the U.S. Domestic Market", **Highway Research Record**, 213, 1968.

DE VANY, A., "The Revealed Value of Time in Air Travel", **Review of Economics and Statistics**, vol. 66(1), 1974.

DE VANY, A., "The Effect of Price and Entry Regulation on Airline Output, Capacity, and Efficiency", **Bell Journal of Economics**, 6, 1975.

GRONAU, R., **The Value of Travel Time. Theory and Measurement**, Croom Helm, London, 1970, 213p.

IPPOLITO, R.A., "Estimating Airline Demand with Quality and Service variables", **Journal of Transportation Economics and Policy**, 1981, pp. 7-14.

KANAFANI, A. G. GEOFFREY and S. TAGHAVI, "Studies in the Demand Short Haul Air transport", **Institute of Transportation and Traffic Engineering University of California Berkeley,** CR137764, 1975, 57p.

LAFERRIÈRE, R., "Une Agrégation Nouvelle des Itinéraires de Transport Aérien (ANITA)", Ph.D. thesis, Centre de Recherche sur les Transports, Université de Montréal, 574, 1988.

LANSIG, J.B., J.C. LAO and D.B. SUITS, "An Analysis of Interurban Air Travel", **Quarterly Journal of Economics**, 1961, pp. 87-95.

LONG, H.W., "City Characteristics and the Demand for Interurban Air Travel", **Land Economics**, 1968.

SOBIENAK, J.W., **Forecasts of Passenger Travel in Canada's Domestic Long-Haul Air Market**, Canadian Transport Commission, 44, 1972.

TRAPANI, J.M. and V. OLSON, "An Analysis of the Impact of Open Entry on Price and Quality of Service in the Airline Industry", **Review of Economics and Statistics**, 1982, pp. 67-76.

15 EVALUATING AIR LIBERALIZATION AGREEMENTS: AN INTEGRATION OF DEMAND ANALYSIS AND TRADE THEORY[1]

David Gillen,
Richard Harris
and Tae Oum

15.1 INTRODUCTION

The agreement establishing the World Trade organization (WTO) came into force on January 1, 1995. The WTO replaced the General Agreement on Tariffs and Trade (GATT) which had governed trading relationships since the late 1940's. The WTO embodies fifty years of multilateral trade negotiations in the GATT that liberalized trade and established a significant body of trading rules. What the WTO did not succeed in doing was delivering agreement on trade in services. It did produce a solid framework of trading rules and obligations but failed to get agreement for applying these to trade in services. An agreement on freer trade in telecommunications was reached in February 1997 but agreements have not been reached in financial services and maritime services. Discussions regarding aviation were not even considered. This at a time when the demand for international aviation services is growing at double digit rates in many parts of the world.

For almost 50 years international competition in civil aviation services has been restricted by a variety of impediments. Their history dates to 1944 when the Bermuda Agreement was established. This agreement introduced capacity regulation, requirements for fair and equal opportunity, independent designation of carriers, and a system of precise route definition. The Agreement established a framework of liberal bilateral agreements whereby governments negotiated the exchange of air freedom rights on a nation by nation basis. A set of 'freedoms'

[1] We are indebted to Michael O'Connor and Steve Lewis-Workman for their contribution to this project.

defines increasing degrees of market access and liberalization.[2] However, these trading rules have come under some pressure.[3]

During the deregulatory period in the United States (1978 and later) the negotiating objective of the U.S. government of equality of operating opportunity for the carriers of both nations and a fair exchange of traffic rights was abandoned. By virtue of sheer market size and the strength of its carriers, the U.S. was able to impart a pro-competitive approach on several nations. The U.S. government saw the new liberal, pro-competitive bilaterals as a means of putting pressure on reluctant governments in the same geographic region. The U.S. took advantage of 5th freedom rights in certain countries to circumvent restrictions in neighboring nations with more restrictive bilaterals. This approach, for the most part, was successful. Under what became known as "encirclement" theory, the UK and Germany were to be pressured by expansion of air service to and from Belgium and The Netherlands. Soon afterward, a new agreement with South Korea was intended to put pressure on Japan. This campaign for "Open Skies" as it became known, was further stimulated by strong criticism within the U..S. of the restrictive terms of Bermuda II.[4] This effect and the more general movements toward free trade internationally means that in all markets, the move will be toward less rather than more regulation. What is up for debate is the pace and form of liberalization.

In negotiating trade agreements, the concern of the negotiating parties is who gains, who loses and what trade might be deflected from or to itself or others as a result of some agreement. Before greater liberalization in (air) services proceeds further, countries need to better understand the consequences of changes to the rules and restrictions governing trade. In any trade negotiation, the participants consider how changes to the rules governing trade will affect consumers and producers in each country including those from which trade might be deflected. Governments are also concerned about the potential loss of tax revenues. These 'trading' considerations which are quite standard when assessing trade in goods were never fully taken into account when negotiating trade in air services. Part of the reason was that negotiation was on a bilateral basis and markets were generally quite restrictive.

The purpose of this paper is to develop a method of assessing alternative changes in the rules governing the supply of international aviation services among countries. The traditional approach would be to undertake a benefit-cost analysis of the alternatives. However, cost-benefit methodology has traditionally concerned itself with the consequences on aggregate economic efficiency within a given national

---

[2] See Transport Canada, "Assessing the Benefits and Costs of International Air Transport Liberalization", Ottawa (1996)

[3] The strains on the regulatory system are a result of extensive domestic deregulation, the entry of new carriers in domestic and international markets, the growth of cross-border controls, code-sharing agreements and the divergent and growing needs of business and tourist travelers and shippers as trade expands under the liberalized WTO.

[4] In 1977, the UK renounced the Bermuda Agreement. The Bermuda II Agreement was accepted by the US and the UK and was aimed at restructuring the air relationships which had developed after 1945. This agreement was, in many ways more restrictive than the agreement that preceded it and was never a model for US bilateral air transport agreements.

market. In practice, much of the emphasis has been on the improvement to consumers' welfare with domestic deregulation.[5] Knowledge of the aggregate price elasticities would be sufficient to calculate welfare gains or losses.[6] When trade liberalization takes place in an international setting there are additional issues such as trade deflection that need to be considered in any evaluation.

Trade policy while concerned with changes in global efficiency following policy changes, tends to concentrate on the distribution of the impacts of these changes across nations and on identifying the winners and losers. In this type of analysis, there is a concern for evaluating the impacts on *both* producer and consumer interests, as a nation's producers may gain while its consumers lose (or vice-versa) from policy changes.[7] Third party effects resulting from trade diversion are perhaps the most important part of any analysis. These calculations can only be made by disaggregating markets.[8] Inter-route and inter-carrier substitution elasticities are needed to assess gains and losses by national carriers. As well trade deflection is estimated by calculating the extent to which consumers will substitute routes or move to third party carriers. In this analysis of substitution fare, quality and national preferences affect market share and welfare effects. National preferences in a multi-county setting have an important influence and can be captured in the quality parameters.

In this paper we present a model to assess the impact of changes in the rules governing trade in aviation services between countries. In section 2 the types of bilateral regimes are presented and the measure of gains and loses presented. Section 3 contains a presentation of previous work in their assessment of changes in international air transport liberalization while section 4 provides a discussion of trade theory applied to trade in services and points out some differences between a traditional benefit-cost approach and a trade theory approach. The formal model of demand side benefits is presented in section 5 together with a description of how the supply side is modelled and the summary is contained in section 6.

15.2 UNDERSTANDING MARGINAL GAINS FROM POLICY CHANGES

The key factors impacting a carrier in a bilateral are market access, designation, capacity and tariffs. Individual bilaterals can be categorized as facilitating, moderately open, and restrictive based on the number of restrictions in place.

---

[5] Governments are also a major gainer or loser through changes in net tax/subsidy revenues particularly as indirect taxation is an important feature or the tax framework or industrial or subsidy policies are in place.

[6] There are a number of elasticity estimates available in the literature. See Oum, Waters and Yong (1992)

[7] Trade policy uses a long-accepted analytic approach to address specific trade questions. However, until now the very question of liberalizing air travel has not been dealt with in a substantial way by trade policy analysts. It is only recently that trade economists have focused their efforts on the service sector.

[8] Any model assessing welfare changes from bilateral liberalization must be capable of capturing the impact on third party as well as national carriers.

Market access, for example, can be constrained by limiting the number of points a carrier can serve, by limiting freedoms -- particularly fifth freedoms -- by controlling the number of designated carriers to participate in the bilateral and by having ownership or other performance requirements imposed. Note that many of these factors also serve to limit capacity or supply. We might think of market access defining the number of firms and capacity as the number of seats, frequencies or share of seats which a carrier can provide in the market(s).

Table 1: Categorization of International Air Transport Policy Regimes

	Restrictive	Moderate	Facilitating
Market Access	-No 5th Freedoms -Single Point Access	-Limited 5th Freedoms -Multiple with Specific Access Points Restricted	-Full 5th Freedom Rights -Open Access to All Points
Designation	-Single Designation -No Foreign Ownership	-Multiple Designation with Restrictions -Limited Foreign Ownership	-Multiple Designation -No Ownership Restrictions
Capacity/ Frequency Controls	-Agreement Between Airlines -Predetermined (Quota)	-Increases Subject to Approval	-No Controls
Tariffs	-Airline Agreement Mandatory	-Refer to IATA -Single Disapproval	-Double Disapproval

Route access is also a major determinant of market access. Route access often generates asymmetrical effects for the countries negotiating a bilateral. Canadian carriers can originate from any point in Canada to a foreign country whereas a foreign carrier can access only a limited set of designated points in Canada. UK, Germany, Netherlands and Mexico have relatively greater access to Canadian points than other countries. With Open Skies, American carriers have significant access to Canadian points and it provides a significant asset value to Canadian carriers to form alliances with carriers who would like to access the US market via Canada.[9]

---

[9] The nature of the Capacity controls to either carrier in a bilateral is important. Restrictive regimes require agreement between designated carriers and approval by both authorities. Canada has very restrictive capacity regimes in all areas except with the United Kingdom, Germany and the Netherlands. In twelve of its largest international markets, Canada has the ability to designate more than one carrier in eleven of them. This benefit could be negated with capacity restrictions in the case of Hong Kong, Japan and Australia, while in France and Italy there would need to be an agreement between the carriers.

In developing our model we are interested in liberalization from two perspectives. First, what particular aspect of liberalization is taking place; market access, capacity constraints, carrier designation or tariff setting? Second what is the relative change in liberalization? Is the regime currently highly protectionist and the suggested move is to a less but still somewhat restrictive regime or is it a move to full liberalization? Does it matter? The model should be capable of answering these questions. Table 1 presents a categorization of policy regimes and policy levers.

15.3 PREVIOUS STUDIES OF WELFARE GAINS FROM LIBERALIZATION

There are two studies that have investigated the gains from liberalization in international aviation. They use different methodologies and examine different areas of the world. The Australian study (Street, Smith and Savage, 1994) attempts to measure the gains to both cost efficiency and improvements in service quality. The American study (Hufbauer, and Findlay, 1996) considers only the cost savings.

An analysis of opening up the Australian market to greater competition illustrates the differences between changes in domestic and international aviation policy. Using a relatively simple model they attempted to examine the trade-offs inherent in any such study. They found (Reported in Table 2 that it will not necessarily be the case that easing the conditions of an air services agreement will always return a positive outcome for the domestic economy, in this case Australia.

Table 2: Summary of Annualized Estimates of Welfare Change (Market Responses to Four Liberalization Scenarios)

	Annualized estimate of welfare change ($ millions)				
	Stage 2	Stage 3	Stage 4a,	Stage 4b or	Stage 4c
World welfare	23	46	21	0	-27
Australian welfare	2	-14	-20	-25	-31
Australia's airline	-14	-33	-33	-33	-33
Australian passengers	9	7	3	0	-5
Australian tourists	4	3	1	0	-2
Foreign welfare	22	60	41	25	4
Foreign airlines	-30	5	2	0	-2
New entrant	21	35	34	33	32
Foreign passengers	34	29	13	0	-18

Source: Street, Smith and Savage (1994)

Note: Included within 'Australian welfare' and 'Foreign welfare' is the profit repatriation from Australia's airline to its foreign owner. Hence, these totals differ from the sum of their displayed components by the amount of this repatriation.

Canada has the right to Designate additional carriers, without capacity restrictions for 3rd and 4th freedom services to the United Kingdom, Germany, Netherlands, Jamaica, Mexico and Trinidad.

The analysis is undertaken in stages to assess how welfare changes occur with an evolution from liberalization. In *Stage 1* Australia has one airline offering four frequencies per week between Australia and a foreign country. The foreign country's airline offers six frequencies per week. A third foreign carrier is in the market with two frequencies per week. The assumed elasticities are -0.75 business passenger, -1.5 for leisure passenger, 0.15 flight frequency elasticities for business and 0.05 for leisure passengers. The ratio of business to leisure is ¼ and 80 percent of travelers are foreigners. In *stage 2* entry of a foreign carrier occurs increasing capacity and reducing fares. *Stage 3* represents the withdrawal of the domestic carrier from the market, thereby reducing competition. In stage 4 three possible outcomes are considered due to the uncertainty of some effects. In 4a, air fares rise by 8 percent, in 4b fares rise by 8 percent more and in 4c fares are based on a collusive industry.

The trade-offs which policy makers must evaluate are those that occur between what is best for the world versus what is best for Australia, and what is best for Australia's international airline interest versus the tourism industry versus the consumers of air travel. Recognizing the welfare trade-offs are being assessed within a partial equilibrium framework and these would most likely have to be considered within a broader trading framework. The gains and losses must be considered from different perspectives. It may make economic sense from a global viewpoint for an airline, Qantas, to cease operations in a particular market if a foreign airline were able to operate more efficiently. Or it may be globally beneficial to increase competition in one of Qantas's markets with the intent of stimulating price competition and lowering fares for consumers. Yet from a national perspective if the market is dominated by a foreign passengers, does it make sense to reduce Qantas's profit by carrying these passengers? These are fair policy questions and ones which face negotiators.

Table 3: Possible Cost Savings To Users From Competitive Aviation Service In 2010 And For The Period 1997-2010 ($Billion)

Country	Cost savings in 2010	Cumulative cost savings, 1997-2010
Australia	$1.0	$7
Canada	$1.5	$11
Hong Kong	$2.2	$15
Japan	$9.4	$66
Korea	$3.9	$27
Malaysia	$1.0	$ 7
Singapore	$2.7	$19
Total	**$21.7**	**$152**

Source: Hufbauser and Findlay (1996)

A second study of the benefits from liberalization investigated the gains across countries. The method of calculation is relatively crude and assumes no strategic interaction among carriers. The gains are all in the form of cost savings and are assumed to be transferred to consumers through competition. The starting point of the calculation is 2010 GNP (in 1993 dollars) calculated as the 1993 GNP growing at growth rates of 2.5 to 3.5 percent for Australia, Canada and Japan and 6 - 7 percent growth for Hong Kong, Korea, Malaysia and Singapore. The total operating revenues of the country's largest carrier are used to calculate the proportion of aviation activity in GNP. A 25 percent cost reduction is assumed. The gains are then measured as (Aviation Revenue$_i$/GNP$_i$) x GNP$_i$ x .25 for each year. The calculations are illustrated in Table 3.These numbers appear to be too high. The assumption of a 25 percent cost saving is somewhat generous given the cost efficiency of most of the Asian carriers.

The numbers contained in Table 3 are ad hoc and gross measures. There is no underlying model and the distribution of gains and losses are not identified. On the other hand the results reported in Table 2 are model based. The value in this Australian study is that it treated the entry/exit issue as well as frequency changes. It distinguished between more competition and more supply. It also identified the sources of the gains and losses, it identified gains or losses to foreign and domestic travelers and it examined the downstream impact on tourism. This study is a good example at a first attempt at integrating trade related issues into an traditional evaluation of changes in aviation markets. It serves as a starting point for our modeling.

15.4 TRADE THEORY APPROACH

Trade policy analysis introduces a long-accepted framework for the analysis of specific trade issues. It is able to handle a number of increasingly complex assumptions regarding market structure and product differentiation. International trade policy examines the (unilateral, bilateral, regional or multilateral) distribution of the gains and losses among countries, owing to changes in trade policy instruments. The policy instruments usually consist of changes in the level of either tariff or non-tariff barriers, expressed either as price distortions or quantitative constraints on exports or imports. These gains or losses have two sources: (i) a country's increased specialization in industries in which it enjoys a relative advantage, compared to other countries' industries; and (ii) relative price changes which favour one country at the expense of another. Trade policy analysis is often concerned with the redistribution of factors employed in the impacted industry and their incomes, as a consequence of policy changes. Lastly, trade policy analysis is often conducted with a strategic view in mind: the evaluation of trade-offs between one industry versus another at the domestic level and redistribution with other industries as well. This multi-industry focus is quite different from the single-industry regulatory approach which has characterized the air transport industry.

Trade policy analysis has historically been interested in, among other things, changes in factor prices arising from trade. For that reason, it is often conducted in a general-equilibrium analytical framework, or at least tends to model the relevant factor markets explicitly. In addition, virtually all trade policy models explicitly adopt a multi-country framework in which both producers and consumers are distinguished by national origin. This can be done at either the partial or general-equilibrium level. In many instances there is an explicit treatment of the national factor supply curves in order to account for policy-induced wage changes across countries.

Trade policy analysis generally adopts a multi-country approach to trade flows, but also uses a bilateral approach in special cases. The discussion of both bilateral and regional liberalization invariably deals with the important third- party effects of these types of agreements. In considering bilateral or regional agreements, one must account for the effects of the diversion of trade away from, or toward, third countries not involved in the bilateral agreement. The bilateral liberalization of air transport must deal with exactly the same type of problems. A U.S.-Netherlands liberalization on the North Atlantic may divert traffic away from French national carriers on a New-York Paris route, for example, due to the lower fares on New York-Amsterdam which follow from the bilateral liberalization. Accounting for these effects in quantitative work is a matter of judgment. In the case of Canada-U.S., the effects are potentially large in almost all industries given (i) the geographic proximity of the U.S. market to Canadian consumers and producers, and (ii) the large share of Canadian supply accounted for by U.S.-based producers.

There are three sets of cases to keep in mind when discussing the role of trade diversion. Consider a three-country framework involving Canada, the United States and a third country called X.

(i) A more liberalized U.S.-X bilateral agreement may divert traffic away from Canadian carriers toward U.S. and X-based carriers on Canada-X routes. It may also divert traffic which is currently on-going from X through Canada to the U.S., toward a X-U.S. direct route.

(ii) A more liberalized Canada-X bilateral agreement may give rise to diversion away from U.S.-X toward Canada and thus increase Canada-U.S. traffic.

(iii) A Canada-U.S.-X multilateral agreement relative to two existing bilateral agreements could lead to increased Canada-U.S. traffic but substantial reductions in either Canada-X traffic or U.S.-X traffic. U.S. hubbing advantages would be an important factor in this type of calculation.

15.4.1 Other International Issues

There are a number of international issues that must be resolved in any trade policy analysis, namely exchange rates and international cost comparisons; international differences in taxation; and the evaluation of changes in international policy regimes.

Probably the singly most perplexing problem in international industry analysis is the choice of an exchange rate concept at which to convert local currency values into a single and comparable number. This is an entirely practical and unavoidable measurement issue which must be dealt with in any methodology in which international cost comparisons are central to the empirical evaluation of relative national competitiveness. Some studies use current exchange rates to convert all costs to a single comparable unit, say U.S. dollars, in a particular base year. It is widely recognized this may be inappropriate due to the substantial short-term volatility in these rates. The second most common method is to convert all local currency nominal values using Purchasing Power Parity (PPP) values of the exchange rate. PPP exchange rate values are widely available. They suffer from a number of severe problems however. One is that they are derived from a particular assumption regarding initial parity values in the base years, which is usually arbitrary and may be far from the true PPP value in that year. Another is that PPP fails to account adequately for changes in the *equilibrium exchange* rate due to differential productivity growth differentials between countries. This is a key issue when making comparison between the Asian economies and those in North America or Europe due to large differences in growth rates. The recent moves to floating exchange rates and the turmoil in Asian markets exacerbate the problem.

Current exchange rates may actually do much better than PPP when considering shifts in demand or changes in competition for an internationally provided service. Thus, if we look at labour costs in Japan for example, and correct them using the PPP value of the Yen, this would suggest that Japan would have a much larger wage cost advantage than it actually has, as the PPP value of the Yen is far below the current 120 Yen/U.S. dollar exchange rate. There is currently no widely accepted methodology for dealing with these problems other than to recognize them. An average of the exchange rate over the last economic cycle is probably a better approximation than PPP numbers to the equilibrium value of the exchange rate for purposes of competitive analysis. It is hard to overstate just how important this adjustment is to actual measures of benefits and costs in these types of exercises.

Finally, in the multi-country context, one must typically come up with dollar figures for losses and gains in welfare *by country*; these dollar figures are sometimes compared across countries. It is at this stage that a PPP correction to measured surplus changes might be useful, in that changes in real income by country need to be measured in standardized units that correct for local price-level differences.

Another area of concern are international taxation differences. Changes in the demand for air travel will affect the revenues collected by the national governments by levying taxes on goods, wages, airport services, etc. The change in these revenues, and induced changes in deadweight losses due to taxation, have to be accounted for in principle as part of the cost-benefit analysis. Secondly, differences in the tax treatment of profits and wage income may induce shifts in the locations of particular activities of air transport firms in the event of a liberalization.

Trade policy analysis has become adept at evaluating changes in trade barriers in the form of tariffs or non-tariff barriers to trade in goods. The literature concerned with changes in preferential trading arrangements is the most relevant to the case of bilateral agreements to liberalize air transport. It has been much less successful at dealing with barriers to trade in services or impediments to trade due to international differences in regulatory regimes. Adequately capturing changes in entry restrictions, for example, in a practical and easily quantifiable way remains an unresolved issue.

15.5 APPROACH TO MODEL DEVELOPMENT AND ESTIMATION

The modeling approach is based on an integration of the economic cost-benefit model with the conventions from trade theory to account for issues that arise when analyzing the structure of international trade in services. In particular it needs to be able to distinguish the effects of entry and shifts in supply through flight frequency changes of incumbent carriers. The model is placed in a network context and must therefore also be capable of representing the impact of these changes on trade flows over different routes. Finally, it needs to distinguish classes of service and nationality to measure the distribution of gains and losses between producers and consumers and between domestic and foreign users.

The model developed below uses a two tier approach. The first tier builds the analytic foundations based on the conditions of demand, the conditions for supply and market clearing yields equilibrium quantities and prices (equilibrium conditions developed for two dimensional market i.e., a two carrier one route OD pair).

The second tier utilizes numerical methods to solve for market equilibrium in a multidimensional airline market i.e., composed of multiple carriers for multiple routes in an origin destination pair. The approach uses a generalized Armington-type model[10] which allows for changes in the number of services (carriers) available to consumers distinguished by country of origin and commodity type. In our analysis the commodity 'type' refers to both the OD market and the carrier. Moreover, we allow commodities to have different characteristics. Carriers may have different frequencies, for example and this is a measure of service quality that will affect demand.

Aviation services are supplied in a network and a requirement of the model is integrating all of the dimensions of international air travel into the framework. The starting point is the representation of the relevant OD markets for a given network. In general terms this would be all the OD markets in the relevant region. In Figure 1, we illustrate such a network as in the North Pacific. In this case it is simplified to represent OD traffic between Vancouver (YVR),Tokyo (NRT), Seattle (SEA) and Seoul(SEL). In this international network there are four countries, each country with a single airport, and three (3) potential OD markets in each country. For example, in Vancouver all originating traffic is assumed to be Vancouver based and destined for one of the three alternative destinations. Each OD market is served by several alternative routes and several carriers serving a particular route. Each route has one or more segments where a segment is a flight between two airports. Each carrier will carry passengers traveling from YVR-NRT, as well as passengers to YVR from other cities in Canada (Toronto-YYZ for example) and passengers traveling beyond NRT (to Seoul, for example). The model dimensionality therefore means that the passenger must be indexed by nationality, destination, fareclass, trip purpose, carrier and route.

A major question regarding liberalization is what will happen to the characteristics of this network in response to a bilateral liberalization between Canada and Japan. While this liberalization will pertain only to Japanese and

---

[10] See Spence (1976), Helpman and Krugman (1985) and Dixit and Stiglitz (1977).

Canada carriers and the network segments connecting YVR and NRT, the evaluation of these effect will depend on the network wide demand and supply responses. For example how traffic between SEL and YVR or SEA and NRT might be diverted through either NRT or YVR in response to the liberalization. Both the demand and supply side specification attempt to take into account these system wide interaction effects.

Figure 1: Illustrating Four Country North Pacific Air Transportation Network and Canada-Japan Liberalization

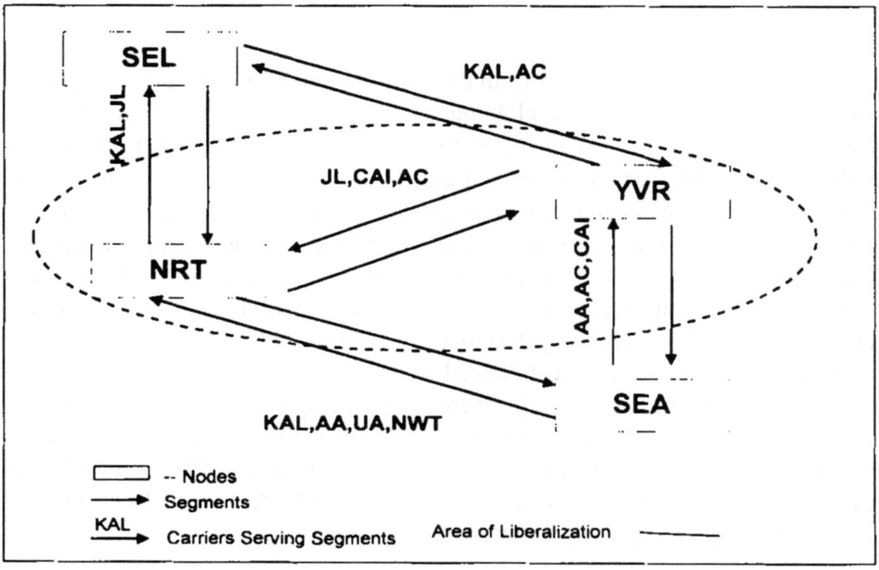

15.5.1 Demand Model Specification and Estimation

The demand model must be capable of incorporating differentiated products to correctly capture changes in the level and quality of air services delivered by incumbent as well a new entrant carriers. One way of introducing preferences for differentiated services and products is to assume variety of services. This follows from the idea that there are more products than characteristics and re-bundling characteristics results in another product. A car, stereo, vacation, restaurant, wine and air trip are well defined products. However, each of these products can and does have many varieties; American, Australian, Canadian and German wines, for example. The way this 'many dimensions' for products can be handled is by placing structure on the underlying preference functions thereby yielding manageable demand functions.

The preferences can be represented by a two level utility function sometimes referred to as multi-stage decision-making. This means in stage one consumers allocate their budget across broad categories of expenditures and optimize this mix.

In the second stage individuals allocate their within category budget across the variety of products within that category.[11] For example, we can think of people allocating their budget across broad categories of food, clothing, shelter, recreation and savings. They would optimize this allocation in this first stage dependent on the relative price indices for categories and preferences. In the second stage they would allocated their within category budget to optimize each category given relative prices for each product in the category. This type of preference can be represented by a two-level utility function

$$U = U\left(u_1(\bullet), u_2(\bullet), \ldots, u_k(\bullet)\right) \qquad \text{Equation 1}$$

where $u_i(\bullet)$ is the subutility derived from the consumption of expenditure category i. For example, these might be food, clothing, shelter, recreation, etc..[12] The structure we impose is to assume $U(\bullet)$ is increasing and homothetically separable. If an expenditure category has only one product or the products within it are homogeneous, $u_i(\bullet)$ will depend only on the quantity consumed q_i. If the expenditure category has many products or much variety, $u_i(\bullet)$ will depend on the quantity of each variety consumed. Furthermore, we can think of there being a taste for variety; more variety even if not every one is consumed, makes people better off. In effect, variety will be valued in its own right, (Dixit and Stiglitz, 1977).

Modeling of greater variety has followed the use of concave symmetric subutility functions such as $u_i\ (q_{i1}, q_{i2}, \ldots, q_{il})$ where q_{il} is the quantity of variety l to be consumed out of expenditure category i.[13] If all varieties are closely priced consumers will choose to consume all in relatively equal quantities. As relative prices diverge some varieties will not be consumed. A useful form of the [homothetically separable] utility function often used is

$$u_i(q_{i1}, q_{i2}, \ldots) \equiv \left(\sum_l q_{il}^{\beta_i}\right)^{1/\beta_i}, \ \beta_i = \left(1 - \frac{1}{\sigma_i}\right), \sigma_i > 1 \qquad \text{Equation 2}$$

where σ_i is the elasticity of substitution of varieties. The reason this form is considered useful is that each pair of varieties is equally substitutable for each other. Furthermore the degree of substitutability of any pair of varieties does not depend on

---

[11] Consumer preferences must be bugetable and decentralizable. Consumer preferences are said to be bugetable if it is possible to allocate income optimally across m budget categories knowing only the m aggregate category prices and without information of within category products. Preferences are said to be decentralizable if it is possible to optimally allocate the category expenditures knowing only the intra-category prices (Oum and Gillen, 1983)

[12] While these restrictions on preferences may seem excessive, they are implied in any travel demand model which uses OD or route aggregate data, which most all do.

[13] In theory an infinite varieties could be consumed but not produced. Rising marginal costs place an upper limit on variety. The selection of how much variety will be determined by relative prices; California wine, Australian wine and French wine.

the size of the market and is independent of the demand for any other variety.[14] From this CES form of the subutility function it is possible to show that the subutility level achieved from expenditure level E_i , the expenditure on product i, and n_i the variety of product i, and price p_i the price of product i, is

$$u_i\left(\frac{E_i}{n_i p},\ldots\right)=(n_i)^{1/(\sigma_i-1)}\frac{E}{p_i} \qquad \text{Equation 3}$$

Equation 3 shows that for a given level of spending on a product and a given price for the available varieties, welfare increases as the number of varieties increases. For our purposes this is an interesting result since it addresses the issue of whether adding more carriers to an OD market improves consumer welfare.[15]

From the two stage optimization process, the demand functions produced for variety from the first stage will be

$$q_{iz}=\frac{p_{iz}^{-\sigma_i}}{\sum_{z\in\Omega_i}p_{iz}^{1-\sigma_i}}E_i \quad \text{for } z\in\Omega_i \qquad \text{Equation 4}$$

where p_{iz} is the price of variety z and Ω_i is the set of available varieties. It can be shown, Dixit and Stiglitz (1977) the price elasticity of demand for the ith variety is σ_i provided n is sufficiently large; i.e. $\sigma_i = \sigma_i(n_i)$. This is a powerful result since it says that the sensitivity to price changes will be fairly represented by the degree to which varieties are substitutes as measured by the elasticity of substitution. Therefore, in our demand model knowledge of the substitutability between carriers will play a key role.

This idea of variety and nationally differentiated products was introduced into the international trade literature by Armington (1969). Our demand model follows these ideas to derive demands for substitutable but "differentiated" services. This approach was chosen for a number of reasons. When new carriers enter the market it represents a new 'variety' of an already traded service. Also this approach allows for market size as well as carrier shares to change. In the air travel liberalization model the services are alternative route/carrier combinations over a given origin-destination pair. The basic model is amended to incorporate quality or non-price factor which can vary across route-carrier alternatives. The specification of the demand side, described below, is designed with the goal in mind of measuring all of the benefits of changing the rules affecting the supply of [international] air travel services. We need to account for all changes to consumer benefits and therefore

---

[14] This assumption is precisely what Spence (1977) uses to simplify the analysis of the introduction of new products into a market.

[15] Commodity type in our analysis refers to both the OD market and the carrier.

must measure demand at the level of the route segment and aggregate to the route and market level.

The demand side distinguishes between aggregate OD demand, and demand for individual routes connecting an OD pair. For every OD pair there is a home demand aggregator at each end of the route for each fare class. Each OD group can thus be thought of as an individual consumer with a [Marshallian] demand curve given by

$$Q=f(P) \qquad \text{Equation 5}$$

Q is an index of total passenger demand over the particular OD market, connected by a number of route/carriers indexed $r=1,\ldots\ldots,R$. For simplicity, we refer to any given r simply as a route. The index of aggregated demand is a function of the price index P; P is the real price index for this route and is a function of the individual prices p_r on the routes existing in an OD market.

Q is referred to as the real quantity index of demand -- it can also be interpreted as being measured in "utils"of *aggregate real air service.* Let q_r be the individual route demands measured in conventional passenger unit terms and let p_r be the route prices. If we assume that the utility function generating Q is positive linear homogenous so that:

$$Q=U(q_1,\ldots,q_R) \qquad \text{Equation 6}$$

then the dual to $U(.)$ is the exact price index function $P(p_1,\ldots\ldots,p_R)$. It is convenient to work with the price index function rather than the utility or quantity index function. In the Armington literature one assumes that $P(\bullet)$ is of the Constant Elasticity of Substitution form so that:

$$P(p_1,\ldots,p_r)=\left[\sum_{r=1}^{R}\delta_r p_r^{-\sigma}\right]^{-1/\sigma} \qquad \text{Equation 7}$$

Here the δ_r are the weights on individual routes r and σ is the Allen-Uzawa common elasticity of substitution between any two route pairs. Demand for route r given the level of aggregate Q, is given via Shepherd's Lemma so that:[16]

$$q_r=\delta_r\left(\frac{p_r}{P}\right)^{-\sigma}Q \qquad \text{Equation 8}$$

[16] Given a list of prices p_r on all routes, demand on route r is calculated in the following manner: compute the value of the aggregate price index P using equation 7; calculate the aggregate real quantity index Q using the aggregate demand curve (using equation 5); calculate individual route demands using equation 8.

In consumer equilibrium total consumer expenditure in this OD market is given by:

$$E = \sum_{r=1}^{R} p_r q_r \qquad \text{Equation 9}$$

Note that by construction $E=PQ$; actual expenditure on all routes is equal to the product of the price index and the aggregate real quantity index.

In our multi-country demand analysis welfare as well as market shares are dependent on quality differences. This would include the effect of national preferences. In order to accommodate differences across routes in quality characteristics, the linear quality model is used (which is closely related to the hedonic price approach to quality adjustments).[17] The quality index for route r with a vector of characteristics 'x' could be represented by quality function as $a_r(f_r, t_r, other)$ where a_r is an increasing function in all variables corresponding to an increase in quality attributes such as frequency (f_r). The particular function form for a_r(.) is taken to be iso-elastic.

The basic model starts with a definition of quality adjusted units of real service, interpreted as units of the particular service measured in efficiency units with the quality function a_r(.).

$$q_r^* = a_r(x_r) q_r \qquad \text{Equation 10}$$

The number q_r is referred to as the "unadjusted demand" or physical demand; in measurement terms it corresponds to the observable quantity of service r purchased by the consumer. In this case it corresponds to the number of passengers on a route in the relevant OD market. Higher a_r coefficients correspond to higher quality. Corresponding to the quality adjusted demand q^* in efficiency units is a price p^*; i.e., the price per unit of q^*.

Given the linearity of q_r* in q_r it follows that:

$$p_r^* = (1/a_r(x_r)) p_r \qquad \text{Equation 11}$$

The quality units are chosen such that for a service with quality level $a_r=1$, $p_r=p_r^*$. As the quality level rises for given p_r, the real price per unit of quality, p_r^* falls. Consumers actually buy the physical quantity q_r at price p_r, but from a utility point of view purchase q_r* at price p_r* per unit of quality-adjusted demand. This is the figure which affects the calculation of consumer surplus, our measure of benefits. Depending on the nature of the supply side of the model, consumers take both p_r and p_r^* as given and choose q_r^* and thus q_r.

[17] See Chapter 2, Tirole, Jean. Theory of Industrial Organization, for a complete exposition of this model.

The approach in the previous section to deriving individual unadjusted route demand curves is applied in exactly the same manner with quality adjustments except that all prices and quantities are expressed in quality adjusted units.

$$Q^* = f(P^*) \qquad \text{Equation 12}$$

$$P^* = \left[\sum_{r=1}^{R} \delta_r p_r^{*-\sigma}\right]^{-1/\sigma} \qquad \text{Equation 13}$$

$$q_r^* = \delta_r \left(\frac{p_r^*}{P^*}\right)^{-\sigma} Q^* \qquad \text{Equation 14}$$

To empirically implement such a procedure it is necessary to have information on the quality coefficients a_r so that the real quality adjusted prices p_r^* can be calculated and substituted into the price index and demand function. Having derived a quality-adjusted individual route demand via the same process outlined in the previous section, demand in observable units (passenger volumes) is given by:

$$q_r = \frac{\delta_r}{a_r}\left(\frac{p_r^*}{P^*}\right)^{-\sigma} Q^* \qquad \text{Equation 15}$$

One of the benefits of this particular demand specification is that it allows explicitly for calculating consumers' welfare and demand consequences of adding new routes or reducing route choices in a given OD market and for quality changes on those routes.

In equation 15 it is impossible to empirically distinguish between shifts in demand due to changes in δ_r and changes in a_r. In order to identify the model we set all δ_r equal to 1. The implication of this assumption is that if all routes offer the same quality and the same prices then demand by assumption would be equal on all routes. Demand differences therefore must be attributed in the benchmark and counterfactuals to either quality or price differences across routes. As a simple illustration, suppose there is a market where there are only two routes, so $R = 2$ and both quality adjusted prices are equal to 1.0; thus demand on both routes is equal. Under these market conditions, the aggregate price index is given by:

$$P^*(2) = (\delta 1^{-\sigma} + \delta 1^{-\sigma})^{-1/\sigma} = (2\delta)^{-1/\sigma} \qquad \text{Equation 16}$$

Now suppose a new route is introduced that offers the same characteristics (price and non-price characteristics) as the previous routes so that its hedonic price is also unity, but now R = 3. In this case the new aggregate price index is given by:

$$P^*(3) = (\delta(1)^{-\sigma} + \delta(1)^{-\sigma} + \delta(1)^{-\sigma})^{-1/\sigma} = (3\delta)^{-1/\sigma} \qquad \text{Equation 17}$$

We see in comparing these two equations that the real price index falls if $\sigma > 1$; i.e. the elasticity of substitution between route/carriers exceeds unity. If $\sigma = 2$ $P^*(3)/P^*(2) = 0.81$; an increase from 2 to 3 routes is equivalent to a 19 percent reduction in the real price of aggregate travel. When substituted into the demand function the increase in real quality adjusted demand is approximately $\eta^d \bullet \Delta P^*$. Note that in the case of exit the adjustment would be in the opposite direction.

This demand model is also explicitly structured to deal with the issue of inter-route substitution in a network context such as that outlined in the previous section. In Figure 1, for example, changes to the bilateral between Canada and Japan and liberalization of the of YVR-NRT market is likely to induce substitution between alternative routes connecting Japan and Canada, but passing through third countries. For example, a route such as SEA-NRT would be serviced by a U.S. carrier but with the liberalization the route SEA-YVR-NRT would draw some traffic. The extent of inter-route substitution in response to liberalization and its welfare consequences for consumers will depend on key parameters such as the route substitution elasticity and the relevant quality characteristics of competing routes.

15.5.2 Framework for Supply Model

The supply modeling framework captures changes in cost of air carrier services in the market which may be influenced by the rules governing trade in services. Airlines may respond to changes in the rules of international air travel (e.g., flight frequency) by supplying more service or new services. To the extent that airlines experience cost economies, these supply responses will be exhibited by a shift in the cost function.

In the demand model, any OD market may be served by a number of routes and each route is composed of one or more segments. A segment is a flight between any two airports. In a network of multiple OD's, it is probable that changes in one OD will affect passenger demands over the other OD's. For example, if higher frequencies are allowed between Canada and Japan not only will this OD market expand, but additional traffic may be garnered from passengers who are traveling to Korea via Japan. The flight segment YVR-NRT will carry more than simply the O-D traffic and this will affect costs through economies of traffic density. The base unit for the cost function will therefore be the flight segment. Once the segment costs are calculated it is possible to construct a route cost by aggregating the relevant segment costs. The total carrier costs are calculated as the sum of all passenger costs and segment costs.

In describing a carrier's costs we distinguish costs which vary by segment and those which vary by route. In many cases the source of cost differences will be in the airline system or station costs. For example, if carrier *i* were to extend its operation from point B to point C, when it was already in an AB market, the additional costs would include the increase in flight operating costs and passenger costs. However, since it is already serving airport B, the cost of adding an operation will be quite low. This is quite different from a circumstance of entering an entirely new market. Clearly, both volume of passenger and flight frequency are important.

Total cost for a flight segment, C_s^T can be written as:

$$C_S^T = C_S^q(q_S) + C_S^f(f_S) \qquad \text{Equation 18}$$

where q is the total number of passengers on a segment and f_s is the flight frequency on that segment. The first term of equation 12 is the segment costs which relate to passengers while the second term relates to costs which are associated with flight frequency.

C^q (•) are passenger costs on a segment and are obtained from Form 41 data by subtracting flight related costs from total costs.[18] These calculated total indirect costs are allocated to each segment by multiplying systemwide total indirect costs by the ratio of segment revenue to systemwide total revenue.[19] C^f(•) can be measured by adding the cost per block hour multiplied by the number of block hours required for the flight segment and a measure of the opportunity costs of flight capital.[20]

These two costs which are treated as constant unit costs to the airline is analogous to the concept of constant marginal cost in the usual competitive model. These are unit flight costs and unit passenger costs, w and v respectively. Unit costs will change (UC will shift down) as the volume of passengers changes and as flight frequency and load factors change.

Total costs are then defined as:

$$TC = vQ + wF \qquad \text{Equation 19}$$

where F is segment frequency and Q is segment passenger demand

Carrier load factors are calculated as follows:

$$z = (Q/F)/G \qquad \text{Equation 20}$$

where: G is gauge (available seats or plane capacity)

Average per-passenger segment cost, u, can be computed by dividing the total segment cost by the number of passengers. The approximate average cost per

---

[18] Form 41 data are the cost figures submitted by the US carriers to the US Department of Transportation. The costs are comprehensive and cover domestic as well as international operations. These data are not available for non-American carriers.

[19] Indirect costs are not available on a segment basis. This is one method of allocating them.

[20] The Form 41 data do not provide an accurate measure of the economic costs of capital invested in aircraft and therefore the block-hour costs need to be adjusted upward by the amount of interest cost on the capital tied up in the aircraft (opportunity cost of flight capital).

passenger is obtained by dividing the total block hour costs (flight costs) for the segment plus the total passenger costs by the number of segment passengers.

Unit cost on a per passenger basis are expressed as follows:

$$u = TC/Q = wF/Q+v = (w/Gz)+v \qquad \text{Equation 21}$$

In the event of two segment routes unit cost is defined as the sum of segment unit cost using load factors on each segment. We then define profits on a route basis: i.e. (fare on route minus route unit cost multiplied by route demand). In this way, load factors are endogenized in the model. This has important implications for dynamic efficiency effects. Entry affects costs in two ways. First, entry of a low cost carrier affects incumbents' costs by putting pressure on input prices and productive efficiency. Second, it changes incumbents' passenger volume, which, in turn, changes their per-passenger segment costs by being at a different point on the economies of density curve.

These cost functions can be used to represent the costs of non-US carriers by adjusting for productivity differences among carriers. Building on work by Oum and Yu (1995) who compute productivity indices for a number of international carriers, we are able to represent cost differences between carriers of different nationalities operating in a given market. Productivity information is also used to adjust costs in markets as the level of competition rises with entry of lower cost carriers.

In assessing the gains or losses from changes to the bilaterals the market structure was assumed to be [perfectly] competitive. The alternative scenarios are based on an analysis and simulation of the market response to changes in the bilateral relationship. These changes will be reflected in changes in fares, changes in frequency, and entry of new carriers. The fares in the alternate case are determined in two ways. First, the competitive price case calculates the market clearing prices based on the supplied capacity. Prices are adjusted such that each carrier's aircraft are filled according to their supplied capacity and their optimal load factor. Upon liberalization, all carriers' fares either drop to the marginal cost of the chosen benchmark airline, allowing for differences in input prices and factor productivity or they continue to be regulated. The second fare adjustment mechanism allows the model to iterate on price until supply equals demand. This approach allows for each carrier to either make or lose money depending upon their ability to fill capacity at fares above marginal cost. Equilibrium is achieved when a zero economic profit for the highest carrier occurs. If other carriers in the market are more efficient they may end up with some positive economic profits.

The empirical results from the model are reported elsewhere in this volume (See D. Lewis) they need not be repeated here. It is useful however to briefly remark on the operation of the model. A base case is defined using information on the routes, carriers and markets under consideration. The model is route and segment based therefore the market conditions for an international city pair are required. The key variables used to describe the base case OD route are: the airlines serving market, the type of aircraft, the passenger volume by airline, the fares by airline, the frequency by airline, the travel time by airline and the carrier specific preference (Nationality) factor.

The alternative scenarios are based on an analysis and simulation of the market response to changes in the bilateral relationship. These changes will be reflected in changes in fares, changes in frequency, and entry of new carriers. The fares in the alternate case are determined in two ways. First, the competitive price case calculates the market clearing prices based on the supplied capacity. Prices are adjusted such that each carrier's aircraft are filled according to their supplied capacity and their optimal load factor. Upon liberalization, all carriers' fares either drop to the marginal cost of the chosen benchmark airline, allowing for differences in input prices and factor productivity or they continue to be regulated. Several of the policy modeling scenarios use price regulation. The second fare adjustment mechanism allows the model to iterate on price until supply equals demand. This approach allows for each carrier to either make or lose money depending upon their ability to fill capacity at fares above marginal cost.

15.6 SUMMARY AND CONCLUSION

Domestic deregulation has been introduced more broadly, in part, because individual countries can act unilaterally within their borders to change the rules governing industry behaviour. This is not true in an international setting, where countries view access to their markets as an asset, and negotiate with potential trading partners on this basis. Bilateral negotiations for international air services often consider the impact on the domestic airline(s), possible trade-offs among industries and potential trade diversion to other countries.

Trade negotiations for new sets of rules either for goods or services are concerned with the following questions: What are the benefits and costs of liberalization to consumers and producers? How are the gains and losses distributed among foreign and domestic consumers and producers? What is the nature of the transition to a more liberalized trading regime? What policy instruments will yield the largest total net welfare gain and the largest net welfare gain to the domestic economy?

The potential movement toward liberalized international aviation markets presents these questions to all countries involved in bilateral negotiations for international aviation services. Most countries approach negotiations with broad experience in negotiating trade in services but relatively less experience in establishing the rules for trade in services. It is not clear that experience in the former can provide insights into the consequences of having different trading rules, or levels of liberalization, for trade in services.

Trade in services is fundamentally different than trade in goods because service quality plays a more significant role than in the trade of goods and national preferences from cultural and language differences matter. Differences in factor prices and productive efficiency certainly will affect the profitability of an enterprise but just as important are product differentiation and international trade flows. Because services involve direct contact with people, they cannot be produced in the home country and exported through a domestic distribution system to satisfy customer demand.

The demand model described in this paper grew out of a concern that traditional benefit-cost analysis did not provide a sufficiently comprehensive assessment of the welfare outcomes of changes to aviation bilaterals. Liberalizing trade in air services between countries must go beyond the single issue of economic efficiency. The impacts on producers and third parties from trade deflection must be measured. In effect distributional concerns are as important as economic efficiency. The model therefore needed to be disaggregate to incorporate inter-route and inter-carrier substitution. Inter-route substitution explicitly allows us to identify the trade deflection consequences of liberalization on third country carriers. The aggregate elasticities used in conventional benefit-cost studies are readily available but carrier and route substitution elasticities are not. Detailed market share data by carrier and route are necessary to estimate these values. Furthermore, estimate of the impact of quality on welfare and market shares needs to be considered. It is in this way the important role of national preferences can be integrated into the demand model.

The model is designed to usefully examine partial (bilateral) liberalization on OD routes involving three or more national carriers. It can be used to address the key areas of concern for policy makers. The first broad set of questions related to the implications of changes in trading rules are: Who gains? Who loses? What is the extent of trade deflection? And, how are the gains/losses distributed? One of the key insights to be gained is the identification of which policy levers are more successful in generating net welfare gains. Related questions are: What is the impact on the carriers as well as third parties and, why and what can, or should, be done to ease any losses suffered? Extensions to assess the impact on downstream industries such as tourism can be integrated into this framework.

References

Armington, Paul S. (1969). "A Theory of Demand for Products Distinguished by Place of Production," IMF Staff Papers.

Caves, D.W., L. R. Christensen, and W.E. Diewert. "Multilateral Comparisons of Output, Input, and Productivity Using Superlative Index Numbers." *Economic Journal*, 92, 1982, pp. 73-86.

Crumley, Bruce. "EU Liberalization After 2 Years: The Government." *Air Transport World*, January 1995, pp. 45-53.

Dempsey, Paul Stephen. "Turbulence in the 'Open Skies': The Deregulation of International Air Transport", Transportation Law Journal, Vol. 15, 1987, pp. 325-42.

Dixit, A.K. 1992. "Optimal Trade and Industrial Policies for the U.S. Automobile Industry," in G.M. Grossman (ed.) *Imperfect Competition and International Trade*, (Cambridge, Mass.: MIT Press).

Dixit A. and J. Stiglitz (1977), "Monopolistic Competition and Optimal Product Diversity", American Economic Review 67: 297-308.

Doganis, Rigas. "The Bilateral Regime for Air Transport: Current Position and Future Prospects" in International Air Transport: The Challenges Ahead. Paris: OECD Publications, 1993.

Gillen, D.W., T.H. Oum and M. Tretheway. 1990. "Airline Cost Structure and Policy Implications: A Multi-Product Approach for Canadian Airlines," *Journal of Transport Economics and Policy*, vol. 24: 9-34

Harris, R. 1989. "The New Protectionism Revisited" Canadian Journal of Economics, XXII, No. 4, November 1989, pp. 751-78..

Harris, R. 1991. "Market Access in International Trade: A Theoretical Appraisal" in R. Stern (ed.) *U.S. Canadian Trade and Investment Relations with Japan* (University of Chicago Press), 1991

Harris, R. and D. Cox. 1992. "North American Free Trade and Its Implications for Canada: Results from a CGE Model of North American Trade," *The World Economy*, vol. 15: 31-44.

Harris, R. 1993. "Trade and Industrial Policy for a 'Declining' Industry: the Case of the U.S. Steel Industry," in P. Krugman and A. Smith (eds.) *Empirical Studies of Strategic Trade Policy*, (NBER and University of Chicago Press).

Helpman, E. and Paul Krugman, *Market Structure and Foreign Trade: Increasing Returns, Imperfect Competition, and the International Economy* (1985) MIT Press, Cambridge MA

Hufbauer, Gary and Christopher Findlay (eds), Flying High: Liberalizing Civil Aviation in the Asia Pacific, Washington, Institute for International Economics, Washington, 1996

Hurdle, G.J. et al. 1989. "Concentration, Potential Entry, and Performance in the Airline Industry," *Journal of Industrial Economics*, vol. 38: 119-139.

Oum, Tae Hoon. and C. Yu. "A Comparative Study of Total Factor Productivity of World's Major Airlines." *(Forthcoming, Journal of Transport Economics & Policy, 1996)*.

Oum, Tae Hoon and Yu, C, "A Productivity Comparison of the World's Major Airlines," Journal of Air Transport Management, vol.2, No.3/4 (1995), pp. 181-195

Oum, Tae Hoon, William Waters and Jong-Say Yong, "Concepts of price Elasticities of Transport Demand and Recent Empirical Estimates", *Journal of Transport Economics & Policy* (May) 1992 pp: 139-154

Spence, Michael, "Product Selection, Fixed Cost and Monopolistic Competition", *Review of Economic Studies* 43 (1976):217-236

Street, John, David Smith and Scott Savage, "An Analysis of the Trade-Offs in International Aviation", *19th Australian Transport Research Forum*, 1994

Tirole, Jean (1988), *The Theory of Industrial Organization*, MIT Press.

Transport Canada, "Canada's International Air Policy", TP12276, December 1994.

Windle, Robert., "The World's Airlines: A Cost and Productivity Comparison." *Journal of Transport Economics and Policy*, 1991.

Windle and Dresner, "Partial Productivity Measures and Total Factor Productivity in the Air Transport Industry: Limitations and Uses." *Transportation Research*, Vol. 26, 1992.

16 AN INDUSTRY PERSPECTIVE

DeAnne Julius

What I want to talk about is the changing structure of the air transport industry not over the past 50 years, but looking ahead. What I shall do is address this under three headings: First, what is happening, at least from the point-of-view of an integrated long-haul carrier based in Europe. Second, why are these changes happening, and what is driving the process of structural change in our industry. Last, how should public policy react?

First, what is happening? Consider first the US market which is both the largest and, in a regulatory sense, the most mature market in that it has been deregulated for longer than others. But maturity does not imply stability. Since the 1970s there has been a rash of start-ups, a wave of bankruptcies and consolidations. It has not been a stable market structure at all.

Is it stable today? Well that is anybody's guess, but from our perspective, there appears to be a three tier market structure in the US. There are the three large integrated domestic-international carriers; American, United and Delta. All are profitable, though possibly with over hanging cost problems that will reemerge when the economy turns down again. There are then four intermediate carriers, USAir, TWA, Northwest and Continental, occupying what is probably a rather precarious ledge of being an intermediate carrier in the US market. This ledge probably is not a stable or large enough one for four carriers to occupy for the long term future. Then there are many regional carriers and low cost, no frills operators, some profitable and some not. The market share of those carriers has yo-yoed over the last 10 years, between 10% and 21%. Our view is that it probably will not exceed 15% on average over the next 10 years, and it will probably continue to be a story of new entrants, exits and consolidations.

There is still some evidence of over capacity in the U.S. market. Even the profitable players have lower seat factors than British Airways, even adjusted for stage length. The question is, why, in a mature and competitive market, during the 6th year of fairly strong economic growth, is there still over capacity? The over capacity may be due in part to the ease of market entry; the high price elasticity of demand -- particularly the high cross price elasticity in our industry -- and the supply discontinuities. In this regard, supply discontinuities refer to the fact that planes come in certain sizes such that when one frequency is added to a route, capacity is often increased by 20-30%. The discontinuities are at the route level, not at the firm level. The over capacity is also due in part to selling a perishable product. That is, if a seat is not sold before the plane departs, the revenue from it is lost forever. This encourages deep price discounting.

Given these characteristics, there is a very real question as to whether the air transport market will reach sustainable equilibrium positions. There is not a lot of evidence of that in the US case. If not, if the industry is doomed to structural turbulence, then this raises some quite different regulatory issues than if it is a market which is always headed for equilibrium.

In Europe, the industry structure has four segments. First, there is a small segment of profitable, integrated carriers. This segment includes British Airways, KLM, Lufthansa and SAS, all of whom over the medium to long term have been profitable, although not every carrier in every year. These carriers have cost and revenue structures, and marketing strategies that are in some sort of sustainable alignment. Second, there are a large number of loss-makers, including Iberia, Air France, Alitalia, Sabena and Swiss Air. Certainly from a financial point of view, being a loss-maker year after year is not a sustainable position, even with government subsidies. In Europe the Commission is imposing more discipline on state subsidies in an attempt to replicate the effect of private shareholders. The days of European carriers operating without any budget constraints are all but over.

Third, there is a small but growing number of no frills carriers that mostly operate inside the domestic European market. This segment includes Ryan Air, Debonair and EasyJet in the U.K. It includes Deutsch BA in Germany, and within France TAT and Air Liberté. The low frill carriers are making gains domestically, but it is difficult to foresee them making significant gains across borders in Europe. Part of the reason is that there is not as much potential for market stimulation across European borders, as in the US market. Most people living in Britain don't have relatives in Italy or Switzerland, whereas many people who live in New York do have relatives who live in California or Chicago. The so-called visiting friends and relatives (VFR) market is much smaller intra-Europe than it is intra Canada or the United States. There are also issues on the cost side in Europe, which make any carrier higher cost predominantly because of the social overhead cost of labour and, to some extent, airport related costs.

Finally, a fourth segment of market structure in Europe is the charter market. This segment accounts for over 30% of European travel; that is all flights that touch Europe or are intra-European, and it includes both long and short-haul. The charter market has been shrinking as a share of the total, and it will probably continue to shrink. As the integrated carriers become more efficient and more able to fill their seats, and use yield management in an effective way, as has been the case in the US, they will gain and make inroads on the charter market. But for the next 5-10 years the charter airlines will remain an important competitive force.

In Europe, the structure of the industry is also unstable, but I think it is not going to change rapidly, partly because of the existence of subsidies. I was interested to hear Marc Gaudry talk about the way the French decision on TGV funding had been made, if the amount of money the French poured into Air France in the last three years had instead been spent buying BA shares, we would be 2/3 owned by the French Government today. At least so far, it would have been a better investment for them! In any case there are still political and regulatory barriers to consolidation in Europe, and without consolidation there will not be significant changes in the market structure.

In the Asia Pacific region, the situation is again different. That is a region of the world where demand is growing very rapidly. At the same time the airport infrastructures as well as the number of planes and carriers are also growing very rapidly. It is reminiscent of the situation in North America or Europe back in the 1960s, when it was very much a high growth industry and where there were not as many constraints on the infrastructure side as there are today. Since over capacity is not evident in the Asia-Pacific, there is very little interest in the intra-Asian alliances that one otherwise might expect to see. There is also not a great deal of interest in extra-Asian alliances, with the exception of Qantas whose domestic market, as you have already heard yesterday from Mr. Wolf, is similar to the deregulated US/UK.

Finally, if we do lift our eyes above this regional level, and think about the kinds of structural changes in the industry that are happening across regions, the most significant development is, of course, the cross regional alliances that are being built. They often include an intra-European element. The Lufthansa-United alliance, for example, is a cross regional alliance which has full anti-trust immunity as well as an intra-European element (Lufthansa-SAS). The regional carrier, British Midlands, is also 40% owned by SAS. Our own alliance with American Airlines, which is being looked at by three sets of regulators at the moment, includes Qantas as the Asian component. The Lufthansa-United relationship is blessed with anti-trust immunity, and therefore is able to do many more things together than we could do with American Airlines without that immunity. The KLM-Northwest alliance is of course the 3rd one. It does have anti-trust immunity, but does not have an Asian partner at the moment. Then there is the Swiss Air-Sabena combination in Europe, with Delta as the American partner, again with anti-trust immunity, and Singapore Airlines as the Asian partner.

It is important to remember that although alliances are forming, the history so far is that these are not easy partnerships. They have been difficult to cement and to implement. The difficulty relates mainly to the regulatory structure. I can compare the situation to that in the oil industry, from my days working at Shell. There are lots of strategic alliances, both in the chemical industry and in developing major oil fields around the world. It was almost always the case, at least if it was a big, risky investment, that a joint venture would be formed to share the risks and the rewards. When you have a joint venture and a shareholding pool, then it is much easier to develop common policies that benefit both partners. If there is no pooled share holding, as there isn't in most of the airline alliances, at the end of the day, the directors of those two companies are legally and rightly responsible to their own shareholders. That it is why it is fundamentally very difficult to build deep alliances in our industry. The question one needs to ask is why are people trying it at all?

The industry, at least as I see it, is perhaps midway through a fundamental transition from having national monopolies, to having global competitors. There are two parts to that; one is the national to global, and the other is monopoly to competition.

In regard to the national to global part, what is happening in the airline industry is only an example of what is happening in many many industries, particularly networked industries, such as computer software and telecommunications. The motivations may vary, but in these industries it is more often about achieving network economies than simple cost-reduction or scale economics.

Professor Sickles suggested that alliances are being driven by cost savings. This may be true on the domestic front but recent data indicates that for British Airways unit cost savings are not significant when benchmarked against American carriers, correcting for sector length. In our discussions with American Airlines leading up to the our alliance with them, it became clear that in some areas they are able to operate at lower costs than we, and in other areas we operate at a lower cost than they. We would expect this result because we have different patterns of capital and labour input cost.

If the rational is not cost savings, what about economies of scale? Academics have been telling us for years that once you get past the level of about 15 or 20 airplanes in your network, there are no firm-level scale economies. What drives alliances is network economies and it is demand-side externalities that are the main justification. Customers prefer to connect on the same carrier, if at all possible, or if not, then connect on a code-share. When looking at how customers book through CRS systems, it is clear that even when CRS systems have all bias eliminated, customers prefer connections on the same or code-share linked carriers.

There are also network economies on the supply side. Connections with a partner enable you to build hubs in different parts of the world to connect the two networks at third points around the world. There is some evidence now in the US market that perhaps hubbing has gone too far in the sense that there is now scope for new entrants to bypass hubs and build point to point traffic. The European and Asian carriers' situation is that hubbing has not gone far enough to reap its full benefits. We did an analysis to compare inter-continental hubs in the US and Europe. An intercontinental hub was defined as an airport that had at least 20 intercontinental destinations offered from it. Europe has 22 such intercontinental hubs – airports from which you can fly to at least 20 different places beyond Europe. The US, with a similar size and wealth as Europe, has only six such hubs. These six intercontinental hubs are in five cities, with New York having two of them. So, hubbing has occurred in the deregulated US with a very different result from that in Europe. I do not think Europe will reach the same point because population distribution is different, among other things. But those benefits behind hubbing and the passenger preference for code share or single brand on the whole route are the things which are driving this industry to look at global market places, not just at a national market place.

Does global mean monopoly? Not if we follow the pattern of other industries. Consolidation occurs when liberalization comes, and then greater competition among stronger players. For example, many countries had their own auto industry.

There was consolidation, first at the national level, then at the regional level. Today, the largest five auto companies account for 45% of the world market, and yet very few people, economists included, would claim there is monopoly power in the auto industry or that customers do not have sufficient choice. I should also say that those top five car companies have alliances among themselves. General Motors and Toyota are the top two and they have a strategic alliance. So, deregulation and globalization lead both to consolidation and to greater competition. It is competition across alliances, among alliances, with new entrants on short-haul routes, on long haul-routes, and on different market niches around the pattern of one's network.

That brings me to my final topic which is the public policy issues that these changes in the structure of the industry raise. In my mind, the public policy issues really boil down to one issue in the long run -- competition policy. There are certainly other elements, other aspects in which governments will and should remain involved. On the safety side, for example, I would never suggest that governments withdraw. On bilateral route negotiations, we heard from Mr. Michalski this morning, about where he sees that going, and as a member of his committee I firmly subscribe to his view. Slot allocation is also a very big issue in Europe. All of these have a different order of magnitude in terms of the structure of the industry, the benefits to consumers and the economic efficiency of producers in the industry. They are all second order issues compared to competition.

The key competition question for the policy maker is: "Under what circumstances does greater consolidation lead to inefficient market outcomes?" We have many academics and researchers in this audience. I do not suggest that people do research on whether deregulation will lead to consolidation, as I think it almost certainly will. But the analysis should not stop there. Rather, one must trace the steps in the argument from liberalization leading to consolidation, at least at hubs, to the share of operations at individual hubs by certain carriers. That itself provides greater passenger benefit, because the connecting time through the hub becomes less if a carrier builds up its operations there. It probably also provides lower operating costs. That could indicate that prices would go up or down at that hub depending on whether the benefits to the customer, and the customer's willingness to pay, offsets or does not offset the potential for lower costs.

Competition authorities are concerned only if prices go up. So, if prices go up it is still necessary to disentangle, statistically speaking, how much of that increased benefit reflects the customer's willingness to pay for something that was not there before the airport became a hub, and how much of that increase in price is due to the simple fact that the infrastructure is constrained. We all know as economists that when you have constraints, prices often do rise, depending on the substitute available. I would particularly like to see research on a comparison of what happens, from a competitive point of view, in cities that have more than one airport. The Southwest strategy and those of other new entry carriers, is not to set up at large constrained hubs but, rather, to offer something which is a substitute from another airport. The reason I am particularly interested in such research, of course, is because London has four airports: Heathrow, Gatwick, Stansted and Luton. The low cost carriers that operate in London are not setting up at Heathrow, not because

British Airways would drive them out of business, but because of the costs and the unavailability of slots. It would not be sensible from an air policy point of view either to have tiny planes fly in and out of Heathrow. The competitive scene in London, with its four airports, (five, if you count City Airport) is different compared from other cities in Europe which have a single airport. There must be interesting data sets that one could look at in the US market on multiple airport cities. I think there is a whole range of areas where transport research could help us answer these key competition policy issues.

Having discovered what conditions there are that might, do, or have, led to anti-competitive outcomes of consolidation, then the second question is, "Is there anything peculiar about those conditions to the air transport industry?" If so, we need to continue to regulate consolidation in air transport differently. But if not, we need to subject the airlines and their activities to exactly the same anti-trust surveillance that other industries have to face. In my own view, and I do not claim to speak for the industry, this kind of shift by government, from transport policy to a rather sophisticated view of competition policy, drawing upon evidence that is available from economists and others, is the logical regulatory counterpart of the shift in the air transport industry from public to private ownership. I think that those two shifts need to go hand in hand in the future.

17 ON THE FUTURE ROLE OF ALLIANCE

Joseph Berechman
Jaap de Wit

17.1 INTRODUCTION

The chicken and the pig met for negotiations on an alliance and out of the talks was born the idea of ham and eggs. Initially the two were very pleased with the idea, but suddenly the pig became uneasy. "This is all very well", he said," but while you are producing eggs I end up dead." The chicken smiled knowingly. " That's all right" she said, "that's the way it is with alliances."

The organizers of this symposium invited us to speak (or rather to speculate) on the future role of alliances in world aviation, where, as we understand it, the emphasis is on the words: "future role of'. As transport economists, who usually deal with laborious and, at times, tedious technical modeling and statistical analysis, we take a great pleasure in having to surmise about future events such as this one. It is particularly enjoyable since we know that it is quite unlikely that we would ever have to face the consequences of having arrived at the wrong conclusions. The world in general, and the aviation industry in particular, is so complex and subject to so many uncertainties that, even if someone would remember our wrong predictions, we would probably still be able to find a neat explanation (or rather a learned excuse) for our erroneous inferences. The need to say something intelligent about the "future role of..... forces one to think (a purported favorite pastime of academicians) about conceivable approaches for tackling such an issue. And short of a detailed methodological and statistical analysis, which the organizers of this conferences dissuaded us from undertaking, all of these approaches contain a significant element of intuition and plain common sense. Hence, the pleasure we have had in accepting the invitation to speak on this subject.

A second introductory remark is that the title of the presentation: "the future role of alliance", implicitly presumes that we all agree on what "aviation alliance" actually means and what its future is likely to be, so that what remains to be explored is its future *role* in shaping up aviation markets. We will argue that, in fact, neither of these suppositions is valid and we will try to explain what we understand by "aviation alliance" and how it may evolve over time. Afterwards, we will be able to surmise about its future role.

Given these preliminary remarks, the key objectives of this paper are: (1) to explain the economic underpinnings of aviation alliances and the future development in this field; (2) to describe the underlying rationale for our assessment of the future role of aviation alliances; and (3) given this reasoning, to explicate our conjecture that, in the long run, aviation alliances will have a limited impact on the structure of aviation markets.

We would like to emphasize at the outset that this is not a technical paper with the analytical style and approach much favored by academic economists today. While founded on economic reasoning, the paper addresses a wider audience, including practitioners and policy makers. Thus, in section 2, we briefly define aviation alliance and elucidate its economic underpinnings.

17.2 FUNDAMENTALS OF ALLIANCES

The term "alliance" as it is commonly used nowadays in the aviation jargon, is rather vague and undefined, at least from an economic point of view. Essentially, it seems to convey the idea of some form of *mutually beneficial cooperation* between more or less *autonomous airlines.* [1] Below we will use the terms "alliance" and "cooperation" interchangeably and we will examine the source of these reciprocal benefits. Prior to that, however, it is worthwhile to briefly look at possible forms of alliance.

Economic cooperation between carriers can be described as a spectrum of coordinated activities the overall objective of which is to lower costs and increase revenues. Thus, depending on specific strategic objectives, available resources and regulatory constraints, an alliance between airlines engulfs a broad spectrum of arrangements.

The strictly regulated international airline industry has already been demonstrating various forms of interfirm cooperation for a long time. Examples are IATA interlining agreements, pooling agreements, and partial or complete wet leases. However, the characteristics of cooperation have changed substantially after deregulation.

At present the most prevalent form of alliances in the airline industry are code sharing agreements. Although a cooperation can take many forms, most forms are combined with a code-sharing arrangement. As a consequence the complexity of

[1] In this concept an alliance covers a whole spectrum of integration tendencies excluding the two extremes: completely independent firms at one side, and a completely integrated firm through full mergers or takeovers at the other side. (See also Lorange and Roos, 1992). This goes back to the distinction between intrafirm and inter firm, based on the Coasian transaction-cost concept (Coase, 1937).

these arrangements is very diverse. Since statistics on airline alliances can hardly reflect this diversity, premature conclusions on alliances are sometimes tempting.

Conceptually, the diversity of alliances can be related to the level of *cohesion* between the code sharing partners. This level is reflected in

- the network scope
- the commercial commitment of the non-operating carrier(s) in the alliance
- the degree of integration of the other marketing-mix components
- the operational integration of the airline product
- and equity aspects of the alliance.

■ *The network scope* of a code-sharing agreement can range from route-specific arrangements, or subsets of routes of both alliance partners to the complete network of one partner. *Point-specific* (also called "gateway-to-gateway") alliances are the lion's share of today alliances. Since a pointspecific alliance requires a more limited commitment of the alliance partners, this partially explains the instability of the actual alliance picture in the airline industry. Examples can be found on the routes between the capitals of several Central and Western European countries. A few examples in intercontinental markets are the arrangements between Quantas and JAL, Singapore Airlines and AA, TAP and Delta.

The involvement of *complete networks* in alliances is actually limited to feeder airlines in cooperation with their major carriers. Originally, this type of code sharing was strongly stimulated in the deregulated U.S. domestic market by the emerging hub-and-spoke systems and the growing popularity of computer reservation systems (CRS). In today's liberalized European market domestic as well as cross-border feeder companies are also closely tied to the major carrier, like Deutsche BA, GB Airways and TAT European Airlines, Brymon European, BA Regional, CityFlyer Express, Logan Air, Manx Airlines and Air Liberté to BA, and KLM Cityhopper, Air UK, Maersk Air and Eurowing to KLM. Each of these commuters uses the code of their hub carrier.

If subsets of routes of different alliance partners are involved, this is often referred to as *strategic alliances*. Not only gateway-to-gateway services but also points beyond are included in this network integration. Examples are the NorthWest-KLM alliance, the United-Lufthansa cooperation and the intended BA-AA alliance.

■ *The commercial commitment of the non-operating carrier in the alliance* [2] is another cohesive factor in alliances. As Beyhoff cs. (1995) indicate, there is a

[2] Sometimes the role of the operating and non-operating carrier alternates between the partners on a code-shared route if each of them operates one or more aircraft on this route. Sometimes the role of the non-operating carrier in the alliance is only played by one of the partners, like BA versus its franchising partners.

broad range of options to allocate the commercial risk between the operating and non-operating airline. A free sale arrangement implies fundamentally different responsibilities compared to a blocked space (partial wet lease) arrangement, a full wet lease arrangement, a franchising agreement or a joint venture on a subset of routes. The last one has some resemblance to the traditional revenue/cost pooling agreements and provides the highest level of cohesion, as illustrated by the KLM-NW alliance. [3]

- Code-sharing focuses on the product component of the *marketing-mix*. From this point of view, the synergy between code-sharing and other components in the marketing mix strongly determines the cohesive power between the partners. For example, the impact of code-sharing cannot be isolated from the alliance partners' decisions to coordinate other customer-service aspects of the airline product, like integrated schedule planning on each other's hub, and the combined use of airport, handling and maintenance facilities.

The interaction between code-sharing and other components of the marketing mix is obvious. We only mention the integrated CRS use on code-shared routes (product-distribution tool), the linking of the frequent-flyer plans [4] of the partners (product promotion tool), and coordinated yield management and fare integration (product-pricing tool) on code-shared routes.

We conclude that code sharing is mostly not a independent phenomenon in an alliance. The larger the network scope of the alliance, the higher the probability that code sharing is a component in an integrated marketing strategy of the partners involved in the alliance.

- The cohesive role of *equity stakes* in airline alliances is not that obvious now as some authors suggest. Lindquist of the Boston Consulting Group (1996), for example, concludes from his surveys in 1992 and 1995 that alliance survival rates are substantially higher for equity alliances than for non-equity alliances. He also indicates that equity alliances generally form part of wider-ranging partnerships, whereas non-equity alliances are mostly dominated by simple code sharing agreements alone.

Lindquist expects that, as soon as government-imposed restrictions on foreign ownership in most countries will be mitigated, these cross-border minority equity deals may well be converted into majority control positions or outright acquisitions.

Until now this expected step-wise development towards a limited number of single-entity global airlines is not reflected in actual airline alliance behavior. Equity stakes in the leading alliances are absent or even terminated, as is shown by

---

[3] This requires an anti-trust exemption from at least the US authorities.

[4] These loyalty schemes not only reflect horizontal integration between cooperating airlines but also **vertical integration** within the supply chain of the airline industry: most FFP's now have tie-ups with other travel-related businesses like hotel chains, car-hire companies, telecommunications and restaurants. In the eighties these were takeover targets for the airline industry (e.g. KLM and the Hilton chain), but now these vertical ties also have taken the form of weak (non formalized) alliances.

the recent KLM-NW alliance. Also the share of equitybased alliances in the total number of alliances decreased in 1996/97, as table I indicates. [5]

Table 1 Airlines Alliances

	1997	*1996*	*1995*	*1994*
Number of alliances	363	390	324	280
▪ with equity stakes	54	62	58	58
▪ without equity stakes	309	327	266	222
New alliances	72	71	50	-
Number of airlines	177	159	153	136

Source: *Airline Business*, June 1997

These figures for the first time raise the question, whether there are limits to such forms of cooperation between airlines, and if so, whether this results from the structure of the aviation market and from strategic considerations of airlines. To answer this question we need to examine the airlines' benefits from cooperation, as well the costs (financial and strategic) involved. In brief, we need to examine, in some detail, the rationale for cooperation between airlines.

Essentially, economic cooperation between firms like airlines, will develop if these firi-ns stand to gain some tangible financial benefits. It is particularly so in markets which have been sufficiently liberalized to render phenomena such as home carrier, public ownership and cross-subsidization of routes obsolete and unprofitable. Such benefits may include reductions in the operating costs, an increased volume of traffic, an increased ability to enter new markets, or the possibility to bypass international regulations (e.g. of fifth freedom), to impede attempts by other carriers to enter markets, to use an inadequate number of slots more efficiently, and to exploit economies of scale, economies of scope and, most importantly, economies of network. Thus, in exploring the rationale for cooperation between airlines and the boundaries of this cooperation, it is necessary to examine which of the elements is present.

Consider, for example, a code-sharing agreement between two carriers. What are the likely benefits from such an arrangement? Here is a partial list of benefits:

1) Following the agreement, each of the two carriers enjoys marketing economies as additional destinations to their respective networks can be advertised at very low costs.

2) The two carriers can circumvent operational barriers, erected by bilateral services agreements between states (for example, fifth-freedom or third-country code-sharing [6]).

---

[5] Again: the diversity of alliances involved in these figures prohibits making too strong conclusions.

[6] Depending on the angle of observation third-country code-shared services either touch a third country or involve a carrier from a third nation.

3) The feeder services of each carrier potentially increase the number of passengers for the other one.

4) Programs such as the frequent flier program can be shared.

5) The position on the CRS screen may improve after code-sharing the same flights.

6) Potentially there is room for fare reduction to improve load factors.

Thus, there are quite substantial benefits to be gained from code sharing as well as from other forms of alliance. It is, therefore, of interest to ask whether there are limitations to alliances which eventually will constrain their extent and, consequently, their effect on the structure of the aviation market. The overall analytical structure of this paper is given by Figure I below.

Figure 1: Analytical Framework

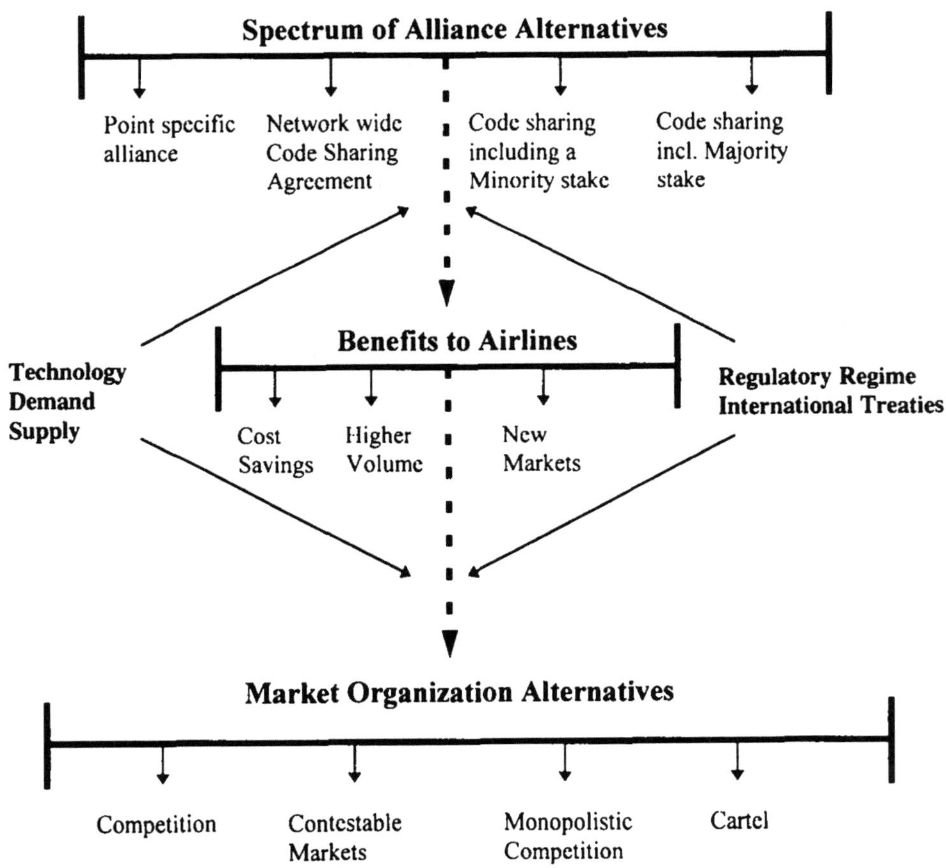

17.3 FACTORS AFFECTING ALLIANCE: REGULATION, TECHNOLOGY, DEMAND, SUPPLY-SIDE ECONOMIES, AND MARKET ORGANIZATION

Limitations to alliances and, for that matter, to any form of cooperation between economic concerns, can result from several sources: regulatory constraints imposed by overseeing agencies, changes in technology (e.g. in aircraft size), trends in the demand level and in distribution, supply-side economies such as scale, scope and network economies, and market organization determinants such as the nature of competition or market entry strategies. We will briefly survey some of these factors with the objective of assessing their impact on the future of alliances.

Figure 2: Economic Factors Affecting Alliance

1) Regulatory Effects
   - State or market regulation
   - International treaties
   - Anti-trust legislation
   - Non-uniform environmental regulations
   - Non-uniform airport charges

2) Technology
   - Aircraft type
   - ATC
   - CRS
   - Baggage handling

3) Demand Factors
   - Longitudinal Trends
   - Geographical Distribution
   - Preferences (price, travel time and frequency elasticities)
   - Competing modes (e.g., rail)

4) Supply-Side Factors
   - Horizontal integration between airlines
   - Economic complementary in production: network integration
     - common (shared) factors of production
     - demand complementary
   - Global network economics
   - Product (scope) economies
   - Diseconomies of Size and of Coordination

5) Market Organization Factors
- Effective market entry barriers
  - Slots (un)availability and hub dominance
  - State subsidy
  - Price cutting, frequent flier and other type of barriers
- Effect of hub-and-spoke network
- Market entry by new upstarts
- Anti-trust immunity
- Extent of network economies
- Market equilibrium and stability

17.3.1 Regulatory Effects on Alliance

Fear of monopolistic behavior, or attempts to protect state interests induce many countries to adopt regulatory measures which limit the extent of cross border cooperation between airlines. These restrictions are clearly demonstrated in issues like the foreign ownership of an airline, code-sharing in bilateral air-service agreements, and the role of different regimes of competition policy and environmental regulation applied to the airline industry.

Restrictions on foreign ownership are closely tied to the bilateral system of air service agreements. These agreements rely on principles like substantial ownership and effective control of an airline by the citizens in the country of registration. National aeronautics acts usually reflect these principles by stipulating a maximum percentage of foreign ownership in the range of 25 to 49 % of the voting common stock (OECD, 1997). As a consequence of these restrictions, alliances become a secondhand option in those situations where a cross-border merger or acquisition would be a more effective way of realizing synergetic effects between carriers.

An additional complication in this context is the continuing public ownership of airlines in many countries. Inflexible public ownership can substantially frustrate a market-based restructuring of this industry in different forms of cooperation.

The restrictive impact of bilateral service agreements on alliances is primarily explained by the inability of the bilateral system to handle the multilateral nature of the traffic flows in the codeshared networks of alliance partners. As such code-sharing might even become a threat to the bilateral system by undermining the bilateral limitations on market access and capacity control. This explains the tendency of regulatory authorities to encapsulate code-sharing into the regulatory framework. Since the mid-eighties, for example, the US require that a foreign alliance partner of a US carrier must have the underlying traffic rights for all code-shared points served in the US domestic market. And nowadays, in addition to the underlying traffic rights, a specific authorization is also required for each code-sharing operation. Other countries have followed this approach and in some instances have extended this practice to both code-sharing partners while also adding other criteria (e.g.: code-sharing should be allowed in a developmental market and no excessive circuity is allowed in the routing of the code-shared services).

Although ICAO (1997) concludes that until now code-sharing is not treated systematically but rather on an ad hoc regulatory basis dictated by general aeropolitical considerations [7], the danger that codesharing will become a 'quasi-traffic right' is not imaginary.

The transition from a restrictive bilateral context towards a more liberalized multilateral framework is therefore essential to the future of alliances.

ICAO (1997) emphasizes that international alliances raise the issue of competition in two ways: either as an enhancement of competition by the provision of better service, or as a reduction of the competition forces at work in the market. The latter effect requires a consistent and predictable application of competition rules. However, until now the application of competition laws from different countries can be involved in this cross-border cooperation, thereby compromising the efficiency of the restructuring process. The proverbial example is the intended AA-BA alliance. This has resulted in the involvement of US antitrust authorities, the UK Office of Fair Trading and the European Commission which, for the first time, is trying to extend its competence to apply EUcompetition rules to third country routes.

A consistent framework of competition rules will be a major factor of influence in the future development of international airline cooperation.

An issue of increasing importance is the impact of non-uniform environmental regulations on existing and potential alliances. Unilateral national policies regarding the environment would substantially affect the competitive position of individual alliance partners. For example, an aviation fuel tax or a value added tax on tickets, to be introduced by individual countries or the EU to internalize external environmental effects of the airline industry, are important environmental issues in Europe nowadays. Actions of individual countries or even individual airports to accelerate the phasing out of noisy aircraft are not imaginary. If the airport involved is one of the vital hubs in the alliance network, such a policy can strongly influence the position of an airline as an alliance partner. A recent example in this context is the noise abatement policy in the Netherlands. This national policy has resulted in noise contours around Amsterdam Airport Schiphol, which appear to be far more restrictive on the short run than the actually available operational capacity of this airport. These new restrictions may even frustrate the future role of Schiphol as the central European hub in the NorthWest-KLM alliance during the next few years. Therefore, in the recently concluded long-term agreement on closer cooperation between NorthWest and KLM a proviso was made by NorthWeSt. [8] The agreement assumes sufficient hub capacity to be available at Amsterdam Airport Schiphol in the near future.

---

[7] 7 As a consequence significant differences are found in the US granting of code-sharing rights. In the US/Netherlands, open skies' agreement the KLM/Northwest code-sharing is granted full antitrust immunity. The US/Germany agreement, however, is more restrictive. This latter model is also applied by the US to other European countries.

[8] This agreement has taken the place of KLM's equity participation in NorthWest.

Table 2 Cost Composition on Passenger Services AEA 1995

cost categories	long haul	Europe	domestic
aircraft acquisition	10.4%	11.7%	*10.5%*
fuel	*13.3%*	*6.0%*	*66%*
maintenance	9.6%	8.5%	10.1%
landing fees	*3.7%*	*8.4%*	*9.1%*
en route charges	4.0%	5.6%	4.6%
flight-deck crew	8.0%	7.4%	8.2%
cabin crew	9.5%	5.2%	*5.0%*
ground handling	*9.1%*	*17.3%*	*18.3%*
inflight service	6.8%	7.0%	5.8%
sales administration	9.6%	8.3%	6.9%
sales commissions	9.1%	8.7%	9.4%
miscellaneous	6.9%	5.9%	*5.5%*

Source: *AEA Yearbook 1997.*

The same impact can be attributed to differentials in total turn-around costs of hub airports. A substantial part of airline operating costs is determined by cost categories that vary per airport: airport charges, fuel costs, handling costs and local ATC charges. If the airport involved is a central hub in an alliance network and the airport-related costs per standard visit are high, the competitive role of an alliance can be undermined. Economic regulation of airport charges and ground handling services are becoming increasingly important components in cost-cutting policies of the home based alliance partner. The relative importance of these cost components in different markets is underlined in table 2.

All in all, the effects of regulation on alliances are very important. Non-uniform regulation affects the stability of existing alliances as well as the viability of new alliances yet to be formed.

17.3.2 Technology

The impact of technology on the future role of alliances in the airline industry is divers and complicated.

In the next decade a wide array of aircraft types will become available to the airlines, ranging from 30-seater jets to at least one 650-seater mega-jumbo. In between the various aircraft types the capacity increments are becoming smaller and smaller (Airline Business, 1997). At first sight this growing diversity is contradictory to the increasing need for fleet commonality between alliance partners. Commonality is an important issue in alliances from the point of view of the demand side as well as from that of the cost side. On the demand side it is an important instrument to induce brand loyalty to the alliance product, especially if alliance partners are alternately operating on the same routes in the alliance network. On the cost side fleet commonality or at least cockpit commonality is an important opportunity for cutting the maintenance and labor costs of the alliance. Indirectly an integrated maintenance system in an alliance also improves the reliability of operations. Economies of fleet standardization therefore have a major impact on the competitive position of alliances.[9] The answer of the airframe manufacturers to a maximum diversity in aircraft capacity and a minimum diversity in aircraft types is found in families of closely related aircraft types, thereby maintaining optimal operational and cockpit commonality and at the same time providing the necessary diversity in the capacity. This creates new opportunities for alliance partners to strengthen their alliance by intensifying their cooperation in the areas of fleet renewal and expansion. On the other hand, given the limited number of aircraft types, fleet compatibility of potential new partners in an new alliance is getting a more discrete rather than a continuous character.

Therefore we may conclude that the actual and future composition of the alliance partners' fleets is strongly related to the viability, stability and competitive power of an alliance.

The most outspoken role of technology in the development of alliances has emerged in the distribution of the airline product. Information technology and especially the development of modern computer reservation systems (CRS), have been conditional to alliances in the airline industry. Codesharing found its origin in the CRS screen priority rules in the U.S. domestic market. The market transparency created by the CRS during the last decade is closely related to the market presence of individual carriers in as many city pair markets as possible. This drive toward network expansion is also reflected in the fact that alliance partners are sharing airline codes. As a matter of fact, the CRS can be seen as the indispensable information infrastructure for modern airline alliances. Today, after a period of dehosting and a transition to less biased global distribution systems, the use of different CRS in the same alliance is no longer a major impediment in the common marketing of code-shared flights. But this picture may rapidly change due to new developments in information technology and their impact on the distribution of the airline product. Electronic ticketing, introduced by airlines with the aim to cut distribution cost by by-passing existing CRS facilities (see also table 2), has now rapidly been followed by on-line access to internal reservation systems of airlines through the Internet. Although the actual on-line booking facilities through Internet are still limited, a growing number of independent Websites offer travel services, that are not tied to a particular carrier.[10] The question now is whether these new reservation service providers that have entered cyberspace will become a derivative of existing airline alliances, or independent incentives to new forms of airline cooperation. Hence, an important question with respect to the future viability of airline alliances might be: will the airline brand loyalty of the frequent flyer determine the success of a future alliance, or will the Website loyalty of the frequent browser determine the success of the independent reservation service provider? In other words, the question is whether the airlines will be the managers of the future alliance networks, or merely the capacity providers to transport networks, virtually linked by an information provider from outside?

---

[9] An illustration of alliance fleet commonality are the plans explored by BA and Quantas to use each other's B747s during the downtime in the other partner's home country.

[10] Examples are Expedia, ITN, PCTravel, and Sabre's Travelocity (Airline business, February 1997)

Another aspect of computer technology that will stimulate further integration between alliance partners is the new yield management technology, valuing passengers on the basis of their O&D characteristics rather than on individual flight segments. Especially in code-shared networks with anti-trust exemptions to develop coordinated pricing strategies this is a new opportunity to a further optimization of the overall network yields of both partners.

Hub efficiency, to accommodate more and/or larger waves, will become an strategic factor in the success of future alliances. Also in the liberalized European market the number of waves on the central hubs is now rapidly being extended by their home-based carriers, as is illustrated by Bootsma (1997). Especially so-called 'global' alliance partners are improving the connectivity of the alliance network through their hubs. KLM extended the number of waves at Amsterdam airport from 3 to 5, Sabena is doing the same in Brussels, whereas Lufthansa is expanding from 4 to 5 waves in Frankfurt, and Swissair from 3 to 4 in Zurich. Air France has recently introduced a 5 waves system at Paris airport CDG and Alitalia is preparing Milan Malpensa to accommodate different waves in 1998.

The viability and stability of future alliances seems to be closely related to increased hub efficiency. Hub efficiency improvement is strongly technology driven. Minimum connecting times are increasingly becoming dependent on high-tech bar-coded baggage handling systems. Also the optimization of passenger flow throughput is receiving more attention., but this requires complete concepts of airport design.

It is not obvious, however, that the new airport-related technology of airport ticketing and check-in machines will improve this throughput. Even if these machines accept smart cards storing the information needed to buy a travel product and to check at the gate, this new technology might simply reallocate throughput congestion inside the hub.

Runway and local ATC capacity are another technology-driven phenomenon related to hub efficiency. New opportunities to increase airport capacity by advanced technological systems like GPS or MLS can strongly influence the structure of hub and spoke networks in an alliance. Especially in Europe increasing capacity restrictions on the major hubs will stimulate more decentralized multi hub systems in alliance networks. Multiple hubbing will stimulate a further concentration of the European airline industry however. In other words, the need to incorporate more European hubs in a 'global alliance' network will require the involvement of more home-based carriers.

The management of new ATC technology is another item that is relevant to the punctuality of hub and spoke systems. Within a limited area like Europe, the fragmented approach seems to be further away from an integrated en-route system than ever. National competences in the air space can become a major obstacle to institutional changes towards technological coordination and integration. This means that the divergence between the pace of concentration and cooperation in the airline industry and the pace of coordination and integration in the European ATC system appears to grow wider and wider.

17.3.3 Demand

Demand characteristics of air transport are intensively interacting with alliance developments, be it that causal relations are not always unidirectional. In general, a passenger's utility from air travel is affected by two main factors: air fare and total travel time.

With air fare elasticities of -1.8 and -1.2, for non-business and for business passengers respectively, an alliance can expect increases in passenger volumes and a positive effect on overall profitability if air fares decline (Oum et al., 1993). The crucial point therefore is whether alliances bring down air fares. Essentially, this question concerns the relationship between deregulation, alliances, network structure and competition. Without elaborating this too far here, it can concluded that, following the USA deregulation, concentration and cooperation in the airline industry have continued until now, and airfares have substantially declined for most routes on which effective competition has developed (Morrison and Winston, 1986; Borenstein, 1989).

This at first sight contradictory effect is explained by the increased competition of alternative hub and spoke systems on individual city pair markets through different hubs (DoT, 1990). The opportunities for reducing air fares through cost reduction in integrated multiple hub and spoke networks of different alliance partners, are discussed in 3.4.

The same developments, but at a slower pace, have emerged in the liberalized European air transport market. After a period of ten years, passenger yields on European routes had fallen by nearly 30% in 1996. Airline networks are now rapidly being restructured into more effective Euro hub and spoke systems (Bootsma, 1997) and international concentration in the EU has taken off through crossborder alliances between major airlines systems. At the same time, competition on individual city pair routes is increasing slowly (AEA, 1997).

A major theoretical and empirical result from the introduction of hub and spoke networks is the significant increase in frequency (Morrison and Winston, 1986; Barrett, 1990; Oum et al., 1993; Berechman and Shy, 1996). Bootsma (1997) shows that there is a dynamic growth relation between the number of waves and the average operating frequency. If the value of the latter variable exceeds the value of the former one, there can be a reason to increase the number of waves. For example, in 1997 average frequency on the KLM feeder network is 3.9 a day, based on a 3-waves system, whereas Air France has an average of 3.4 in a recently introduced 5-waves system. This frequency increase, in turn, significantly reduces waiting times for departing passengers and produces more favorable multiple departure times. This affects demand through demand elasticities of -0.047 and 0.206 for non-business and business passengers respectively, which in the latter group is larger than their travel time demand elasticity (-0.158). (Morrison and Winston, 1986).

Demand characteristics thus are an important incentive to expand the hub and spoke systems of cooperating airlines. The use of these expanding networks can be explained on the basis of increased revenue resulting from increased traffic, given the cost level.

The geographical distribution of demand also has a major impact on the attractiveness of alliance partners. As long as the national airport is the primary hub of each European airline, the location of such a hub in the continental market is a strategic factor for a European airline as a potential alliance partner. For example, the position of the Lufthansa hub in the gravity center of the European market provides an optimal omnidirectional connectivity of intra-European spokes. The duration of the hub repeat cycle can be confined to a rather short period without looming too many connections in the successive waves.

Another alliance related aspect of the geographical distribution of demand concerns the size of the local market around a hub. The larger this market, the larger the airline network and the more attractive the airline as an alliance partner. This is illustrated by BA: in spite of the eccentric position in the European market, BA's home base accommodates a very strong local demand. If these two factors concerning the geographical distribution are unfavorable to one and the same airline, likein the case of SAS, this also determines the attractiveness of such an airline as a full-fledged partner in a global alliance.

A role of importance on the global alliance playing field increasingly requires the ability to cover at least one's own continental market fully and adequately. This is partly explained by the marketing abilities of individual airlines, but also or even mainly by the geographical distribution of demand on the continent.

17.3.4 Supply-side Economies

From an economic viewpoint, regular forms of alliance, such as code-sharing, amount to horizontal integration between firms (airlines). In contrast with vertical integration (takeovers and mergers), a precondition for horizontal integration is economic complementary in production processes. In aviation, such complementary mainly applies to network integration where, for operational purposes, the individual networks of two individual airlines function as one combined network. Two key factors underlie such integration. The first factor is that the two networks do indeed complement one another. This, in turn, implies that the two airlines must share a common factor of production, e.g. their operation from the same airport, or, from demand side, a sufficient number of passengers flown by one airline who wish to reach their destinations serviced by the second one.

The second factor is network economies. Several authors (e.g. Bailey et al., 1985, Morrison and Winston, 1986; Keeler, 1991; Brueckner and Spiller, 1991; Hendricks et al., 1992) have argued that cost considerations, mainly economies of aircraft size coupled with scope economies, underlie the intensified use of combined hub and spoke networks. What this argument essentially implies, is that the use of expanding hub and spoke networks has two major effects:

1) it increases traffic density on each served route and, as a consequence, enforces aircraft-size economies;

2) the use of a major hub, through which all traffic is funneled, introduces conditions of joint production, which in turn, intensifies scope economies.[11]

It should be emphasized here again, that from theoretical as well as empirical viewpoints, traffic density economies do not imply scope or scale economies. In fact, airline costs in some markets (e.g. local or feeder services) can be explained on the basis of traffic density economies only whereas costs in other markets (e.g. trunk services) are strongly affected by scope and scale economies. (Caves et al, 1984). This seems to correspond with the results Brueckner (1997) recently reported. He concludes that two opposing forces are at work in the integrated networks of alliance partners: one on the prices between the hubs, where the alliance partners create a monopolistic power and thus increase prices, and the other on the spoke routes where prices are reduced due to a fall in marginal costs created by density economies. It is important however that according to Brueckner the second effect in his simulations are much greater than the former. In other words, strategic alliances have a substantial positive net effect on demand in these integrated networks.

A plausible conclusion is, that, both from the demand side and the cost side, there are important incentives for expanding hub and spoke systems through closer cooperation between carriers in the same continent as well as between carriers from different continents.

17.3.5 Market Organization

Alliances probably strongly interact with market organization. Airline cooperation between incumbents through expansion or combination of hub and spoke (HS) networks strongly affects market entry barriers and competition between incumbents and new carriers.

Market entry barriers: it should be observed that entry deterrence or accommodation market arrangements are *not* due to any possible asymmetry between the incumbent and entrant airlines but rather ensue from the heterogeneity of passengers relative to their value of time (Berechman and de Wit, 1996). Under certain conditions the adoption of the HS network has been shown to be an effective market entry mechanism due to favorable economies of density, of network and increased flight frequency.

Obviously, if an entrant intends to actually carry out his entry threat, he needs to maintain slots at relevant airports. Hence, another useful entry deterrence approach is for the incumbent to exercise socalled grandfather rights at airports, thereby hindering new entrants from gaining slots there. The importance of hub dominance was highlighted by Borenstein (1989), who showed that airlines with a dominant position in hubs also charged much higher prices when compared to those who did not have such a preponderate position. On the other hand, Borenstein (1992) showed that the airfares on routes which are served by more than one carrier are

[11] When compared with the former 3-wave system structure, KLM's new 5-wave system structure has resulted in an expected increase of 36 % in handling efficiency at the Amsterdam hub (Bootsma,1997).

likely to be significantly lower than those on comparable routes served by a single carrier or by a carrier with a dominant position in that market. Hence the importance of entry deterrence mechanisms being available to incumbent airlines.

Button (1989) in this context, emphasized the role of experience, providing incumbents with extra buffers against new entrants through goodwill to the passenger, knowledge of the markets being served and learning costs in the new entrant's organization. These economies of experience could explain the attractiveness of franchising agreements to new entrants: this agreement at once provides the new entrant (the franchises) with the market knowledge and the goodwill of the incumbent (the franchiser). The absence of economies of experience could also be an additional explanation for the limited viability of many new entrants.

From 1993 until today, 88 new airlines have started up in the EU. In 1996, 56 of them were still operating, whereas from the 177 carriers already operating in mid 1992 another 51 had suspended operations in 1996 (AEA, 1997). The most volatile group are the small-aircraft operators, with 70% of the failed and 60% of the (as yet) successful start-ups. The main reason for suspending operations seem to be the effective market entry barriers erected by the major carriers. The (un)availability and control of slots in busy airports (e.g. Heathrow, Frankfurt) is a major mechanism used by established carriers to hinder the market entry by start-ups. This explains why in many cases these new airlines operate from secondary airports (e.g., Ryanair from London Stansted), thereby circumventing the slot availability barrier in major airports in aneffort to emulate the successes of Southwest in the US.

Competitionfrom new start-ups: notwithstanding the above barriers, new start-up airlines have often been able to introduce significant competition into markets previously controlled by a single major carrier. Especially so-called 'no-frills' start-ups, like EasyJet and Virgin Express do not segment the market with the traditional advance-purchase and minimum-stay rules. In stead, they use escalating price structures which give early-booking passengers the best chance of obtaining the cheapest seats. This new competition has a major downward influence on the ticket prices for the routes involved. However we do not know to which extent the decreasing yield on European routes is influenced by a) route-specific impacts of new entrants, b) EU-wide pricing freedom and competition between incumbents on routes with two and more carriers, or c) 'hub fares' with transfer-connecting services undercutting the tariffs for direct flights.

These hub fares strongly reflect the growing roles of Euro hubbing and ICA-Euro transfer within the expanding and intensifying hub and spoke networks of European incumbent carriers and their alliance partners.

Furthermore it is uncertain whether European liberalization will actually result in a sustainable increase of the total number of airlines, which has been surprisingly stable at about 180. On the longer run, the economies of experience might lead to an incorporation of most entrants into the limited number of global alliances, be it directly through mergers or indirectly through franchising agreements.

The market structure in Europe may well change dramatically in the future, but the role of new entrants seems to be of some importance in such a typical transition stage. New entrants will certainly create a downward pressure on fares. Network-wide price competition in the EU, however, is primarily expected from larger alliances, who are expected to extend their combined hub and spoke networks in the EU.

17.4 ASSESSING THE EFFECTS OF THE ABOVE FACTORS ON THE FUTURE ROLE OF ALLIANCE

17.4.1 On the Stability of Alliances

The impacts of various factors on cooperation tendencies in the airline industry have been discussed in the previous paragraphs. We found that the airline industry as a typical network-oriented service industry is getting important economic stimuli towards intensified cooperation on a national as well as on a continental and global scale.

At the national level this consolidation process is realized through the full range of cooperation options, be it that mergers and takeovers play a more prominent role here than they do in the international arena. Cross-border cooperation concentrates primarily on non-equity based codesharing. The limited role of equity swaps or equity stakes in cross-border airline cooperation can be connected with regulatory restrictions on foreign stakes in national airlines (excluding mergers, takeovers or majority stakes). These restrictions can be based on supposed public utility aspects of air transport, on anti-trust arguments or on national defense arguments. Besides, the existing international bilateral system of air transport regulation is an obstacle to a more rigorous consolidation of the global airline industry.

Under these conditions code sharing provides a flexible opportunity to alliance partners on different continents to cash in on the advantages of larger intercontinental hub and spoke systems. On the cost side, these advantages emerge through important network economies, and on the demand side through the various elasticities.

Without the above mentioned regulatory restrictions 'flag' carriers would be ordinary transport firms. In that case, the airline industry would probably get involved in a familiar 'ham and eggs' process towards global consolidation. The telecom industry already showed that the network economies will be the major drives.

However, as long as the 'ham and eggs' cooperation model cannot be applied to the international airline industry, code-sharing alliances seem to be the most obvious way to intensify international airline cooperation. Consequently, as we already discussed in paragraph 2. the nature of cooperation remains highly unstable. This is not only explained by the limited role of equity-based alliances, but also by the more tactical rather than strategic nature of many so-called alliances that only focus on a route-specific approach. [12]

---

12 Actually this explanation implicitly refers to the vague definition of alliance.

In general we can distinguish between two kinds of factors that can affect the success of an alliance: organizational factors and economic factors. Button (1997) provides the following list of factors [13] :

- The objectives of the cooperating airlines are set too broadly
- These objectives are not congruent
- Asymmetry between partners
- Unrealistic expectations
- Incompatible product service standards
- Conflicting or competitive priorities
- Contrasting corporate styles

Another rationale for the instability of alliances is embedded in the dynamic nature of the economic environment in which airlines operate. Here we must differentiate between institutional changes and pure economic changes. The former relate to the interests (economic, operational and strategic) of the various parties involved, including labor, airports, suppliers and passengers. [14] The latter relate to the underlying size economies (which provide the grounds for alliances in the first place), such as decreasing scope or network economies, the emergence of new economic opportunities, for example, British Airways' alliance with USAir ended when BA expected a cooperation with American Airlines to be more profitable) or conflicts arising from the arrival of new competing airlines, etc.

17.4.2 Asymmetry and Instability of Alliances

Asymmetry in internal alliance relations is an important factor in testing the stability level of international alliances. The probability and complexity of asymmetry increases disproportionately with a growing number of alliance partners. The following diagram illustrates this.

[13] See also Flanagan and Marcus (1993) and Lindquist (1996).

[14] Button (1997) describes these interests within the framework of the coalition theory, where the formation and break down of alliances is assumed to be due to the mutual (dis)advantages that such collaboration offers to various interest groups.

Figure 3: Possible Conflict in Mutual relations of an Alliance

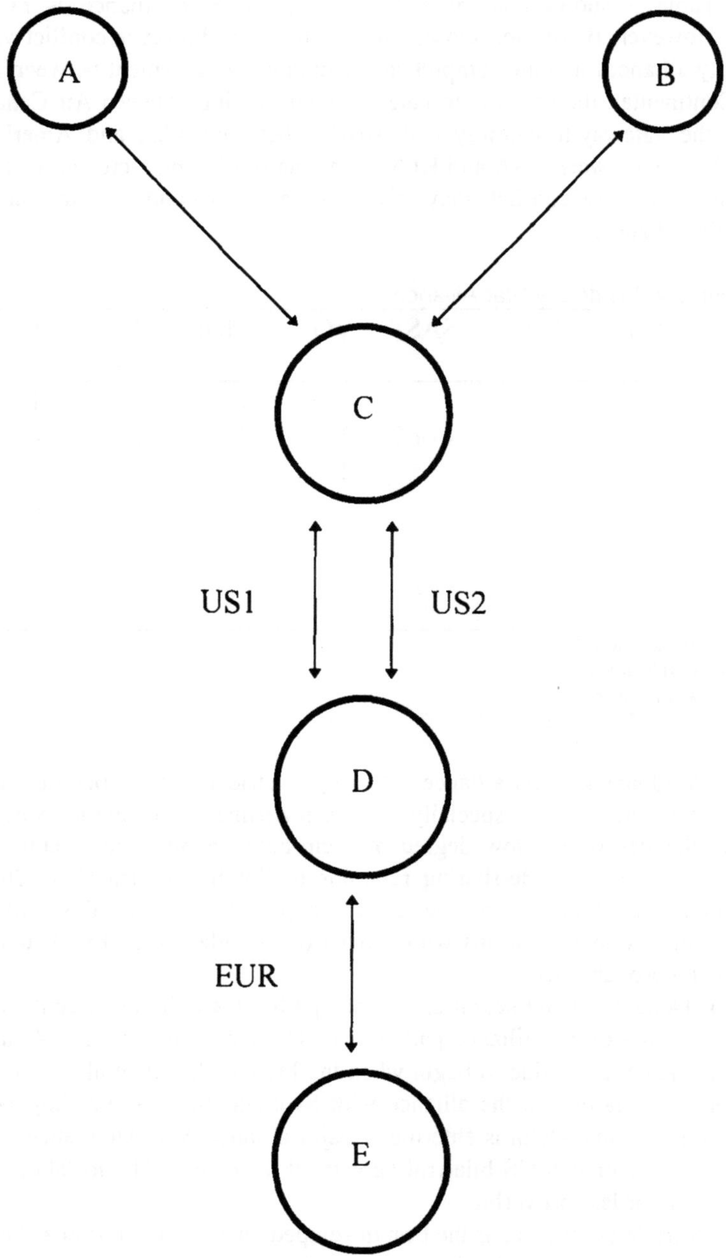

A closer look at the existing global alliances reveals various degrees of asymmetry. Table 3 shows that, at a first sight, the Star alliance is rather symmetrical. However, if we look closer this alliance may however conflict with other third-party alliances like the comprehensive marketing agreement between Air Canada and Continental, the gateway to gateway code sharing between Air Canada and Swissair, the gateway-to-gateway code-sharing between SAA and American Airlines, and the one between SAA and KLM. The major binding factor in the Star alliance is Lufthansa. New conflicts may arise as soon as a second Far East carrier is included in the alliance.

Table 3 Cooperation Inside the Star Alliance

	LH	UA	SAS	VG	Thai	Air Can.	SAA
LH		1	1	1	1	1	1
UA			1 or 2	2	2	1 or 2	-
SAS				2	2	-	-
VG					-	-	-
Thai						-	-
Air Can							-
SAA							-

Source: Airline Business June 1997
1 = strategic network-wide alliance
2 = gateway-to-gateway alliance
3 = continental point-specific alliance

The BA - AA- Quantas - CAI alliance is less symmetrical, due to specific third-party alliances involved in this. Especially American Airlines is developing various other satellite alliances with a low degree of reciprocity in other continents, for example rapidly expanding code-sharing relations in South America (Lan Chile, Aerolineas Argentinas, Avanca and the Taca group). In the Far East AA is following the same strategy: link-ups with Asiana (also code shared by Quantas), China Airlines and probably JAL.

The roles of Delta and Continental as alliance partners are the most confusing. Continental is focusing on the alliance partners Air Canada (Star alliance), Alitalia and possibly also Air France, due to begin when the French-US bilateral agreement is signed. Delta is a partner in the alliance with Swissair, Sabena and Singapore Airlines. At the same time Delta is entering a major alliance with Air France, also due to begin when the French-US bilateral agreement is signed. The instability of the relations is more or less proverbial.

The KLM - NorthWest alliance is the best developed airline cooperation as far as the North Atlantic marketis involved. The recent change towards a non-equity based alliance has resulted in an extended and more symmetrical cooperation in the Far East, where NorthWest has canceled the link with Asiana. Both partners have linked up now with a major Japanese carrier, JAS. Recently KLM's access to the Japanese market substantially improved. Tokyo has already been a bridghead to NorthWest for many years.

17.4.3 On the Future Role of Alliance: Some Predictions

Scientific knowledge is a body of statements of varying degree of certainty - some most unsure, some nearly sure, but none *absolutely sure.* (Feynman, 1989).

As final comments we would like to propose the following 'body of statements of varying degree of certainty' on the future role of alliance:

- The airline industry is a network-oriented service industry with a strong tendency to consolidation in national, continental and global markets. In these three types of markets this process of concentration continues at different speed. depending especially on the level of deregulation.

- Within the existing regulatory framework of international bilateralism, alliances are the only opportunity to benefit from networks economies of cooperating airlines.

- In national markets, consolidation will continue through mergers, takeovers and franchising feeder agreements.

- Concentration will also take off in the deregulated international markets, be it through takeovers or through bankruptcy of weak incumbent carriers. (For example those EU carriers that no longer receive traditional state aid.)

- At the same time, lean and cost-efficient start-up carriers will challenge the monopolistic position of incumbent airlines and their alliances on contestable fringe markets, thus destabilizing existing alliances.

- Most continental markets are fragmented by many national markets, as in the Far East and Europe. Airport infrastructure in these continents is a decisive factor in airline concentration. Congested hub airports compel home-based carriers to cooperate with other carriers on the same continent in order to be able to acquire additional hub capacity.

- The nature of global alliances is inherently unstable, since too many alliance partners have to be involved in the development of a true global network. The asymmetry in these alliances cannot be eliminated.

- The volatility of these international alliances will ultimately end in a more definite concentration of the global airline industry. The progress of international deregulation will be the major constraint on this process, but at the same time that progress will be influenced by the intensifying cooperation between international airlines.

- In a globally concentrating airline industry the role of alliance will rapidly fade.

References

AEA: Association of European Airlines, 1997, *1996 Yearbook, Statistical Appendices,* Brussels.

Bailey, E. E., Graham, D. R., and Kaplan, D. P., 1985, *Deregulating the Airlines,* MIT Press, Cambridge MA.

Barrett, S. D., 1990, Deregulating European Aviation, *Transportation,* 16, 311-327.

Beydorff, S., Ehmer, H., and Wilken, D., 1995, *Code-sharing in internationalen Luftverkehr der* BRD, Forschungsbericht 95-23, DLR.

Berechman, J., and Shy, 0., 1996, "Airline deregulation and the choice of networks", *in Advances in Spatial Equilibrium,* P. Nijkamp (ed.), Forthcoming.

Berechman, J., and De Wit, J. , 1996, An Analysis of the Effects of European Aviation Deregulation on an Airline's Network Structure and Choice of a Primary West European Hub Airport, *Journal of' Transport Economics and Policy,* September 1996, 251-274.

Bootsma, P.D. 1997, *Airline Flight Schedule Development, - Analysis and design tools.for European hinterland hubs-, PhD thesis* University of Twente.

Borenstein, S., 1989, Hubs and High Fares: Dominance and Market Power in the U.S. Airline Industry, *Rand Journal of Economics,* 20(3), 344-365.

Borenstein S., 1990, "Airline Mergers, Airport Dominance, and Market Power, *American Economic Review, 80,* 400-404.

Borenstein, S., 1992, The Evolution of US Airline Competition, *Journal qf Economic Perspectives,* 6, 45-74.

Brueckner, J. K., and Spiller, P. T., 1991, Competition and Mergers in Airlines Networks, *International Journal of Industrial Organization,* 9, 323-342.

Brueckner, J.K., 1997, *The Economics of International Codesharing.. an Analysis ofairline Alliances,* August, University of Illinois.

Button, K.J., 1989, Contestability in the UK Bus Industry, and Experience Goods and Economies of Experience, in J. Dodgsonand N. Topham (eds.), *Bus Deregulation and Privatisation.. An [nternational Perspective,* Gower, Aldershot.

Button, K.J., 1997, *Why don't all aviation marriages work?* Aviation Policy Program, George Mason University.

Coase, R.H., 1937, The Nature of the Firm, *Economica,* November, 386-405.

Feynman R., 1989, *What Do You Care What Other People Think?,* Bantam Books, New York.

Hendricks, K., Piccione, M., and Tan, G., 1992, The Economics of Hubs: The Case of Monopoly, *Review of Economic Studies,* 62, 83-99.

ICAO, 1997, *Study on the Implications of airline Codesharing,* Attachment to State Letter EC 2/7497/17, Montreal.

Keeler, T. E., 1991, Airline Deregulation and Market Performance: The Economic Basis for Regulatory Reform and Lessons from the US Experience, in Banister D., and Button, K., (eds.), *Transport in a Free Market Economy,* 121-176, Macmillan Ed.

Lorange, P. and Roos, J., 1992, *Strategic Alliances, -Formation, Implementation and Evolution-,* Blackwell, Oxford.

Morrison S. A., and Winston C., 1986, *The Economic Effect ofairline Deregulation,* Washington D.C.: The Brookings Institute.

Morrison S. and Winston C., 1990, The Dynamics of Airline Pricing and Competition", *American Economic Review,* 80, 389-393.

OECD, 1997, *The Future ofinternational Air Transport Policy, Responding to Global Change,* Paris.

Oum, T. H., Waters, W. G., and Jong-Say, Y., 1992, Concepis of Transport Demand Elasticities and the Recent estimates: An Interpretive Survey, *Journal of Transport Economics and Policy,* May, 13 9154.

Oum, T. H., Zhang, A., and Zhang., Y., 1993, Inter-Firm Rivalry and Firm-Specific Price Elasticities in Deregulated Airline Markets, *Journal of Transport Economics and Policy,* 27(2), 171-192.

Oum, T. H., Taylor A, J., and Zhang, A., 1993, Strategic Airline Policy in the Globalizing Airline *Networks, Transportation Journal, 14-30.*

US Department of Transport, 1990, *Secretary's Task Force on Competition in th US. Domestic Airline Industry,* Washington, D.C.

18 WRAP UP: THE WAY I SEE IT

John Panzar

What is the most predicable result of liberalization? Well, it is unpredictability. I am old enough to remember attending conferences like this 20 years ago where we discussed the prospect of de-regulation in the United States. In spite of the wide body of deregulated experience with the intra-state California market to make predictions, economists and the industry people as well got it largely wrong! Among the major things that were not predicted were hub and spoke networks, yield management techniques, and frequent flier plans - three areas of major contribution to the U.S. industry today.

I will try to say something concerning what we've learned in the U.S. regarding the impact on alliances, the evolution of networks and, what I think is probably the most important, the evolution of airport competition which we heard a little bit about yesterday.

18.1 ALLIANCES

We heard from four economists who essentially agreed that alliances are an artefact of the current heavily regulated structure and they won't last beyond the opening up of markets. An alliance is like a lesser form of a merger. Like a network merger, an alliance has both horizontal and vertical effects. Horizontal effects occur when head-to-head competition results and tend to be anti-competitive. When an alliance results in the extension of the network of the carrier, that alliance has a vertical effect and tends to benefit consumers through new options as we've heard discussed.

However, once one get to open skies, or 7th freedom operations, or whatever one wants to call it, these network extensions can be done by carriers themselves. They will be done by merger only if that proves more effective than expansion.

It is the job of the anti trust authorities to see that mergers are largely end to end rather than overlapping as many of the alliances that we are talking about have been. This is something that should be learned from U.S. experience where there are only two merger authorities. Maybe six or eight merger authorities are needed to ensure that one is ready to step up to the plate and stop anti competitive airline mergers.

18.2 THE EVOLUTION OF NETWORKS

Why do we have 22 intercontinental hubs in Europe? Obviously because of the crazy bilateral structure which permits Air Austria to fly to New York and then permits Swiss Air to also fly to New York. That would never happen in a liberalized free system.

Some kind of rationalization is necessary. And this rationalization is going to emphasize the formation of hub and spoke networks within the European Community. There has to be a premium for coming up with the best hub to serve these European markets. You may not agree with this and I think that Dr. Julius likely knows more about what is likely to happen than I.

Maybe we will not get down to five or six intercontinental hubs. I am willing bet that the number of hubs will be less than half of number that exist today. The question remains, how will those hubs be determined? If you look at the U.S. experience, hubs are determined on the basis of geography. A hub should be centrally located. You rarely see hubs on the periphery. You do not see hubs on the periphery in the U.S. and you have to wonder about London. London, however, has the other things going for it.

O & D traffic volumes are essential. Airlines have determined that it is hard to establish a hub where there are not a lot of people. They have tried to establish hubs out in the middle of nowhere - the green field approach. There was a view that if you build it people would come. Well they did not come. Airlines had to abandon their attempts at hubbing at these more remote locations.

18.3 AIRPORT COMPETITION

The third feature is airport attractiveness. How good a facility in terms of airport infrastructure can one have? In this respect the Europeans are a way ahead of the U.S.. The Europeans have adopted privatization as the way to stimulate innovation and technical change in airports. I think that this will play a key role in the future. In Benedickt Mandel's paper, using the coloured map of Germany, it is just fascinating to see how a private or public airport manager has a tool to strategically optimize his operation and forecast his market share.

This gets me to my final point. We are soon going to move one stage up. Airport competition is going to replace flag carrier competition as the national rivalry. The European Union is going to have to engage in some serious thinking about airport anti trust policy for want of a better term. They are not off to a good start! It is my understanding that while airports in London are being privatized, all three major airports in London are being considered as a bundle. While this might be good for raising money for the treasury, from a public policies perspective, I think I would want independent airport managers competing to offer the best mix of services and rates. However, the British are always better at selling monopolies than promoting competition. It goes back to the 13th century when King Henry sold the first Royal monopoly.

MIX
Papier aus verantwortungsvollen Quellen
Paper from responsible sources
FSC® C105338

If you have any concerns about our products,
you can contact us on
ProductSafety@springernature.com

In case Publisher is established outside the EU,
the EU authorized representative is:
Springer Nature Customer Service Center GmbH
Europaplatz 3, 69115 Heidelberg, Germany

Printed by Libri Plureos GmbH
in Hamburg, Germany